THE ART OF DEFIANCE

THE ART OF DEFIANCE

Dissident Culture and Militant Resistance in 1970s Iran

Peyman Vahabzadeh

EDINBURGH
University Press

Edinburgh University Press is one of the leading university presses in the UK. We publish academic books and journals in our selected subject areas across the humanities and social sciences, combining cutting-edge scholarship with high editorial and production values to produce academic works of lasting importance. For more information visit our website: edinburghuniversitypress.com

Edinburgh University Press Ltd
The Tun – Holyrood Road
12(2f) Jackson's Entry
Edinburgh EH8 8PJ

First published in hardback by Edinburgh University Press 2022

Typeset in 11/15 Adobe Garamond by
IDSUK (DataConnection) Ltd, and
printed and bound by CPI Group (UK) Ltd,
Croydon, CR0 4YY

A CIP record for this book is available from the British Library

ISBN 978 1 4744 9222 5 (hardback)
ISBN 978 1 4744 9223 2 (paperback)
ISBN 978 1 4744 9224 9 (webready PDF)
ISBN 978 1 4744 9225 6 (epub)

CONTENTS

FIGURES

ACKNOWLEDGEMENTS

This book is the product of years of research and discussions with friends, Mohsen Saffari, Mohammad Safavi, Hadi Ebrahimi, Sara Naderi and Siyamak Ghaffari.

I am grateful to Saeed Yousef for pointing out some key sources relevant to Chapter 2 and to Mohammad Kharrazy, whose knowledge of music and the musical context of Iran shed light on discussions in Chapter 4. I thank Vahid Ahmadi Sarbast for his assistance with the data that appears in Chapter 1. Many thanks also to Mandana Karimi: this book would not have been in its present shape if it were not for her indispensable assistance. I am deeply grateful to my talented friend Siyamak Ghaffari, who generously provided the original artwork for the cover of this book.

I thank the Interlibrary Loan Desk at University of Victoria Library for obtaining research materials. A visit to the International Institute for Social History in Amsterdam in 2016 helped me retrieve some resources and I thank Touraj Atabaki for facilitating this visit. I acknowledge a Social Sciences and Humanities Research Council of Canada (SSHRC) Insight Grant (435-2018-0010) that provided funding for this research.

This work has in part been inspired by Professor Hamid Dabashi, the defiant scholar par excellence, whose multiple works dwell on the intersection of arts, politics and action. Readers will notice how the *spirit* of his work gingerly roves across the plateaux of this book.

I thank Louise Hutton, Emma Rees, Bekah Dey and Eddie Clark at Edinburgh University Press, and copy-editor Michael Ayton, for their superb professionalism and care that made the publication of this book a smooth and enjoyable process.

Earlier and shorter versions of Chapters 1 and 2 have been published as chapters in *Persian Language, Literature and Culture: New Leaves, Fresh Looks*, ed. Kamran Talattof (London/New York: Routledge, 2015) and in *Iran in the Middle East: Transnational Encounters and Social History*, ed. Houchang Chehabi, Peyman Jafari and Maral Jefroudi (London: I. B. Tauris, 2015).

No book is ever solely the product of its author. As always, my friend and life-companion Giti and our intellectual son Emile have been a part of this book, especially through our 'family poetry nights'. I am also deeply indebted to my parents, Mahin Mousavi Yeganeh, a poet and teacher, and the late Ahmad Vahabzadeh, a librarian and translator – two outstanding humans who whispered in my youthful ears poetry and rebellion and cultivated in me the ever-flowing spirit of imagining another world better than this oppressive, colonial and collapsing world we have globally inherited. Every page in this book reflects the trace of their loving parenting.

NOTE ON TRANSLATION AND TRANSLITERATION

The unenviable task of translating the vast majority of poems and excerpts from Persian sources and providing the reader with readable English translations of them fell to me. Unless noted otherwise, all translations are mine. Where possible, I tried to rely on the existing translations of the poems I quoted, but this only applied to translations done by outstanding scholars in the field, whom I have acknowledged.

In translating some polysemic Persian words, I acceded to their contextual meanings. At times, this necessitated introducing the word's etymological significance or historical context, or inserting the Persian words in parentheses. In transliterating certain Persian words or concepts, I followed the simple rule of approximating the sound of Persian letters to those in the English alphabet. I avoided using typographical ciphers and diacritics that are used to designate Persian letter-sounds involving scanning and accentuation (as in *Encyclopedia Iranica*). The exceptions to this rule pertain to Persian or Arabic proper names or names of the persons that have already appeared in English and/or on the internet with a certain spelling (e.g. Mohammad, Mahmoud, Muslim). I have ignored the distinction between long and short vowels in Persian, but I have used the inverse apostrophe (') to mark the vowel 'Ayn' when Ayn appears in the middle of the word (as in *she'r*). I have dropped the inverse apostrophe when the Ayn appears as the first vowel of the word (e.g. Ali or Elm).

I have used a regular apostrophe (') to mark 'Hamza' in the middle of the word (as in Ra'is Ali), with the prominent exception of the word 'Fadai'. My objective is to maintain a style of writing that captures the nuances in a discourse as a subset of language that locates, conditions and makes possible the articulation of the subject matter.

Ask in the mirror
the name of your Saviour.

Forough Farrokhzad

Where is the earth's gravity?
Where in this world am I standing
with this burden of dormant and bloody cries?
O, my homeland,
where in this world am I standing?

Khosrow Golesorkhi

INTRODUCTION

READING THE INVISIBLE INK

The outcome of the final clash between my heart and my mind
was a pleasant mistake
I grew up in this war
a war that motivated me toward a fresh start
under my hand there was a handful of prose poetry
above my head the cracks on my home's ceiling.

Bahram Nouraei, *Khub* (Good)

I was about thirteen years old when, one summer afternoon, my father casu-ally handed me a cassette tape upon arrival home from work. He was a dedicated and unassuming librarian, and his peculiar mannerisms revealed his eternal love of books, while his personal library had become legendary among friends and family, owing not just to the sheer number of collected books in Persian, English and French, but more importantly to numerous rare and banned books, aside from a mostly secret collection of lithographs and handwritten books from the Qajar period. His present was an audiobook of the then famous 'children's story', *The Little Black Fish*, written in Persian by the Azerbaijani educator and author Samad Behrangi (1939–67). Originally published in 1968 by the Centre for Intellectual Cultivation of Children and Youth (CICCY; *Kanun-e Parvarsh-e Fekri-ye Kudakan va Nojavanan*), founded in 1965 by Empress Farah Pahlavi, the book, like those associated with its production, was to experience the most curious destiny. Having received the 1968 Children's Book Board Special Award, the book depicted the allegorical story of a young little black fish which, living in a trivial creek and dreaming of exploring the world, embarked on the perilous journey to join other fishes in the ocean, facing mortal dangers on the way. This particular rebellious fish, brimming with youthful zeal and idealism, succumbed neither to the reproaches of sedentary and lethargic elders nor to the threats of assorted waterways masters. The Persian language is not gendered, and so our protagonist did not have a specifically assigned gender, and expectedly, on the audiobook (nowadays available online) a female voice-actor's slightly high-pitched, androgynous voice embodied the little black fish's sonic presence. In my young mind then and to this day, the heroic fish has been simultaneously female and male. I travelled shoulder to shoulder with the fearless little fish in this timeless saga. I could not stop listening to the story and became very keen on reading the actual book, which was hard to obtain at the time because it was banned. But not for my father. I received a book that brought to life the little fish through the amazing illustrations of Farshid Mesghali, which brought him international awards including a Hans Christian Andersen Medal in 1974. With the book, my sensory experience of the fiction was complete. Upon listening to and reading the story, I became 'political', a revolutionary indeed – at the age of thirteen. Such a formative experience: I am still living that spirit.

The audiobook was produced in 1971, the very turbulent year in which young men and women, mostly university students and graduates, changed the Iranian political scene by launching urban guerrilla warfare through a parochial but legendary attack on the Gendarmerie Post of the village of Siahkal in the Caspian province of Gilan, followed by the daring assassination of Military Prosecutor Lieutenant General Zia Farsiu, who had handed down the execution sentence of thirteen Siahkal militants, and the founding of *Cherikha-ye Fadai-ye Khalq*, People's Fadai Guerrillas (PFG or Fadaiyan) that founded and spearheaded armed struggle in Iran.

As is well-known, this 'children's story' became the manifesto of young Iranian Marxist revolutionaries who had come of age under the repressive regime of Mohammad Reza Shah Pahlavi in the 1960s. *The Little Black Fish* is rightly considered to have attracted more revolutionaries to Iran's short-lived but influential urban guerrilla movement, spearheaded by Fadaiyan, than any Marxist or PFG treatise (Vahabzadeh 2010: 134). That the state-funded CICCY published a revolutionary treatise in disguise that was later banned is amazing in itself. But the curious fate of its author also added to the aura of the book.

Coming from a humble background in Tabriz, Behrangi had graduated from the two-year teacher-training programme in 1957. He taught in the villages of Azerbaijan, and aside from writing short stories, Azeri-Turkish folk tales and children's stories, and translating fiction from Turkish and English, he had written a critical work on pedagogy in which he had scorned the Tehran-centric pedagogical works based on American and European educational psychology used in teachers' training programmes, flagging the major chasm between the state's (imported, colonial) educational reforms and the harsh realities of the provinces, especially rural Iran (Behrangi 1970). Behrangi accidentally drowned in the River Aras in the Arasbaran region of Azerbaijan in August 1968 while accompanied by an 'unidentified officer'. Precisely because of the latter's presence, Behrangi's death was attributed to a SAVAK (Iranian intelligence) conspiracy within dissident circles. Although aware of the truth, key cultural figures – playwright, novelist and psychiatrist Gholam Hossein Sa'edi (1936–85), essayist and novelist Jalal Al-Ahmad (1923–69) and cultural writer Amir Parviz Puyan (1947–71) – had decided that the 'movement' (no actual movement existed at the time!) needed a martyr, and Samad's untimely death would serve as just that. In an uncanny way, these authors had *anticipated* the Fadaiyan movement, that was yet to come. The reason? Puyan, who later co-founded the PFG, was in contact with the Azeri dissident writers and cultural figures Behruz Dehqani (1939–71) and Ali Reza Nabdel (1944–71) in Tabriz, close friends of Behrangi. Nabdel created a cell later that joined the PFG upon its foundation. Thus, Samad had posthumously become something of a mythical figure for Fadaiyan and for thousands of university students and dissident intellectuals that supported the PFG. In any case, a Special Issue of the literary magazine *Arash* (no. 18, November 1968) served to propagate the conspiracy theory in subtle but effective ways. In his shrewdly ambivalent editorial in the issue, editor Eslam Kazemiyeh set the tone for the contributions that *suggested* the conspiracy surrounding Behrangi's death, comparing his life to that of the little black fish in the book that had been published just before Samad's departure. Behrangi had left his comrades in a drowning accident only to emerge in the public imagination as an immortal martyr – a witness to the country's injustices.

This was the second such conspiracy story in late 1960s Iran: the first involved the widely propagated idea that SAVAK had caused the untimely death of the popular world-champion wrestler Gholam Reza Takhti (1930–68), an affiliate of the legalist-reformist opposition, the National Front (*Jebheh-ye Melli*), who had in fact committed suicide in January 1968 because of depression in Tehran's Hotel Atlantic. In this case, too, Al-Ahmad also propagated the rumour about SAVAK conspiracy (Takhti 2019). Takhti's funeral procession was turned into a protest rally by dissident students and publics.

Although Samad's brother insisted on conspiracy (Behrangi 2000), in 1991 the 'unidentified officer' stepped forward with the truth. Hamzeh Farahati (d. 2021) was Samad's comrade who had accompanied him for a swim in the River Aras while off-duty as an army officer. Al-Ahmad, Sa'edi and others 'consented to announce Samad as a martyr . . . on the condition that there should be no mention of me, only of that "officer"' (Farahati 1991: 12; see also Farahati 2006: 153–66; Vahabzadeh 2010: 23–4, n. 1). Mythmaking has its victims.

Regarding that particular audiobook: it was also produced by the CICCY. It was professionally voice-acted, but, perhaps more importantly, it was sonically enriched with a soundtrack by Esfandiar Monfaredzadeh (1941–), which was borrowed from the soundtrack of a 1970 (box-office hit) movie, *Reza Motori* (*Motorcycle-Rider Reza*), directed by Massoud Kimiai, and containing a hit song, 'The Lonesome Man' ('Yek Mard-e Tanha') with lyrics by Shahyar Ghanbari, who, along with a few others, created the New Iranian Song-writing (*Taranehsarai-ye Novin-e Iran*) school. The soundtrack received an award at the Sepas Film Festival in Tehran. The presence of the melody of 'The Lonesome Man' suggested to eager ears that Ghanbari's words 'that man' who 'stood like a mountain' in 'a pulseless night' referred to Behrangi and his death (Parand 2011a). A complex turn of events also connected Monfaredzadeh to the little fish. He was imprisoned from August 1973 to May 1974 in relation to a SAVAK sting involving rounding up a dozen or so poets, writers and filmmakers and charging them with a conspiracy to kidnap the Royal

Family (Parand 2011b; Samakar 2001: 164; see Vahabzadeh 2010: 218–19). In retrospect, it seems the rebellious little fish yearning to join comrades in the sea had already braided together the arts and politics.

The thirteen-year-old me had inadvertently inherited this complex history, amazingly woven together through politics, arts, literature and social history. The little black fish which breaks away from the norms of society and refuses the temptation of a safe and rewarding but tedious and humiliating life in a forsaken creek was now embodied by the immortal Fadai Guerrillas, who mysteriously appeared in our home when my eager ears heard, every now and then, my father whispering to my mother about *cherikha* (guerrillas) in an unmistakably laudatory tone.

The Arts that Outlive the Event

Following my previous books on the militant Left in 1970s Iran (Vahabzadeh 2010, 2015a, 2019b), this book offers a glance into this decade from a fresh angle. My personal recollections above, contextualised by my research, show how specific social, political and historical phenomena are received through *lived experiences*, thus constituting a specific *weltanschauung* for those who can (still) perceive the *event* that surrounds them. The ability to be touched by the event through what I will call an 'art-experience' is not a common capacity. Under normal conditions, the citizens of any state are *hegemonised* into subscribing to the state-propagated image of a 'good life', and thus, for the most part, the experiences of the average citizen, to expand on Antonio Gramsci's theory, are *re-grounded* by the *weltanschauung* of the ruling class (Vahabzadeh, 2007a). It is no wonder, then, that when the militants emerged on the Iranian political scene, young people enthusiastically responded to their call in astonishing numbers, in spite of the mortal dangers that they were likely to face, just like our legendary little black fish.

The *thesis* of this book can be summarised as follows: at the time when Iran was undergoing rapid, authoritarian modernisation that was meant to stabilise the country's economic position on the periphery of the capitalist world-system (despite the Shah's claim in the 1970s that Iran was about to become the Japan of West Asia), the state's policy of educational expansion resulted in building a large, educated middle class. With growing state control, censorship and wholesale crackdown on opposition in the 1960s and 1970s on the one hand, and the rise of the *short-lived urban guerrillas spearheaded by the PFG in the 1970s* on the other, *in a dialectical fashion the arts* produced by dissident artists – specifically poetry, songs, short fiction and film – both reflected the militant struggles under the country's skin *and* contributed hugely to the creation of a public, larger-than-life image of otherwise small groups of militants. *These works of art and literature defied the state-propagated weltanschauung and allowed public articulation of dissent to shape up. Militant action was translated into artistic expression and vice versa.* The arts of defiance thus swayed young educated individuals, as well as certain layers of the public, to perceive the Iranian state through the eyes of its most radical critics: the Marxist militants. This book proceeds to show that because of the arts, the PFG militants – who were few in number and whose literature and presence only resonated with the clandestine university student groups and informal intellectual circles – acquired disproportionate heroic dimensions in the eyes of the public and were transported into a mythic and symbolic universe beyond their actual militant existence, and thus, they permeated the collective consciousness of non-conforming Iranians as immortal liberators. A ripple effect also expanded the admiration for active dissidents beyond the PFG to other militants at the time. In *A Guerrilla Odyssey* (2010), which took eleven years to complete, I studied the Fadaiyan's political history and theories and alluded to how the PFG was represented in the larger socio-political context through the so-called 'Fadai Movement'. That study, however, did not investigate the reasons for the unrivalled popularity of the PFG. A subsequent article (Vahabzadeh 2015b) shed light on the path – art and politics in the context of PFG in 1970s – that eventually culminated in this book which focuses on the 'aesthetic dimension of the movement' (Katsiaficas 1987: 230).

In short, this is a case study of the relationship between social movements, on the one hand, and poetry, literature, and film, on the other. This is a global story. Poets, writers, musicians and filmmakers have always contributed artistically to the social or revolutionary movements which they supported and with which they identify, but attending to this is beyond this study. I would like to tell the Iranian version of this global movement here. The arts' contribution to the deep social protest that was embodied by guerrilla warfare in Iran, a movement championed by the PFG, has been acknowledged but never systematically studied. This book offers the dialectical connections between dissident art and militant resistance. I will argue that the PFG's relative popularity in the 1970s, which grew fully and most visibly in post-revolutionary times and in particular between 1979 and 1982 (during and before the state's heavy-handed crackdown), is due to the myth-making aspect of the arts in the years prior to 1979. Within specific genres and styles, the arts created a 'myth', following George Sorel, that brought immortality to the guerrillas. The myth achieved for the public in the 1970s what the PFG literature had tried to achieve for militant students in 1969–70: *the myth rendered militant resistance against the Shah intelligible, even desirable.* Through dissident arts, the Fadai Guerrillas – and *by virtue of their approximation to the Fadaiyan's codified, armed action,* other militants like the People's Mojahedin – emerged as timeless, selfless and immortal liberators that were connected to the Iranian cultural memory of resistances against oppression. This specific junction of arts and politics is therefore at the heart of this study, with universal implications beyond this particular case study. Myths work through a 'delayed effect', and I will show that the guerrillas acquired superhuman proportions, paradoxically by the time the militant opposition had significantly subsided. It was the arts that supplied dissident activists, largely caught in their ideological lexis and thus unable to communicate with the populace they intended to mobilise, with a greater public reach by symbolising their struggles in ways relatable to larger audiences. In short, caught in the endless, high-entropy, all-consuming task of running an underground militant organisation, Fadaiyan (and other militants) were not equipped with the cultural means for constructing of a public image of themselves, nor did they have the resources for that, while dissident artists, writers, poets and intellectuals created a myth of the immortal liberator beyond the wildest imagination of the activists themselves. But prior to this *delayed effect,* just as with my personal memory described above, the arts, poetry in particular, attracted many to the guerrillas: in the age when copies of underground and banned publications were circulated at a snail's pace (see Ghamari 2016: 62–8), scores of surviving activists were attracted to revolutionary action particularly through poetry or other fast-travelling media such a Behrangi's children's stories. We come full circle: either way, we end up with the arts.

My personal memory, narrated earlier, is indeed the story of a generation. The cogent words of the post-revolutionary Iranian hip-hop artist Bahram Nouraei in the epigraph capture the very conflict of heart and the mind that gave the 1970s generation a fresh start.

Approach and Method

This book examines the processes through which the arts have lent themselves to a particular defiant movement – the one pioneered by the PFG in the 1970s. The study will substantiate the link between arts and politics in this context – a link that seems to have been written in invisible ink, although it has been surfacing in the memories of the activists of the time. There have been previous studies of the ideological components of modern Iranian literature (Ghanoonparvar 1984; Naficy 1997; Talattof 2000). This book, however, aims at offering fresh insights on its subject and does not probe this phenomenon in merely ideological terms. Ideological readings seem reductionist, as they simplify complex world-views, social relations and experiences through algorithmic ordering of things. To a probing gaze, these works incline to regard 'political poetry' as ideological (which is true) while almost completely disregarding the ideological edifice of the status quo that this poetry challenges. Paradoxically, this inclination exposes the ideologies of the authors. Ideologies are in the air we breathe. Accordingly, unlike the existing literature, I do not regard the arts simply as a response to (effect of) specific politics (the cause) – that is, as an ideological construct in the sort of common sense that 'art imitates life'. Nor do I advocate the position that ideologically-inclined (Marxist) writers, poets and filmmakers created a specific genre to advocate the same cause as the guerrillas (Talattof 2000: 4, 88–9, 91). I do not seek to establish a causal connection; rather, I aim at the construction of a particular culture of defiance in a specific period, although I am aware that this is a global story across many societies that also underwent similar conditions. The relationship between the arts and militant action in this particular context is more complex than meets the eye. In fact, among other things, this book shows how *life imitates art* and what this change of *weltanschauung* tells about our common experiences and perspectives. The arts, in other words, channelled the world-view of the younger generation of the 1960s and 1970s into a new Gestalt.

My work acknowledges a limitation: when studying various aspects of modern literature in Iran, the existing scholarly works almost invariably equate modern Iranian literature with Persian literature (Ghanoonparvar 1984; Naficy 1997; Talattof 2000), thus revealing a certain Persian-centric bias. Iran embraces an irreducibly multilingual nation, and although Persian literature solidly constitutes the bulk of literary production, modern Iranian literature cannot be solely Persian. Deserving particular mention here are Azeri and Kurdish literatures. I was born in Tehran into a mixed Persian and Azerbaijani background, but despite my love of Azeri language I was assimilated into Persian. That is why despite my efforts I have not sufficient command of Azeri to include Azeri literature in this study. This caveat is meant to alert the reader to the unwitting biases in our works.

There are several reasons for my focus on the PFG in this book: in the historical background of the Fadaiyan's emergence, there were many attempts at instigating armed struggle in the 1960s, but they all failed because they were mostly activities of isolated groups of intellectuals (with the exception of the repressed Kurdish uprising in 1968). Informed by Islamic or Maoist ideas, these were in fact inspired by the revolutionary movements of their time: Algeria, Cuba, Vietnam (Sohrabi 2019; Vahabzadeh 2010: 5–13). The Fadai Guerrillas were *inaugurators*: their militant resistance against the regime was accompanied by their own theories cleverly built around a *movement*; like other New Left militants, they relied heavily on the student movement as their social base, successfully contacted the revolutionary movements or states in the Middle East, and received support from Iranian student activists in Europe and the United States. In short, though small in number, they were unique in vision and execution, the elite of a vast network of dissidents. Fadaiyan also produced considerable and original revolutionary literature and encouraged literary works within their logistical capacity and ideological ambits. The PFG was the only group with a clear, long-term vision of armed struggle based on a brilliant theory of 'armed propaganda', adeptly crafted for the Iranian reality, by the PFG's indirect originator Bijan (Bizhan) Jazani (1976a; 1978: 46–7; 1976c; Vahabzadeh 2010: 97–104; 2019b: 133–4). The other key militant group, the Organisation of the Iranian People's Mojahedin (*Sazman-e Mojahedin-e Khalq-e Iran*, or OIPM), did not have such an elaborate understanding of armed struggle, and although the group had spent several years preparing for armed struggle, its direct entrance into action was only a reaction to the SAVAK raids that nearly destroyed the group's networks in August 1971. Although the OIPM officially dates its founding five years prior to Siahkal, it had not engaged in any direct activity before Siahkal, and by its own admission launched armed struggle after the PFG's emergence because had it not joined the struggle it would have left the leadership of the movement to Fadaiyan (Behrooz 2000: 61). Smaller Marxists militant groups for the most part simply emulated PFG or OIPM and had very limited resources. Thus, it is important to understand that the PFG is the standard-bearer of this era of militant opposition in Iran. My previous in-depth study of the PFG also allows for a rich contextualisation and social history necessary for this study. For the purpose of this study, it must be clarified that no other militant group, not even OIPM, had a cultural aspect and vision like the PFG, which was joined by many militant artists.

It is not my intention in this book to provide a survey of any kind or establish how ideology connects arts to movements or vice versa. I am concerned with the *construction* of a particular, in this case defiant, generational *weltanschauung*. As such, the poems, songs, fiction or films I discuss are selective in that they provide us with the discursive and symbolic contours of an emerging Gestalt. The reader will notice the organic connection between the foregoing and my phenomenological approach: as in my previous studies, I deploy in this study an extension of my radical or temporal phenomenology, inspired by Reiner Schürmann's philosophy, according to which each era produces, with relative distinctness, its own mode of thinking and acting, and as such, truth has an epochal character. Borrowing a concept from Michel Foucault, militant opposition dwelled in a specific savoir-faire in 1970s Iran. The savoir-faire that came with the world-view and action of the militants emerged through the prior construction of a rebellious Gestalt primarily through poetry, while in turn it mobilised truth-claims in subsequent artistic expressions. Thinking about the subject matter in such a phenomenological way requires that we seek an epoch's *hermeneutical master code* that allows for a specific, context-sensitive and Gestalt-oriented interpretation of otherwise heterogeneous phenomena. The overall approach will be neither causal nor positivist, neither arbitrary nor conjectural. It is about how a certain savoir-faire, a specific mode of revelation of Truth in acting and thinking, emerges through a long process, then dominates (relatively speaking) and captures a generation's imagination for a while before it slowly withers away. Accordingly, in treating its subject matter under the directions of a phenomenological gaze and through an era's hermeneutical master code, this book offers a multi-dimensional and 'mixed-methods' approach, and navigates its way through political history, social history, literary theory, discourse analysis and semiology.

A Glance at the Book

Chapter 1 offers the historical contexts and theoretical approaches of this book. These entail brief histories of the PFG and student movement, as well as an extended interpretation of George Sorel's theory of the 'myth of the general strike' and a new, tropological interpretation of Jazani's theory of 'armed propaganda' as the guiding theory of this study. These approaches are enriched by the phenomenological theory of Gestalt and by Karl Mannheim's Sociology of Knowledge. Chapter 1 discusses the myth and event, and it offers an *interpretive extension* of Jazani's theory for understanding the Siahkal operation as an event that clarifies how a master code emerges in Iranian political Gestalt. The subsequent chapters will use *embedded theories* when needed for each specific analysis.

The Iranian *weltanschauung* is profoundly poetic. Chapter 2 investigates the curious relationship between poetry and politics in Iran by offering foundational approaches informed by phenomenology, hermeneutics and sign theory, that will be used in subsequent chapters as well. Chapter 2 shows the connection between poetry and militant resistance through interpretation of some key poems. Modern Persian poetry (which this chapter focuses on) contains the discursive and poetic elements which, as early as the 1940s, allowed 'political poetry' not as disguised ideological manifestos but as expressions of a modern *weltanschauung* that contributed immensely to the poetic formation of dissidents some thirty years later. Because modern Persian poetry was foundational to the politicisation of other arts in Iran, this chapter is, judiciously, the most extensive. Chapter 3 studies the 1970s protest songs that popularised political consciousness among the youth. Fighting censorship, protest songs were organically connected to both poetry and the guerrilla movement with the added element of music. Chapter 4 probes short fiction and its connection to armed struggle by focusing mostly on the works of Samad Behrangi, whose fiction anticipated the guerrilla movement he never witnessed. Chapter 5 attends to the few cinematic works that worked through censorship in reflecting the guerrilla period. The Conclusion reflects on the study by resituating the study of arts and movements.

1

EVENT AND MYTH: PREPARATORY CONSIDERATIONS FOR THE STUDY OF PARALLEL MOVEMENTS

All power to imagination.

(Paris 1968 slogan)

The 1960s are rightly characterised as the 'world historical' age of national liberation movements in Asia and Africa as well as of movements against the capitalist world system in Latin American and Western states. These and other movements of the 1960s – women's, civil rights, gay liberation, student and indigenous – also inform today's world (see Debray 1967; Katsiaficas 1987; Varon 2004), as the latter movements mark the birth of 'new social movements' and identity politics (Vahabzadeh 2003). In Fredric Jameson's cogent words, 'for a time, everything was possible . . . this period . . . was a moment of universal liberation' (1988: 207). The 1960s, in particular at its 'hour', 1968, brought to the view the 'international connection between social movements' (Katsiaficas 1987: 3). 'It was not by chance alone that the Tet offensive in Vietnam occurred in the same year as the Prague Spring, the May events in France, the student rebellion in West Germany, the assassination of Martin Luther King, the takeover of Columbia University, riots at the Democratic National Convention in Chicago, and the pre-Olympic massacre in Mexico City', observes George Katsiaficas. 'These events were related to one another, and a synchronic analysis of the global movement of 1968 validates Hegel's proposition that world history moves from east to west' (1987: 4). Nineteen sixty-eight has been rightly characterised as the year of global revolution.

Historically, the idea of popular armed uprising rose in such turning-point events as the American War of Independence (1775–83) and the Haitian Revolution (1791–1804), while *conceptually* the militant action of intellectuals who were intent upon instigating a popular uprising can be traced back to the nineteenth-century revolutionary violence of Russian Narodniks (see Hobsbawm 1963; Vahabzadeh 2019b: 100), which influenced Lenin and Mao (Laclau 2005: 9–10). However, I do not intend to pinpoint the historical and conceptual lineage of armed struggle in order to explain the PFG-instigated urban guerrilla warfare in Iran. The global events of the 1960s, in particular the rise of guerrilla movements in Latin America (Gott 2008), have been widely credited for the rise of Iranian militants (Vahabzadeh 2010: 14–15, 24), although I take the Latin American influence, while important, to be partial. The turn to militantism by young Iranians in late 1960s must mainly be traced back to their *specific experience* of living in a rapidly developing society in which modernising the country's infrastructure was meant to take Iran into global capitalism as a significant, geostrategic participant (the Japan of West Asia, in the Shah's words), while the capitalist world system in fact incorporated Iran only as a peripheral participant: economically a sure supplier of petroleum and politically an unwavering ally against Iran's neighbour, the Soviet Union, in the age of Cold War. In general, the country's developmental projects clearly lifted sectors of the populace into modern, urban life, but this was carried out through the increasingly autocratic rule of Mohammad Reza Pahlavi (reign: 1941–79) and a political establishment that fed a gluttonous ruling elite. The result was the process of 'repressive development' that created a situation in which *economic* development was pushed forward without *political* modernisation and thus public consultation and input (Vahabzadeh 2010: 1–5). The Shah had built a curious 'rentier state': 'The state's main relationships to Iranian society were mediated through its expenditures – on the military, on development projects, on modern construction, on consumption subsidies, and the like. Suspended above its own people, the Iranian state bought them off, rearranged their lives, and repressed any dissidents among them' (Skocpol 1994: 244). The result of antimonial 'repressive development' was the appearance of visibly gross social injustices and at times stark class polarisation that taunted the Shah with his claim about the country moving towards a 'Great Civilisation'. The generation of post-secondary students who came of age in late 1960s Iran found, in dismay, their specific existential world in this chasm.

Modern university is the locus of socialisation of the young, aspiring women and men who, entering the domain of higher education from different social, cultural and class backgrounds, learn to communicate with one another over their often differing and diverging world-views and values. Coming from a plurality of subject positions, modern students create an environment for self-expression, listening and debating, as they learn to be individuals while appreciating the power of the collective. This is how *the university is a utopian, democratic society*. Like the juggernaut, repressive development was a machine intended for gigantic achievements over short periods of time, and as such, the regime did not have the patience to allow students to experience participation and democracy, which define student life. This is how the existential chasm between a potentially democratic student life and a paternalistic regime obsessed with producing mindless functionaries grew deeper and wider. In the absence of democratic participation, the defiant young women and men quickly learned activism.

The Student Movement

This generation had inherited two major recent setbacks: the 1953 CIA/MI6 engineered coup that had toppled the democratically elected Premier Dr Mohammad Mosaddeq, and the 1963 crackdown on legal opposition following parliamentary elections and the semi-relaxed political atmosphere that had started in 1960. In other words, the living memory of socially conscious university students in the late 1960s was the *traumatic memory of defeats*. It was this knowledge that by 1964 had caused Bijan Jazani and his comrades to lose faith in legal opposition and convinced them that the country's political modernisation had encountered an impasse – the Shah's autocratic rule – that only armed struggle had a chance to challenge. By the late 1960s, the aforesaid processes had wrought out a political binary between the regime in its totality and a new, defiant generation of university students – both Marxists and leftist Muslims.

The PFG arose directly from the student movement, and that is why its militant action succeeded in having a public impact in the country in contrast to several earlier attempts (by Maoists) in the 1960s to instigate guerrilla warfare (Vahabzadeh 2010: 5, 15), although the latter's membership mainly came from university students and graduates. The PFG originators attribute their turn to militant methods to their losing hope in democratic reforms through legal means (Ahmadzadeh 1976; Jazani 1978; Puyan 1979; see Behrooz 1999: 33–4). Their final proof came in the form of the crackdown on all opposition in 1963. In fact, the defence statements of two original founders of one of the PFG constitutive groups unequivocally attest to their democratic aspirations (Mohajer and Baba Ali 2016).

But the student movement would not have borne the militant opposition had it not been for an important demographic fact: to actualise its ambitious modernisation plans, the regime needed trained experts and thus invested heavily in post-secondary education, as a result of which the college and university student population increased more than tenfold in 24 years: statistically, 14,500 students were enrolled in four universities and 2,538 in technical colleges in 1953; by 1977, the number of undergraduate students enrolled in sixteen universities stood at 154,315 while 227,507 were studying in 800 technical training schools (Abrahamian 1980: 22). In other words, university and college students had become a *formidable social force*. They would constitute the unwavering constituency of the militants by 1968 and after: from a dialectical point of view, the regime had produced its own anti-thesis. It was indeed the radicalised factions of student activists who were impressed by the ideas of the New Left and created armed struggle. This radicalisation and the turn to militant action was indeed a global trend: like the PFG, the German *Rote Armee Fraktion* (RAF) and the US Weather Underground sprang out of student movements and bore the signature non-conformism of the New Left (Varon 2004: 9). The same is true of the student movement worldwide from Africa to Latin America (Katsiaficas 1987: 34–5), indicating that 'the guerrillas of the third world and radical movements in the core were intimately tied together in theory, and in practice, they forged a unity against a common enemy (US "imperialism") and a common rival (Soviet-style "radicalism")' (Katsiaficas 1987: 37). Their global context was Cuban revolution, the Algerian war of liberation, and Vietnam's heroic resistance against American imperialism.

With the post-secondary students emerging as a formidable social force, in the absence of the institutional means for genuine political participation, and given the intrusive securitisation of society, student activists increasingly staged targeted protests and sit-ins across university and college campuses. Because genuine student associations were not allowed, student activists self-organised across campuses in semi-clandestine fashion, mostly around loose ideological inclinations, and established lateral connections with like-minded circles in other universities. These diverse circles had generally amicable relations with one another and collaborated against a common enemy. This is why it is much harder to map the Iranian student movement in the 1960s than their European counterparts where student associations were legal. Most of the Iranian students' collective actions concerned concrete grievances or *motalebat-e senfi* ('guild demands'), but these often escalated into political demonstrations, leading to arrests or suspension of student activists. Unfortunately, there are no reliable sources for surveying student unrest in the late 1960s, and state-controlled newspapers of the time did not report such incidents. Thus, researchers like me could only rely on scattered activist reports. These were dress rehearsals, so to speak, as many student activists learned to participate in public events in order to turn them into political rallies. Suffice it to point out two prominent student mobilisations that constituted the backbone of mass rallies in the late 1960s. The first was the mass rally at the funeral procession in January 1968 of the world wrestling champion Gholam Reza Takhti, who had committed suicide, though his death was attributed to a SAVAK conspiracy. The second took place on 22–3 February 1970 when students and workers staged mass violent protests against a change in Tehran Transit bus routes that led to a doubling or tripling of bus fares. By the second day, the protest became a mass uprising that resulted in several protestors being shot to death or wounded and hundreds arrested. According to daily newspapers, the protestors had torched or seriously damaged sixty Tehran Transit buses. The Shah intervened immediately, forcing the government to pay off the Tehran Transit deficit so that the company would resume the old fare rates (Aqeli 1997: 237). In a political climate where the government would not tolerate freedom of assembly and speech, the student movement tactically turned public events into protests against the regime. While the campuses witnessed waves of protests and sit-ins regarding various student and political issues, the newspapers remained silent. They only reported the 22 December 1970 protest in University of Tehran where the students had shouted slogans against the regime (Aqeli 1997: 248). It was at this time that an undercurrent gradually shaped up beneath these mobilisations. Some students were radicalised and adopted militant approaches which – *à la* radical student and urban guerrilla movements of the 1960s – aimed at instigating a popular uprising to overthrow the Iranian monarchy. Although both groups go back to the mid-1960s, the future PFG and OIPM concretised at this time, through the student activist networks.

The raison d'être of the rebellious generation of Iranian students must be sought in the social and political conditions resulting from the Shah's 'repressive development'. It is true that this generation was inspired by the revolutionary spirit of the 1960s (Matin-Asgari 2002; Shannon 2011). But we must point out how extensive socio-economic and social mobility under a police state alienated the growing student population. To this, we must also add the stark inequalities that stained the state's claims of progress. In retrospect, we can observe that the student-based guerrilla warfare captured the audible protest of this particular generation against its non-responsive parent generation that had gathered around the state, its promises and its material rewards.

The fact that small networks of militant intellectuals and university students could elusively but effectively challenge one of the most powerful states in the world at the time, a state known for widespread abuses of human rights and mistreatment of political prisoners (Nobari 1978), is often rightly attributed to the dedication of the activists and the influx of support they continually received (Behrooz 2000: 50; Vahabzadeh 2010: 214). Asef Bayat succinctly captures the conditions under which militants were socialised at this time:

At the time activism did not mean doing civil society or NGO work . . . rather it meant enacting and engaging in political education. So each ideological camp [Islamic and leftist] on college campuses developed its own organization, reading groups, library, hiking trips, dress code, and, most important, a distinctive language for everyday exchange. Both groups would compete avidly in their efforts to recruit new members. But at times they would make tactical alliances, for instance, during strike planning, handing out leaflets, and similar sensitive activities. (2017: 35)

In this context, the PFG was born.

People's Fadai Guerrillas: A Brief History

I have already offered a detailed study of the PFG (Vahabzadeh 2010). Founded in April 1971 following a number of armed operations in Tehran and Tabriz, *Cherikha-ye Fadai-ye Khalq* or the People's Fadai Guerrillas emerged upon the unification of two independent Marxist militant groups consisting largely of university students and graduates, as well as young writers, educators and cultural figures, and a handful of young workers and union activists.

The older founding group, Group One, consisted of young activists from the early 1950s whose formative lived experience was that of the 1953 coup that toppled the democratically elected government of Premier Mosaddeq and his National Front. Affiliated with the Tudeh Party of Iran Youth Organisation, they were disillusioned upon witnessing Tudeh's lethargic response to the coup, as the Tudeh leadership decided not to mobilise its vast membership and clandestine Officers Organisation to counteract the coup. Bijan Jazani (1937–75), a social sciences graduate, and Hassan Zia-Zarifi (1939–75), a lawyer, returned to activism with the advent of the Second National Front in 1960–3 when the Shah had relaxed political restrictions in response to the conditions imposed by the Kennedy administration for granting Iran a US aid package necessary for the Shah's ambitious reforms. This short and precarious period of controlled freedom was terminated with the state's heavy-handed repression in June 1963 – a turning point that brought the country back under the Shah's autocratic rule. Jazani and three others founded the nucleus of the group in April 1963, and Jazani was joined by Zia-Zarifi in March 1966 (Anon. 1976b: 12, 19). For Jazani, Zia-Zarifi and their comrades, the experience of two waves of repression within a decade meant that legal opposition was hopeless. They secretly organised an armed group that had twenty members by 1968, when Jazani, Zia-Zarifi and most members of the group were arrested, tried and received heavy prison terms.

The group's survivors regrouped and recruited new members. Two original members of Group One – Ali Akbar Safai-Farahani and Mohammad Saffari-Ashtiani – returned to Iran after training and fighting in the Palestinian resistance. The group carefully planned an attack, and on the evening of 8 February 1971 a team of nine armed men attacked the Siahkal Gendarmerie Post in Gilan Province. Planning to hold the extravagant Celebration of 2,500 Years of Monarchy in Iran (12–16 October 1971), the regime quickly militarised the region and subsequently arrested the militants (killing two) and their support network. The military court expedited the trial of fourteen members of Group One and executed thirteen militants on 18 March 1971. The operation was parochial but daring; most importantly, it provided Iranian dissidents, especially intellectuals and university students, with a much-awaited *event* that soon led to a contemporary cultural *myth* of gallantry and resistance against the repressive regime. Operation commander Safai-Farahani had reportedly told his interrogator in prison: 'You're mistaken. We've not failed. The next day after our execution, the triumph of Siahkal will resonate throughout Iran' (quoted in Madani 2011). He was right. This small operation was soon celebrated as *rastakhiz-e Siahkal*, the 'Siahkal resurgence' – embodying the *perceived* bold resurgence of a people through its selfless vanguards. The event had given rise to a movement that persisted in the years to come: in the revolutionary streets of 1978–9, scores of leftist protestors shouted, 'We will make all Iran a Siahkal!' A handful of activists from Group One, led by Hamid Ashraf (1946–76), survived the police raids and co-founded the PFG.

The younger founding group, Group Two, came of age in 1960–3 with the experience of the ebb and flow of the student and nationalist movement and was loosely associated with the religious figures around the Second National Front. Amir Parviz Puyan (1947–71) and Massoud Ahmadzadeh (1947–1972), friends from Mashhad, met Abbas Meftahi (1945–72) at Tehran University. Together, they formed a group and gradually adopted Marxism-Leninism. Influenced by Che Guevara and the Cuban revolution, the Brazilian Carlos Marighella, the Frenchman Régis Debray and Uruguay's Tupamaros, they chose armed struggle in 1969–70. Ahmadzadeh and Puyan each wrote a treatise that allowed for the radicalised wings of student activists to accept armed struggle. The group succeeded in rapidly building underground networks with around fifty members, but was soon raided by

SAVAK, in late 1970. Ahmadzadeh, Meftahi, Puyan and Ashraf held meetings in March and April 1971 and founded the PFG in April. The PFG bore indeed the theoretical signature of Group Two. Within a few short months thereafter, Ahmadzadeh and Meftahi were arrested, tried and then executed (1972) and Puyan was killed in a shootout (1971), leaving Ashraf to become the elusive and legendary commander of the PFG and Iran's most wanted man until his death in June 1976, to the extent that reportedly 'almost every day the [S]hah asked his increasingly agitated security chief, General Nasiri, about him' (Milani 2008: 96). Ashraf had brilliantly led the PFG from the verge of annihilation in 1972 to a small but formidable clandestine group that maintained the upper hand in their psychological warfare against state security between 1973 and 1975 (Behrooz, 2000: 63). Their success is partly owing to support by university students and intellectuals, funds from the Confederation of Iranian Students-National Union (CISNU) abroad, and weapons and funds gifted to them by Libya, the Democratic Republic of Yemen, and the People's Front for the Liberation of Palestine (led by George Habash) (Anon. 1976a, 1976b).

The PFG emerged on the political scene as the response of a younger generation of Marxists to the failure of Tudeh Party in 1953. In the eyes of this generation, this was the defeat of conventional, Soviet-style Marxism. Attested by the fact that the founding groups of the PFG bore the signature modes of acting and thinking of the global New Left, they aimed at a communist *re-foundation* or what they called the 'new communist movement'. The PFG still declared Marxism-Leninism as its ideology; although many of its recruits did not have knowledge of Marxism, declaring (nominal) adherence to Marxism-Leninism was required for membership. In this case, 'Marxism-Leninism' was really the signifier of a global solidarity of sister movements for social justice, rather than what it meant for the Soviet Union. The PFG was in fact an ideologically flexible group, as its members in fact believed in different shades of Marxism, despite their proclaimed allegiance to Marxism-Leninism proper. The PFG's guiding theory between 1971 and 1973 was Ahmadzadeh's *Armed Struggle: Both Strategy and Tactics* (summer 1970), according to which guerrilla warfare would compensate for the lack of objective conditions of the revolution (a Leninist requirement, ironically) as armed struggle would soon mobilise the masses towards a popular uprising.

The PFG was perceived as a small motor of intellectuals that would ignite the larger motor of the masses (Ahmadzadeh 1976). The claim that anti-imperialism and armed struggle would make up for the objective conditions of revolution was a common conviction among the urban guerrillas at the time, and West Germany's RAF and the American Weather Underground, among others, also asserted it as a principle (Varon 2004: 7, 8).

While serving his prison term, and until his assassination in prison in April 1975, Jazani monitored the developments of the PFG and his younger protégé, now PFG commander, Hamid Ashraf. He felt the need to provide directions to the group and wrote several key theoretical treatises in prison on how armed struggle and a popular movement should be strategically implemented. For Jazani, armed struggle was only a preparatory stage for political organisation and popular uprising (Jazani 1976a). His miniaturised writings were copied onto cigarette papers and smuggled in belts by about-to-be-released prisoners, usually young pro-Fadai students who were serving short prison terms (Negahdar 2008); the PFG leadership began to take new directions by 1974 towards organising social support networks, abandoning Ahmadzadeh's ideas. Iranian security finally managed to break into the hermetically sealed network of the group through telephone surveillance, which led to the PFG's near-eradication in the spring of 1976 and the death of its legendary commander Ashraf. As the few surviving members tried to rebuild the group, Jazani's ideas also gradually faded away, and by 1979, and in post-revolutionary times, the larger factions of the PFG rejected armed struggle. That a handful of guerrillas managed to keep the group alive until they were joined by released Fadai prisoners on the eve of the Revolution is due to the (universal) principle of identification of the militant with the group, as stated in the RAF slogan: 'the guerrilla is the group' (Varon 2004: 9). After the Revolution, the PFG fashioned itself as a popular, leftist, *political* party – one that nonetheless owed its popularity to the collective, lived memory of the generation that remembered Fadaiyan as heroic and immortal freedom-fighters. Their defence of the rights of the ethnic minorities – notably, Turkmens, Arabs, Kurds – made them popular in the provinces, although they remained astonishingly silent about the new regime's abuses of women's rights. The OIPFG's post-revolutionary popularity came with theoretical and strategic confusion about the new conditions.

Between 1971 and 1979, aside from bank robberies and sporadic shoot-outs with the police, the PFG carried out a dozen carefully chosen and planned operations: their most prominent operation was the assassination of Lieutenant General Zia Farsiu, Chief Prosecutor of the Military Court, in April 1971, who had handed down the death sentences of the Siahkal guerrillas. In addition to armed clashes, the PFG bombed power-lines, military posts and police stations. Through these operations, as the state tried to demonise the guerrillas as terrorists and saboteurs (*kharabkaran*) in the pages of state-controlled daily newspapers, the guerrillas permeated the Iranian social psyche. I remember clearly how state employees mocked the security drills in the government buildings as '*cherikbazi*' ('guerrilla play'), suggesting the guerrillas had actually 'played' the distressed security forces, and that despite such drills, the guerrillas would still succeed in bombing government buildings if they so wished. These years of heightened urban guerrilla presence were commonly dubbed the 'guerrilla period'.

Of course, the 'guerrilla groups and "new communist parties" formed . . . in the belief that they could accomplish what actions of millions of people had failed to do: destroy the existing system so that a new society could be born' (Katsiaficas 1987: 181–2). However, aside from such cases as Nicaragua and El Salvador, the guerrilla movements by and large did not succeed in instigating popular uprisings, and that is to be understood as a global trend, as 'the New Left proved itself incapable of reconsolidating a popular base and moving to the second phase of struggle: going from the contestation of power to the building of a hegemonic bloc capable of leading an entire society in a new direction' (Katsiaficas 1987: 183). The Iranian guerrillas were no exception either, and thus, calling their mode of activism a 'failure' (Behrooz 2000) reports not only a gross misunderstanding, but also lack of knowledge of the global trend of the New Left.

By my count, 237 Fadai members lost their lives between 1971 and 1979, the original phase of PFG activity (Vahabzadeh 2010: 16–77, 257–9). The Fadaiyan played a catalyst role in instigating the 10–11 February 1979 armed uprising that toppled the monarchy (Vahabzadeh 2010: 58–9), and on 10 February the OIPFG established its first open headquarters in the School of Engineering at Tehran University, thus transforming itself from an underground group into a political organisation. As is well-known, the Fadaiyan grew into Iran's most popular leftist organisation following the Revolution – thanks to the 'mythic' presence of the selfless guerrilla in the popular imagination. One account surprisingly claims that in Iran's first (and only free) parliamentary elections (March 1980), the OIPFG candidates received approximately 10 per cent of the total ballots cast (OIPF-M 2010). In this specific parliamentary election (Friday 14 March 1980), 10.87 million cast their votes (out of the 20.85 million eligible voters; a 52% participation rate), which translates into a million votes cast in favour of OIPFG's 64 candidates across Iran. This claim cannot be verified: it sounds exaggerated as in more than half of the country the OIPFG did not even nominate candidates. The election took place amid many claims and complaints about electoral irregularities and fraud. So much so that, in protest at such irregularities, the Advisor to the Premier, Dariyoush Foruhar, resigned from his post (*Kayhan* 20 February 1980, p. 2). The OIPFG also filed official complaints, citing rigged process in several electoral districts, and even called (inconsistently) for a new election (*Kar* 1980c: 2, 1–7; 1980d: 8–9; 1980e: 14). The Ministry of the Interior never published the number of votes in each electoral district, only the votes that elected candidates and runners-up had received. Among the OIPFG candidates were the dissident playwright Said Soltanpour and the writer Nassim Khaksar (see *Kar* 1980a: 14). Both Soltanpour and Khaksar were among the writers who promoted the Fadaiyan through their poetry and fiction and had served prison terms under the Shah.

That said, the OIPFG's popularity might not be measurable in electoral numbers, but there are other indicators: on May Day 1979, hundreds of thousands rallied under the OIPFG banner in Tehran (*Kar* 1979: 1–2). Likewise, on 7 March 1980, in a mass demonstration invited and held by the OIPFG in Tehran's Azadi Square, hundreds of thousands (possibly close to 300,000) Fadai supporters participated (*Kar* 1980b: 8–9). Immediately following the Revolution, Fadaiyan grew very popular in the Plains of Turkmen on the eastern edge of the Caspian Sea where Turkmen OIPFG members mobilised peasants to occupy and redistribute agrarian lands of major landowners, many of whom were from the ruling elite under the deposed monarchy, and organised them into exemplary grassroots, autonomous red councils that, in the absence of a strong presence of the state, took control of their own affairs. Fadai cadres leading the

Cultural-Political Association of the Turkmen People and Headquarters of the Turkmen People in the town of Gonbad Kavus organised the peasants. Alarmed by the strong influence of Marxist Fadaiyan in the region, the new regime clashed with the locals in staged conflicts, which led to two brief armed clashes in March 1979 and February 1980. In the case of the latter, the regime, now prepared for a full-fledged crackdown, heavily militarised the region, repressed the Turkmen movement and kidnapped and assassinated four OIPFG-Turkmen leaders (Vahabzadeh 2010: 68). Although the Democratic Party of Iranian Kurdistan and the Party of Toilers of Iranian Kurdistan dominated the Kurdish regions in western Iran, the Fadaiyan also enjoyed significant popularity among the Kurds before the civil war in the early 1980s and some Fadai factions in fact fought alongside the Kurds during the conflict (Vahabzadeh 2010: 68–9).

From a small, student-based clandestine militant group to the largest leftist organisation in the short-lived 'Spring of Freedom': this book shows how this is largely owing to the 'mythic' effect promoted by dissident arts, that immensely contributed to the construction of the *weltanschauung* through which the Fadaiyan gained popularity.

The OIPFG's dearth of theoretical and ideological approaches eventually caused its disintegration. A first split in 1977 took away a dozen PFG members who joined the Tudeh Party in 1979, while a small faction went back to the now-expired guerrilla methods in 1979. In June 1980, the most popular leftist group in 1979 underwent a series of major schisms that split the OIPFG into several factions: a minority faction (later splitting into several groups) began fighting the new Islamic regime without any clear theoretical or ideological road map, while a majority faction (later split in two) turned to Soviet Marxism and the Tudeh Party, thus abandoning the group's New Left origins, and shamefully supported the repressive, Islamic state for three years before the scythe of the regime's security forces began mowing them down. Whatever their strategy, all Fadai factions were repressed by the mid-1980s. Hundreds, possibly over a thousand, of Fadai activists and supporters lost their lives between 1979 and 1988 (in the summer 1988 massacre, out of 4,486 political prisoners executed 169 were registered as Fadai prisoners of different factions). Thousands were forced into exile and tens of thousands sought refuge in the anonymity of society.

Of the heroic Fadaiyan nothing is left today: ageing leaders, mostly in exile, either quit or engaged in Web-based and exile politics, which do not seriously resonate with the younger generation or today's realities. And yet, the *aura* of that very group whose militants forever marked a period of recent history with their selfless activism still shines in memories and literature written about that era.

The Myth of the General Strike

My original theoretical approach entails the convergence of three distinct theoretical trajectories: myth, event and armed propaganda.

As my first theoretical pillar, 'myth' does not allude to fable or to passive and received traditional beliefs. For me, *myth refers to the active process of collective co-construction of a social narrative linked to present reality.* I dwell on the theory of revolutionary violence by Georges Sorel (1847–1922), who has influenced various, even opposing, ideas from Italian fascism to Frantz Fanon – evidence of his theory's wide-ranging applicability. As an anarcho-syndicalist, he offered the concept of the 'myth of the general strike'. His concept remains abstract, as he did not offer concrete referents to exemplify the myth, which registers a 'lack'. But this abstraction expanded the reach of his ideas. His 'messianic' concept of the 'myth' bears compelling affinities with the epistemological grounds of millenarian or epoch-making movements from Christianity to the French Revolution. Sorel's *Reflections on Violence* (orig. 1906) provides a potential framework for understanding rebellious action in the age of anti-colonial national liberation movements in the twentieth century. Here, his theory assists me in arguing that *a constructed cultural myth (of dissent) creates a political weight often unattainable politically.* So, here I offer a workable exegesis of Sorel in order to *expand* it in the light of my case study.

Sorel's 'philosophy of violence' involves a defence of anarcho-syndicalism (2004: 56). Distinct from 'savagery' or 'force' (2004: 118, 171), violence 'should be employed only for acts of revolt . . . the object of force is to impose a certain social order in which the minority governs, while violence tends to the destruction of the old order' (Sorel 2004: 171). Thus, *violence arises from the generative power of social change* and should be understood as pure and non-judicial (and non-criminal). Sorel compares violence to calculated military campaigns in classical warfare (2004: 115) – the goal-oriented activity of challenging an enemy. This is why Hannah Arendt suggests that Sorel's concept of 'violence' must be understood as an instrumental and rational activity (1970: 79). This conception of violence allows Sorel to discover the essence of the final revolutionary conflict of humanity, he asserts, as perceived by Marx but untheorised by him. The name of this pure violence is the 'general strike'.

In defending revolutionary syndicalism against parliamentary (reformist) socialists, Sorel seeks to theoretically situate revolutionary violence in both *ontological* and *epistemological* terms. Participants in a 'social movement always picture their coming action as a battle in which their cause is certain to triumph', he observes. 'These constructions [i.e. pictures] . . . I propose to call myths; the syndicalist "general strike" and Marx's catastrophic revolution are such myths' (2004: 41–2). The myth is therefore 'identical with the convictions of a group, being the expression of these convictions in the language of movement' (Sorel 2004: 50). In terms of the conceptual genealogy of revolutionary violence of the 1960s, whose connection with the arts this book illustrates, we should consider *certain* affinities between Sorel's 'myth' and the concept of 'utopia' in Karl Mannheim, meant to designate 'that certain oppressed groups are intellectually so strongly interested in the destruction and transformation of a given condition of society that they unwittingly see only those elements in the situation which tend to negate it' (Mannheim 1969: 36). Obviously, Mannheim's 'utopia' primarily relates to the *knowledge* regarding revolutionary action, rather than perceptions of action (Sorel). I will return to this point.

The key component of the ontological aspect of the myth is *action*. It is action that distinguishes revolutionary syndicalists from sedentary claimants of socialism, and thus, it can be understood as an *epistemological marker*. Accordingly, socialism is primarily defined by engagement in revolutionary action. Because they lack action, parliamentary socialists offer only a *semblance* of socialism (Sorel 2004: 120). To Sorel, 'action' means *leaving the present*: 'To say that we are acting, implies that we are creating an imaginary world placed ahead of the present world and composed of movements which depend entirely on us. In this way our freedom becomes perfectly intelligible' (2004: 48). Since action is future-oriented and thus open-ended, it involves 'the *framing of a future, in some indeterminate time*' (Sorel 2004: 124; original emphasis). Its 'indeterminacy', *counter-intuitively*, enables, encloses and anticipates 'all the strongest inclinations of a people, of a party or of a class, inclinations . . . which give an aspect of complete reality to the hopes of immediate action by which . . . men [*sic*] can reform their desires, passions, and mental activity' (Sorel 2004: 125). The myth of the general strike, therefore, captures the essence of genuine social transformation. Thus the 'question whether the general strike is a partial reality, or only a product of popular imagination, is of little importance. All that it is necessary to know is, whether the general strike contains everything that the socialist doctrine expects of the revolutionary proletariat' (Sorel 2004: 127). Reading this in a Freudian light, by conjuring up images, desires and expressions, we see that the myth of the general strike replaces comprehensive knowledge of the revolution with a *condensed, symbolic* version. For me, symbolic action is key: it is symbol alone that allows the transcendence of reality, and thus, symbol is a gateway to liberation from the status quo. Sorel concludes:

> Strikes have engendered in the proletariat the noblest, deepest, and most moving sentiments that they possess; the general strike groups them all in a co-ordinated picture, and, by bringing them together, gives to each one of them its maximum of intensity; appealing to their painful memories of particular conflicts; it colours with an intense life all the details of the composition presented to consciousness. (2004: 127)

With the proletarian revolutionary and future-oriented action that aims at the total transformation of society the myth of general strike emerges (Sorel 2004: 125). This is the *ontological* foundation of the myth. Reformist, parliamentarian socialists can only feign this ontology (Sorel 2004: 78).

Replacing existing social relations will *inevitably embody* an expression of violence, and the general strike embodies this *foundational violence* (Sorel 2004: 57). Thus, proletarian violence expresses the ontological moment of the foundation of the new. *The myth prepares for this moment* that is yet to come and makes sense of all preceding and existing forms of action that push the existing system to its ruins and create room for future innovation. And yet, *this ontological moment needs to be registered* in the knowledge of the working class and its vanguards. The myth is the principle of intelligibility of the future, reconciled humanity as well as the inevitable, transformative violence that prepares for it. So, we arrive at the epistemological aspect of the myth: the general strike becomes a way of conceptualising the proletarian violence (Sorel, 2004: 119). In other words, 'General strikes not only sum up new historical epochs of class struggle by revealing in utmost clarity the nature of the antagonists, they also indicate the future direction of the movement – its aspirations and goals, which, in the heat of historical struggle, emerge as popular wishes and intuitions' (Katsiaficas 1987: 9). Moreover, the myth places socialist knowledge above all strands of socialist representatives of the proletariat (Sorel 2004: 129). This is how the syndicalists solve the epistemological problem of socialist revolution and revolutionary syndicalism becomes an educational power (Sorel 2004: 123, 242).

The myth of the general strike, however, is by no means objective or 'scientific' (Sorel 2004: 124), although it allows for the orientation of the working class towards a meaningful future (Sorel 2004: 49). Nonetheless, one should not try to compare the 'accomplished fact' and the image of myth shared and formed by the people (Sorel 2004: 42). Antonio Gramsci likens Sorel's myth to Machiavelli's 'Prince': neither 'a cold utopia nor . . . learned theorizing', but instead 'a creation of concrete phantasy which acts on a dispersed and shattered people to arouse and organise its collective will' (1971: 126). Let us also note Arendt's observation: Sorel 'ended up proposing nothing more violent than the famous myth of the general strike, a form of action which we today would think of as belonging rather to the arsenal of nonviolent politics' (1970: 12, 78).

To understand guerrilla warfare and the arts (poetry, song, fiction, film) in 1970s Iran, and how the latter contributed to the popularisation of the former, this chapter focuses on how the activists of the time collectively created a *myth* of the immortal guerrilla. The *social-psychological* presence of the guerrillas was possibly as important as their physical obstinance under a police state; the guerrillas' omnipresence significantly amplified the effect of the operations of underground groups which, compared with similar movements worldwide, were small in membership and their operations few in number.

Sorel's theory of revolutionary violence explains how the myth stages revolutionary action within a specific epistemological frame, thus rendering it intelligible. Before proceeding, though, we also need a theory of event.

Event and Movement

Sorel's theory is useful in theorising how revolutionary action creates its own *raison d'être* through a 'myth' that functions as a common ground for understanding and contextualising action within a future that is to-come (*a-venir*). But my approach will be lacking if I do not theorise that which in our particular context held the myth to reality. For that, I need a concept of 'event', my second theoretical pillar, for which I turn to Robin Wagner-Pacifici's work.

Contrary to common perception, an event is not a happening of extraordinary and captivating proportions. Any *incident* that has a potential social significance can become an *event* proper if it introduces a *rupture* (Wagner-Pacifici 2017: 72). Yet the *incident* itself is nothing but 'a series of actions that only gradually and with difficulty cohere into an *event* that can be categorised, located in time and space, and given a name' (Wagner-Pacifici 2017: 1; original emphasis). The component of time is important because it indicates a (perceived) 'turning point in history' (Wagner-Pacifici 2017: 5). Unlike habitual happenings that create the illusion of linear time, an event challenges the linearity of history, announcing a *new era*. Therefore, a turning point, properly understood, redirects history according to the ground the event has created. So, the event is both that which has happened and that which is about to happen (Wagner-Pacifici 2017: 44). It creates its own *ground* because it cannot appear within the established structure. For something to be properly known as an 'event', it should step out of the existing ground and constitute its own.

But no event can be known as such unless it deploys particular *political semiotics*: an event is always *communicated*. When the rupture happens, a number of possibilities are revealed. In and by themselves these possibilities are not coherent. It is political semiosis that in appropriating, even colonising, these possibilities give the event its *identity* (Wagner-Pacifici 2017: 62). In fact, in the absence of a particular semiosis as well as in the presence of multiple semiotics, an incident may never rise to an event. An example of this is the Paris Commune of 1871 (Wagner-Pacifici 2017: 103–13): because diverging discourses attempted to explain this multifaceted movement, each according to its own logic and concern (communists, anarchists or feminists), this spectacular experiment in popular self-governance never attained the status of an event. Therefore, without communicating particular political semiotics – its own lexis, symbols, intimations – an event may appear and disappear without being properly noticed. Communication and ground enable the event to produce its *figure* (Wagner-Pacifici 2017: 49). Once emerging as an event through particular political semiotics, an event lives on within its own particular space, one that retains its identity.

With the concepts of myth and event, which, respectively, pertain to psychological and historical aspects of revolutionary action, before turning to my third theoretical pillar we are now equipped to properly understand the founding moment of Iran's generational militant insurgency – birth of the event.

The Siahkal Resurgence

Pre-dating the PFG's formation in April 1971, an armed attack on the Gendarmerie Post at the village of Siahkal in Gilan Province on 8 February 1971 inaugurated the emergence of a rebellious generation. The Siahkal operation was by no means the country's first or even most significant armed operation in the 1960s, but it was the one that attained the status of an *event*. Let me be clear: the PFG was not the first underground militant group in 1960s Iran. In early 1960s, Maoist student activists in Europe, led by Parviz Nikkhah (1939–79), had returned to Iran to instigate guerrilla warfare. They were arrested after the assassination attempt on the Shah in Marmar Palace in Tehran in April 1965, although the group had nothing to do with it. Moreover, two years before Siahkal, a vast Kurdish armed uprising had taken place in western Iran, a movement that involved hundreds and led to the militarisation of the region (Jahani Asl 2017: 193–202). Undeservingly, the Kurdish movement did not register with the intellectuals because at the time the dissident intellectuals regarded it as a regional movement (*jonbesh-e melli*) rather than a national movement (*jonbesh-e sarasari*) – the latter being what they sought to instigate. Lastly, as early as 1969, a group of young Iranian activists from Europe returned to Iran and founded the Liberation Organisation of Iranian Peoples (*Sazman-e Rah'ibakhsh-e Khalqha-ye Iran*) as an unmistakably urban guerrilla group. The group carried out a bank robbery, but was exposed after its unsuccessful attempt to kidnap the US Ambassador to Iran in 1970, and its members were arrested. By and large, these movements did not permeate the Iranian collective memory due to lack of a constructed political semiosis. As a *foundational act*, the Siahkal operation enabled an era (1971–9) overshadowed by armed struggle and laden with collective perceptions of the immortal, omnipresent and elusive freedom-fighter. To properly understand the 'Siahkal effect', let me offer a brief report of the operation.

The operation was carried out in the context of the security preparations for the Shah's grandiose and extravagant celebration of 2,500 years of monarchy in Iran, held on 12–16 October 1971 at the relics of Persepolis, and attended by heads of states from sixty-nine countries, at the cost of US $200 million. SAVAK planned major security preparations that included a major crackdown on all opposition. In the months prior to the celebrations thousands of student activists and intellectuals were jailed. To show off the power of the state, the head of Internal Security of SAVAK, Parviz Sabeti, staged a televised briefing on 23 December 1970, in which he showcased one of the most able SAVAK agents, Abbas Ali Shahriyarinejad (Shahriyari), who was responsible for several high-profile sting operations that had led to the arrest of dozens of revolutionaries in the 1960s (including Group One). Shahriyari (assassinated by the PFG in 1975) appeared on television with his face obscured, posing as a foreign agent, now exposed by SAVAK. Sabeti introduced him as Eslami or 'the man with a thousand faces', and bragged about SAVAK's (supposed) one million agents and informants. In this 'island of stability', he asserted, nothing moved without the knowledge of Iranian security. Just a month and a half after this televised power-talk, a small team of Marxist guerrillas carried out the attack in Siahkal, smashing the image of the 'island of stability', ridiculing Iranian security. The guerrillas had chosen the Caspian region because of its lush ecology, just as half a century earlier Gilan had been home to the Jangali movement and the short-lived Soviet Socialist Republic of Iran in 1920–1 (see Chaqueri 1995), whose collective memory still lingered in the region.

The operation was rushed in reaction to SAVAK's raid on the team's logistics networks and arrest of several members on the evening of 6 February 1971. Eight out of the nine militants of the mountain team, led by Ali Akbar Safai-Farahani, took part in the attack on 8 February, killing two men. The team was then chased by, and engaged with, the Army from 9 to 28 February. With seven militants finally arrested and two killed, the authorities claimed the quick 'eradication' of the 'insurgents and saboteurs'.

Partial publications of the interrogation records of the Siahkal militants reveal that the attack was rushed to force the release of a militant captured earlier that day (8 February) by the villagers and handed over to Gendarmerie personnel. The eight men seized an old Ford van and took its passengers hostage in the woods under the watch of an armed militant. In the five-man attack on the Post, an officer and a civilian were killed, and a militant was accidentally injured by friendly fire. Two other militants were supposed to simultaneously attack the nearby forest ranger's base (unarmed), but somehow they did not. The team seized the rifles in the Post without taking ammunition. They had planned to blow up the Post but forgot their explosives in the building in their haste to get out of the area (Naderi 2008: 191–9; Rohani 1993: 293–5).

The regime's reaction was surprisingly disproportionate: the Shah ordered the Gilan Gendarmerie Regiment, Provincial Police, SAVAK counter-insurgency unit and several helicopters to descend on the region to suppress just eight guerrillas. Lieutenant-General Oveysi, Commander of National Gendarmerie, directed the operation (Ashraf 1979: 105). Strangely, though, the remaining militants did not escape the region, as they had planned. It was chiefly the freezing temperature and exhaustion that defeated them. During the next three weeks, three insurgents were captured by the frightened villagers of Chehel Sotun, who took the liberty of torturing their captives before handing them over to the authorities. Others engaged with the army on several occasions. Having fled the scene alone and totally exhausted, one militant ended up being captured by an unarmed villager eight days later. When the remaining four tried to surrender, two were shot by the frightened gendarmes (Naderi 2008: 199–221; Rohani 1993: 296–303; Vahabzadeh 2010: 25–30).

With the capture of the militants from both urban (logistical) and mountain teams, the military court rushed the trial and the appeal court proceedings against the fourteen arrestees, and death sentences on thirteen guerrillas were hurriedly carried out on 18 March 1971 (Figure 1.1). The regime declared its conclusive success in eliminating the guerrilla networks in a press release dated 27 March 1971.

Just ten days later, on the morning of 6 April 1971, a team of militants gunned down Chief Military Prosecutor Lieutenant-General Zia Farsiu in Tehran. The assassination not only made a mockery of the security forces,

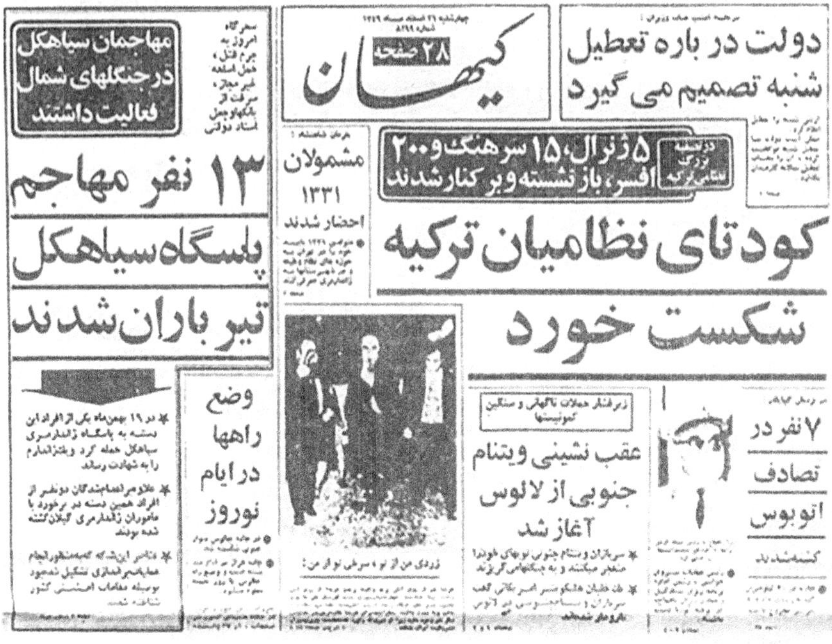

Figure 1.1 *Kayhan* daily (17 March 1971), headline. The headline (upper left) reads: 'This morning, indicted with murder, carrying illegal weapons, bank robbery, and forging legal documents, THE 13 ASSAILANTS OF SIAHKAL POST WERE SHOT.' The insert box reads: 'The Siahkal assailants were active in northern [Caspian] jungles.' Other captions read: 'On 8 February [1971], members of this band attacked the Siahkal Gendarmerie Post and killed an officer. In addition to those executed, two other members of this band were killed in the clashes with Gilan Gendarmerie personnel. The elements of this network, which was created for subversive operations, were identified by the intelligence authorities of the country.'

it left the impression of the presence of a large, well-organised and elusive underground movement. Iranian security conceded a psychological defeat in May 1971 when SAVAK distributed posters of Iran's most-wanted men, nine PFG members, with a bounty of 100,000 Tomans (roughly US$ 15,000 at the time; one could by a condo in hip northern Tehran with that money [Madani, 2011]) for information leading to the arrest or death of each. Contrary to SAVAK's intentions, these posters reinforced the social perception of

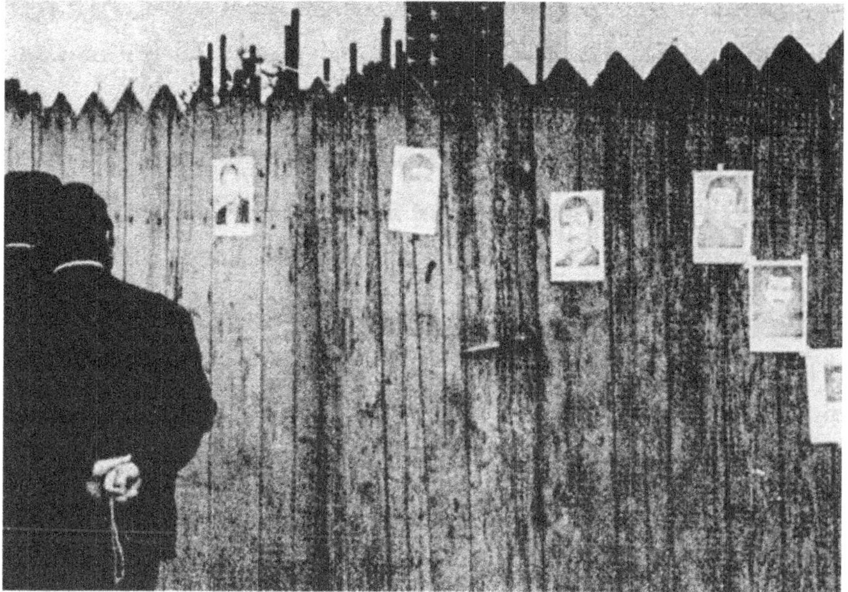

Figure 1.2 Posters of Iran's most wanted men, members of the PFG, spring 1971 (source: Naderi 2008).

the PFG as an elusive, hermetic and impermeable organisation. The posters (Figure 1.2), in fact, increased the popularity of the heroic militants in the eyes of dissident Iranians.

Although the facts show that the operation was a military failure, the mere audacity in rising up in arms and in small numbers to challenge the Iranian state, one the world's top military forces, fascinated dissident Iranians – above all, university students and intellectuals. Once the news reached the public, the operation was celebrated as an *epic* turning point: it was now called the 'Siahkal resurgence' (*rastakhiz-e Siahkal*) – the revival of dissent after the 1953 coup and the 1963 crackdown. It was not just any 'resurgence': armed uprising, albeit small in scale, conveyed a clear message of dissident and revolt. In that naming, *the event was born*, history was suddenly *ruptured*, and the *ground* had shifted – all encompassed through deployment of particular political semiotics: the guerrilla literature. Clandestine circles of dissident university students were quickly mobilised to support the elusive guerrillas. The event had created its own *figure*. Soon, in the communications around Siahkal, in particular poetry and other artistic expressions, the operation was transformed into 'myth': after Siahkal, revolutionary action became possible, even necessary. The event had enabled it, just as the myth demanded it. Indeed, thanks to Siahkal, and the discursive ambit that surrounded it, armed movement became intelligible, even desirable (see Vahabzadeh 2021).

Once the event is publicly marked *qua* event, the conditions of possibility of myth appear. Now the myth, extending the present into a future, founds the principle of intelligibility that rationalises a particular mode of action. The myth lives in collective imagination and empowers those hands that reach for arms to engage in battles against oppression. In the political discourse surrounding the *event* of the 'Siahkal resurgence', militant defiance profoundly touched intellectuals and students, but what took the myth to the public were the works of art.

Cultural and Literary Origins of the PFG

A comparative review of Iranian militant groups in the 1960s and 1970s reveals that the Fadaiyan were distinct in terms of their cultural and literary origins. There is a reason for this: in the 1960s, while ideas of launching militant opposition were still simmering within student and dissident circles, many future PFG members and supporters had engaged in the only means of resistance available to them in the repressive post-1963 atmosphere: writing and publishing in cultural and literary magazines. This is especially true regarding poetry and literary criticism (Chapter 2). Members of the other significant militant group in the 1970s, the OIPM, came from religious backgrounds that mostly did not encourage participation in the cultural milieu dominated by secular and leftist intellectuals. Although some members – for example the Mojahedin leader Reza Reza'i (1948–74) – had written poetry, OIPM members and supporters were significantly absent in the cultural expanse. This is primarily a matter of socialisation: while young women and men from non-religious backgrounds associated with the cosmopolitan cultural currents of their time, young people from religious backgrounds generally socialised in religious circles and attended religious high schools. However, in the 1960s the two solitudes – secular and religious – converged in the universities, which is another story. Members of other, smaller militant groups, few in number, did not register on cultural compass either. In short, among the first generation of Fadaiyan, 'cultural figures' stood out (Yousef 2017b: 586). The PFG was distinct in terms of its cultural presence.

The PFG was mostly made up of university students and graduates, but interestingly, a good proportion of PFG members were in science and engineering. For this book, I conducted a survey of the education levels of 156 PFG 'martyrs' between 1971 and 1979 (out of a total of 237), which produces a reliable indicator of the education of PFG members (and other militant groups). Out of 156, 44 had high school diploma or under, 84 were university students, 23 held bachelors or honours degrees, three were engineering graduates, and two held MD. Of the 84 university students, 34 were engineering students.

From their early days, Fadaiyan were aware of the importance of cultural work, although ideological and biased memoirs deny this, picturing activists in wide brushstroke, 'mostly unfamiliar with knowledge, insight, and culture' (Sarkuhi 2002: 16). Evidence suggests otherwise: Saeed Yousef was one of the younger pro-Fadai poets and proponents of the guerrilla/Siahkal poetry (Chapter 2). While he was studying in the Faculty of Literature of Mashhad University in 1971, he reminisces, in response to a comrade who had asked why he was not recruited for guerrilla teams, his other comrade, fellow student and PFG member Bahman Azhang (1947–72), had replied, 'What Saeed is doing [writing poetry] now is more important' (Yousef 2017b: 608). Years later, Yousef published a photo snapped on the occasion of the farewell party of the Dean of Faculty, Dr Rajai. Twelve men and one woman appear in the photo: of the men, six were arrested in 1971, of whom three (Bahman Azhang, Hamid Tavakkoli and Gholam Reza Golavi) were executed, while two (Yousef and Razi Khodadadi) received a three-year and one (Jahangir Mohammadzadeh) a two-year sentence. The future left-leaning poet and critic Mohammad Mokhtari (1942–88) is also in the photo (Yusof 2017b: 609).

One of the founding teams of the PFG was the leftist 'Tabriz circle' whose prominent members – Samad Behrangi (1939–68), Behruz Dehqani (1939–71) and Ali Reza Nabdel (Okhtay, 1944–71) – were well-known cultural figures in Azerbaijan. Behrangi and Dehqani were classmates in Tabriz Teachers Training College. Rural teachers in Azerbaijan by choice, the three collaborated with the Friday Literary Supplement of *Mahd-e Azadi* newspaper in Tabriz, publishing translations, poetry and Azerbaijani folklore. The editorial of the paper's eight-page first issue (23 September 1965) declared its objective to be an 'effort in reflecting what goes on in the world of arts' (Behrangi 2000: 112–13). The *Mahd-e Azadi* Friday Supplement immediately astonished the Tehran-based literary community for its quality (Behrangi 2000: 113). Interestingly, the second issue of the Supplement (30 September 1965) opened with an article entitled 'The Role of Commitment [*resalat*] in Poetry' (Behrangi 2000: 120), a growing debate at the time (Chapter 2). Bahrangi became the posthumous face of the Fadaiyan (Chapter 4). Dehqani had translated the Irish dramatist Sean O'Casey and the American writer William Faulkner. He had written about Azerbiajani and Italian folklore and authored short stories and literary criticism (see Orang Khadavi 2005). Nabdel had written a book, *Azerbaijan and the National Question* (late 1960s), and published Azeri poetry. His Azerbiajni folklore was published as early as 1961 in the pages of *Ketab-e Hafteh* (no. 1 [23 September 1961], 127–8).

A founding member of the PFG, Amir Parviz Puyan was also an aspiring cultural figure who associated with many key dissident writers. He was the author of a key PFG treatise, *The Necessity of Armed Struggle and the Refutation of Theory of Survival* (1970), his literary legacy remaining lean but pointed. Aside from his translations, short fiction and articles, he wrote an article on the occasion of the death of Jalal Al-Ahmad, Iran's most prominent dissident intellectual, in which he launched a critique of dissident intellectuals who do not partake in revolutionary action: 'Although he was not in our [militant] ranks, he was not in the enemy's ranks either. Thanks to his fighting our common enemy, he was our friend in a specific and limited way. Because of our irreconcilability the enemy too considered him a friend in a specific and limited way. The realization of the socialist movement would have been a challenging test for Al-Ahmad' (Puyan 2012: 193). Under a pen name, Ali Kabiri, he also wrote a short elegy for Behrangi in the special issue of *Arash* (no. 18, November 1968). His Behrangi 'read, went, worked hard, ran, observed, experienced, and learned. [Behrangi] was one of the small group of people who connected reading with seeing and experiencing' (Puyan 2012: 129).

To these cultural figures, one must add known PFG members or supporters who also wrote poetry and fiction but hardly, or never, published them. These include the poets Farhad Sediqi Pashaki, Said Payan and Abbas

Kaboli. Mostafa Sho'aiyan, who had joined the PFG for a short period in 1973–4, was a published poet, essayist and revolutionary theoretician. Of particular mention are Fadai women who were poets and writers: Marzieh Ahmadi-Osku'i, Roqiyyeh Daneshgari, Ghazal Ayati and Sediqeh Serafat. Several other rank-and-file PFG militants were also poets, but neither their works nor their names as artist-militants were ever made public: we know only through memoirs of their comrades (see Setwat 2019). I must point out that the proponents of guerrilla/Siahkal poetry were invariably male, and masculinist tropes and personalities frequently permeated this genre (Chapter 2). However, the Fadai women challenged this trend and introduced feminine world-views in their literature. Lastly, Saeed Yousef, Saeed Soltanpur, Ali Mirfetros, Ali-Ashraf Darvishian and Ne'mat Mirzazadeh (M. Azarm) were the poets and writers who received prison terms for their support for the PFG (Yousef 2017b: 586). This list is not exhaustive, but it solidly reveals the cultural and literary background of Fadaiyan activists. It explains why the PFG stands at the core of this study.

Armed Propaganda: In the Language of Nimble Symbols

Now to my third theoretical pillar. Between 1971 and 1976, the PFG carried out a *limited* number of carefully devised operations and assassinations that were meant to connect Fadaiyan with their actual and potential social constituencies – students, workers, political prisoners and intellectuals – as well as launching psychological warfare against state security (Vahabzadeh 2010: 38–9, 50–1, 99–103). Fadaiyan followed specific rules of engagement: for instance, unlike their Muslim counterpart, the OIPM, they did not assassinate foreign nationals – specifically, the US military personnel stationed in Iran – or target the royal family, because such operations would not contribute to popular mobilisation of specific social groups. In contrast to Fadaiyan, Mojahedin had assassinated US nationals – namely, Airforce Major General Harold Price on 21 May 1972 and Lieutenant Colonel Lewis Lee Hawkins on 3 June 1973. Moreover, they had attempted to kidnap Shahram Pahlavinia, son of Princess Ashraf Pahlavi, on 23 September 1971. Also, they bombed a Bank Omran branch and Kourosh department store in Tehran because the Pahlavis were their shareholders (see OIPFG and OIPM 2014: 100–1). Let us mention that in 1972 the PFG and the OIPM had one joint plan to assassinate an American national (see OIPFG and OIPM 2014: 104–5), but it did not materialise and this was before Jazani's theory was adopted by the PFG.

The success of the the Fadaiyan's operations – some two dozen bombings and half a dozen assassinations in the span of five years (1971–6), excluding shootouts with the police – was owing to Jazani's brilliant theory of 'armed propaganda' (*tabligh-e mosallahaneh*), to which I have previously dedicated due analysis (Vahabzadeh 2010: 38–41). The concept can be traced back to Russian Narodniks and Lenin's appropriation of it through his vanguard party 'propaganda' programme (see Vahabzadeh 2019b: 100). Strictly, though, 'armed propaganda' was formulated through the simultaneous experiences of Vietnamese and Cuban liberation. In *People's War, People's Army* (1961), General Võ Nguyên Giáp proposes armed units under this designation tasked with the 'first period of the preparation for armed insurrection' (2014: 39). In *Guerrilla Warfare* (1961), Che Guevara suggests a similar idea: armed fighters should approach villages and speak to the peasants about the struggle (1998: 16). For Che Guevara, 'armed propaganda' meant the presence of the guerrillas in the liberated or conflict areas, involving the guerrillas explaining their actions and trying to win the support of the peasants (1998: 87; Debray 1967: 47). When the concept reaches Brazilian Marxist revolutionary Carlos Marighella, it appears in a new light in his *Mini-Manual of the Urban Guerrilla* (1969): 'The coordination of urban guerrilla activities, including each armed action, is the primary way of making armed propaganda. These actions, carried out with specific objectives and aims in mind, inevitably become propaganda material for the mass communication system' (Marighella 1969). The brilliance of Jazani resides in his transforming a primarily organisational *term* in Giáp and Che into a *concept* akin to Marighella's understanding, but a superior one (see Vahabzadeh 2010: 100).

Thus, for the first time here, I offer a *hermeneutic* reading of this theory that intends to *reveal the hidden message* embedded in, and sheltered by, his explicit writings. By focusing on the *said* in his theory, I wish to excavate the *unsaid*, that which lies at the heart of his theory, *assumed* by him, and thus never theorised. Between 1971 and 1976, the PFG assassinated two military personnel, two SAVAK interrogators, a SAVAK agent and infiltrator, a factory owner, and a defecting member. While reflecting in prison on the increasing popularity of the Fadaiyan among the educated classes, Jazani, who regarded the PFG as his brainchild, offered the *concept* of 'armed propaganda' to capture the *socially symbolic* and thus *mythic* presence of the elusive guerrillas. He departed from Che's notion, as the latter, capturing the Cuban experience, assumes the presence of a guerrilla force that can create a liberated zone. Iranian guerrillas had no significant military might, nor could they force a liberated zone. This is a major dissimilarity between the two cases. However, by drawing on the similarities between Iran and Latin America (fighting against imperialism and its domestic agents in the state), Jazani deploys 'armed propaganda' (*tabligh-e mosallahaneh*) to emphasise the *symbolic and metonymic* character of guerrilla operations (1978: 47), although due to his lacking proper semiotic phraseology this aspect of his theory remains *under-articulated*. That said, however, my interpretation reveals the hidden components of his concept, as follows:

(1) First, carefully chosen targets allow the guerrillas to send a *clear message* to a particular public, state functionaries or movement supporters, and each operation (bombing and assassination) is accompanied by distribution of tracts that explain how the operation was in support of a specific group (students, workers, intellectuals, peasants, urban poor, etc.); I call this aspect the *communications effect*.

(2) Second, an operation makes the guerrillas, who are measurably multiple times weaker and thousands of times smaller than their adversary, *appear* larger and more capable than they actually are; I call this the *metonymic effect*.

(3) Lastly, the operation renders the regime susceptible and confused in the eyes of the people, as it is unable to block or counteract such assaults; I call this the *political effect*.

These effects are released from armed operation and the subsequent discourse emerging and centring around it simultaneously. Jazani must have had such a model in mind, however tacitly, when he thought armed propaganda an efficient method. *This triangular effect of armed propaganda lends itself to the connection of dissident arts and militant resistance in 1970s Iran* (Figure 1.3). Armed propaganda, therefore, should involve activities and operations that

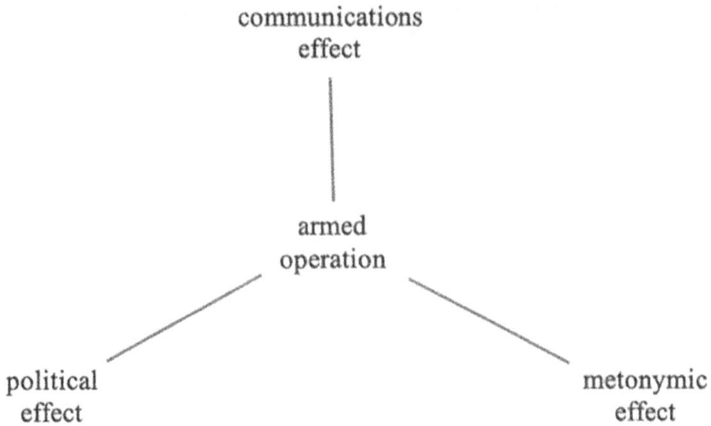

Figure 1.3 Triangular theory of armed propaganda, extrapolated from Jazani's theory.

can be decoded by politically uneducated publics (Jazani 1978: 47). Thus, Jazani's 'armed propaganda' is fit for urban guerrilla warfare where there cannot be any rebel-controlled zone (as in Vietnam or Cuba). Stated differently, Jazani considered armed action – using weapons for specific political targets in the rebels' war against the state – as the source of *production of collectively-receptive meaning*. With each bombing and assassination, the guerrillas' weapons would fire a cluster of symbolic gestures and messages targeting simultaneously multiple fields, groups, supporters and enemies. Armed propaganda distinguishes a political assassination from blind terrorism (Jazani 1978: 36, 45–6). Since Jazani was clear about the fact that the guerrillas – made up of intellectuals and educated individuals and thereby detached from the masses – were too small to even imagine unseating the state, and since he believed that the dissidents were not able to contact, let alone communicate, with people in order to mobilise them, he strategised that proper operations of the intellectuals' armed struggle could lead to a popular uprising. But between the two discrete points, the first actual and the second projected, armed propaganda serves to ensure the symbolic and metonymic presence of the guerrillas that would eventually connect armed struggle to the perceived popular revolt. Thus, his proposed means of popular mobilisation was *not*, strictly speaking, political, but heavily symbolic. Indeed, without being equipped with theories of *social semiotics*,

Jazani proposed a theory that heavily relied on collective signs and symbols. We can see how Jazani's original interpretation and inventive application of the Cuban experience actually produced a semiotic theory of politicised social symbols that has been obscured by ideological and doctrinal readings of his work, obscured up until now and in these lines. This is how the myth surrounding the event of 'resurgence' shaped the 1970s rebellious politics.

'Armed propaganda', therefore, has *certain conceptual affinities* with the 'myth of the general strike'. Whereas Sorel's theory belongs to the time of rising working-class movements in the West, 'armed propaganda' reconstructs the 'myth' in the age of anti-colonial national liberation. Jazani's observation about the metonymic effect of small guerrilla operations, however, was already experientially and intuitively at work in the minds of the activists of the time, as they communicated the political message of these operations. In Jazani's words, 'Although these [guerrilla] groups are extremely small in comparison to the forces of the regime, their militancy and immortality [*fananapaziri*] in the face of the regime's great power puts an end to the one-sided and absolute reality of the regime' (Jazani 1978: 43).

The collectively constructed and vehemently publicised mythic and epic depiction of the guerrillas, despite state censorship, amplified the news about the insurgents. The Siahkal *event* had released great synergy. The metonymic presence of the guerrillas in dissident view appears in this follow-up 'report' on Siahkal operation in an issue of the short-lived publication *Nabard* (published in Europe):

Continued Armed Struggle in the Caspian Jungles

Currently in the Caspian jungles, outside [the towns of] Shahsavar, Sari, and Amol, the guerrillas, in bands of three, are fighting with the armed forces. Due to the guerrillas' continued attacks, frightened Forest Rangers and Gendarmerie Forces have evacuated parts of the wooded areas and this has caused the local residents to be able to use the jungles at will.

To take away the guerrillas' ability to use natural camouflage, the regime has sprayed the region using poisonous chemicals that destroy green vegetation and tree leaves. (*Nabard* 1971: 4)

The 'report' is completely fictional, a work of imagination. *Nabard* (Combat) was published by some activists of the splinter group from the Revolutionary

Organisation of the Tudeh Party of Iran stationed in Europe. Supporters of armed struggle, these activists included Mehdi Khanbaba-Tehrani (the key figure behind the publication), Bahman Nirumand, Homayun Qahreman and Esfandiar Ashja'i (see CSHD 2004: 351, 357–8).

Readers who, like this author, are old enough to reminisce upon televised images of the Vietnam War in the 1960s and 1970s recognise the source of the claim about spraying chemicals to destroy the guerrillas' natural camouflage! It never happened. Reports like these, drafted and distributed without the Fadaiyans' knowledge but never denied or acknowledged by them, helped the guerrillas attain a metonymic presence. Those who knew the facts did not speak out about such fabrications because they regarded these 'reports' as a part of psychological warfare against the state. In all fairness, the PFG never engaged in such unrealistic hyperboles in its official literature, but they apparently enjoyed such superhuman depictions of their activities. To show the extent of reach of these rumours, suffice it to document that, while in prison, Jazani acknowledged such exaggerated accounts: 'after Siahkal, it was rumoured that the jungles of the North [Caspian region] are full of guerrillas' (1976a: 56).

It was the Siahkal operation that allowed narratives of heroism and epic guerrilla presence to surface in arts and poetry. Clearly, the Siahkal event in and by itself had already produced the triangular effect of armed propaganda before Jazani had proposed it, but obviously his gaze was not remiss regarding this, and for that he must be credited. Clearly, the images conjured up in such 'reports' stem from the event itself: *we do not create myths; we discover them.* These sentimental depictions within the emerging public discourse of a rebellious generation did not escape Jazani, who reflected in prison on the 'immortality' of the guerrillas, seeing in these widespread, collectively shared fables the materialisation of his theory of 'armed propaganda':

The people have taunted the regime by communicating news and hundreds of rumours in favour of the guerrillas. Fallen guerrillas have left behind themselves tales of heroic deeds. Following the attack on the Siahkal Post and even after the execution of the thirteen [militants], the jungles were filled with guerrilla bands. After the execution [assassination] of [General] Farsiu and announcing the bounty for the 9 guerrillas, the people made fun of the regime through jokes. After his death, Puyan came back to life many times. In his clashes [with police] Saffari [Ashtiani] attained super-human powers and at the time of his martyrdom he had been fighting the enemy single-handedly for hours. Mehrnush [Ebrahimi] jumped from one rooftop to another, killing enemy agents with her machinegun . . . These are the positive signs of the sympathy and love of the people toward armed struggle. (Jazani 1978: 78; see also Jazani 1976a: 56–8)

This passage contains my proposed communications, metonymic and political effects of the operations of the guerrillas that created a social text, a public counter-discourse, that annulled the regime's propaganda. A guerrilla version of the 'myth of the general strike' now comes to life via a revolutionary generation that founded in Iranian politics something utterly new: Marxist-Leninist, urban, intellectual-based, guerrilla warfare. Despite mortal setbacks by 1976, the PFG resurrected in 1979 as Iran's most popular leftist political party, primarily due to the success of its vast and talented supporters in reconstructing the myth of the immortal and selfless fighter for freedom and justice. I noted that Sorel's theory tends to *render revolutionary violence intelligible* within the proletarian politics of his day. The Siahkal resurgence, in our case, immediately became a source of inspiration for a defiant generation, as it rendered guerrilla insurgency intelligible, constructing a generation's unifying horizon of liberation. Haloed with gallantry, Fadaiyan and other militants were elevated to the status of hagiographised liberators in underground publications and in the hearts and minds of dissidents and discontented publics. Guerrilla action, just like general strikes, 'create[s] a new reality, negating previous institutions, rupturing the hegemony of the existing order, and releasing seemingly boundless social energies which normally remain suppressed, repressed, and channelled into more "proper" outlets. The liberation of the life instincts in these moments creates unique qualities of social life' (Katsiaficas 1987: 10). Inspired by the event, and in the context of the triangular effect of the armed presence of elusive guerrillas, the arts re-emerged as the articulators and perpetuators of the myth.

On Censorship

The entrance of print media in Iran in the nineteenth century gave birth to rival twins: freedom of expression and state censorship. While the Iranian state had ensured a monopoly over radio and television broadcast up until the age of the internet, print media has remained an arena of expressive challenges. No wonder that exile media, where freedom of expression is exercised, has always been a part of contemporary Iranian culture – a phenomenon aided these days by multipolar social media (aided in turn by VPN and proxy) despite the state's failing attempts to curb and filter them.

As it pertains to my study of the literary and artistic defiance of the status quo and advocacy of an emerging, militant movement, a quick glance at the post-1953 institutionalisation of censorship, consistently nicknamed *momayezi* or screening, is necessary. The 'Screening Committee', renamed the 'Writing Bureau', under the Ministry of Culture and Arts was tasked with (print) publication licensing under the auspices of the Fourth Division of SAVAK (founded in 1957). In 1963, the Bureau was moved under the newly established Ministry of Information, renamed in 1973 Ministry of Information and Tourism, and was mandated with screening all media and not just print. Around the late 1960s, the process was set in this way: before distribution, a printed book must obtain a National Library Registration Number, and in order for that to happen, a copy must be submitted to the 'Writing Bureau', which, upon examination of its content, would approve, approve subject to content changes, or ban publication (Khosravi 1999: 166–7). This way, the onus was on the publisher: in case of banned materials, the publisher, having already paid for typesetting and printing, would lose his investment. So, the publication licence now caused self-censorship. Publishing magazines also required a licence, but it could be revoked if any issue of a magazine contained content deemed inappropriate. In 1974, at the peak of the battle between the guerrillas and Iranian security, fifty newspapers and magazines were shut down by the government (Khosravi 1999: 168).

The screening process sounds rigorous, but, aside from obvious things like insulting the Shah, ridiculing the monarchy or offending against Islamic values, there was no uniformity in approach, and the extent of censorship could vary depending on the screener (*momayez*). There were not even agreements among the screeners, and often a book would be screened by more than one *momayez* (Khosravi 1999: 179–80). Noticeably, the government recruited some well-known writers and poets as screeners. Some prominent writers in this list include: Amir Houshang Ebtehaj (b. 1928), Hossein Pejman Bakhtiyari (1900–74), Rahim Mo'ini Kermanshahi (1922–2015), Simin Behbahani (1927–2014), Nader Naderpour (1929–2000), Yadollah Royaee (b. 1932), Fereidoun Moshiri (1926–2000) and Shahyar Ghanbari (b. 1950) (Jannatie Ataie, 2005: 29, 32). Sometimes censorship allowed the classicists who worked as *momayez* to simply impose their preference without any obvious political reason (Jannatie Ataie 2005: 27–8). To complicate matters, the Fourth Bureau of SAVAK had a free hand in all this, its decisions superseding that of the Writing Bureau; it even banned, removed from bookstores and destroyed books that had been previously published (Khosravi 1999: 214). While print censorship has a long history, song, soundtrack and film screening and censorship came in the early 1970s (see Chapters 3 and 5).

There is a curious memo (218/2) titled 'Preliminary Plan for Monitoring Literary and Artistic Works' that contains recommendations for a unified screening process. It is not clear which organisation is the author of this document. Amazingly, the long memo uses the word *sansur*, stating that 'advanced countries' have relinquished censorship altogether and censorship has proven ineffective. Putting a positive spin on screening, the memo suggests a 'foundational approach', a new organisation under the Premier's Office. A committee of educated and reputable writers and artists, it is suggested, should screen all publications as well as theatre and film productions, to filter out works (1) contrary to the Imperial Constitution, (2) containing violence, malice and pornography, and (3) 'outside the aforesaid political and moral bases'. The memo also recommends awards for artistic works that uphold the values promoted by the state (OMCP 2000a: 1,048–57). Whatever this memo yielded remains unknown: censorship continued in the ways described earlier, but it is important to note that the government wished to have a proactive role in censorship.

Let us remember that enhanced restrictions on publication in the 1960s were a response to the growing cultural activism of intellectuals and the expansion of higher education institutions – a sociological fact. A survey of the number of published books illustrates my point: 751 books were published in 1963, 1,048 in 1964, 1,752 in 1965 and a staggering 4,709 books in 1969, the highest in the entire Pahlavi era (Khosravi 1999: 177, 166).

Censorship was not just imposed on political texts. A survey of published books after 'alterations' (year unknown) in different areas shows that 54 altered titles were in the social sciences, 45 in history, 39 in philosophy, 38 in literature, 38 in religion, 33 in the arts, 30 in geography, 17 in languages, and 26 in other categories (Khosravi 1999: 185). As might be expected, censorship was the most important grievance of the Iranian Writers Association (founded in 1968).

The laundry list of how censorship was implemented requires an independent study, but for readers who may not be familiar with the Iranian reality in this period, let us go through a number of amusing examples extracted from the archives of the Writing Bureau or SAVAK. Generally, screening targeted particular expressions, allusions and suggestions deemed 'inappropriate' and 'sensitive'. Aside from the obvious words (like 'tulip', 'comrade', 'forest', 'winter'), strange cases abound. Look at these recommendations extracted from screening files: 'the book attacks "night" and "darkness" and that causes concern'; 'change the title from "Behind This Tall Mountain They Plant Light" to "The Winds Die Wailing"'; 'Change the title "Rich King"' (Khosravi 1999: 184, 186). Even Plato's comment on the unjust nature of trials in the *Apology* was removed (Khosravi 1999: 188). Lastly, a children's book, *How the Red Flower Grows*, was printed with full colour illustrations on glossy paper in 5,000 copies. Its publication coincided with the trial and execution of the poet and critic Khosrow Golesorkhi (Vahabzadeh 2010: 218–19; see Chapter 2). Golesorkhi in Persian means 'of red flower' (or 'red rose'). The police raided the print shop and seized all copies of the book. The publisher was told that 'this book . . . is the story of Golesorkhi'. All copies were burned (Khosravi 1999: 190–1).

They may seem random, but these cases reveal that in the 1960s and 1970s, to quote Umberto Eco, a 'semiological guerrilla warfare' preceded and was concomitant with militant activitism. Clearly, *those who controlled the linguistic and visual signs controlled also the political imagination.* The socially conscious writers, poets and filmmakers of this decade knew this by heart. They had at their imaginative disposal a vast array of metaphors, tropes and symbols that, using artistic licence, they released into literary and artistic works with the intention of conveying uncommunicable defiance, testimony and mourning. Poetry reveals this best. State censorship was tasked with decoding, curbing and banning ever-emerging tropes. One day the river is a river; the next it represents a solitary life's flow towards the sea of solidarity. Then at some point the symbols get fixed: they are articulated as a point of antagonism and cannot be read otherwise: the forest becomes the secret bastion of guerrillas. And the antagonists now knew what it meant. Ferdinand de Saussure tells us that the linguistic sign (and sign in general) is a matter of convention. So, to keep semiotic defiance fresh and provocative, the artists needed to dispatch new tropes and symbols or redeploy the existing ones in nuanced and oblique ways. Steadfast, Iranian poets, writers and filmmakers mastered this art. Censorship forced the nimble situating of signs – literary or visual. Often, writing meant engaging in the perilous undertaking of political imagination at this time of defiance.

Conclusions: Acting and Tropes

Every age arises from a founding event immortalised through a myth – an organising principle that connects the present to a future and allows for the ordering of activity under the existing conditions to be imagined, rationalised and aligned with an *a-venir* collective self.

Under the conditions of repressive development, Iran's ruling class produced a new social class of trained professionals, expected to man the ambitious developmental projects that would land Iran in the orbit of international capitalism. Yet this ambitious class of professionals – university students and graduates – was impeded from genuine political participation. Political disenfranchisement of the otherwise prosperous middle class alienated Iran's younger generation, and, gnawing appallingly on its collective soul-searching, censorship ruined its chances to create its *weltanschauung* in a participatory fashion. Armed struggle, *in nuce*, represents an attempt at bringing about political opening. Against the backdrop of the brutal security forces, the selfless actions of the militants invoked in the Iranian collective psyche age-old fables of gallantry and heroism. Such cultural dispositions in turn shaped the political behaviour of the Iranian leftist movement, while the Pahlavi Dynasty was appealing to an archaic ideology of Persian Empire largely unrelatable by the average citizen, let alone the poor and marginalised.

For the rebellious younger generation a new myth was needed. The PFG and other militants created their own 'myth of the general strike' through armed struggle: their myth made oppression vivid and resistance to it possible. *This myth rendered a particular coded action (militantism) intelligible, even desirable.* Following an event, the construction of a myth is the *foundational gesture* of a new age and deploys an array of available but also 'compatible' symbols and tropes. The myth is simultaneously real and imaginary, political and artistic. It grows into the *organising principle and the point of convergence of future dissident tropes and symbols.* It perpetuates itself through the *tropes* it begets and nourishes. So, the cultural study of social movement activism will inevitably yield the study of a tropological universe. That is why, as Jazani clearly saw but left underarticulated, an armed operation immediately acquired communications, metonymic and political dimensions that were relayed to the public in the hopes that armed action would overcome the psychological defeatism internalised by the populace. In Jazani's words, 'What will impress onto the cold steel of the masses during a period of inertia is the blazing fire of the vanguard' (1976e: 25). The question of the mobilisation of the populace was at the heart of Sorel's and Jazani's theories (and the entire Marxist and revolutionary movements from the nineteenth century up until today).

Here is the issue: in every moment of an intended revolutionary change, as Sorel recognised, it is necessary, even inevitable, *to create a myth that unifies diverse experiences of dissident groups and renders revolutionary violence indispensable and justifiable.* Understanding this 'myth' as an ideological façade, while not quite incorrect, will detract from its significance. Acting needs to be linked, *in perception*, to a life-altering experience, while in fact action remains connected to its projected purpose. This is when we notice the cohort of images (surrounding the Fadai Guerrillas) that are capable of instigating 'the noblest, deepest, and most moving sentiments' (Sorel 2004: 366) of the revolutionaries and their supporters.

To be precise, Sorel refused to consider the myth in terms of any measurable step. 'In employing the term myth I . . . put myself in a position to refuse any discussion whatever with the people who wish to submit the idea of a general strike to a detailed criticism' (Sorel 2004: 43). Understandably, his refusal to 'concretise' the myth arises from safeguarding the myth against endless factional debates among socialists. Through this refusal, Sorel conceptualised the myth as a super-ideological point of convergence of all revolutionary socialists. Utopia, as an image of a desire and a measure of a want, need not have 'realistic' aspects, but it still exercises power over us (Sorel 2004: 126). This is where the work of Mannheim (1969) once again comes to mind. Tropes compensate for the realities that *a-venir* action wishes to undermine.

The sacrifices of young men and women – who otherwise could have had a comfortable life but had instead chosen to fight for political inclusion and justice – did not go unnoticed in the eyes of a vast array of Iranians suspicious of commanded modernisation. As such, without knowledge of literature on revolutionary violence (like Sorel's), this generation *instinctively and existentially created* its own liberationist 'myth', a key element in revolutionary mobilisation. This myth, in turn, became part of the Iranian social psyche and culture. That the vanguards of this generation turned to Marxism-Leninism and guerrilla warfare (*à la* Latin America) must be understood in the context of the 1960s. The ideological inclinations and violent methods of this generation must be viewed as secondary to the 'myth' they had created. The Fadai Guerrillas re-emerged after the 1979 Revolution as Iran's largest leftist group not due to their ideology or violent methods but because of the cultural impression they had left on society as selfless lovers of the oppressed (Vahabzadeh 2010: 244–5).

The reach of the PFG was limited to its support network, due to police conditions and censorship. It had neither the resources *nor the proper means of expression for communicating with the populace*, given its consistent use of leftist lexis that alienated the average reader. This is where the arts stepped in: *the guerrillas were gradually and symbolically, and thus culturally, reconstructed through artistic, literary and visual allusions, cues, expressions and tropes* by the intellectuals who promoted the image of the selfless freedom-fighter in the public eye, and helped promote a political binarism in which one should have sided either with the regime or with the dissidents. Thanks to the dissident artists, this binarism permeated the collective psyche of the people and *inadvertently* prepared them for the diverse revolutionary movement of 1978–9 that was eventually exploited by the clerics (Vahabzadeh 2010: 215).

To understand how this cultural construction of dissent, in connection with my tripartite theory of myth, event and triangular aspect of 'armed propaganda', rendered militant activism intelligible and desirable, we need to attend to how poetry, songs and soundtracks, short fiction and film *communicated* the *political message* of the dissidents through the artistically iterated *metonyms* of action.

2

LIFE IMITATING ART:
THE THIRTY-YEAR POETIC HISTORY

Poetry arises from life and is the fruit of life. But it is certainly not the outcome of our feelings, although it might be connected to our feelings and select our feelings or impressions.

Nima Yushij (1945)

We had all the words of the world at our disposal and
we did not say
> *that which would be of use*
Because there was one word
> *only one word that was missing:*
— freedom!

We did not say it.
You visualise it!

Ahmad Shamlu (1972)

Poetry-loving Persian speakers from my generation are fortunate to have within their collective memory the relayed yet tangible experience of modern Persian poetry's advent – the historic break from the age-old, captivating and rich tradition, over a millennium long, of classical

Persian poetry. This ground-breaking feat was championed by Nima Yushij (Ali Esfandiyari; 1897–1959) and his *she'r-e no* (New Poetry, or modern poetry). Yushij and his (often forgotten) predecessors and contemporaries on the path of poetry modernisation relentlessly campaigned to 'release' Persian poetry from the classical metrics, structures and imagery that these vanguards regarded as imposed limitations on their expressing their shifting realities in a rapidly modernising country (Akhavan-Sales 1990; Ariyanpour 1988; Karimi-Hakkak 1995; Naficy 1997; Talattof 2000). Although it resulted from a collective endeavour, the eventual and vigorous entrance of Iran's poetic modernity, in the face of resistances from defenders of the tradition, is undoubtedly tied to Nima Yushij. History has its own curious logic.

Yushij's unwavering commitment to poetic modernity, expressed in his works and those of contemporary or subsequent generations deeply influenced by him, was a part of an era's Zeitgeist following the Constitutional Revolution (1906–11) – a period that marked the beginning of the long, painful and interwoven process of solidifying Iranian modernity through the authoritarian Pahlavi state. This Zeitgeist was also registered through the then-emerging modern Persian fiction, advocated by several contemporaries of Yushij, which intrigued Nima as a literary movement braided with his New Poetry. In the realm of literature as well as in the cultural milieu, a revolutionary spirit was in the air in the early-to-mid-twentieth century. The poetic style of *she'r-e no* that Yushij founded was collectively named after him: *she'r-e Nima'i* or Nimaic poetry. The naming of phenomena, events and styles is never innocent, and in the case of Nimaic poetry, we will see why.

The debates over *tajaddod-e adabi* (literary modernisation) came to an ascertainable conclusion, and modern Persian literature won the day by breaking new paths. History always stages its heroes in an uncanny fashion, just as triumph often overshadows the many who brought it about. I have shown elsewhere that the Nimaic poetic modernisation came at the cost of overshadowing some key figures among Yushij's contemporaries (Vahabzadeh 2007b). For the record, Tabriz-based Taqi Raf'at (1889–1920), poet and Constitutional revolutionary, was one of the earliest pioneers of poetic modernity whose debate with traditionalist (*Malekolsho'ara* or Poet-Laureate) Mohammad Taqi Bahar (1886–1951) over poetic modernity is often cited as an early source of the process that culminated in Nima's innovations (Ariyanpour 1988: 445–66; Karimi-Hakkak 1995: 16–18; Shams-Langarudi 1991a: 50–6). According to Ahmad Karimi-Hakkak, however, Raf'at's advocacy of poetic modernity, although important in providing an intellectual context, 'did not result in any change visible to the naked eye or immediately perceptible in other ways' (1995: 234). Let us note that neither traditionalists nor modernists constituted monolithic groups; and one must acknowledge their internal diversity. That said, because this historic-poetic advent stands at the roots of a subsequent phenomenon in the 1970s, I must acknowledge two of Nima's contemporaries. The first is Abbas Shamseddin Kia (1909–87), a.k.a. Partow Doctor Tondarkia, who was influenced by French literary modernity (like Nima) and proposed his '*Shahin*' (falcon) as a poetic style intended to collapse the age-old distinction between poetry (*nazm*) and prose (*nasr*) as a model for poetic modernity. He called it '*nasm*'. Tondarkia exceeded poetry and reached philosophy. His proposal was perhaps too radical and abstract for his time, so much so that his '*Shahin*' poems were scorned by his contemporaries. He was silenced by traditionalists and modernists alike (see Karami 2019; Shams-Langarudi 1991a: 192–210; Vahabzadeh 2007b: 37–51). The second figure, Houshang Irani (1925–73), also faced a similar fate when his radical poetic style became the subject of unending ridicule. Some traditionalists flagged Irani's radically modernist and nonconformist (and Buddhist) poetry in order to scorn Nimaic New Poetry. He chose silence and withdrew from the public spotlight before dying in oblivion (see Shams-Langarudi 1991a: 452–66, 497–507; Tahbaz 2001; Vahabzadeh 2007b: 23–5).

Phenomenology and Literature

My allusions to the last two, marginalised figures bring me to a key proposition with implications for this study. Phenomenology, my guiding school of thought, is the study of appearances: to be precise, the study of how the inter-subjective frames and the structures within frame things in specific ways that cause phenomena to appear to our view as endowed with specific meanings. By exposing how such collective but tacit constructions veil the 'things themselves', phenomenology intends to *re-activate* original meanings buried under layers of *sedimented* meanings and thus allows for new beginnings. Accordingly, phenomenology and literature have always been kinsfolk (Vahabzadeh 2015d). Phenomenology helps us understand the *emergence* of modernist poetry properly. As discussed elsewhere, *genuine* poetry, as opposed to imitation poetry, is always about *beginnings* and a breaking away from traditions, norms or styles. Poetry is an *event*: it *happens* at the moment of subverting the existing 'logic' (of style) and the experience of the *death of meaning* and the moment of astonishment. With the experience of the death of meaning, and subsequent *wanderings*, fleeting as these experiences are, we move away from the familiar and are drifted into the unfamiliar and wandering that leads us to caesura. Where poetry appears, phenomena, now defamiliarised, shine forth in a new light and a new world becomes possible (Vahabzadeh 2007b: 17, 18, 20, 22) – whence arises the *prophetic* aspect of genuine, life-altering poetry that, at least in part, motivated the young revolutionaries of the 1960s and 1970s. To foreshadow an argument of this chapter, it is precisely in this 'shining forth' that the poetry of the 1960s captured the imagination of the young generation, motivating them towards revolutionary praxis. *In poetry, 'another world is possible', so reality can be directed towards that poetic possibility.* That is why poetry has always aided struggles for social justice globally.

From a phenomenological viewpoint, every beginning opens up possibilities, and as such, it is always diverse. From a humble beginning, *one* among many possibilities rises to dominate an entire subsequent era and capture the imagination of a community. Nimaic poetry and Persian poetic modernity are no exception. Yushij revolutionised poetry, but in turn, he contributed to a certain stylistic, *poetic-symbolic fixity* through which modernist poetry continued to expand and multiply. The fixity in question was achieved through the simultaneous deployment of symbols and tropes and creation of a poetic community that, by and large, would adhere to and co-interpret such symbolism. Without such fixity and community to energise it, the poetic rendition of militant resistance three decades later would not have been possible.

Sign, Suggestion and Symbols

We need to understand how language works, or else we end up (re-)producing theoretically-feeble assertions without proper justification. This chapter on poetry is indeed a *foundational* chapter in that structural analysis offered here also applies to songs and soundtracks, short fiction, and cinema in subsequent chapters. I need to refer to Ferdinand de Saussure and his structural analysis: the linguistic *sign* consists of *signifier* (word, visual image, the sensible) and *signified* (concept, mental image, the intelligible), or put differently, the sensible word-image and the intelligible concept-image (Saussure 1959: 65). The two refer to the intellectual or mental allusions that enable language to communicate ideas in abstraction. The linguistic sign has nothing to do with the material, concrete object or reality of the sign's allusion that Saussure calls the *referent*. For example, the word 'cat' has nothing to do with the common domesticated feline; it is only a designation, and it works as long as a *linguistic community* adheres to its conventional use. 'The linguistic sign unites, not a thing and a name, but a concept and a sound-image', avers Saussure. 'The latter is not the material sound, a purely physical thing, but the psychological imprint of the sound, the impression that it makes on our senses. The *sound-image* is sensory, and if I happen to call it "material," it is only in that sense, and by way of opposing it to the other terms of the association, the *concept*, which is generally more abstract' (Saussure 1959: 66). We should be reminded that Saussurian linguistics is pitched against the rationalistic approaches of his contemporary linguists. Hence one of his most controversial assertions: 'The bond between the signifier and the signified is arbitrary . . . Since I mean by sign the whole that results from the associating of the signifier with the signified, I can simply say: *the linguistic sign is arbitrary*' (Saussure 1959: 67; original emphasis). Because of the arbitrary character of the linguistic sign, the role of the historical community is accentuated. This is why the signifier 'cat' invokes in our minds a quadruped and furry feline of, usually, a domesticated breed: the tacit agreement of a historical community of speakers has made this particular signifier–signified pair to persist. The word 'cat', therefore, has no logical or organic connections with the actual animal, the referent.

Taking a step further, we need to explore the power of 'suggestion': according to Ernesto Laclau, suggestion is possible due to the *unfixity* between signifier and signified. This inherent unfixity requires that the pairing of signifier and signified, that of *word and meaning*, be determined by conditions outside of the sign itself, a process called *overdetermination* (which comes with underdetermination), 'by which a particular word condenses around itself a plurality of meanings' (Laclau 2005: 22). Overdetermination means the meaning of a word is actually determined by an outside-word (*dehors-mot*), *the context,* and this implies that there is always more than one possible meaning for the word. Stated plainly, a word can simultaneously contain a number of meanings. We may call this, *à la* Freud, 'condensation'. In the context of Nimaic poetry, I can observe that night, darkness, oppression and hopelessness are condensed under the signifier 'night'. Suggestion is enabled by this structural feature of the sign. Yushij *writes* 'night' but he *suggests* political suffocation. This particular trope indeed enabled a whole range of poetic possibilities that linguistically mobilised the articulation of experiences of a whole rebellious generation. When tropes and metaphors find their community *reality yields to symbols* and the possibility of the act of writing in literary concert emerges. I will soon return to this.

Origins: Hermeneutical Community of Deliberate Inferences

Yushij broke with the long and rich tradition that was still vehemently advocated by a culturally influential literary community in the early twentieth century. *She'r-e no*, in turn, created a community of its own. To quote the revolutionary Marxist and poet Mostafa Sho'aiyan (1936–76), poetic modernity grew 'from the few to the many'. In the context of rapidly changing Iran – from Reza Shah's authoritative modernisation to the 1941–53 period of political and expressive freedom – the New Poetry had a time to build a *community* of staunch advocates and earnest adherents. But this was not simply a community of rising poets like Ahmad Shamlu (1925–2000) and Mehdi Akhavan-Sales (1928–90). It was, rather, a *hermeneutical community of active co-interpreters* that viewed the world through the prism of *she'r-e no* and its symbolic possibilities. And this was not simply a community of freestanding agents: they were *at the mercy of literary significations* and bound to the structure of the sign as indicated above. Hence, to understand this community one must trace certain privileged signifiers back to their original deployments in *she'r-e no* and reveal their *power* in shaping up a certain *weltanschauung* within the Gestalt of a rising militant generation. This is where sign and experience converge.

As is well-known, poetic modernity emerged in the immediate aftermath of the Constitutional Revolution (1906–11). Persian literature has always been 'politically conscious' (Dabashi 1985: 153). This is particularly true about Mirzadeh Eshqi (Seyed Mohammad Reza Kurdestani, 1893–1924),

Abolqasem Aref Qazvini (1882–1934) and Mohammad Farroki Yazdi (1889–1939) during the constitutionalism era and the reign of Reza Shah, whose poems brought political messages in the age of print media to an audience in a country in which an illiterate majority relied on rhymed verses to memorise and convey ideas. These constitutionalist poets offered a poetry that was closer to 'natural speech', thus breaking away from the convoluted poetry and prose of the Qajar era. Most constitutionalist intellectuals also advocated literary and linguistic reforms (Ajudani 2003; Parsinejad 2003). Mirzadeh Eshqi, in particular, had discovered an expressive poetry released from the classical metrics and rhyming, and he made efforts to enact a new poetic style that entailed accessible and naturalistic prose, captured in his narrative poem, 'Three Sketches of Maryam' (or 'The Ideals of a Countryside Old Man in Three Sketches', 1924). This long narrative poem is said to have been influenced by Nima's 'Afsaneh' ('Legend', 1922), although by Yushij's own admission this claim remains unfounded (Yushij, quoted in Ajudani 2003: 140, n. 15; see also Ariyanpour 1988: 377). Yushij came of age in the post-constitutional era and the reign of Reza Shah; so naturally he dovetails the constitutionalist poets, sharing their advocacy of natural expressions.

Born in 1897 in Yush in the Caspian province of Gilan, Nima had spent his childhood living a rural life, often shepherding in the highlands. He came to Tehran at twelve years of age to attend the Catholic St Louis school and learned French (Ariyanpour 1995: 579–81). As he reflected many times later, he had brought with himself to the city a 'naturalistic' imagination and poetry – a particular imagination which informs his 'Afsaneh', a poem celebrated as inaugurating *she'r-e no* as it presents a 'natural' way of speaking, and for which he should be credited as the founder of modern 'nature' poetry (Naficy 1997: 19, 78). The referentiality of 'nature' in Yushij's poetry has been the subject of several explanatory letters that he wrote to his friends. In lieu of the *aruz* rhythm of classical poetry (borrowed from Arabic poetry and dominant until the late nineteenth century), Yushij gradually propagated the *natural* rhythm of speech and liberated Persian poetry from the *aruzi* structure as a pre-given frame of expression. But what does this 'naturalistic' tendency mean? The break with classical style is often attributed to European ideas (Karimi-Hakkak 1995: 7) and to the fact that almost all the advocates of poetic modernisation were familiar with a European language, in particular French. But this claim is simplistic. Thinking of classical and modern poetry in binary terms distorts reality by associating progressive ideas with poetic liberation and subversion (Karimi-Hakkak 1995: 3, 25). The construction of European ideas, 'particularly Russian and French', 'remained superficial, sketchy, and indirect'. European poetry, however, served the constitutionalist intellectuals, and the subsequent generation of Yushij, by characterising classical poetry as the 'negative background' against which they could justify their New Poetry (Karimi-Hakkak 1995: 33). Phenomenologically, attributing modern poetry to European influence, naive as it seems, overlooks the lived experience of Nima, who had come from a particularly-expressed Gestalt in his childhood in rural Caspian, a world in which the symbolic universe had already constructed in young Nima's mind a poetic imagination that came only to fore through its opposite: the alienating, urban life. Yushij bemoans this alienation repeatedly. Hence his exposure to French could at best be regarded as an oblique catalyst, not as an influence. Thus, 'naturalistic' poetry would draw its *imagination* from the *lived experience* of the poet and audience insofar as this experience is *linguistically expressed*. This process has already begun before Yushij.

In contrast to Qajar literature, modern Persian poetry (and fiction) dwelled in the *im*-mediate (not mediated) experience of the world through the poem. Famous constitutionalist poems relied on a similar concept to varying degrees, but still relied on classical imagery, symbolism and tropes. So, most of these poets had not yet released themselves from the classical imagination. The best example is Aref Qazvini's song (c. 1911) with the captivating lines cauterised in the Iranian collective consciousness: *az khun-e javanan-e vatan laleh damideh / az matam-e sarv-qaddeshan sarv khamideh* ('tulips have blossomed from the blood of our homeland's youth / the cypress tree is bent in mourning our cypress-tall youth'). In Farrokhi Yazdi's well-known poem (undated), we witness a move towards more naturalistic expressions: *an zaman keh benhadam sar beh pay-e azadi / dast-e khod ze jan shostam az baray-e azadi* (the moment I devoted myself to the cause of freedom / I washed my hands of my life for the cause of freedom). Because of the particular experience of Nima, there is something uniquely personal about Yushij's deployment of 'nature' as a poetic *master signifier*. Once deployed, 'nature' yielded a political symbol. 'In the many letters he has written to his relatives, friends and acquaintances during his lifetime, we can follow the discourse of nature, both as a nostalgia for his hometown, Yush, and as an ideological device' (Naficy 1997: 39, 38). As a signifier of personal nostalgia, through repeated iterations, nature is transformed into a political symbol. *Once the experience is mediated by the symbol, any symbol, a universe is bound to emerge.* It is now clear why we need a phenomenological understanding of symbols – these 'plenary words':

> On the shore of a lake surrounded by pine trees, I say 'this lake is surrounded by pine trees.' As soon as the words are spoken, immediacy is lost. Wherever I turn, words are already there . . . The technician rejoices at this. It is by means of words that he organizes, transforms, and fabricates what he calls the universe of things. (Schürmann 1997b: 52)

The world is organised by the symbols that already precede me and organise my potentially *originary* and *primordial* experience. This is how *she'r-e no* was brought forth by a Caspian child: a primordial experience already formed symbolically founds an entire epoch-making poetic movement that was alien to the existing poetic world of traditionalists. *Symbols allow me access to the primordial experience.* Therefore, the 'region of language whose structure is determined by double meaning and mystery is the symbol' (Schürmann 1997a: 21). As such, following Schürmann, symbols

> take the common word and render it uncommon, thereby taking the listener to the world that is different from the one sanctioned by received convention. Symbols open up the difference within words, and they do so by means of gathering of meaning, and thus take us from the ordinary to the sacred. Symbol is a word or a noun, as opposed to myth, which is an element; an allegory, which alludes to the unsaid; a metaphor, which annuls itself to establish meanings otherwise than literal; or analogy, whose double meaning is artificially constructed. (Vahabzadeh 2015d)

This double meaning, in the context of Yushij's poetic modernity, may yield or be appropriated by 'ideology', as some scholars argue (Ghanoonparvar 1984; Naficy 1997; Talattof 2000). But ideology has no existence without the power of symbols in constructing a world through words – a world not 'intended' by the word as such. It all depends on the *context*. As we will see, these poetic symbols played a crucial role in *articulating the experiences of a rebellious generation* that otherwise would not be capable of expressing its concerns and *weltanschauung*, and the latter, of course, always already insinuates a community – indeed, what I call a hermeneutical 'community of deliberate inferences'.

This brings us back to an important point: just as Saussure had recognised in the early twentieth century, the *linguistic community* is key to the perpetuation of an emerging discourse. Ahmad Karimi-Hakkak rightly submits that the emergence and consolidation of *she'r-e no* as the *new discursive universe required the collective decoding of the poetic signs to be determined in advance* (1995: 67). He suggests that a certain reception and reading of the poetic signs established the means through which such discursive universe could self-perpetuate. 'I assume the presence of an expanding discursive universe, forged and fostered through a system of social communication which includes political, journalistic, and other social activities around the texts under analysis' (1995: 67). A community of deliberate inferences, I argue, dwelled in the symbolic universe that allowed activists to infer from the poems of Yushij, Shamlu and Akhavan-Sales political messages. Emerging poetic communities became increasingly radicalised in their political views precisely when the Shah's authoritarian rule intensified in the 1960s.

Literature is always, inevitably, immersed in its historical context and responds to the turbulences of its times. In the post-1941 Iran, social and political conditions were relaxed and provided Nima with the conditions that gave him wider public recognition for his poetic innovations. His most important public appearance was at the First Congress of Iranian Writers, held as the Irano-Soviet Cultural Association (Vox) in Tehran in June 1946, in which seventy-eight writers and poets presented (Abedini 1990: 121–6; Al-Ahmad 1962: 65). He was never a member or supporter of the pro-Soviet Tudeh Party of Iran, but the editors of the pro-Tudeh literary bi-weekly, *Kabutar-e Solh* (*The Peace Dove*, founded in 1941), published 'The Slain's Attire' ('Jameh-ye Maqtul', 1926, in modified classical style), an anti-war poem by 'Master Nima', in the journal's inaugural issue (6 May 1951), although the editors reputedly did not understand or even believe in Nima's innovations (Shams-Langarudi 1991a: 253). This kind of appropriation attests to the clear presence of 'political' elements in Yushij's poem. The attention Nima received from young Ehsan Tabari (1917–89), a rising Tudeh Party cultural, and future theoretical, figure, caused his symbolic poems to have a 'leftist' significatory connotation in the collective conscience of 1940s–50s literary circles. In the 1940s, Nima cautiously associated himself with the Tudeh publications in order to publish his poems: 'behind the curtains of that [Tudeh] Party's power he sought a refuge from the conspiracy of silence that surrounded him' (Al-Ahmad 1962: 70). Regarding the Tudeh Party, Nima had written: 'I am greater and purer to be a Tudeh member. That is to say, it is impossible for a thinker to follow the decisions of such and such [a] youngster who is the middleman and broker (*karchaqkon*) of our northern enemy [the USSR]' (Yushij 1962: 51). After the split in the Tudeh Party in 1948, he also published in the Party's splinter journal *Elm va Zendegi* (*Science and Life*) (Al-Ahmad 1962: 70). These connections inevitably associated Yushij with leftist cultural circles.

Let us quickly consider a review of Nima's 'The Filthy Hope' by the Tudeh Party theoretician Ehsan Tabari as an indication of how a community of deliberate inferences is socially and culturally formed. There is an important context to this poem: throughout his career, Yushij constructed a romantic symbolism of nature, poetically deploying natural contraries like 'day' and 'night' – also common in classical poetry and thus culturally familiar for Iranians – that primed readers to *infer* antagonisms in the social realm. In such poems, the signifier 'night' is split between a natural phenomenon and a literary metaphor (Naficy 1997: 93). This is how the poetic-conceptual journey of Yushij proves interesting. 'By the time that Nima began to write his unrhymed verse with variable line length in the late 1930s, he threw away his romanticism, though not the discourse of nature. To the contrary, he uses it as an ideological device alongside the catchword "the people" that he picks up from this time onward' (Naficy 1997: 53). Consequently, 'While the struggle between night and day is not without precedence in Persian poetry, its depiction in this particular way and in such an expanded manner is unprecedented' (Karimi-Hakkak 1995: 253). Tabari praised 'The Filthy Hope' as a modern poem, fit for this time (Karimi-Hakkak 1995: 253). Unlike previous engagements with Yushij's poetry that hinged on traditional worldviews and poetic imaginations, Tabari's indeed offered a modernist's review of another modernist's poem. Tabari wrote a short preface to 'The Filthy Hope' in the Tudeh publication *Nameh-ye Mardom* (9 May 1943), where there also appeared a version of the poem with many errors in it. The preface irritated Nima, who replied to Tabari in a famous long letter (13 June 1943). In the preface, Tabari credited Yushij with breaking away with traditional styles and advancing poetic modernism, comparing the two to carriage and automobile: although the noise and sluggishness of early automobiles made them appear inferior to 'ornamented carriages', no one ever believed the automobile to be behind the carriage in the evolution of transportation (Tabari in Yushij 2012: 38). Although unfamiliar (*nama'nus*), the New Poetry was on its way to perfection. 'The Filthy Hope', Tabari stated, was a 'symbolic' poem in which morning (*sobh*) was a trope (*kenayeh*) referring to a 'new society and a new life order. Night (*shab*) is reaction, backwardness, ignorance, and corruption of the present society' (Tabari in Yushij 2012: 38; Naficy 1997: 99–100). Tabari is correct in pointing out the bifurcation of symbols (in a society that had just emerged from, and thus had living memory of, dictatorship), and his preface shows how the emerging poetic symbolism of *she'r-e no* was immediately sanctioned by a community of readers with political commitments. In his rejoinder Yushij insisted, *inter alia*, that his poetry was primarily driven by a commitment to arts, stating, 'With a foundation different from science or morals, albeit influential on the arts, the arts try to achieve their aesthetics and then create along with itself that which is within us and the nature of life' (Yushij 2012: 24). What Yushij seems to argue is that the artist must primarily be *committed* to his/her art. Stated differently, he was against the *instrumentalist approach* to the arts. These two points are important: Yushij's commitment to his poetry *theoretically* diverged from commitments extraneous to poetry, and yet they converged socially and culturally. Note the *paradox*. This community of readers and writers whose poetic *weltanschauung* was deeply influenced by Nimaic poetry with their *deliberate inferences* created a movement in the 1960s and 1970s called 'committed literature' (*adabiyyat-e mote'ahedd*) in which the paradox made its brightest appearance. This particular symbolism and commitment, that defined around thirty years of the literary and poetic history of Iran (from the 1940s to the 1970s), is reductively attributed to 'ideology' by some scholars (Ghanoonparvar 1984; Talattof 2000; Naficy 1997), but I am not sure if this designation sheds any light on the paradox. If Nima's admitted commitment to his art precedes his other commitments, how can we explain that much of his poetry is clearly politically and socially committed to justice and freedom, without implicitly accusing him of duplicity? Ideology is everywhere, and insofar as we live under modern states, we are all 'ideological' in the Althusserian way. 'Literary commitment' cannot be thought of outside a symbolic world in which, by virtue of the uttered word and its inevitable mediation of experience, reality also produces that which is unreal, imaginary, phantasmic.

Poetic Tropes and Symbols: A Genealogy

My point of departure here is to show how new poetic discourse and dissenting politics gradually converged and constructed a symbolic world that reached its zenith in the 1970s poetry (and following poetry, other art forms). This symbolism rendered poetic dissent against an authoritative state possible. This task requires me to read history 'backwards' and seek to unravel the origins of such convergence. Now, I will need to offer (playing with Jazani's book title, *The Thirty-Year Political History*) a 'thirty-year poetic history' that will genealogically unveil the sources of symbols and tropes in the prior decades of poetic creativity that in the 1970s ultimately led to the short lived 'guerrilla poetry'.

We established that the new poetic style emerged through forging specific poetic symbols. Yushij himself appropriated some key metaphors that later were deployed beyond his wildest imaginings. In short, as *she'r-e no* appeared, carving out its own symbolic universe, it allowed Yushij and his contemporary poetic modernists to express their lived experiences in a disjointed time when the collective memory of fighting for freedom in the Constitutional Revolution was still alive while these poets had to live under a repressive state, at least during the nascent years of *she'r-e no*. Nima's poem 'Afsaneh' ('Legend', 1922) captures this historic moment. A symbol makes a common word uncommon; so, my point is that *the diremptive experience of wanting freedom under repression necessitated a deployment of a naturalistic lexicon in a manner that was anything but natural.* Signifiers taken from nature – night, mountain, slumber, and/or people – were now mobilised to *suggest* the signifieds that were further away from their immediate referents – *signifieds intentionally inferred only within a particular political imagination.* In its due course in the next thirty years, *naturalist poetry increasingly became a poetry of deliberate inferences by a community of artists and activists with shared and overlapping political horizons.*

Nima's lyrical poem 'Afsaneh' is celebrated as the birth of New Poetry (Ariyanpour 1995: 587) – a turning point in Yushij's poetic excursion towards innovatively bringing poetry closer to real-life experience. 'Afsaneh' was first published in *Qarn-e Bistom* (*The Twentieth Century*), a journal edited by the revolutionary republican and literary figure Mirzadeh Eshqi, whose 'Three Sketches of Maryam' (1924) had heralded an innovative approach to poetry, and whom Nima had considered would be a promising poetic modernist had he lived on (in Shams Langarudi 1991a: 143). Mirzadeh Eshqi was assassinated by Reza Shah's agents at the age of thirty-one because of his mocking poems aimed against his dictatorship (Shams Langarudi 1991a: 143–53). These details reveal the political undertone of the time, a response to political repression under the two Pahlavi Shahs, during whose reigns poetic modernity emerged and flourished.

Nima's approach in 'Afsaneh' was unambiguous: in a preface to the publication of 'Afsaneh' in *The Twentieth Century*, addressed to the 'Young Poet', Yushij declared: 'this structure which contains my "*Afsaneh*" shows a natural and free style of conversation, and it may not be interesting for you at first, but I believe it is the best structure, since it can be allocated to "play" (*namayesh*)' (1989: 81). This 'structure entertains your guests in that it allows them to speak as much as they want, whether in one or a few hemistiches, in a word or two, out of will and nature', Nima avers. 'What in particular has convinced me about this structure is to observe meaning and nature, and there is no greater merit for poetry and poet than *describing nature better and present the meaning with simplicity*' (Yushij 1989: 82; my emphasis). Two aspects are important here: first, Yushij makes reference to *namayesh* or stage-play, that is, the 'performative' aspect of his revolutionising poetry. Second, the New Poetry provides a way out of the rigid classical structures and brings poetry to the 'natural' iteration and articulation that borders simplicity. This performative and the natural simplicity, we will soon see, immensely aided the poetry of the 1960s–70s in depicting political dissent.

Nima's poetry gained increasing political-symbolic overtone within his new style after the abdication in 1941 of Reza Shah forced by the occupying Allied forces (Ariyanpour 1995: 598). His poems in this period and later indicate his sensibility regarding social justice and his envisioned (utopic) transformation of the country. Poems like 'Phoenix' (1938), 'The Filthy Hope' (1941), 'The Bell' (1944), 'Manli' (1945), 'Moonlight' (1948), 'The Amen Bird' (1952) or 'The Boat' (1952) – among his most celebrated poems – attest to his social and political sensibilities. In these, he deployed the performative component that leaned on relaying immediate experience through natural expressions.

In 'Phoenix' ('Qoqnus'), as in many other works by Yushij, 'the main motif . . . is the metaphorical struggle between dawn and night. Nima was one of the first poets who used political symbolism in his poem *Chicness* ('Phoenix') in 1937 and then in many other poems' (Naficy 1997: 93):

Phoenix

. . .

From the moment when the sun's gold on the wave
withers and the tide rises on the shore
a jackal's howl, and a village man
has kindled the fire concealed in his home.
A slight flame, crimson to the eye
blushes a line under the night's two wide eyes
and farther from here,
the people pass by.
She, that rare bird, cloaked as she remains
flies away from where she rests.
Amidst the things tangled together
with the light, and the darkness of this long night
she goes through.

. . .

This earth has not any charm, nor does life
She feels as though the hopes of the birds, like his,
are sombre like the smoke. And if their hopes
like a blazing pyre
reflect in their eyes, alluding to a bright morning.
(Yushij 1991: 222–3)

When the Phoenix's mythic rebirth in this poem (dated February 1938) – depicted in a rural (Caspian) setting and coloured with imagery of day and night, pyre and darkness – represents a people's renaissance, the poem has already entered a social lexicon, inviting a 'political' reading.

So, it would be correct to surmise that one of the best examples of the emergence of political symbols appears in Yushij's 'night poems' (*shabaneh*). In fact, *shabaneh* poems became a tradition of their own, continued by many poets and excelled in by Shamlu, 'this free spirit in an increasingly unfree society' (Karimi-Hakkak 1977: 201). The concept of 'night' as a political symbol first appeared in his poem 'The Filthy Hope' ('Omid-e Palid', March 1941). Written within the last few months of Reza Shah's authoritarian reign, this poem dwells on the contrast between night and day, light and darkness, to symbolise a political message about the hope of 'that hasty, narcissistic body' destroying a new beginning, the sunrise:

> So this dark night stays forever
> it sucks in the smiling, bright morn.
> It devours, where it sees,
> a people's thought on the rightful path.
> That grows hope in their heart.
> It watches
> it watches
> so no one would converge on this path,
> underneath its cold, filthy tears
> . . .
> It weighs brightness and darkness
> in its heart
> the hope for the diminishment of the sunrise. (Yushij 1991: 291)

Ever since this poetic moment, night (*shab*) has emerged in modern Persian poetry as a prevailing image (Talattof 2000: 7). From this point onwards, the reader is introduced to 'the political symbolism of . . . "Night Poetry," in Nima's work, in which "night" represents poetical evil and the sun symbolises freedom and happiness' (Naficy 1997: 50). The signifier 'night' has a natural referent. With Nima's *contextually (and thus politically) allusive* poetic articulation, nature and politics are connected and mutually implied in poems (Naficy 1997: 80). Furthermore, as a key symbol, 'night' inaugurates the advent of a community of symbols, metaphors and tropes shaping the (political) symbolism of two generations of poets, from the 1940s to the 1970s, whose yearning for freedom of expression under two dictatorships urged them to deploy ever more complex metaphors, tropes and symbols. Here is a useful catalogue that indicates my point:

> night (*shab*), which referred to dictatorial conditions, spawned many related metaphors, such as *zharfa-ye shab* (the depth of the night), *shab-e harzeh darayan* (the night of idle talkers), *shab-e lashkhoran* (vultures' night), *shab-e dardalud* (the painful night), *shab-e khunin* (the bloody night), *shab-e ashkalud* (the tearful night), *shab-e sangi* (the stony night), *shab-e asman-e sard* (the night of cold sky), *shab-e barani* (the rainy night), and *shab-e por az setareh-ha ye zendani* (a night full of imprisoned stars). (Talattof 2000: 88)

The alluding of 'night' to political oppression is made possible through *suggestion*, that is, in the Saussurian moment when the signifier is detached, for the time being, from its commonly shared signified and attached to another. But as a nodal point and powerful symbol, through juxtaposition with contrasting metaphors and tropes *shab* also serves to hint at the possibility of triumphant overcoming by those heroic figures who selflessly withstand oppression:

> *bidari-e shab* (the awakening of night), *payan-e shab* (the end of the night), *shab-e por setareh* (the night full of stars), *sepidehdam* (the dawn), *khorshid* (sun), *khorshidha-ye shabaneh* (nightly suns), *rastakhiz* (resurrection), *shekufeh* (blossom), *moj* (wave), and *ofoq* (horizon). (Talattof 2000: 88)

A metaphor taken from the earth's *natural* rotation, night will inevitably yield to day. This is how symbols grow into articulatory nodes of experience for two generations of poets. Now imagine, as actually happened, poetic symbolism employing 'non-natural' signifiers, those with more directly political signifieds. A master-signifier of the 'guerrilla poetry' (see below) is indeed *khalq* (people):

> In the past, the word *khalq* did not carry this overtone and was used equivocally to mean people, the ordinary crowd, mob, or nation. For example, in the works of Mirza Malkom Khan, one of the writers of the years that led to the Constitutional Revolution, the word 'khalq' was used to imply 'nation.' Nima

in his first poem of 'The Tale of Pallid Color/Cold Blood' uses words 'nation' (*khalq*), 'folk' (*qowm*), and 'people' (*mardom*) interchangeably. This poem was written much earlier than the time that the Soviet regime became dominant in Tajikistan, where people speak Tajiki, which is close to modern Persian, and the word *khalq* was used in a Marxist sense to distinguish 'people' from 'nation.' Later on . . . the word *khalq* bloomed to a whole social and literary discourse . . . (Naficy 1997: 50; original emphasis)

In 'Phoenix', Yushij deploys another explosive symbol that further suggests the poet's *commitment to justice for people*. Let us note that Nima's younger brother, Ladbon Esfandiyari (1899–1931), who had also attended St Louis school in Tehran, joined the Jangali movement (1915–21) – a movement led by Mirza Kuchek Khan (1880–1921) in response to the failure of the Constitutional Revolution to bring about justice, a movement that liberated parts of Gilan province for a short while – and fled to the young Bolshevik Russia in the aftermath of the movement's defeat. He attended the KUTV (Communist University of the Toilers of the East). A poet in the classical tradition, Ladbon stayed in the USSR as a Party Cadre who, among other things, rewrote and translated Communist Party literature into Tajiki. He was among the first Iranian communists to be killed in Stalinist purges (see Chaqueri 2002: 13–21). In light of Ladbon's tragic fate, Nima's inclination towards social justice and freedom, his literary commitment, was pursued at a measured distance from actual political stances and parties. Personally, Yushij had certain religious inclinations and was critical of Communism, as is attested by his diaries: 'I am not a communist', he declared, 'I know some of their ideas are close to those of mine but I know that they [Communists] have many weak points' (Yushij 1962: 50–1). This measured distance was also kept by the subsequent dominant poetic figure, Shamlu, who mastered the 'night' poem (*shabaneh*) style and created a poetic world of defiant self-consciousness that inspired young Iranians to partake in the struggles of their age in the 1970s.

I will show soon that the deployment of a specific array of linguistic signs in modern poetry leading up to the 1970s enabled poetry to create 'manifestos' of the emerging rebellion generation. This was best shown in the short-lived 'guerrilla poetry'. It would be a mistake to assume that these linguistic signs had any *organic* relationship with one another – although at times we witness that signifiers such as forest, tree and dew appear (somewhat organically) in a poem by Khosrow Golesorkhi (1944–74) to conjure up a particular (symbolic) ambiance. Following Ernesto Laclau's discursive theory (1985; 2005), I argue that it was due to a specific *articulation* of the poetic-dissident community that certain 'relations of equivalence' were established between signifiers and around the particular 'nodal point' of *defiance and dissent*, thus creating a specific and recognisable *poetic discourse*.

In his celebrated 'The Amen Bird' ('Morgh-e Amin', 1952), Yushij launches afresh an unprecedented mythological bird that converses with the people, in natural speech rhythm, and conveys the message of 'the oneness of the people's wishes and the bird's vision' (Karimi-Hakkak 1995: 262):

> The Amen Bird is a pained soul who has remained a vagrant.
> He has travelled to the farthest end of this house of injustice,
> has returned, no longer desiring water or grain, because of his sufferings.
> Now he awaits
> the day of opening.
> . . .
> In the rain of voices that say,
> 'may the unjust sufferings of the masses come to an end!'
> – while unjust sufferings of the masses increase by the moment –
> the Amen Bird begins to speak of the people's pain.
> (Yushij, trans. Karimi-Hakkak 1995: 263–4)

In 'The Amen Bird', the two principles that Yushij conceived as pillars of his poetry make their appearances: 'Our poetry both in its rhythmic form or in its essence (*baten*), like prose, should be descriptive of all happenings (*vaqaye'*)', and 'our prose mirrors nature and full of poetic imagination' (Yushij 2004).

Stricto sensu, night and day stand as *contraries* as a natural, cosmic rotation causes the presence of one in the other's absence; thus, there is no conflict or antagonism between day and night. Their mutual exclusivity, however, is appropriated by politically-minded poets and their political-symbolist poetry in order to *transposition* the *antagonistic* visions of Iran's future (authoritarian versus participatory). Hence, Nima's 'nature poetry', in due process and with the changing social context of the country, yields the famous *shabaneh* or 'night poetry'.

In 'The Amen Bird' (and other poems), the *performative* and the *natural simplicity* of *she'r-e no* converge. Nima wished for *poetry to imitate life*. Such a poetry *becomes 'actable' because it opens new horizons before the readers' imaginations*. As such, a poetic community is born, and within that, a community of deliberate inferences.

The Poetry of Defiance

In light of the theoretical and historical summation that showcased the formation of a poetic community converging around specific tropology and symbolism that annexed poetry to the poets' social and political 'commitments', we can now move beyond Yushij and trace a movement in the 1950s and early 1960s that increasingly shaped the poetic imagination of the late 1960s and 1970s. To this end, I must refer to selected 'paradigmatic' poems in order to locate the thread that strings together a long and complex process of symbolic transformation of poetic imagination that captured the hearts and minds of a new generation of poets and activists. Therefore, the following poems are not simply exemplars; rather, they are (social) *phenomena* that contain the *poetic truth of life* in a rapidly changing and increasingly repressive (post-1953) society. I intend to reveal, *stricto sensu*, the dialectics of the arts and political action: through its foundation, modern Persian poetry enabled a certain poetic imagination that as early as the 1940s had anticipated, in part, the poetic *fixity* of the 1970s. This is how Iranian political history in this period pushed poetic modernisation to become associated with a particular conception of social and political 'commitment' within the arts. *Poetic self-consciousness in this experience was accompanied by political self-consciousness –* evidence of an elective affinity between the two. In poetry of the 1960s, lived experiences converged and were tethered by a shining, unifying liberatory horizon; victory appears within reach, for the moment at least.

As is well-known, the 1953 coup ended an unprecedented (twelve-year) period of relative freedom of expression and smashed the nation's democratic dreams. It pushed Nima into reclusiveness until his death (1959) out of fear of the regime's reprisal for his 'political' poems. This observation illustrates that the community of deliberate inferences is not a private salon of aloof artists:

those inferences, sanctioned by political interests (in Nima's case, the political interests of the Tudeh philosopher Tabari), vividly marked public and political discourses. Embodying a vision of a free Iran, Yushij's symbolic poetry, after having grown into the dominant genre for almost a decade, had subsided by this time. Not surprisingly, so did the poetic works of the main protagonists of *she'r-e no*, and in particular, Mehdi Akhavan-Sales. Born in Mashhad, he was well-versed in the traditional 'Khorasan Style' (*sabk-e Khorasani*) of poetry, but also vehemently advocated *she'r-e no*, and not just in his poetry: he is also the author of a voluminous treatise on Yushij, once widely read and cited (Akhavan-Sales 1990). He was imprisoned a few times for political reasons, once after the coup, when he spent several months in prison for refusing to pledge in writing to stay out of politics. He worked in various capacities for provincial and national television networks and briefly taught at Tehran University. After the revolution he was forced into retirement without pay. Reportedly, after the 1979 Revolution he had turned down a phone invitation by Ali Khamenei (current Supreme Leader and a fellow Mashhadi) to employ his poetry to support the Islamic Republic, to which he had purportedly responded, 'We've always been against domination, not for domination.'

Akhavan-Sales excelled at Nima's social and political symbolism (Shams-Langarudi 1991b: 296) and arguably became the single most important voice of the post-1953 period of political shock. What distinguishes him among his contemporaries is his epic symbolism and imagery. Following the coup, his cauterising longing for a bygone time of free expression and political liberty won for Akhavan-Sales's works the designation 'defeat poetry' – a symbolism of despair that captured the mood of the late 1950s. His Selected Poems, *Zemestan* (*The Winter*), published in 1956, was titled after a famous heart-wrenching poem that unambiguously limns the helpless submission of freedom-loving individuals in his generation to the post-coup repression – those whom he brilliantly called 'exile[s] in [their] homeland' (*dar vatan-e khish gharib*). This collection contained works in New Poetry and Nimaic classical styles. 'The Winter' is dated December 1955, and it opens:

> No one wants to answer your greetings,
> > the heads are tucked in collars.
> None raises his head to meet and greet comrades,

and one's view goes no further than his next step.
For the path is dark and precarious.
And should you stretch out a caring arm to another,
he'll only reluctantly show his hand,
for the cold is brutally piercing.
Coming out of a warm chest, your exhale becomes an opaque cloud,
which obscures your view like a wall.
When you exhale like so, what would you expect
from your close or distant friends?

The poem's imagery of winter clearly paints an ambiance of retreating into private life due to the brutal cold of repression. It depicts precisely how activists withdrew from public life out of fear of post-coup reprisal. Old friendships and camaraderie were no more. The poem concludes:

What do you mean time's come, it is dawn, morning has arrived!
It is deluding you, this isn't the reddish sky right after sunrise

. . .

My friend! Go light up the goblet of wine, for night and day are the same
No one wants to answer your greetings
The air is choking, doors are shut, heads tucked in collars, hands concealed
breaths are clouds, hearts fatigued and broken
trees crystal-wrapped skeletons
the ground lifeless, the sky's ceiling low
dusty are sun and moon.
It is winter.
(Akhavan-Sales 1956: 97–9)

This particular poem became one of the most widely read poems by the activists in the 1960s–70s: a sort of background imagery to a movement they were about to launch to overcome despair. Its symbolism and imagery allowed for the rising generation of militants, most of whom were too young to have experienced the coup, to experience the mood of defeat that Akhavan-Sales's generation had experienced. The symbolism of the 'The Winter' found its way to the next generation.

A bird's eye observation of the 1950s political symbolism, however, reveals a very interesting aspect: this symbolism of defeat and despair, typical of

Akhavan-Sales's poetry at this time and indicative of the years immediately following the coup, is preceded by a symbolism of honour and resistance. In *The Winter*, the same volume in which the said poem appeared, there also appeared another famous (and long) poem, *Sagha va Gorgha* ('Dogs and Wolves'), dated November 1951 (Akhavan-Sales 1956: 97–9), describing the days of heightened mobilisation in support of Premier Dr Mosaddeq. 'Dogs and Wolves' is a long epic depicting the dogs' loyalty to their master for food, comfort and security, which come at the cost of abjection, obedience and occasional torment. In contrast, the wolves brace themselves against cold and hunger and are hunted down by their human enemies, and yet they refuse to become domesticated. A masterpiece in Nimaic rhythm, the poem presents three sections: that of the poet, followed by the 'Song of Dogs', and then the 'Song of Wolves'. Listening briefly to the 'Song of Dogs' brings the poem's dialectics to light:

– 'Eating those leftovers,'
– 'And if not that, a piece of bone,'
– 'What a comfortable life, a wonderful world
What a dear and kind master!'

– 'But the lash . . . that's such a curse . . .'
– 'Yes, but one must endure that;
true, it's really painful,
but the master will at the end take pity on us,

as his rage calms, he lets us,
to lay our head on his feet and shoes,
he will attend to our wounds and we
cherish his care.'

The concluding lines, narrated through the 'Song of Wolves', tell it all:

– 'And . . . now . . . the third enemy . . . who startlingly
jumped out of ambush and attacked
Fire arm . . . ruthless . . . ruthless
. . . No vigour left, neither to go on nor to return.'

'Drink on, O Snow! Grow red, fire up
this blood is ours, the homeless.
This blood is the blood of hungry wolves
this blood is the blood of the children of the plateau.'

– 'In this cold, hungry, wounded,
we run hurriedly like the wind, heads low in the snow
but the honour of being free
we guard. We are free. We are free.'
(Akhavan-Sales 1956: 66, 69)

Just like the militants of the 1970s, in this poem Akhavan-Sales privileges the perilous life of rebellion over the safe, servile life within the master's house. Revolt against masters gives us dignity, that which is absent in servitude. In an uncanny way, Akhavan-Sales *anticipates* the emergence of educated young men and women who refused to be soulless functionaries serving the Shah's repressive regime: *informed by the struggle for justice and liberation, the dignity of defiance overrode the tedium of servitude.* The reader needs no cues from me to see clearly how the struggle of the wolves, who, unlike dogs, do not submit to domination and safeguard their rebellious freedom with dignity and pride, represents the ardour of those who challenged authoritarianism. This story never grows old.

These two poems by Akhavan-Sales clearly represent the collective moods of activists before and after the coup, and how under the despair of defeat there still glowed the embers of defiance. In the 1950s, another emblematic poem was published: the long, epic *Arash-e Kamangir* (*Arash, the Bowman*, dated 14 March 1959), published in 1959, by the Tudeh Party member Siavash Kasra'i (1926–95), a Nimaic poet who dedicated his poem to Major Khosrow Ruzbeh (1915–58), head of the Tudeh Party's clandestine Officers Organisation who was captured after the coup and executed. Named in *Avestan* and in passing mentioned in Abolqasem Ferdowsi's *The Book of Kings* (*Shahnameh*, 1010 CE), Arash is a mythical character: upon the defeat of the Iranians by their central Asian Turanian rivals, the myth goes, the border between the two countries was to be decided by recording how far an arrow, released from Mount Damavand, would go to the east. It was a humiliating condition for Iranians, imposed by Turan. Arash is tasked with firing that momentous arrow. Knowing he is the hope of an entire nation, he climbs Mount Damavand (the highest peak in Iran, north of Tehran today), becomes one with his bow, and launches an arrow that travels for an entire day and lands on the trunk of a walnut tree on the banks of Amu Darya River (running from present-day Uzbekistan to Afghanistan and Tajikistan). Upon firing the arrow, Arash disappears. He dies and became ether. Kasra'i revived this old story into a modern-day long epic that became a manifesto of hope in the 1960s. The poem became so popular that it was taught in Persian Literature textbooks in the 1970s. Kasra'i uses frame narrative in three layers, in which an arrivant from the snowstorm finds a shelter where he listens to Amu Nowruz (he who heralds the vernal equinox or Nowruz) telling the tale of Arash to children. Amu Nowruz declares:

> 'Life deserves an engulfing flame,
> And the flames need a burning log.
>
> You are a forest, O Human!
>
> O Forest, born free
> generously stretching your skirt over the mountains
> . . .
> your soul serving fire
> stand tall and stay green, O Forest of Human!'

The symbolism is clear: the battle of a defeated people (Iranians) with the invading army (the Shah and his imperialist supporters). Arash's self-sacrifice (which the word '*fadai*' in Persian captures) opens new horizons before a nation. Kasra'i's array of symbols and imagery works for the epic, as *Arash* promotes the vanguard's self-sacrifice for a greater cause, one that brings peace for the people:

> Yes, indeed, Arash put his life in the arrow
> He achieved the works of hundreds of thousands of blades.

And when the story is told and Amu Nowruz and the children go to sleep, it remains for the unnamed arrivant to reflect:

> It snows outside the lodge.
> Snow falls on bushes and stones.
> Mountains are silent,
> valleys heavyhearted;
> the roads await the sound of a caravan's bells . . .
> The children are long asleep,
> and so is Amu Nowruz.
> I put a log in the hearth,
> and a blazing fire ascends . . .
> (Kasra'i 2001: 14, 28–9)

Are not these sleeping children indeed the Siahkal guerrillas who would wake up twelve years later to spark anew a blazing fire?

Yushij, Akhavan-Sales and Shamlu, as outstanding figures of the first generation of *she'r-e no*, shared a certain conception of literature and poetry: that literature in general and poetry in particular are socially *committed* forms of art. As suggested, this shared conception can be traced to the particular historical advent of Persian poetic modernity: it was concomitant with the post-Constitutional Revolution social and political context, followed by nearly two decades of dictatorship and then a relatively free period when collective aspirations for fair and just collective life grew. Thus, the key protagonists of poetic modernity advocated *she'r-e mote'ahed*, 'poetic commitment' (literally, 'committed poetry'). Here, 'commitment' (*ta'ahod*) meant the commitment of the poet/poetry to the pressing social issues of the time and avoidance of privatism and romanticism. *Commitment* reigned supreme between the 1950s and the 1970s. But 'commitment' is open to interpretation and thus a divisive notion. But just as 'literary commitment' was expanding into a collective tendency, there emerged exceptions, the most notable arguably being Houshang Irani (1925–73) and the short-lived literary circle called *Khorus Jangi* (*The Fighting Cock*), which included Jalil Ziapour (1920–99, modernist painter), Hassan Shirvani (playwright, critic), Gholam Hosseim Gharib (1923–2004, novelist) and Manouchehr Sheybani

(1924–91, poet, filmmaker). A defiant parody of the Tudeh literary bi-weekly, *Kabutar-e Solh* (*The Peace Dove*, founded in 1941), the designation *Khorus Jangi* clearly mocked 'party literature' and Nima's loose association with these journals. Quickly marginalised and with its publications dismissed, the circle published five issues of its magazine, *Khorus Jangi*, between April and June 1951, before slipping into oblivion (see Tahbaz 2001). For *Khorus Jangi* associates, the artist was committed only to the art (i.e. modern arts and literature), not to values outside of the arts. In short, they stated, if literature has a social and/or political message, it must arise from literature itself, not be imposed on it.

Anyway, the 'poetry of defeat' of Akhavan-Sales soon, almost simultaneously, gave way to one of resistance. The dialectics of despair and revolt could not be clearer when we put Akhavan-Sales's 'The Winter' (dated 1955, published 1956) right next to Shamlu's 'Fog' ('Meh', written 1953, published 1957). At this time, Shamlu also wrote 'The Fairies' ('Pariya'), a 'children's' rhyme written like a traditional *matal* (rhymed folk fable), 'an allegory of political change' (Karimi-Hakkak 1977: 204) heralding a revolution to come (Ghanoonparvar 1984: 131). This poem has invited different interpretations (Ghanoonparvar 1984: 129–47; Karimi-Hakkak, 1977: 203–5). I skip this poem here and will discuss its protest-song version in Chapter 3. Published in *Hava-ye Tazeh* (*Fresh Air*, 1958), 'Meh' ('Fog') and its images turned out to be influential for the next generation of 'committed' poets:

Fog

Fog has covered all over the desert.
The village light is concealed
there is a warm wave in the desert's blood
the desert – weary,
   silent,
     out of breath –
       sweats slowly and entirely
        in the fog's warm delirium

'Fog has covered all over the desert,' murmurs the passer-by
'the village dogs are silent,

cloaked in the fog's mantle, I reach home. *Golku* doesn't know. She'll see
    me suddenly at the threshold. A teardrop in her eye, a smile on her lips,
    she'll say:
Fog has covered all over the desert . . . I thought, should the fog persist till
    dawn, the daring men would return from their hideout to visit their
    loved ones.'

Fog has covered
              all over
                    the desert.
The village light is concealed; there is a warm wave in the desert's blood.
The desert – weary, silent, out of breath – sweats slowly and entirely in the
    fog's warm delirium . . .
(Shamlu 1993c: 48–9)

The poem is self-explanatory and the foggy, bucolic ambiance both mythic
and real. Despite its appearance as prose poetry to untrained eyes, there is
actually a remarkably creative Nimaic metric concealed in the poem's natural
rhythm of spoken Persian, and this reinforces the narrative structure of the
poem. One might imagine that, depicting the secret return of the guerrilla
to visit his loved one, 'Fog' was written in the aftermath of the Fadai Guerrillas and the Siahkal operation. But the poem is actually dated 1953: it was
written following the coup, although published in 1957. The *anticipation*,
expressed in this poem (and differently in 'The Fairies'), of the liberator's
return to his loved ones makes the advent of the guerrillas an even more
curious phenomenon from a cultural and literary standpoint. Imagine reading this poem after the 'Siahkal resurgence'. Visualise how the ambiance
lends itself to the image of the nine daring men who attached the Siahkal
Gendarmerie Post trying to return home after the operation. In the collective imagination of dissident students and intellectuals of the time, 'Fog'
was an embodiment of the elusive and omnipresent urban guerrillas, among
whom the Fadai Guerrillas stood out. In its description, the poem is eerily
exact. The concrete Siahkal guerrillas now personified the figurative and
ethereal presence of the transcendental liberator in the poem. The literal and
living militant was now the figurative and poetic liberator. The fusion of the
horizons of real-life militants, on the one hand, and artists and poets, on the

other, could not be clearer, nor more explosive (pun intended). *Yushij envisaged art imitating life* (through natural imagery and speech); however, this poem of Shamlu, the 'poet-prophet' (Ghanoonparvar 1984: 141), proved the opposite. *For this poem* ('Fog', 1953) *to be realised, to conjure up its tangible referent, one should have waited almost two decades (1971).*

In 1970s Iran, it was life that imitated art.

Defiance in Spirit

I must pause here to point out what we might call, following Gilles Deleuze and Félix Guattari (1986), 'minor literature' – literature that has been persistently overlooked but remains important for this study. In this book, 'defiance' is conceptualised in a *political* way, and the defiant temperament of the generation of PFG and OIPM is connected to artistic defiance and the passion that the selfless guerrillas sparked in artists. This constitutes a general attitude towards revolutionary spirit. Phenomenologically, however, we should unravel and appreciate the very *spirit of defiance* that informs defiant and rebellious arts *before* they 'become' political. In other words, the 'spirit' (of defiance) precedes its moment of being lent to politically symbolic art forms. Here, I think of the *spirit* of Nima's *break* with the classical tradition before he began writing political poems. In fact, I submit, without that spirit of defying the age-old tradition, he would not have written politically defiant poems. The same is true about Forough Farrokhzad's poetry as the work of a defiant woman who expresses her naked experiences as in her famous lines, 'I sinned, a pleasurable sin / in a bosom that was warm and fiery': here, in the absence of metaphors waiting to be decoded, the poet's passion is directly felt by the reader. Farrokhzad's defiance of established, sanctioned symbolism that identified Nimaic and post-Nimaic poetry allows for her steering towards her own singular 'genre'. The 'spirit' I am thinking of is perhaps better shown in Houshang Irani and his rebellion against modern poetic norms, to some extent against meaning itself, that led first to his marginalisation and then his silence: *genuine poetry ends up in silence.*

In the context of this particular study, two honorary mentions are in order: the defiant poetry of Karo (Karapet) Derderian (1927–2007) and of Nosrat Rahmani (1930–2000). Neither was deemed 'political'. Interestingly, they were both influenced by the romanticism of some earlier Nimaic poets like Fereidoun Tavalloli (1919–85). An Iranian Armenian, Derderian signed his books and poems as Karo and was (and probably remains) one of Iran's most popular poets. Consistently ignored by the Nimaic poetic circles and classicist figures alike, he wrote both in modern and classical forms and was regarded as a 'folk' (referring to '*avam*', in a pejorative way) poet. I think the designations 'folk poet' or 'lay poet' fit him best. Unlike the poets I have discussed or will discuss in this chapter, Karo published his collections not with established literary publishers but with small-time trade publishers, and not in intellectual journals but in popular, non-literary (even gossip) magazines that literati deemed banal (*mobtazal*). He wrote about folkish concerns: a dying son, an ugly girl, romantic betrayals, an Abadan construction worker, or a prostitute giving birth (Karo 1955; 1966) – the materials esoteric Nimaic poets would not touch. And he wrote about these lay concerns with a steadfast objection to the injustices of this world. He shared Akhavan-Sales's voice of despair, not politically but *existentially*, such that his work had great resonance with young (non-political) people in particular. Uncommitted to prevailing literary genres and symbolisms, and ignored by the poetic establishment, he deployed 'untidy' imagery as well as gripping, naked expressions that others dismissed as 'sentimental'. His poetry and prose are too close to his uninhibited imagination to offer coherent meaning out of converging tropes and metaphors, and thus, an irremediable cacophony permeates his writings. The laypersons in the teahouses of southern Tehran would not recount by heart poems of Yushij, Farrokhzad or Shamlu; they would recite Karo's 'lay' poetry. During my time in the Iranian army, I, who come from an elite literary background, reading modern post-Nimaic poetry, was struck by the extent of Karo's popularity among young conscripts with the education level of high-school diploma or under. They introduced me to Karo and deeply related to his candid poetry and prose about love, sex, betrayal and death. Karo's prose-and-poetry *Breaking the Silence* (*Shekast-e Sokut*, 1955) was one of the most popular books of all time: bootlegged versions of it are still sold everywhere. This is Karo's reaction to the post-1953 coup repression:

Twist O lash! Smash, break my bones!
Annihilate in darkness, the opaque shadow,
burn the bars of injustice's fire of this age of suffering,

the night-lighting gaze of my eyes!
Trample under injustice, humiliate, destroy!
In the dungeon of dreadful death!
. . .
I sing resolutely and fearlessly! In the humane future . . .
On the peak of power, the toiling human
I raise proudly the flag of my ideals in my callus-covered hands.
(Karo 1955: 23; original emphasis)

Signification and symbolism, while clear, are not convergent on a central idea and yet the overall picture remains relatable and graspable. This aspect is characteristic of Karo's poetry and prose and the reason for his being shunned for his 'sloppy' (*shelakhteh*) work by the poetry elite. But in raising his voice against injustice and torture, Karo shows his defiant spirit, interestingly not against the state but in defence of the 'toiling human'. One of his best poems reveals his defiance against the entire order of things – against the injustice of poverty and against the poetic beautification of rain:

Rain Again

Rain again, without a song
Rain again with all the night's dereliction
strikes the lonely man
drips on the carpet in the house
The dripping sound of sorrow again
Desperation again

I stand behind the glass of loneliness
I don't know, I don't understand,
how these drops of dereliction can be beautiful?

I don't understand, why don't people understand
the child that badly shivers under the lashes of rain
how is his desperation beautiful?
I don't understand.

The tears of a dad
when a ceiling of mud and iron under the boots of the rain
have calmly rained on his dead wife and butterflies,
how does this express love?
I don't know.

I don't know why people don't know
that rain is not just love
the incessant sound of rain moves along the pain of these hearts
how is our death beautiful?
I don't understand.
. . .

Listen to me, my child
before the eyes of tomorrow's man
yes, the rain is beautiful for the beautiful people of higher-up
and the rain that has love only falls on drunken lovers
and the rain of you and me has pain and sorrow
and god knows well
that this earthly justice, lacks justice.
(Karo 2015)

Karo's defiant spirit radiates out of these words, and yet the poem is not politically pointed. This poem resonates with laypersons because it does not try to teach or shake off a conscience in slumber or mobilise a torn one. It simply depicts the infernal reality concealed by aesthetic depictions of other poets, revealing the tangible misery of poverty and thus impressing this damning reality upon readers.

To illustrate my point, let me momentarily digress and see how the very same idea appears in a poem by Esma'il Kho'i (1938–2021) – a celebrated 'political' poet – in his 'The North Too' (dated February 1969). He contrasts the rain in Tehran's poor south and rich north, a dualism he seeks to prophetically dismantle as an advocate of social justice. In the political ambiance of the late 1960s, this now-famous poem was received widely by the dissident readership. See how these two poets view the same phenomenon – a reflection of their divergent world-views:

The North Too

Rain will destroy the south of the city

Rain
    will destroy
                the south of the city . . .
And I, amazingly, am not sorrow-stricken.

. . .

I must celebrate the fall of sorrow in me.

At this moment
I am expressive and explosive, like wrath
and, like wrath, I am capable.
And I can pick up the Divan of Hafez
and shred its pages
                to pieces
                    with my bare hands
and I can – like a blade, like the subtle shifts of whittling
believe in the need for blood and autumn,
and I can stand on the storm's path
and devastate a garden of buds and dew,
and I can even
        even up close
            witness the beheading of one to one thousand young lambs.

. . .

The south of the city will be destroyed
and there's no reason to feel sad, no reason to feel sad
South of the city ought to be destroyed
Cruel?
        No, this is not cruelty
cruelty is in pitying the puddles
cruelty is in pitying the brush in the valley
to be on the mountain-peak, and to feel pity for the valley
cruelty has always been thus
        The flood says so
           I say so.

Cruelty has always been like this.

. . .

The south of the city will be destroyed
and there's no reason to feel sad –
the tumbling of water will destroy the south
and the south's destruction
      will destroy the north.
(Kho'i 1995: 93–6; trans. Karimi-Hakkak and Beard)

This contrast serves us immensely: with striking intensity and emotional flow, Karo's poem depicts the misery that rain brings to the shanty towns (presumably of southern Tehran) from the worm's-eye perspective of the poor and unprivileged who live the narrated abject conditions. Karo's poem indicates, in Reza Barahani's words (in a different context; see below): 'poetry shows, it does not state' (Barahani, quoted in Yousef 2017a). The sorrow-filled mood of Karo's poem is not only compelling and absorbing, it is relatable, weighing heavy on the conscience. In anyone with a heart, Karo's 'Rain Again' arouses compassion, empathy and a yearning for justice. Karo shows the injustice of this world first hand. In contrast, and despite his advocacy of justice and his association with the PFG co-founder Puyan, Kho'i's poetic representation, laden with decrees and diktats ('rain will destroy', or 'I say so'), is detached and abstract, expressed from a bird's-eye perspective, the vantage point of a middle-class intellectual in his comfortable cocoon. Notwithstanding the poet's professed rage, the poem sounds sterile in communicating the wretched effects of rain. As a dialectician, it seems, he is entitled to bracket his emotions and instead announce, with a certain conceit, that he 'celebrates the fall of sorrow' in him when confronted with the misery of the poor. It is an interpretive error to read his 'celebration' as an irony. There is no irony in being 'on the mountain-peak, and . . . feel[ing] pity for the valley', because this poem is a philosopher's statement that is informed not by empathy but by a calculative theory of class warfare which gives him hope that once the poor of southern Tehran are pushed to the brink, they will pour into northern Tehran and destroy the rich! Although Kho'i is sometimes associated with 'jungle' or 'guerrilla poetry' (Shafi'i Kadkani 2001: 79; Yousef 2017a; 2017b: 597), this association is more affective than genric or aesthetic, as his work is too aristocratically personal and distinct to have been contributing – through imagery, symbolism or dynamics – to the poetic movement that was unfolding before his eyes in the late 1960s. As early as 1970, Golesorkhi had criticised Kho'i's poetry from a Marxist-literary stance. In his review of three poetry books Kho'i had published in 1970, Golesorkhi speaks about a poetry that is entangled in 'rules, interests, and selfishness of the so-called intellectual class' and a poet (Kho'i) who, being a 'rightful child of Akhavan-Sales', 'trapped in dry and lifeless philosophies', 'must be sought in his own class contradictions' (Golesorkhi, quoted in Shams-Langarudi 1991d: 69, 72, 70). In other words, Golesorkhi judges Kho'i on his inability to commit to the emerging poetry of defiance.

Back to our discussion. Karo's poem stands out as dynamic, Kho'i's as idyllic. I hope this contrast reveals why Karo was Iran's most popular living poet *outside* intellectual circles.

Nosrat Rahmani appeared differently within the poetic public. He was not as popular as either Karo or key figures of poetic modernity, but trailblazed through the post-Nimaic movement because of his public and poetic panache and in-your-face personality, and was invited to events such as the Khusheh (1968) and Goethe (1977) poetry festivals. As a young man, he lived a fairly unconventional life; in contrast to his urbane counterparts who enjoyed a middle-class hygienic lifestyle in which drinking and smoking opium was regarded as an acceptable 'perversion', he associated himself with the rugged, even lewd, toiling masses of southern Tehran. After all, not many poets carry a switchblade in their pocket! In the 1960s, apparently in response to Barahani's published criticism of Shamlu, Rahmani assaulted Barahani with a knife in Café Firuz (Ostad Mohammad 2014). Rahmani was indeed so fond of his switchblade that he wrote a famous poem, 'Knife' (from *Fire of the Wind*, 1970): 'In the solitude of its bed, calmly / – in the tomb of my pocket – / has discharged itself to sleep, / my knife! / Perhaps it's dead / thirsty / with head tucked in collar / and its lips cold / my knife.' The poem continues by reciting the knife's memory, suggesting that this poem was written as Rahmani was finally quitting his rebellious lifestyle and settling down. 'It's not my knife's fault / it's thirsty / thirsty for a sip of salty-tasting blood / it's been created / to cut through a chest / and to bathe in blood / so, behold the bliss of my knife / my knife' (Rahmani 2000: 88–9, 94). Associating poetry with youth, insisting that 'in the crossword[s] puzzle of life there is no room for an old poet', he wrote, in a short preface to an anthology of his poetry: 'In the course of our lives everything, including living itself, is imposed on us. We position ourselves and rebel against things that are contrary to our nature and beliefs, but sooner or later our vigour deteriorates and we submit to things like aging, illness and death' (Rahmani 2000: 12, 9). Rahmani never shied away from politically lacerating poetry although he remained unwaveringly apolitical: 'Defeat is never humiliation / victory / never guards captivity / this old fable / the broken chains have told me' ('Bluff' [1957] in Rahmani 2000: 164). His declaration makes it clear: 'Poetry is not entirely a matter of will. Otherwise, I would like my poem to be fragrant like a flower instead of smelling of gunpowder . . . One must be truly insincere with oneself and one's surroundings to remove politics from one's work in this age and in a dark world such as this' (Rahmani, quoted in ISNA 2020).

With his poems being reminiscent of Akhavan-Sales's 'poetry of dismay' in mood and presentation, Rahmani was not just poetically defiant but existentially rebellious. His 'dismay' went deeper than the political. See this rebellious soul's discovery of the absurdity of life in one of his most famous poems 'Congregating in Slime' (1957), which references cheap street gambling with the flip of a coin. Non-Persian speakers please note, in Iran the two faces of a coin are *shir* (heads, literally, 'lion') and *khat* (tails, literally 'line', also 'script'), and I keep 'lion' and 'line' here to show the poem's subtlety:

Congregating in Slime

It danced
flew and soared
flanged off his fingertip
the coin.
I said: line

The copper butterfly
flew away
flipped, flipped
winged and dropped at the bottom of the slime-filled street gutter

It shone, burning the air, and the gazes
met one another
wiggling through each other
in their chests, wasted loves cried out
O, Despair! O, Hope!

Hurriedly, we ran towards the coin
from the border of being and nothing
to the slime-filled street gutter
we rushed together and then
we knitted our gazes to the body of the coin

The copper butterfly
mirror-like, stood up on the field of slime
and on both sides
there was line
a line toward nothing, a line to the border of void

Sorrow silted
on his quasi-heart
and a smile sucked in the lines around his lips to say
– then, oh . . . the lion's figure?
Tears grew,
and he grew silent

I said:
A field of slime is not the den of lions, it's not.
Line and spots
are passages of the worms.
This is not the field of love and pride
it's the congregation of ugliness and debasement

We ran from one another
on the line of fate
We shed blood serum
We both lost
We both lost
(Rahmani, 2000: 158–61)

This is the loss of everything meaningful in life. We lose. Permanently. Just as the line (*khat*) of the coin draws us towards a line of fate that ends in worms, so the slime of society impedes the den of lions (*shir*) from being. Is this not a reflection to the post-1953 society, one that goes deeper than politics? Profoundly, repression is deemed to be in a state of decay in a society depicted as the slime of street gutters. This poem is politically suggestive. The following is one passage (out of seven) of another poem published in *Congregating in Slime* (1957):

Exile in the Chain's Seven Coils

O Pure
What are you thinking about,
locks?

Free hands
are the greatest gifts to the walls, chains, and shackles
and the best gift of the chain to the free hand
is lock, lock

O Pure
The locks are brokers
The locks are relationships
The locks are debauchees of doors and chains
The locks . . .?

By the way, the brokers are sometimes right, too
By the way, prostitutes are sometimes right, too
The secret of freedom is in the coil of every chain
Lock also means hope
Lock means there is a key
Lock means key
(Rahmani 2000: 140–1)

The poem is self-explanatory, does not offer complicated symbolism and is relatable to readers.

To understand the politically defiant poetry of the 1960s and 1970s, what is key is to appreciate the *poetic defiance* that preceded and informed it. Defiance is always already within poetry itself; defiance lives within and breathes with any genuine poetry and is not alloyed with poetry through the intervention of political consciousness. In fact, without the defiant essence of poetry, defiant arts and literature would not be possible.

Into the Deep Sixties: Dignity of Defiance

Literary commitment confronted the poets of the 1950s and 1960s with a hermeneutical dilemma. Although it sounds reductive, in a nutshell '[c]ommitment means a presuppositional engagement with and concern for social causes, revolutionary ends, and ideological statements' (Dabashi 1985: 149). Commitment is actually more complex. It is based on the principle that the arts are essentially social, and so artworks inevitably should reflect social issues. In other words, 'As sensitive and responsive human beings . . . artists are not, nor could they be, indifferent to the social conditions surrounding them and their art' (Dabashi 1985: 151). But then questions arise: how exactly does a certain message permeate the artistic work? How can we know if a poem is expressive of pure meditations or is an imposition of non-literary values? Curiously, there is a deeper concern informing this debate, and that is the anxiety of both the literary commitment adherents and their opponents who argue that the work might be reduced to statements bereft of artistic and literary merit. Poets do not want their *she'r* (poem) to be *sho'ar* (slogan, declaration). In fact, issuing slogans (instead of writing poetry) was the single most common charge against the 'guerrilla poetry'. This dilemma was indeed a major source of the rift between 'committed literature' and those who basically followed the ideas of *Khorus Jangi* in the 1960s, when a sort of defiance against this specific idea of commitment arose from a new generation of very diverse poets who had come of age in the post-coup era. The word 'commitment' was vigorously probed and vastly re-interpreted. Irani, who had grown silent after the coup, had unwittingly and obliquely influenced the 1960s *Moj-e No* (New Wave) poetry. This *wave* can be regarded as a 'poetic protest' in a double sense: it was a protest against traditional poetry, thereby defending Nima, while it also challenged Yushij's particular poetic modernity, clearly not to reject but to *radicalise* it. Advocating an arts-centred imagination, *Moj-e No* poetry, founded by Ahmad Reza Ahmadi (1940–), unleashed a whole range of experimental poetry informed by a certain, self-reflective (as opposed to socially oriented) poetic consciousness. The New Wave poetry gave birth to *She'r-e Hajm* (*Espacementalisme*), championed by Yadollah Royaee, and *She'r-e Nab* (Pure Poetry) (Nooriala 1994; Shams-Langarudi 1991c: 15–52). Key figures of the New Wave (Ahmadi, Mohammad-Ali Sepanlu, Esma'il Nooriala, Nader Ebrahimi and Qaffar Hosseini) created the Torfeh publication house, which published two issues of *Torfeh* magazine in 1964 and then *Jozveh-ye She'r* (11 issues in 1966–7) to promote New Wave literature. To theorise it, Nooriala published the voluminous *Imagination and Instruments in Iranian Poetry Today* (Nooriala 1969).

Their different philosophies aside, the rising self-styled poets believed that genuine poetry should have no commitment outside of itself. Social and political commitments render poetry the instrument of unpoetic causes, New Wave poets believed, as they imply socialist realism. The poet's noblest and primary commitment is to poetry itself: this is how poets can remain true to themselves. Although many New Wave adherents were far from being apolitical, they refused to measure poetry according to imposed political and social values – expectations that were extraneous to poetry (Nooriala 1994: 92–5). The New Wave *implied* the urban, middle-class value of privatism. But to this group we must add two singular and prominent voices: the distinctly feminine poetry of Forough Farrokhzad (1935–67), which spoke of a woman's experience, and the neo-Nimaic poetry of Soharab Sepehri (1928–80) which dwelled on Buddhist and bucolic imagery.

Here is where there appeared a rift in the socially and politically rich symbolism of *she'r-e no* brought about by Yushij. All in all, a new generation of poets rose to prominence in the 1960s who did not adhere to the narrow vision of social-political commitment of their predecessors. If we attribute New Poetry to the context of Iran's political modernisation, then by the same token we should agree with Shams-Langarudi and attribute New Wave poetry to the Shah's institutional modernisation and the resultant urbanisation and westernised lifestyle in the 1960s, that is commonly known as *tajaddodgarai* (1991c: 15–17). The New Wave was indeed good news for Persian poetry, allowing poetry to surpass Nimaic innovations and the original configurations of *she'r-e no*. It continued to introduce new expressions and experimentations in the 1970s, with the advent of the concrete poetry of the female poet Tahereh Saffarzadeh, who, in her *Tanin dar Delta* (*Echoes in the Delta*, 1970), like Farrokhzad, broke new ground compared with the male-dominated Persian poetry (see Shams-Langarudi 1991d: 83–7).

As I write these lines, history has already been concluded; and the 'committed' (*mote'ahhed*) poetry had dominated the 1960s and 1970s, interestingly, not for any particular or immanent aesthetic or poetic merit, but in large part due to the increasing repression of the 1960s as well as the rise of the revolutionary 1960s with their grammar of rebellion. The 1960s were the age of certain dominant idioms: liberation, egalitarianism, freedom-fighting, self-assertion. Indicative of the decade's rebellious Zeitgeist, these idioms also informed the Fadaiyan's discourse of national liberation (see Vahabzadeh 2010: xxi, 6). The dominant idioms of this age had organic connections with dominant symbols of modern (Nimaic and post-Nimaic) Persian poetry, symbols that indeed preceded the 1960s but curiously awaited their fruition later in this decade and the next. Therefore, it is not surprising that the New Wave poetic genre and its privatism stood in contrast to literary commitment. The refutation of artistic privatism under the conditions of a dictatorship is captured in Shamlu's succinct reflections, some twenty years later in the 1980s, on the poetry of Sohrab Sepehri:

> I have a hard time believing in this ill-timed mysticism. Innocent people are beheaded at the street gutter and I stand a few feet away, advising, 'Don't muddy the water!' [a famous line of Sepehri's poetry]. I think one of us must be totally off, him or me. Rereading him might completely convince me [that he was right] and then I would kiss his hands in my dream and memory [of him]. [His] poems are sometimes very beautiful, even outstanding, but I don't think we can be in the same company. For me at least, 'pure beauty' is not enough. What can I do? (Shamlu, quoted in Siahpoush 1994: 264)

Even more directly, in a *sho'ari* poem dated 1954, Shamlu had declared:

> Today poetry is the weapon of the people [*khalq*] . . .
> today the poem is not a stranger
> from the common pain of the people
> he smiles with the people's lips

he adjoins
the people's hope and pain
with his own bones.
(Shamlu, quoted in Ariyanpour 1995: 625–6)

Indeed, Shamlu believed, 'poetry is life, not stringing together beautiful words . . . Poetry means all [of us]. "Poetry must be composed by all of us, not just one person"' (Shamlu 1985: 20).

Polarised politics and a complex society's divergences inevitably bifurcated poetic ontologies, as evidenced by the literary commitment and New Wave disagreements. Literary criticism reaches its heights in this atmosphere: it elevates itself to the means of asserting the highest ontological value. In his lecture 'The Basis of Poetry: Poetry of Resistance, Poetry of Submission', the poet Ne'mat Mirzazadeh (M. Azarm, 1938–) critically responds to Yaddolah Royaee's essay 'Beyond Espacemantalisme' and asserts that poetry should reflect the values and challenges of society, as a result of which, a duality between poetries of *resistance* and *submission* has emerged. Mirzazadeh characterises the latter as 'the poetry of praising the dominant power, reactionary poetry, a poetry of concerns of non-concern [*gham-e bighami*], a poem that consequently is detrimental to culture', while the former stands out as 'poetry of creation, committed poetry, popular poetry [*she'r-e mardomi*], the poetry of necessary concerns, a poetry that contributes to the evolutionary movement of society' (Azarm, quoted in Shams-Langarudi 1991d: 129; on this 'debate' see ibid.: 127–50). Mysteriously, the date of this lecture is February 1971 – coincidental with the Siahkal operation – and it was delivered to students at the Faculty of Technology, University of Tehran – the birthplace of the PFG.

Despite the sentiment and the position regarding commitment, amazingly, the domination of literary commitment did not come with the exclusion of the New Wave and its offshoots in the pluralistic ambiance of the 1960s, one of the most diverse and fruitful intellectual periods in Iran's modern history. The best representation of this pluralism is possibly the anthology *Khusheh* (*Cluster*, 1968), edited by Shamlu. Based on the poems recited in the celebrated Khusheh Poetry Festival (evenings of 15–19 September 1968), hosted and held by Tehran Municipality Employees Club and well-attended by the public, the anthology entails both poetic streams of the two post-Nimaic generations (Shamlu 1968a; Shams-Langarudi 1991c: 576–605). Literary commitment advocates like Shamlu, Akhavan-Sales, Kho'i and Golesorkhi appeared alongside Irani, Ahmadi, Nooriala, Royaee and other New Wavers. The event was organised by the literary periodical *Khusheh* (ed. Shamlu) and it also contained painting (Mansureh Hosseini) and caricature (Ardeshir Mohasses) exhibits, as well as a memorable staging of Samuel Beckett's *Waiting for Godot* directed by Davud Rashidi (1933–2016) and performed by him, Parviz Kardan (1938–2021), Parviz Sayyad (1939–) and Sirus Afkhami. Beckett's play, in the sensitive ambiance of 1968, certainly suggested a politically anticipative mood. *Khusheh* began publication in 1967 and continued until it was shut down by SAVAK in 1969. The prominent critic and poet Reza Barahani (1935–) had called the festival 'the greatest event in the history of Persian poetry in Iran' (in Shamlu 1968b: i). Another reviewer of the event spoke of 'social poetry . . . [through which] the poet provides a metaphorical depiction of society' (in Shamlu 1968b: ii). The anthology published the poems of 110 poets, who sadly included only nine women, but Shamlu did not publish in it some of the radically political poems read at the event (by Said Soltanpour and Mirzazadeh) (Shams-Langarudi 1991c: 588), while an eyewitness account holds that Soltanpour left the deepest impression on the audience and had 'incited everybody' (Yousef 2017a). Said Soltanpour (1940–81) was a young unknown poet at the time; reportedly, after reading a couple of poems that attacked the regime he was asked to leave the podium, but the crowds cheered him, insisting that he continued reciting his poems (Shams-Langarudi 1991c: 584–5). 'His guerrilla poems that had stirred up a storm in one of those nights [of festival], despite the wide and enthusiastic reception of the people, were attacked by many poets' (Shams-Langarudi 1991c: 584). This caused 'the likes of Shamlu and Barahani to . . . take a position against "slogan" (*sho'ar*)' (Yousef 2017b: 591). Barahani captured this position in his dictum 'poetry shows, it does not state' (Barahani, quoted in Yousef 2017a). In his Preface to the volume Shamlu quotes Barahani, who issues the verdict: 'Slogan (*sho'ar*) is not poetry (*she'r*) . . . Slogan does not show; it states.' Then, clearly annoyed by the applause Soltanpour had received at the Khusheh festival, Barahani continues, 'The excitement that is caused in the audience by poetry will later reveal its lasting impression . . . Artistic excitement is not fleeting. Being excited about slogans is fleeting, and he who announces slogans and causes people to applaud for him by his slogans is not a poet' (Barahani, quoted in Shamlu 1968b: ii; quoted also in Shams-Langarudi 1991c: 586). It was precisely because of the political poets' popular acclamation that in this event 'the so-called New Wave poets . . . were not well received' (Barahani, quoted in Shams-Langarudi, 1991c: 587). Shamlu justifies his censorship, and lies about it, stating that 'at the end of book printing process we sadly noticed that the names and poems of some of the best and most prolific poets have not appeared in the text, and it goes without saying that this has not been intentional' (Shamlu 1968b: iii). Well, this is perhaps not surprising given that Shamlu had reportedly mentioned to Saeed Yousef that Soltanpour's poems were 'nonsense' and 'are not poetry at all' (Yousef 2017b: 606). The whole discussion of poetry versus slogan did not go unchallenged, and in the 1969 issue of the influential intellectual magazine *Jahan-e Naw* (*The New World*), Mohammad Azimi and Mostafa Rahimi called the distinction outdated and misconceived (Yousef 2017b: 592). Azimi stated, 'What primarily matters to us is the belief of the speaker [in] what she/he says' (Azimi 1969: 165). In a bold move that challenges the mainstream and rationalises his choice, as poetry editor, of the poems published in *Jahan-e Naw*, emphasising the social impact of poetry, he continues: 'Let us not forget to remind ourselves that many "slogans" are preferred to "poems"' (Azimi 1969: 167). According to Yousef, who had attended the poetry festival, Soltanpour had won the hearts and souls of the young at the event. So, it is important to echo Yousef, that the reason for Shamlu's censorship was that 'he did not want to see another poet on his own left [wing]' (Yousef 2017a). We will soon see that the next hugely attended poetry event, at the Goethe Institute in Tehran in October 1977, marked the beginning of the end of monarchy. In hindsight, the Khusheh Poetry Festival was a dress rehearsal for the Goethe Poetry Festival, but in the latter event we see the clear domination of literary commitment – the effect of urban guerrilla warfare in the country. The Khusheh poetry nights were the first significant attempt at presenting poetry to the populace after the 1953 coup – in fact, it was the first 'public poetry' event – and asserted the presence of the Iranian Writers Association, founded a few months earlier (21 April 1967) (see Soleimani 1981: 123–8).

For the record, in both events, Khusheh and Goethe, Soltanpour appeared as the most popular poet and was received most enthusiastically by the audience (Yousef 2017b: 617).

Paradoxically, New Wave poetry and its challenging of the dominant notion of 'literary commitment' also created the context for 'guerrilla poetry' (*she'r-e cheriki*) to emerge in the early 1970s. With the rising radical temperament of the 1960s, the esotericism and privatism at the heart of the New Wave's poetic protest forced 'literary commitment', and thereby socially and politically conscious poetry, to return in multi-dimensional fashion. The works of Shamlu, despite his claim to the contrary, represent the most creative *mélange* of lyrical (and even privatist) and socially committed poetry (see below). He spoke of love in the same breath when he symbolically poetised about martyrdom, revolt and the horizon of a liberated nation. No wonder his poetry became a dominant genre until the 1980s. I insist on the importance of this fusion of lyrical and social: it enabled the growing *community of deliberate inferences* to collapse the division between privatism and the socially-committed and read political messages between the lines of seemingly lyrical poems. And this brings us to an emblematic poem by Hamid Mosaddeq (1939–98) – a popular poem among university students. *Blue, Grey, Black* (*Abi, Khakestari, Siah*), dated November–December 1964 and published in a book with that title, is a long lyrical elegy, a unique blend of Nimaic rhythm, Sepehri's imagery, Farrokhzad's romantic sensibility and Akhavan-Sales's symbolism. The 1950s mood of despair and the 1960s mood of defiance converge in this beautiful lyric, rendering it a protest poem. Although Mosaddeq himself reportedly insisted that this was a lyrical (*asheqaneh*) poem, and he had no intention of writing political commentary (Ebrahimi 2018), the poem was read by university students and dissident intellectuals exactly as that. The poem's magic, and thus its reach as a 'political' poem, I argue, rest actually with its lyrical imagery –

In the nights of my solitude
I pray to your expressive eye
In this consuming opaque night, I
make a pilgrimage to the dark of your hair
messier than my thought, your hair
my endless night, your hair

and the poem becomes even more directly lyrical:

> I must appreciate sleep
> where the silent state reigns
> I see the flowers of my hope blossom in my dreams
> and a whisper that tells me:
> 'though this night is long,
> stay strong in your heart, sunrise is near.'

We can see how Nimaic signifiers and symbols associated with the 'night poems' gingerly permeate the romantic expression, thus leading the expectations of alert readers towards interpretations others than those possibly intended by the author. And the expressions of love continue:

> The sky's blue
> and blue are the feathers of birds of sincerity
> In the mirror of the morning, my gaze beholds you
> from your bosom, the true morn
> stretches its wings
> You are my rose,
> You are a jasmine flower
> You're like the pure morning dew
> No!
> You're purer than that.

Unsettled signifiers continue to push the romantic lines into other directions. Notice the reference to 'oneness in the East':

> I call out:
> 'Open the window!'
> You close the window.
> What's this lethargy, this silence in me now?
> What's this oblivion in you?
> Who wishes you and I
> not to become us?
> May his house be ruinous
> If I don't become we, I'll be alone

If you don't become we
you'll be yourself.
Why can't you and I
summon oneness
in the East again?

Note how, as sentiments regarding this ethereal, but clearly female, loved one are expressed, the poem gently shifts in tone and symbolism. Its romantic expression certainly appealed to wider groups of young people than just the socially conscious ones:

One must become a mountain and stay
One must become a river and flow
One must become a meadow and sing. . .
. . .
Words must be spoken
pain must be expressed . . .

The poem's socially conscious message sews the virtue of being rebellious to the romantic sensibility of this generation, on behalf of which Mosaddeq warns the powers-that-be about the descending deluge of dissent in the country: 'don't you think that my silence / attests to my obliviousness.' And then appear the words that were printed in the collective memory of more than one generation. The darling 'you' magically reappears as the rebellious, beloved 'you':

If you rise!
if I rise,
we will all rise.

If you sit!
if I sit,
who will then rise?
Who will challenge [our] enemy?
Who will wrestle down each of our foes?
The meadows will call your name
the mountains will call my poem.
(Mosaddeq 2010)

In its lyrical ambiance, the poem situates the existential cul-de-sac and generational angst of the socially-conscious young Iranians in the face of the Shah's rapid, authoritarian modernisation. Having discovered an imagined alternative based on full participation in forging the country's future, this new, educated class was haunted by the memory of a lost democracy. As Shams-Langarudi accurately observes:

> Although the long poem, *Blue, Grey, Black*, published in 1965 and in the period of revolt against romanticism . . ., did not immediately attract much attention, but a few years later when, with the rise of guerrilla (*cheriki*) atmosphere in Iran, militant (*cheriki*) sentiments had replaced the feeling of gloomy defeat of the fifties, *Blue, Grey, Black* that contains the amazing and emotional *mélange* of politics and love, suddenly became popular with its 1969 second printing, and a few lines [of the poem] became proverbial in the lexis of all, and the slogan of [university] students in their political protests: 'If you rise! / if I rise, / we will all rise.' (Shams-Langarudi 1991c: 281–2)

This is how the community of deliberate inferences, growing out of modernist literary circles, expanded its reach to educated intellectuals, and university students – the social groups that constituted and supported militant activism in the 1970s. This is the key moment when, as Saussure showed, the signifier–signified pair is fixed due to the emergence of a community. Metaphors increasingly give way to symbols: the double (and multiple) meaning of metaphor yields to symbols, these 'plenary words' that allow poetic access to my primordial experience of oppression. These primordial experiences remain otherwise ineffable and thus not fully intelligible: no world can be grasped without utterance. Ideology might offer an expression, but due to its particularly formulaic discourse, ideology can only allow an experience to be expressed in a *reductively mediated* way. That is why, as mentioned, I am hesitant to reduce the construction of this symbolic universe of defiance to ideology, a seemingly popular thesis among scholars (Ghanoonparvar 1984; Naficy 1997; Talattof 2000). Words mediate the reality (Schürmann), but symbols create a world of words that allow for a certain *im*-mediate experience: I have unuttered, personal feelings about living under dictatorship; poetry comes and that feeling becomes effable. *Symbolic defiance in the 1960 allowed an entire generation to access and express, in a particular way, the very experience that had choked it for years.* This age worked its wonders in such a way that the poetry of Mosaddeq – and Shamlu, Akhavan-Sales and others – offered access to that collective experience. Whether a 'political' reading was intended by him makes no difference. As Hans-Georg Gadamer teaches us, authorial intent is irrelevant.

I ask again: as a poem that became the mantra of protesting students in the 1970s (a poem that its writer insisted was lyrical), was *Blue, Grey, Black* romantic or political? Should Shamlu's poetry, with its lyrically memorable poems (especially the ones addressed to his wife Aida), be categorised within the 'literary commitment' group? This *ambivalence* permeates almost every piece of art in this period and is expressed through the rift between New Wave poetry and poems associated with literary commitment. This is counter-intuitive. That is why I cannot uphold this division, despite the philosophical and artistic principles of these tendencies.

We have seen how Shamlu's 'Fog' anticipated the advent of the shadowy liberator as early as the 1950s. We all know about his political commitments. But then we witness a similar idea in a poem by Forough Farrokhzad (1934–67), a celebrated female poet known for her distinct feminine voice and a poetry that boldly dwelled in the vividly expressive lived experience of a woman. Farrokhzad wrote some of the most memorably tangible and emotional expressions of romance and solitude. She mastered the naked depiction of love and lust: 'What sign do I have of his lips / other than tender kisses / I've no other keepsake on my body / than the pressure of [his] iron arms' (1993: 98). 'Ah, I was full of lust – lusting for death / from a dizzying feeling, I had shooting pain in both of my breasts' (Farrokhzad 1993: 325). And of course: 'I've sinned a delightful sin / in a warm and burning embrace / I sinned wrapped in the arms / that were hot, avenging, and iron-firm.' In her reflections on her solitude, Farrokhzad is the poet of this masterpiece:

The Bird Is Mortal

I'm feeling blue
I'm feeling blue

I step in the terrace and rub my fingers
on the stretched skin of the night

The lights of connection are dim
The lights of connection are dim

No one will introduce me
to the sun
No one will take me to the feast of the sparrows
Remember the flight
The bird is only mortal.
(Farrokhzad 1993: 467–8)

And then, this memorable poem from her last poetry collection, *Let Us Believe in the Beginning of the Cold Season* (1963):

When my trust was hanging from the feeble rope of justice
and they tore into pieces the hearts of my lights
in the city,
when they were covering the childish eyes of my love
with the black blindfold of the law,
and blood was squirting out of
the anxious temples of my desire,
when my life no longer meant anything,
nothing, but the ticking clock on the wall
I realised, I must. I must. I must.
Insanely love.
(Farrokhzad 1993: 446)

These lines, written in the unique, feminine voice of Farrokhzad, paint the social and existential anxieties of a generation – one that realised their lives had become 'nothing, but the ticking clock' in an alienating, rapidly developing society that needed not reflective and passionate young persons but soulless state functionaries, and out of that realisation decided to stage a revolution in the years to come. Farrokhzad is indeed narrating the anxieties of the generation that joined the guerrillas.

And the poem steps up the narrative to smash all promises, clearly referring to the world of the Cold War and national liberation movements, to insist on the agency of each one of us:

Ask from the mirror
the name of your saviour
Isn't the earth that is shaken beneath your feet
lonelier than you are?
Did the prophets bring to our century
the dispatch of destruction?
Are these incessant eruptions,
and toxic clouds
the echoes of sacred verses?
My friend, my brother, my blood-relative!
When you reach the moon
record the date of the massacre of flowers.
(Farrokhzad 1993: 447; my emphasis)

Farrokhzad's 'Someone Who Is Not Like Any Other' ('Kasi keh Mesl-e Hichkas Nist'), also published in her last book, takes a more radical turn. Like Shamlu a decade earlier, Farrokhzad anticipates the advent of a liberator, a liberator *unlike* the others:

I've dreamt that someone's coming
I've dreamt of a red star
and I get twitches in my eyelid,
and my shoes are put together all the time
and may I go blind
if I lie
I've dreamt of that red star
when I was not asleep.
Someone's coming
Someone's coming
Someone different
Someone better
Someone who is not like any other, not like father, not like Ensi, not like
    Yahya, not like mother
Someone like the one she should be

. . .

and is not afraid of Seyed Javad's brother
who's gone and worn
the police uniform.
(Farrokhzad 1993: 456–7)

Clearly, her dreaming of the arrival of someone radically different from us has both spiritual and political connotations: the arrivant is 'different', even 'better' – *unique* as 'the one she should be'. Note how the enunciation of her appearance in the first statement is followed by dreaming of a 'red star'. Here she uses the words '*setareh-ye qermez*' as opposed to '*setareh-ye sorkh*' used in Communist discourse. So, her 'red star' does not denote the emblem of Communism, but by virtue of a *suggestion* – the similar colour of the star – Farrokhzad's particular expression, which owes no allegiance to any political discourse, inevitably lends itself to an already established leftist lexis of social change. In short, a signifier (*setareh-ye qermez*) gets subsumed under the discursively-fixed signified of a certainly different signifier (*setareh-ye sorkh*), which is an ideological symbol, and as such will suggest senses other than the author might have intended. Or as Jacques Derrida has announced, there is no signifier that is not at the same time a signified. So, we end up having:

setareh-ye qermez → *setareh-ye sorkh* → revolutionary change
(signifier)   (signifier/signified)   (signified)

This collective reading is enabled by the then growing community of deliberate inferences and the historic context of the time. The enunciatory poetics of a dream thus converge with an established political discourse, thanks to symbols. And of course, this arrivant is 'not afraid of Seyed Javad's brother / who's gone and worn / the police uniform'. The poem was published in the curious year 1963, when Farrokhzad had observed the conclusive demise of nationalist and student movements since 1960, the only period from 1953 to 1979 when limited legal activism had been tolerated by the state. She had possibly anticipated the return of dictatorship. In the eyes of a zealous generation of activists reading her poetry (back then), in just eight years her dream would become a reality. For the activists of the late 1960s, the one who is not like any other is the uncompromising, self-sacrificing guerrilla. I hope the ending of the poem shows that my (unconventional) reading is not far-fetched:

Someone's coming
Someone's coming
Someone who's one with us in her heart, in her breath, in her voice
Someone whose coming
they cannot arrest

handcuff and throw in jail
...
Someone's coming from the sky of Tupkhaneh Square at the night of
	fireworks
who sets the dinner cloth
and shares the bread
and shares Pepsi Cola
and the National Garden
She distributes the Pertussis remedy
and distributes the registration day
and distributes hospital queue numbers
and distributes rubber boots
and Fardin's cinema
She distributes Seyed Javad's daughter's trees
and distributes all that is unsold
and gives us our share, too.
I've dreamt.
(Farrokhzad 1993: 460–2)

In this poem 'commitment' is no longer a deliberate 'decision' to write in such a way as to reflect on the social. This is an evidence of *the social permeating poetry and mobilising the anticipatory symbolism of poetry to address the social itself.* Approaches that take human agency as absolute and 'literary commitment' as volitional, as deliberate choices of genre or style, miss how discursively social concerns, that are in the air we breathe, appropriate our tongues. This is why I hesitate to accept Dabashi's division of twentieth-century Iranian writers into three groups: political authors, for whom 'literature was considered a means, like a rifle, to political ends' (like Golesorkhi and Soltanpour); those writers who were 'atomized and isolated from society'; and lastly, those works 'produced by minds and souls unperforated by total political commitment or anachronistic apathy' (Dabashi 1985: 171–2). This poem by Farrokhzad shows that poetic 'commitment' to social issues is deeper and more lucid than volitional and stylistic commitments.

Is my reading of Farrokhzad far-fetched? The reader will be the judge. But note how Mohammad Reza Shafi'i-Kadkani also identifies Farrokhzad as an early heralder of armed struggle (2001: 79–80) by referring to this part,

'I Feel Sorry for the Flowerbed' ('Delam baray-e Baghcheh Misuzad'), also published in *Let Us Believe* (1963):

> The front yard of our home is lonesome.
> The front yard of our home is lonesome.
> All day
> from behind the door one hears the sound of dismemberment
> and explosion
> And all our neighbours plant mortars and machine guns
> in their flowerbeds
> Our neighbours cover up
> the tiles of their ponds
> and these tiles
> – not that they want to be –
> are secret stashes of gunpowder
> And the children in our alley
> have filled up their school sacks with little bombs
> The front yard of our home is confused.
> (Farrokhzad 1993: 454; Shafi'i-Kadkani 2001: 79–80)

As mentioned, reading such poems in a posteriori fashion invites disagreement. Yousef, who advocated the 'Siahkal poetry' in the 1970s, challenges Shafi'i-Kadkani's interpretation of Farrokhzad, but with a proviso: 'given our knowledge of Forough's spirit, had she lived, it was not improbable that she would zealously defend armed struggle' (Yousef 2017b: 590, n. 9). But focusing on the author is misleading: what lies at the heart of the issue is that there is a set of signifiers, tropes and symbols that lend themselves to such interpretations because they can migrate from one poetic style and genre to another.

One last, particularly important point: note that neither Mosaddeq nor Farrokhzad (willingly) adhere to Nimaic and post-Nimaic symbolisms that enabled poetic protest and, later, 'literary commitment'. In his long lyrics, Mosaddeq deploys fresh and directly tangible expressions unalloyed with the identifiable symbolism of Nima, Akhavan-Sales or Shamlu – an invariably *all-male* new poetic convention. His poem reaches out to a *wider audience* among the youth (after all, its lines were chanted by protesting students) because understanding its message does not require literary decoding in the manner of the community of deliberate inferences. Likewise, Farrokhzad's poetic protest takes on an expression that is almost entirely her own. Avoiding the existing symbolism (of the all-male poetic wave), she builds her imagery on the basis of tangible depictions of 'real' persons and mundane objects. The 'deeper meaning' of her poem does not need the kind of decoding associated with the community of deliberate inferences either. Refusing the growing poetic-symbolic discourse, a legacy of Yushij, Mosaddeq and Farrokhzad stand out in that their poetic protest is built on their specific poetic expressions. *Dissent need not mean conformity in utterance.* This is how *the rebellious spirit of an age permeates all poetry.* The story of the 'deep sixties' Iran.

Return of the Night (Poems)

Just as the political night of repression spread its long and dark wings over the country in the fifteen-year period that ended with the 1978–9 Revolution, so did *shabaneh* or 'night poems' return to the poetic scene. And when it comes to *shabaneh* poetry, Shamlu's name stands out, the one poet who stood steadfast, poetically supporting dissent and freedom, writing poetic tributes to the martyrs of movements, old or new. While in Qasr prison in central Tehran (1955), Shamlu wrote 'Nazli's Death' ('Marg-e Nazli') – a poetic tribute to the young Tudeh Party member Vartan Salakhian (d. 1955) who was his cellmate before he died under extensive torture without revealing the whereabouts of the Party's secret print shop that interrogators sought to extract from him. The feminine nickname 'Nazli' served to conceal the dedicatee's identity and thus to make the poem publishable. This poem soon became one of the mantras of rebellious youth in the 1960s:

'Nazli! The spring's smiling and the Judas tree in bloom.
At home, under the window the jasmine has flowered.
End your doubts.
Do not wrestle with ominous death.
To be is better than to vanish, particularly during the spring . . .'

Nazli did not speak
        She proudly
squeezed her raging teeth and left.

☐

'Nazli, speak up!
The bird of silence
is laying the eggs of a terrible death in her nest!'

Nazli did not speak
            Like the sun
she rose from the darkness and then set in blood before she left.

☐

Nazli did not speak.
Nazli was a star.
She shone in this night before she flew away and left.

Nazli did not speak
Nazli was a violet
She flowered,
        heralding the good news:
            'The winter is over!'
                    And left . . .
(Shamlu 1993c: 73–5)

Aside from the poetically powerful depiction of a person resisting under torture, belittling death, the composition of some key Nimaic and post-Nimaic symbols set in a dialectical way and in Nimaic rhythm report a genuine poem of defiance: night, sun, star, winter, spring – all strung together by the stanza repetition, 'Nazli did not speak'. These imaginative tropes enable the poem to articulate what party tributes, with their dry and detached prose, could not. Shamlu did write a number of other such tributes. It started with 'Qasideh bara-ye Ensan-e Mah-e Bahman' ('Elegy for the Man of February', February 1950), as the title suggests, an elegy for Dr Taqi Erani (1903–40), a prominent scientific Marxist murdered in Reza Shah's prisons, and it appeared in one of Shamlu's earlier collections, *Qat'nameh* (*Resolution*, 1951) (Shamlu 1985).

Of particular mention among these elegiac poems are: 'Of Your Uncles' ('Az Amuha-yat', 1955), 'Behold' ('Negah Kon', 1956), 'That Day' ('Anruz', 1993) – all dedicated specifically to the author and critic Morteza Keyvan (1921–54) who was arrested and executed after the 1953 coup for sheltering wanted Tudeh Party officers; and 'The Birth of He Who Died Lovingly on the Ground' ('Milad Ankeh Asheqaneh bar Khak Mord', 1973), dedicated to the PFG militant Ahmad Zeybarom (1944–72), who was killed following an armed clash with the police in southern Tehran. His stand-off became the subject of a controversial newspaper report that miraculously escaped censorship. The poem 'Ebrahim on Fire' commemorates Mehdi Reza'i (1952–72), an emblematic young militant of the People's Mojahedin who was executed by firing squad at the age of twenty. Here is where Shamlu wrote such memorable lines as:

> What a man! What a man!
>   Who said
> more deserving is for a heart
> to settle in blood
>   with seven swords of love
> and more binding is for a throat
> that would pronounce
>   the most beautiful names.
> (Shamlu 1993a: 32)

If we regard Mosaddeq's lyrical *Blue, Grey, Black* as the (almost unwitting) poetic articulation of a rising, dissident generation's angst that became the anthem of defiant university students, then we should credit Shamlu for his chain of gnawing and disconcerting 'night poems' written between the 1950s and the 1970s. His *shabaneh* converge with the age of poetic defiance, and shaped the poetic sensibility of the younger generation. This poetry found its highest expression in political action. His 'night poems' continued through the 1960s and 1970s, and Shamlu excelled in this category. *Shabaneh* does not really constitute a genre; perhaps it can best be understood as a constellation of individual poems across different collections threaded together by virtue of priming the reader's expectation with the symbol 'night', even though a few *shabaneh* poems are actually lyrical. In the ears of the growing community of deliberate inferences, *shabaneh* itself evoked specific expectations. Let me stress that while Shamlu, as one who inherits the Nimaic legacy, inevitably dwells in the symbolism suggested through *shabaneh* poems, as a dynamic poet he nevertheless supersedes it: the binary of night and day need not be re-stated time and again in these poems since it has already been internalised by the very community of dissident readers that constitutes its audience. I would like to echo Mohammad Mokhtari: 'What I wish to say about the poetic language of Shamlu is indeed [the same as] describing the artistic language of a cultural-political era.' 'Shamlu's poetry basically transforms our era into a metaphor', he observes. 'An era that shaped up in the [nineteen-] forties and fifties, gained a distinct linguistic form in the sixties, and was established as a "linguistic norm" in the seventies that continued after the Revolution as well' (1995: 29). Shamlu did indeed establish a linguistic norm in the *poetry of defiance* in the 1960s–70s, a communally accepted norm that grew into a measure against which the urban middle-class poetry of the New Wave and modern Persian mysticism, as well as the 'excess' of (later) 'guerrilla poetry', were weighed and evaluated.

Interestingly, due to the poetic diversity of the 1960s and the advent of the New Wave poetry, the Night Poetry was rather marginal in terms of presentation. This is how Shamlu understands Night Poetry in 1968:

> *Social poetry* permeates the depths of society through imagery, rhythm, versatility and dynamics of the letter. *With the 'night,' the poet offers an allegorical image of society* and, using a metaphoric language, reveals the situations such that the reader or audience . . . can identify the socially constructive or destructive personages or elements behind the symbols and images. While [the reader] enjoys the unique presentation of allegories, metaphors or rhythms in the poem, behind them [literary devices] s/he reaches a truth superior to the poem itself. (Shamlu 1968b: ii; original emphasis)

Shamlu captures my proposed 'community of deliberate inferences' here. His statement also confirms my interpretation of the *shabaneh* poems: Shamlu's 'night poems' string together his continuing 'commitment' to dissent across a number of decades. About a dozen poems in different collections are titled

'Shabaneh', with five of them alone in his collection *Ebrahim on Fire* (Shamlu 1993a), which contained his poems between 1969 and 1974 – the most intensely politicised (pre-revolutionary) period due to guerrilla activity. In most of these poems a lyrical tempo flows delicately over the symbolism of dissent. In a few, loving sentiments flower: the love of Shamlu's life, Aida (Aida Sarkisian, his Armenian wife), often appears as an unending source of inspiration. In others, the poet's agony of witnessing injustices grips us. It is important to recognise that Shamlu's *shabaneh* poems are not political statements in contrast to the 1970s 'guerrilla poetry'. Here is the evidence – a 'night poem' of this period that leaves no doubt about its symbolism and intentions:

Shabaneh

There is no door
                there is no way
there is no night
                there is no moon
nor day,
                nor the sun,
we stand
                outside of the time
with a bitter dagger
in our shoulders.

No one
        speaks
                to no one
for silence
        speaks
                in a thousand tongues.

We glance
                at our dead
                        with a faint smile,
and await our own turn
without
any smile!
(Shamlu 1993a: 37–8)

Here we witness both intention and expectation: we are aware of our suspense ('outside of the time') and of being betrayed ('a bitter dagger / in our shoulders'), but our silence reveals that we know exactly what goes on ('for silence / speaks / in a thousand tongues'). And taking no collective action ('no one speaks to no one') under these conditions means we will only be joining our dead. Poetically, one could read this poem as exposing a betrayal that is permeated by an ambiguity: being betrayed by those who brought distrust among us; but who, exactly? The poem *suggests* we should overcome the existing (1960s repressive) conditions. This period led to the years of steel and blood as militants and security forces clashed in the cities almost daily ('we glance / at our dead'). The collection *Dagger on a Tray* (*Deshneh dar Dis*), which contains his poems between 1976 and 1977, attests to Shamlu's defence of militant dissent. Note, for instance, these lines from 'The Burial Address' ('Khatabeh-ye Tadfin', apparently dedicated to Che Guevara):

And these

. . .

[are] the protectors of fire
living
       alongside death
              ahead of death
eternally living for they had lived with death
and for the name
        that they had lived with.

. . .

The discoverers of the spring
The humble discoverers of the hemlock
seekers of joy
       in the flow of magma
the magicians of smile
          from out of the pain's hat
with their footprint deeper than joy
in the passages of birds.

□

They stand up to the thunder
light up our home.
And they die.
(Shamlu 1993b: 46–7)

This poem is dated 15 May 1975 and was written following the assassination in prison on 19 April 1975 of Jazani, Zia-Zarifi and five of their comrades, as well as two members of *Mojahedin-e Khalq*, who were serving their sentences in Evin prison. They were murdered extra-judicially by a few SAVAK interrogators who took them outside the prison and to the hills of Evin where they were shot in retaliation for the PFG's and OIPM's assassinations of the regime's officers. Notwithstanding the dedication, Shamlu's reference to the ones who 'stand up to the thunder' is most probably to this group.

Of the 1960s this can be said: by this time, the tropes and symbols of dissent were fully in place – poetically, literarily, cinematically and thus politically. The poetic symbolism Yushij had founded decades earlier had come to fruition. Symbolic binaries and tropes that captured the moods of defeat and defiance were accentuated and grew ever more expressive during the repressive 1960s when state repression was accompanied by an increasing number of institutions of higher education, the breeding grounds of young dissidents and, later, urban guerrillas. This decade was also one of intellectual encounters between Iranian writers and their international counterparts through the pages of numerous cultural and literary magazines – often short-lived due to censorship. This decade revealed the legacy of Yushij's New Poetry in a poetic garden of a thousand flowers – from Sepehri's bucolic, Buddhist poems, to Farrokhzad's existential feminine poetry, to the New Wave poetry of Ahmadi and Royaee's *Espacemantalisme*, all sitting right next to the Nimaic tradition that continued, in different styles, in the works of Akhavan-Sales, Shamlu and Mosaddeq. In the 1960s the seeds of a poetic vision for a new, dynamic and armed defiance against the regime were sowed – in March 1963, to be exact, and by Jazani and three comrades (Vahabzadeh 2010: 17). Neither Iranian security nor the intellectuals and politicians could see this invisible undertow that was destined to appear in the epoch-making 'Siahkal resurgence'. But poetry – as in the poems of Shamlu and Farrokhzad – had already seen with clarity the coming of the liberator, the one who is 'not like any other', while Akhavan-Sales had shown the untameable spirit of wolves and Mosaddeq the fact that if you and I rise, 'we will all rise'. The discursive tropes of defiance were poetically in place.

After Siahkal (February 1971), the birth of PFG (April 1971) and the advent of the urban guerrillas of different ideological tendencies (September 1971), the conditions for the convergence of the poetics and politics of defiance were finally ripe. Poetry no longer played an educational role in preparing the public mindset through its advancement of the symbolism of defiance. It was no longer required of the poetry of defiance to render the *a-venir* liberator intelligible and desirable. After February 1971, the liberators had become a fact of life, revitalising Iranian politics anew through fire and lead, on university campuses and in torture chambers, coming to life in daily newspapers' reports about 'terrorists' and 'saboteurs' as well as in the mimcographed leaflets and handbills of clandestine groups that changed hands in secret. *With its educational task now practically over, its anticipative tone no longer relevant and its social referent already materialised, the poetry of defiance would now celebrate the heroic efforts of the women and men who walked through the dense thicket of ever-flourishing symbols.*

From Nima's watershed in the 1940s to the guerrilla poetry of the 1970s, we have a *thirty-year poetic history* of construction, propagation and suggestion of poetic-political symbols and the concomitant consolidation of the community of deliberate inferences dominated by male poets whose formative poetic experience was rooted in Yushij's innovations. From Yushij to Soltanpour and Golesorkhi (key figures of guerrilla poetry), Persian poetry moved from concrete referentiality to abstract symbolism through a process of discursive coding and decoding – a collective effort of the poetic community. The New Wave, interestingly, defied this process, and it can therefore be regarded as a revolt against revolutionary poetics. But the increasing polarisation of Iranian society did not leave much social space for such nuances. With the guerrilla poetry, a fascinating *reversal* takes place: *it moves from abstract symbolism to concrete referentiality in the years of blood and steel.*

Mirror Image, or Compelling Fact?

What is called 'guerrilla poetry' (*she'r-e cheriki*), I submit, is an *unintended* progeny of the Nimaic tradition, shaped through the works of the aforementioned and other (all-male) poets. A genealogy of the terminology as a reflection of conceptual attempts at capturing this poetry of a highly politicised period is important. Shams-Langarudi coined the term in his voluminous history of modern Persian poetry (1991c, d), but the term invites endless disagreements. 'Guerrilla poetry' refers to a cluster of poems, written within a specific period, that make explicit reference to the heightened guerrilla activity in Iran and in the world, but does it capture a genre? Once we gaze past its explicit political referentiality, the term strikes us as *lacking* aesthetic or conceptual clarity. And similarly with the sister terms of 'guerrilla poetry', those indigenous to Iran: 'Siahkal poetry' and 'jungle poetry' (*she'r-e jangal*). For a critic from the generation that has no lived memory of the 1970s, these designations are concocted: 'In [Shams-Langarudi's] *The Analytical History* announcing the guerrilla poetry as a branch of political poetry is a baseless and unsupported claim' (Ahmadi 2005: 52). Problematising the term 'guerrilla poetry' to dismiss its existence and claiming that the term 'jungle poetry' was made up by Shams-Langarudi as equivalent to 'Siahkal poetry' (Ahmadi, 2005: 52) is simply erasing the question.

Influenced by Saeed Yousef's *A Particular Criticism of a Particular Poetry* (1987), his critical tribute to Soltanpour, and his coinage of 'Siahkal Poetry', Shams-Langarudi discusses the guerrilla poetry as a genre, although he uses the term in broader terms than I understand it. Yousef argues that this was poetry of a specific period marked by the Siahkal operation, but the guerrilla poetry precedes the Siahkal affair. For one thing, there have been other armed uprisings in the country, namely, the Kurdish uprising (1967–8), but 'what distinguishes Siahkal is . . . its continuation through a movement (*jaryan*)' (Yousef 2017a). So the guerrilla or Siahkal poetry was already present in the works of Shafi'i-Kadkani, Kho'i and Soltanpour, as well as Kasra'i and Ja'far Kushabadi (Yousef 2017a). It can also be called the 'poetry of the new movement' (*she'r-e jonbesh-e novin*), to indicate the 'range of influence of Siahkal on different poets' (Yousef 2017a; Fadainia n.d.). Shams-Langarudi agrees with this assessment, adding that before Siahkal the guerrilla poetry created poetic admiration for international guerrillas, 'inspired by the Bolivian guerrillas fighting in the mountains and in praising Che Guevara' (Shams-Langarudi 1991d: 14). So, it seems, the term actually does not refer to a genre per se but to specific content and referents. To be fair, there is some evidence for the way Shams-Langarudi conceptualises guerrilla poetry: one important case is the poetic tribute to Mirza Kuchek Khan, the leader of the ill-fated Jangali movement (1915–21), in the long poem *Kuchek Khan* (1969), by Kushabadi (1941–2009), although Kuchek Khan's movement was too far in the past, more like a fable, a myth, to be registered in the collective memory of Kushabadi's generation. Shams-Langarudi then uses two terms: 'Siahkal poetry', which pertains to 'praising the [Siahkal] jungle guerrillas, without being limited to Siahkal fighters' (1991d: 14), and 'jungle poetry', which captures the 'presence of jungle ambiance in the poems' (1991d: 15).

Readers will observe that, only two descriptive paragraphs into this debate, we already encounter a duality: is guerrilla poetry a *genre*, or does it capture a particular period? Let us pause here and attend to the reasoning of Shams-Langarudi, who observes, quite sociologically:

> But the fact is that alongside the transformation of political struggle (from parliament-oriented to guerrilla struggle) not only did political poetry dominate non-political poetry, the guerrilla poetry also won against the symbolic social-political poetry as well, and in this situation, the form of social-political struggle, rather than aesthetic analyses, was the determining factor in advancing poetry. (1991c: 588)

The idea here is that Persian poetry reflects the lived experience of Iranian society as it goes through periods of consolidation of political power and its contestation by intellectuals and the student and Kurdish movements. The guerrilla poetry, in Shams-Langarudi's analysis, precedes the Siahkal event, but then the Siahkal operation inspired 'Siahkal poetry . . . [as] a branch of guerrilla poetry in praise of the jungle guerrillas without being restricted to them, since even before the Siahkal incident poets like Kasra'i, Golesorkhi, Soltanpour and Kushabadi, impressed by the fighting of Bolivian guerrillas, had spoken in praise of Che Guevara', Shams-Langarudi argues. 'And yet it was with the jungle incident and the execution of the guerrillas that Siahkal poetry was officiated as a part of guerrilla poetry and became popular and covered a decade of modern, political poetry in Iran' (1991d: 14–15). Although Shams-Langarudi coined the *term* 'guerrilla poetry' to unify the poetic experience of a particular political generation, his *concept* is primarily drawn from Yousef's book (1987). This will bring us back to the aforesaid duality. Features of the Siahkal poetry, Yousef (1987: 25–7) holds, are: (a) in Siahkal poetry hope triumphs over despair, since (b) it admires the revolutionary struggle and its heroes and offers a new set of values; (c) in contrast to the previous political poetry, Siahkal poetry does not reproach the masses for having accepted oppression; (d) here, the poet is also a part of the struggle; (e) the content and mood of poems change because of Siahkal; (f) a transformation in image and language takes place; 'Linguistically, a barrage of epic, violent, and stormy words pour into the poetry of this period, and some words . . . became the fixed symbols of poetry' (Yousef 1987: 26); (g) a tendency towards explicit language emerges; even the poetic symbols are now fully exposed and known in advance, because (h) this is a poetry of excitement that borders with 'slogan' (*sho'ar*): 'if it is artistically weak it is nothing but a slogan. One can voice a slogan in a poem, but not every slogan is a poem' (Yousef 1987: 26); (i) this is the poetry of love, dedication and sacrifice, but the lover's (*ma'shuq*) face is now different: 'a class, an ideal, a party or an organization or a heroic comrade' (Yousef 1987: 26); (j) this is a poetry of reason and rejecting one value to affirm another (best displayed in Shamlu's poems in this era); (k) as a result of Siahkal poetry, many poets who did not participate in this movement were pushed to either join it or leave the poetic scene, and the New Wave and other poets mostly chose the latter (Yousef 1987: 27; see also Shams-Langarudi 1991d: 16–19).

The truth of Shams-Langarudi's claim – that the guerrilla movement appeared on the poetic scene and marginalised claims to 'pure' or avant-garde poetry – is actually found in the rather confessional statement by a prominent New Waver, one of the movement's theorists, Esma'il Nooriala (1942–) in his theoretical treatise *Imagination and Instruments in Iranian Poetry Today* (1969). In the Khusheh event, Mohammad-Ali Sepanlu (1940–2015) recited his poem 'The Arab Guerrilla', which reveals the entrance of the signifier '*cherik*' (guerrilla) in the poetic lexicon of a generation – a word that was increasingly received positively by average Iranians who sympathised with the Palestinian cause. And this is before the Fadaiyan included '*cherik*' in their official designation.

Alarmed by the popularity of politicised poetry in Khusheh poetry nights, particularly as evidenced by the impressive reception of the poems of Sepanlu, Soltanpour and Azarm, Nooriala writes:

> In these precious nights it was observed how people's attention is being diverted from authentic (*asil*) poetry containing precise artistic values toward artlessness and slogans of sorts. The more explicit and daring the expressions, even if they were not poetry, the speaker was received as a more authentic and treasured poet.
>
> We are not speaking of [social] responsibility or its lack; the point is that an idea is growing among poetry-reading folks that the value of poetry arises from its being social or political. The outcome is people asking the poet to talk about politics in a gathering intended for reading and listening to 'poetry' . . . This in itself is a disaster, a gift of this day and age in which there is no movement (*harekati nist*) and the poet assumes political leadership and the reader of poetry – weary of silence and repression – seeks guidance from today's poet. (1969: 430)

The angst of the puritan poet, purported to be solely driven by aesthetic values, is clear in these lines. Nooriala misunderstands the place of politics in poetry: post-Nimaic poetry has bred, among other things, 'political poetry' as a literary genre, and despite its oscillating between popularity or unpopularity, depending on the public mood, political poetry holds a crucial place in modern poetry. In short, 'modern poetry owes one of its main characteristics to the political poet' (Estedadi-Shad 2000: 189). Nooriala wrote about his concerns before Siahkal. But soon history issued its verdict: the small Siahkal operation exploded as a moment of liberation and terminated such concerns altogether. No one would write an objection like Noorala's after 1971. 'This was the Siahkal impact, and those who had previously spoken out against political and radical (*tond*) poetry were now silent' (Yousef 2017a). The poet now had to join the movement or choose silence. What exacerbated this situation was SAVAK's repression of poetry (Yousef 2017b: 592–4). As Mohammad Azimi, poetry editor of *Jahan-e Naw*, wrote in 1969 justifying his choice of poems, the standard of poetry was the most matter-of-fact of criteria: 'the belief of the speaker in what she speaks' (Azimi 1969: 165). In short, 'despite a decade of cultural effort of the guerrillas [in various cultural venues and magazines], the guerrilla poetry had never attained such a reception and popularity in society compared to a few days of action by the Siahkal guerrillas' (Shams-Langarudi 1991d: 15). *Poetry is never purely poetic.*

So, we inevitably return to the dual question: is the guerrilla poetry a *genre*, or does it capture a particular period? In his *Periods of Persian Poetry* (2001), the Tehran University professor, poet and poetry historian Mohammad Reza Shafi'i-Kadkani identifies the 1971–9 period as poetically distinct (Shafi'i-Kadkani 2001: 79). His periodisation entails two components: the first pertains to the politically motivated poets specifically writing in the period when 'younger poets are active and their poetic heights take place in this period' (Shafi'i-Kadkani 2001: 79). He names established poets like Shamlu and younger ones like Golesorkhi, Kho'i, Azarm, Soltanpour, Yousef, Ali Mirfetros, Reza Maghsadi, even PFG members Said Payan and Ahmadi-Osku'i (Shafi'i-Kadkani 2001: 79). The second component regards the poetic imagination. Siahkal 'changed the very concept of struggle and the social outlook of the younger generation, and with this form of action the people's mood and understanding of the struggle changed, and thus poetry was influenced by the purple air of machinegun smoke' (Shafi'i-Kadkani 2001: 80). Shafi'i-Kadkani elaborates:

> The poetic language, rhythm, imagination and form are in fact in continuity with the former periods . . . [but] now is the time *to have a century of poetic experience to serve life.* The social cause of this transformation is launching armed struggle . . . From a cultural viewpoint, further translations of foreign poetry as well as underground and partisan literature – that is, 'literature' in its broadest sense – has influenced the poetry of this period. (2001: 81; my emphasis)

In this transformation, in deploying several decades of modern Persian poetry for depicting the oppressive conditions, as Yousef recognises, the *poetic gaze is now diverted*, not inward as in New Wave or Sepehri's mysticism, but outward towards the harshest lived experiences of a generation by 'admiring the heroes of armed struggle, describing torture, prison and execution fields, smashing all the elements of despair and hopelessness in the previous period, and waiting for the coming of something that like the spring will arrive from all sides' (Shafi'i-Kadkani 2001: 81). The symbolic universe also inevitably changes: 'The elements building the poetic images of this period are inspired mostly by the sea, waves, cliffs, thicket, Judas tree, poppy, red star, storm, rifle and explosion' (Shafi'i-Kadkani 2001: 81). As mentioned, though, this symbolism is no longer shrouded in riddles: *the community of deliberate inferences has now grown beyond the literati and poetic publics.* Armed struggle's political and metonymic effects (my reading of Jazani's theory) merge and the exposed symbolism of guerrilla or Siahkal poetry allows for the community of deliberate inferences to embrace the layperson. Perhaps this explains why Shafi'i-Kadkani encouraged Yousef to publish his anthology, *Sher-e Jonbesh-e Novin* (*The Poetry of the New Movement*) (Yousef 2017b: 613), which he did under the pseudonym Safar Fadainia (n.d.).

Just as he opposed the designated terms for this poetry, Hamid Ahmadi blames Shafi'i-Kadkani for starting the whole misunderstanding through his periodisation of modern Persian poetry (Ahmadi 2005: 53). This kind of designation looks at the 'content of poems and does not indicate a poetry with a particular form' (Ahmadi 2005: 54). In other words, caught in the duality that I have mentioned, Ahmadi dismisses the guerrilla poetry because it does not constitute a particular genre or form, scorning Yousef for insisting that it does (Ahmadi 2005: 54). He also dismisses Shams-Langarudi's designation of Kushabadi's *Mirza Kuchek Khan* as Siahkal or jungle poetry (1991d: 15) because this poem was published *before* the Siahkal operation (Ahmadi 2005: 59–60). In contrast, Faramarz Soleimani (1930–2015) affirms that this kind of political poetry was a collective response to an age and its concerns. In his *Poetry Is to Stand Witness* (1981) he disregards the aesthetic question, although, as an accomplished poet himself, he does acknowledge that at times what he calls the catch-all 'poetry of revolution' slips out of poetic imagination and yields to the rhetoric of the revolution. For him, 'guerrilla poetry' embraces lived experience, indeed the spirit of an age:

They came from far away, read their poetry in the streets and neighbourhoods, were captured, and their warm blood congealed on stone walls, but there were other fists and cries from other men who continued on their path. The poetry of revolution that was their feat was the poetry of a specific age and particular conditions. A dark era and repressive conditions. Perhaps these very conditions should not necessitate analysing the technical aspects of their poems. (Soleimani 1981: 18)

Soleimani clearly views poetry as a response to lived conditions, indeed a *verdict*. He relegates, implicitly, the aesthetic question to individual judgement, taste or preference. What matters to him is the impact of poetry. The guerrilla poetry may be dismissed on many grounds, but it cannot be ignored in terms of its unprecedented social and cultural influence (Yousef 2017b: 592–4). Contra to Shamlu's suggestion that poetry must not be explicit, recollects Yousef, his own (and others') 'poetry moved toward greater explicitness (*serahat*)' due to his contacts with pro-Fadai students at Mashhad University (Yousef 2017b: 607). And this is indeed the story of a generation.

With the 1979 Revolution, the age of guerrilla/Siahkal poetry reached its conclusion, although political poetry continues to this day (Yousef 2017a). Anyone studying Persian poetry of the 1960s–70s must inevitably attend to the guerrilla (or Siahkal or jungle) poetry and contextualise it within the era of radical student and armed movements (Yousef 2017b: 585). Some might simply choose to dismiss it (Ahmadi 2005), but they end up leaving a crevasse in poetic history.

The rise and demise of guerrilla or Siahkal poetry are both marked by significant political *events* relating to a social movement with rich poetic imagination. 'Events are central to the ways we experience life, both individually and collectively' (Wagner-Pacifici 2107: x). *I argue that guerrilla poetry is an evental poetry, and not merely expressive of the Siahkal event and the subsequent spectacular movement of the educated young. Siahkal or guerrilla poetry was an integral part of this movement – a movement that imagined the impossible – giving it vision, articulation, imagery, thus making the incredibly perilous, precarious, ardent and arduous life of underground militants intelligible and desirable.* This observation shows us that the duality – the guerrilla poetry as a *periodic* phenomenon or a *genre* – is actually false. It is simply both and neither. It can certainly be regarded as a *genre* due to its particular deployment of tropes and symbols, and this conveniently describes the cluster of poems designated as 'guerrilla'. Yet, the term 'guerrilla poetry' remains an amorphous designation, which tosses us back to the other aspect: its specific time and place in history. 'Does poetry have a shelf-life (*tarikh*)? Should it have one? If a lucky poet relates the feelings of an age, his or her poem is still the poetry of the age for anyone who seeks to connect with that feeling and that age' (Yousef 2017a). The poetic imagination and language that vivified the guerrilla poetry, I have shown, goes back to Nimaic poetry, but it also broke away from Nimaic and post-Nimaic symbolism, because the guerrilla poetry, increasingly converging on fixed tropes and signifiers (so much so that even state censorship could easily identify these poems), lost the richness of *she'r-e no*. Amazingly, though, if we focus on the stream of social justice and liberation that has been present in the mainstreams of Nimaic and post-Nimaic poetry, we come to appreciate guerrilla poetry. The concept of 'liberation' has been present in the thirty-year poetic history prior to the 1970s, but *it did not have a concrete referent* before the Siahkal insurrection. Siahkal, PFG and other militants granted real-life referents for this poetry. Once again, we notice in astonishment, *life imitates art*.

The Guerrilla Poetry

The Siahkal operation constitutes an *event*: it cannot therefore be measured in terms of the ends the operation sought. It was the birthplace of a 'series of actions that only gradually and with difficulty cohere in an *event* that can be categorised, located in time and space, and given a name' (Wagner-Pacifici 2017: 1; original emphasis). This is how an otherwise parochial attack by a handful of militants on a negligible gendarmerie post in a frozen 1971 February (Vahabzadeh 2010: 25–30) transforms itself into *rastakhiz-e Siahkal* in subsequent literature and the collective memory of a generation's activists (see Vahabzadeh 2021). Viewed from the vantage point of the *event* – by reading the poetic movement from the event backwards – Persian political-symbolic poetry and socially-committed literature of the 1960s was ultimately destined to meet the 'resurgence' that the protagonists of this literary movement had anticipated and desired for at least a decade prior to 1971, as previously shown.

Thus, splitting hairs here, it should not be surprising that the guerrilla and jungle poetry actually preceded Siahkal, as Yousef and Shams-Langarudi note also. From my particular, linguistic angle, even the Siahkal poetry did so. A historical-literary register is in order. By the mid-1960s, the protagonists of guerrilla poetry were already finding footholds in the literary scene, thanks to the ascendency of political-symbolic poetry and the community of deliberate inferences. The Khusheh Poetry Festival and left-leaning (often short-lived) journals – namely, *Jahan-e Naw, Sahand, Chapar* and *Arash* – in the late 1960s and early 1970s provided the venues where these protagonists emerged as the oracles of their age. By the mid-1960s, the playwright and poet Said Soltanpour (1940–81) had emerged through explicit and sharp protest poetry that was laden with identifiable lexical cues and dissident-constructed symbols. He became an unwavering pillar of guerrilla and Siahkal poetry (see Shams-Langarudi 1991c: 508). Publishing in the short-lived literary magazines of this time, 'from 1969 onwards Soltanpour becomes the flag-bearer of Iranian guerrilla poetry' (Shams-Langarudi 1991c: 614). Not only did Golesorkhi's poetry, with abundantly sanctioned, symbolically flammable signifiers like jungle, rain, cypress tree, dawn and dagger, begin to define his (and his generation's) restless defiance, but he also arose among literary publics as a serious Marxist literary critic, in particular after his interview with *Chapar* (no. 1, February 1971, simultaneous with the Siahkal operation) (in Shams-Langarudi 1991d: 30–6). Similarly, the late 1960s witnessed the rise of the dissident poets Kushabadi, Mirzazadeh, Mirfetros and Kho'i, the noted proponents of guerrilla poetry. One of the earliest signs of the gradual congealment of guerrilla poetry was 'Another Vietnam' by the pro-Tudeh Party poet Kasra'i that honoured Che Guevara after his death in October 1967 (Yousef 2017b: 589). This poem reveals some key tropes and signifiers of guerrilla poetry:

> With all those weapons
> with that weariness
> with all the bullets that fell upon your body
> Ernesto!
> This time, too, your death turned out to be a lie!
>
> . . .
>
> A man and a gun
> a man and a knapsack of bread and honour
> the vast-forehead and tall-standing free man
> one day presiding steadfast over the Ministry in Cuba
> another day in blood
> in the Bolivian trenches, far from home and loved ones.

O, the leopard of the peak, O the soaring eagle!
If the praises of the people were deservingly yours alone
such a tall death was to be yours alone.
(Kasar'i, n.d.)

Man and gun, bread and honour, leopard and eagle, and a 'tall death', a minister in blood – signifiers of refusal, resistance and defiance, with their allusions leading the reader away from *mediated* impression and closer to an *immediate* emotive imprint, indeed an experience much more direct than allowed by the political-poetic symbolism of Nima, Shamlu and others in their guild of first-generation Nimaic poets. Particular *signifiers* associated with the common, immediately relatable notions of revolutionary action (trench, weapon and bullet in this poem) and *tropes* of wild and untamed nature (leopard and eagle in the poem, and a rich assortment of proceeding poems) gradually appear in frequency and complexity in poetry, thus defining the guerrilla and later Siahkal poetry as a *particular genre*.

The imagery and symbolism of guerrilla/Siahkal poetry was impressively far-reaching, to the extent that even Shamlu, who on no account can be associated with this genre, in fact did write enduring poems that dwelled in the symbolism of guerrilla/Siahkal poetry (Shams-Langarudi 1991d: 15), with a major difference: Shamlu's exalted *lyrical* expressions make his poetry unique, and that is the component that guerrilla/Siahkal poetry generally lacked.

Eerily, Kushabadi's *Kuchek Khan* (dated July 1968) anticipates the *myth* that was collectively constructed around the Siahkal operation two and a half years later. The book was removed from bookstores soon after its publication (Shams-Langarudi 1991c: 670). This long poem (33 pages) offers a constructed epic of the Jangali movement led by Mirza Kuchek Khan – an armed uprising in the jungles of Gilan that led to the short-lived Soviet Socialist Republic of Iran (Chaqueri 1995) before it collapsed due to complicated regional power play. On the run from state troops, Kuchek Khan froze to death on 2 December 1921 near Khalkhal. Kushabadi's epic poem knits together actual places and peoples of this movement. 'Now Gurab Zarmakh / . . . / like cinder under the ashes, / awaits the day of resurrection of the jungles' (Kushabadi 1979: 20):

> In the ambiance of Masuleh [a village in Gilan] where the voice of anvil and sledge hammer is heard along with a remembrance of [revolutionary communist] Heydar Amu Oghlu, [the poet] calls upon Kuchek Khan to rise as [the village of] Gurab expects the resurrection of the jungle and green cries are heard from the [nearby] hills and call for freedom. Then there is a turn to memories from other lands under oppression, from American blacks who are massacred under the stone gaze of Lady Liberty, from Bolivia and other faraway lands. (Soleimani 1981: 44)

Thus, travelling through the ambiance of the mysterious, misty and lush highlands of Gilan, the poem dwells on the figure of an old, local tea-house owner with recollections of Kuchek Khan, and the poem increasingly intensifies a rebellious energy:

> I saw in his weary eyes,
> when you descended like a thunderous deluge from the hills of Kolkaposht
> the storm knitted the clouds in the sky.
> With the roar of the thunder,
> the pulse of the earth was felt in the jungle's branches around us.
> In my eyes the mountains shook like the fists of desperate people.
> From the hills exploding, cries rose
> in the valleys filled with red poppies: 'Freedom!'
> . . .
> Rise up Kuchek Khan!
>
> Rise and perfume the open bosom of the mountains
> with the lovely scent of gunpowder.

And gradually through the narrative, the Jangali movement is connected to the global decolonisation movement of the 1960s. The Jangalis now epitomise the struggles of all oppressed peoples in a common fight. Having died forty-seven years prior to this poem, Kuchek Khan nevertheless resurfaces as our contemporary:

> I saw ports,
> that were being looted and heavily-loaded freighter ships
> cruised on the cold waters of the ocean.

I saw jets that travelled the skies,
like meteorites.
Messy-haired women, holding frightened children on their chest
– amidst exploding bombs and grenades –
homeless, travelled jungle to jungle.

I saw the black people
being massacred
under the stone gaze of Lady Liberty.

This round earth was under the horseshoes of brutality.
I saw that a man under machine-gun fire in Bolivia,
with his iris, blue and loving,
advanced trench by trench and shared with the people,
a part of his heart's sun, right in the fright of darkness.

Intimations of the war of liberation in Vietnam, the African American struggles in the United States and Che Guevara's death are clear. Iran is not a part of this global liberatory movement, and it needs a Kuchek Khan to rise up and lead the country in that direction:

Rise up, Kuchek Khan!
The people's awakening today,
has lit up fires in every jungle.
Rise up and by joining together these jungles,
untie this messy clutter
on this burning earth.

And then, of course, those appear who will partake in this movement:

With the warm singing of their machine guns
fighting men sing the bright morning
from afar.
With their fight the fruit of freedom
is yielding in clusters on green palms.
(Kushabadi 1979: 23, 24, 25, 29, 30, 33)

Kushabadi narrates the story of a generation that 'is looking forward to the day of resurgence of the jungles' (1979: 20). Thus, calling the poem 'an unrealistic poem' and indicative of 'revolutionary romanticism' (Shams-Langarudi 1991c: 67) is a strikingly absurd description and reports the lack of attention to how poetic symbolism opens new paths. Strictly, 'jungle poetry' begins with *Kuchek Khan* as the pivot of the metaphors, signifiers and tropes with which future guerrilla and Siahkal poetry are identified. Although such tropes do appear in the sixties' poetry, they do not point at this sharp invitation to rebellion against oppressive systems.

Upon his murder, Che Guevara immediately became the undying symbol of defiance against the imperialist world order. Soon, *El Che Vive!* became the mantra of Latin American revolutionaries, and Che became the martyr of a global movement. Was it a *coincidence* that, soon after Che's death that preserved him as the immortal fighter of justice, Iranian dissident poets revived Kuchek Khan's image? After all, Mirza had also died in the jungle, and due to the conspiracy of the Iranian state, British imperialism and the Soviet betrayal. Poetically, Mirza stood out as Iran's Che, an immortal fighter to inspire a new defiant generation. Was it also a *coincidence* that the group that launched the Siahkal operation also returned to the jungles where Mirza had fought some half a century previously? Kuchek Khan's repeated poetic reappearance, I submit, must be taken seriously for an analysis of this era.

With the advent of new symbolisms in poetry there also emerged a new cohort of poets. The incipient poetic ambiance soon affected the way jungle and guerrilla poetry permeated the public venue via published magazines. We can observe how the poetry pages of *Jahan-e Naw*, an influential literary and intellectual magazine of the late 1960s, transformed just within two years: the pages that once contained the solely lyrical or social, but clearly 'non-political', poems of Kho'i, Nader Naderpour (1929–2000), Javad Mojabi (1939–), Heshmat Djazani (1930–), Sirus Moshfeqi (1943–2020), Parviz Eslampour (1943–2012), Mahmoud Kianush (1934–2020) and others by 1969–70 presented some pointedly political poems by Sho'aiyan, Akhavan-Sales and Azarm, leading up to the aforementioned defence of Azimi (the magazine's poetry editor) for his poetry choices in 1970. Apparently, though, this choice backfired: the Spring 1970 issue of *Jahan-e Naw* (25: 1–2) contains only translated poetry by non-Iranians (and only one lyrical poem by Kianush), while the Winter–Spring 1971 issue contains no poetry whatsoever, not even translations! The Spring–Fall 1973 issue shows that the journal had given up on poetry altogether. We can read between the lines about how inflammable symbols and tropes had become: *the militants fired machine guns, the poets scorching symbols and metaphors!*

Here is a sample of the poems that forced the journal to drop poetry from its pages. This highly suggestive poem by Sho'aiyan, later known as Red Comrade or 'lonesome guerrilla', should be self-explanatory. He committed suicide upon his arrest in February 1976:

Interrogation

˗ . . . .
˗ . . . .
- that the night is dark
          – but . . .
- that it is still just the beginning of the winter
                  – but . . .
- that yellow leaves are silently
dropping from the branches
        – but . . .

- What do you have to say now?
- I still say:
     – but . . .
I still say:
     – but . . .
(1969: 160)

The poem does not contain complex tropes, which was to be the currency of Siahkal and guerrilla poetry within a year or two. Nonetheless, it constructs the ambiance of interrogation and resistance quite aptly. It was due to publishing such daring poems that *Jahan-e Naw* was forced by censorship to eliminate Persian poetry from its pages and continue publication. The bolder journals that published defiant poetry only expected to be shut down: *Chapar, Faslha-ye Sabz, Sahand.* Some poets preferred publishing books as

Kushabadi had done. Among them, Shafi'i-Kadkani's *In the Garden Alleys of Neishapur* (1971) stood out. With its publication concurrent with the PFG's advent, and with its historical-mystical but tangibly defiant poems being deeply interpretable in terms of life-and-death battles in the streets of Tehran, the book was well-received by lovers of guerrilla poetry:

> May your sleep never be agitated!
> The most pleasant delirium
> is the silky green moss that grows in the pond of your serenity.
>
> May your sleep never be agitated!
> Outside of your quiet and laughter-filled window
> there pass caravans of blood and madness,
> caravans of fire, lightning and gunpowder.
> (Shafi'i-Kadkani 1971: 34–5; poem dated 1968)

Also, consider these lines from a poem that is apparently about the brutal Mongolian invasion of the ancient city of Nishapur in north-eastern Iran:

> The matches of lightning
>   one by one
> go off.
> The night is still night.
> . . .
>
> The matches of lightning
> make the night colourless:
> just as in the eastern country,
> the master of the tartar tribe
> hangs from the dawn's light
> his assonant cry
> (the smoky black lantern).
> (Shafi'i-Kadkani 1971: 56–7, 59; poem dated 1969)

And there is also his poem depicting the public hanging of the Muslim mystic Hossein Ibn Mansour al-Hallaj (858–922 CE), by Abbasid Caliph al-Moqtader. His dead body was dismembered and set on fire, and his ashes were poured into the Tigris:

Hallaj

In the mirror, again, appeared:
The cloud of his chignon in the wind,
and the red anthem of '*analhaq*' [I am truth/God] again
a mantra on his lips.

What did you recite in your prayer of love?
                                     that for years
you have been hanging from the noose and these old guards
are still avoiding
your dead body.

. . .
Wherever
the morning wind
took your ashes,
there grew a man from the earth.
. . .

Your name is still a mantra on our lips.
(Shafi'i-Kadkani 1971: 46–9; poem dated 1969)

The image of the immortal martyr embodies the ideal human of this time. By 1969–71, these anticipatory poems constituted the bulk of the poems we identify as Siahkal or guerrilla poetry.

As we near 1971, the poems become more radical in their symbolic intervention. Mirfetros published two issues of *Sahand*. Its first issue (Spring 1970) is an unapologetic congregation of dissident literati: Soltanpour, Golesorkhi, Kasra'i, Maghsadi, Sa'edi and Al-Ahmad published fiery poems and essays in this issue, while Mirfetros reviewed Mosaddeq's *Blue, Grey, Black*, sanctioning a revolutionary interpretation of it. Al-Ahmad wrote in his article, 'these days the pen has become our weapon', and 'in this country [*velayat*], the arts' function is jihad' (Al-Ahmad, quoted in Shams-Langarudi 1991d: 153). It was in this first issue of *Sahand* that Golesorkhi published his famous poem '*Damun*' (a Gilaki word for the thickness of the forest) (Shams-Langarudi 1991d: 21–4), which evokes the image of Kuchek Khan as the immortal guerrilla and addresses two of Mirza's comrades, Balam Patavani and Anam Abkenari. This poem is filled with the particular lexis of guerrilla poetry, standing out as one of such poetry's clearest representations:

Damun

. . .

Now, my two shoulders
The bullet-wounded wings
               on the fog of the jungle
is a tall rainbow
red, flowing in the rivers of blood.
The dagger pierced within a word
so it would unfurl
a red rainbow in the middle of the jungle.

. . .

Balam,
     Balam Patavani,
Anam,
     Anam Abkenari,
         on the hills of Gaskareh
         in the trenches
what sweet and remote dream embraced you,
that bravely and without a lover,
you scythed ceaselessly
         the bastard wolves . . .?
(Golesorkhi 1994: 77–80)

With the guerrillas fighting in the jungle, the poem explicitly deploys the key symbols of poetic defiance that are decodable by the poetry publics and censorship alike: bullet, jungle, red, blood, dagger, trench, and of course, the images of the two men razing (scything) the enemy soldiers to the ground. After all, 'the jungle / flows / in your green thoughts' (Golesorkhi 1994: 132). Once one thinks of the jungle, the next thing is to pick up a firearm and join the liberators concealed in it. This is how the PFG founders Puyan and Ahmadzadeh resolved the impasse of action for their generation through their treatises. The poet stands with them side by side: it is the poet who makes liberation and martyrdom glorious, intelligible, desirable.

As for *Sahand*, where such a fiery poem was published: given the aforesaid content, as expected the second issue of *Sahand* was banned from publication. To bypass censorship, the issue was published as *Setarehha-ye Javidan* (*Eternal Stars*) in Spring 1971, right after the Siahkal event. The usual suspects appeared in this issue too: Al-Ahmad, Kasra'i, Shafi'i-Kadkani, Kho'i, Golesorkhi and Azarm (Shams-Langarudi 1991d: 20–1, 153–5). Mirfetros's own poem on Siahkal in this issue stands out. As Yousef observes, Siahkal filled the poetic imagery with new references and images (2017b: 599–601). Here is where we see how Kuchek Khan returns as an immortal forebear of the new guerrillas:

One Day You Shall Return Proudly

These days shall pass
One day you shall return
    proudly
O, green mourner of Spring!
     – O, Honourable!
One day you shall return
     from the faraway mythic towns
with convoys of asleep and bloody cries
and the wind
  will take
    the rhythm of your arrival
      to the forgotten yonder
 . . .
Oh . . .
  this is the heart of my homeland
    that is in ruins

This torn
     T
       o
         r
           n
shredded heart of Iran
that is blooming
         thus
            on this soil
this is the defiant and martyred blood of Mirza [Kuchek Khan]

O, you great Kuchek!
O, you space of resistance and revolt!
O, you red spirit of the waking jungle!
Now you blow from Sia[hkal]
         from injured Sia[hkal] –
now you blow
         from the jungle nearby . . .
. . .

We must hold our last prayer
next to Tigris
         or Euphrates
in Balkh
     or Neishapur
(or perhaps
     in the river of turbulent rage of our own blood . . .)
in the river of turbulent rage of our own blood
Here's
     the echo of the muezzin's call:
               – Hasten to the weapon
. . .

O, word
     word
        blood-coloured word!
What charm is there in you?

What charm is there in you
that the sun
       at every dawn

. . .

O, word
    word
       blood-coloured word!
                  – revolution!
       The last word . . .
(Mirfetros, quoted in Shams-Langarudi 1991d: 155–62)

First, a few subtleties in this poem: 'kuchek' in Persian means 'small/little' (in 'O, you great Kuchek!'). Also, in appropriating an Arabic phrase of *azan* (*athan*), he plays with a homophone, changing '*hayya ala salah*' (hasten to the prayer) to '*hayya ala selah*' (hasten to the weapon). In the context of our study, this poem can be regarded as *transitional* in that existing tropes, metaphors and symbols of defiance (mourning, blood, blooming, jungle, river, even Mirza Kuchek Khan) that are shared by the two strands of 'political' poetry of the late 1960s – that of Akhavan-Sales and Shamlu and that of the emerging voices of Soltanpour, Golesorkhi and others – are now shifted away from the purely symbolic field and connected to the signifiers of *actual* revolutionary discourse: resistance, revolt, Sia[hkal] and revolution. We thus poetically switch from a realm of interpretable and *mediated* symbolic representations to the field of *im-mediately* graspable declarations: all power to the symbols! While the community of deliberate inferences remained the foundation of sanctioned interpretations of symbols and tropes in a politically significatory way, by this time, this community recedes in its influence as poetry becomes increasingly tangible and relatable by a growing community of young activists, especially in the universities. *This subtle but decisive fault line in the symbolic allowed the guerrilla or Siahkal poetry to branch off from post-Nimaic poetry, while having stemmed from, and remaining connected to, the robust tree planted by Nima*, and this phenomenon captures the thesis of this chapter.

From a literary standpoint, the sanctioning of such solidified symbols must primarily, though not exclusively, be credited to Golesorkhi, who advanced a Marxist literary critique that advocated a more rigorous form of 'literary commitment' than that of Shamlu and his generation. He unapologetically attacked detached, urban and bourgeois literature, whose sources of inspiration are imperialist notions and their own Third-Worldish inferiority complex (Golesorkhi 1996: 17–26). He urged a 'progressive literature' that exposes the bourgeois binary of poetry and slogan (*she'r va sho'ar*) (1996: 42–5). Interestingly, though, Golesorkhi's work was later called 'poetry-slogan' (*she'r-sho'ar*) (Soleimani 1981: 79), and he was accused of confusing the epistemological boundary that he expressly refuted, an indication of post-revolutionary oblivion of the social and literary conditions under which guerrilla poetry was shaped. This reports the (erroneous) claim about knowing the boundary between poetic and non-poetic regardless of changing historical and aesthetic communities:

> Of the men of No! Khosrow Golesorkhi . . . preferred the most naked and solid relations between the arts and society. He did not recognise any other form of art but the social art (*honar-e ejtema'i*) and by that he believed in its most profound way. He knew that 'social words do not showcase social poetry; without its foundations and origins laid in the social infrastructure, social art won't be social art.' But in this path, he sometimes went so radically he did not distinguish poetry (*she'r*) from slogan (*sho'ar*), thus denying the poetic essence. (Soleimani 1981: 78–9)

A SAVAK conspiracy and entrapment against dissident intellectuals, the details of which are now clear (Samakar 2001; Vahabzadeh 2010: 218–19, n. 1), brought Golesorkhi to a clash with the authorities: accused of planning to kidnap the royal family, a phoney charge unbeknownst to him, Golesorkhi was tried in the only televised military court proceedings in pre-revolutionary Iran. His bold defence statements shook Iranians. I remember as a teenager watching this slender and clearly tormented but unbroken man who stood tall, shaking the courtroom and frightening the military judges. He opened his defence statements with a poem (a stanza of it appears in the epigraph to this book) to identify himself as a poet, and then launched a sharp, postcolonial attack on the regime before being forced into silence. These statements made him an immediately beloved hero for dissidents. He received the death penalty. By refusing to apply for an appeal, Golesorkhi also exposed SAVAK's plan to commute his sentence in the higher court. Although he never was an activist, he signed his last letter as a 'Fadai' of Iranian people. He was executed, along with Karamatollah Daneshian (1946–74), on 18 February 1974. Golesorkhi was a *sha'er*; now he had become a *shahid* who had signed his last letter as a 'people's Fadai'. Kasra'i, Shamlu and several other poets dedicated poems to this singular man who stood tall against an entire machinery of repression, defending his dignity and the right to fight back. Golesorkhi, whose last name means 'of the red flower', became the beloved red rose of a revolutionary generation.

Golesorkhi's status as the poet-martyr of the guerrilla movement has ironically caused neglect in analysing his work as a postcolonial critic and poet. In any case, Siahkal did indeed leave a tangible impact on poetry. He makes references to both Siahkal and Mirza in his poems:

In the Greens of Greens

. . .

The jungle is the sound of our lostness
The jungle is the essence of our unity
And the eyes of Kuchek [Khan]
cannot believe
        that his cry, now
has flowered
in the cold labyrinth of Siahkal
under the jungle's wet eyelid.
(Golesorkhi 1995: 15)

While in 1971 the PFG and other militants were engaged in life-and-death battles, it was poetry that heralded and cherished the coming of 'someone who is not like any other' (Farrokhzad) and brought light to the dark depths of post-1963 repression. At a time when discovery of a PFG leaflet in one's possession by police would guarantee arrest, torture and a hefty prison term, university students and dissident intellectuals avidly sought, read and were inspired by these poems. Haloed with gallantry, the guerrillas, regardless of their ideological inclinations, gradually ascended to the status of hagiographised liberators in the underground publications of 1971 and later. Siahkal was no longer a Caspian township: it was now the mystic birth-place of a generation's rebellious defiance, the allegorical breeding ground of freedom fighters. Poetry aided immensely the collective construction of this image. Poetry achieved this through collective constriction and expansion in deploying certain tropes and symbols at the expense of others – a legacy of Yushij. The symbols that were supposed to be secret language of dissident lexis because they were 'deprived of explicit expression due to dictatorship' (Estedadi-Shad 2000: 191) had now become the open language of defiance, decodable by both dissident readers and security apparatus. Indeed, the guerrilla and Siahkal poetry had educated all in how to decode poetic tropes!

Of course, no discussion of guerrilla or Siahkal poetry deserves its designation without discussing Soltanpour, arguably the arch-poet of this genre – a young, stubborn poet and playwright who withstood opposition to advance a referential, symbolically-militant poetry. He was arrested several times in the late 1960s and early 1970s because of his writings and spent 1974–7 in prison. A few months after his release, he attended the last Goethe Poetry Festival (10–19 October 1977), and just like the Khusheh Poetry Festival nine years earlier he rocked the thousands of attendees with his fiery poetry. After the revolution, he became more politically active, and was arrested and executed by the new regime. Soltanpour inspired many young rebel poets, including poets in the ranks of the PFG, and the songs he wrote in prison became the famous anthems of post-revolutionary Fadaiyan. Cassette-tape production of these poems, *Shararehha-ye Aftab* (*The Rays of Sunlight*), although published without the poet's name, reportedly sold 2.3 million copies after 1979 (see Baran 2018). A review of three consecutive poetry collections by him – *Seda-ye Mira* (*The Mortal Voice*, 1961–8), *Avazha-ye Band* (*Prison Songs*, 1968–72) and *Az Koshtargah* (*From the Abattoir*, 1972–7) – shows the trajectory of increasing symbolic fixity and concrete referentiality through which Siahkal poetry achieved its sharply political genre. Due to censorship, these collections were published as underground publications known colloquially as *jeld sefid* (blank cover).

The Mortal Voice contains social poems and personal lyrics reminiscent of poems by Shamlu and Kho'i. The poems are not pointed, but interpretable: "'Hello!" / You see an acquaintance / an ice cream / a beer / your heart still remains foggy. / You take your friend home / and open the pages of *Kayhan* [daily paper]. / Now a piece of bread / and a sunny-side-up egg, / you rest in bed / the window is filled with moonlight / you see the moon through the window / and invite your friend to see it too!' (Soltanpour n.d.: 1: 27). Its redundancies aside, this poem is clearly not revolutionary, although the collection contains political reflections:

I Sing, Now, Next to Hardship

I come from the land of rocks
from ridges, violence and cry

Will my voice remain
in the rocks of the mountains?
Will there grow tulips from these rocks?
And will buttercups recite to the star
the poem of blood-filled river?
. . .
When the fighting stars
stand against the stone hedge of the night
when the bullets and the guards
aim at the red, awakened tulips
when one hears the sound of death
and one smells blood in the swamp
Nima's strange bird
sings on the wall of the night
I ride like a bird facing the blows of blood and wind
And I sing on the wall of the night.
(Soltanpour, quoted in Shams-Langarudi 1991c: 528–30)

Note how signifiers like mountain, river, swamp and rock, while retaining their 'natural' signifieds, lead the reader to the *suggested* signifieds. Mountain stands for an unconquerable domain or soul, where its rocks remember the cry of the poet and retain his songs. Filled with the blood of previous sacrifices, the river ends up in the swamp of stagnation. All this happens during the night, where the stars stand against a stone hedge, being shot. The symbolic construction of such an ambiance is made possible by using signifiers from everyday language but intending them *suggestively* unconventional. The unconventional, allegorical use of these signifiers then becomes conventional within a specific community of dissident readers so that this poetry makes sense. As Karimi-Hakkak observes, what happened in this era was that 'various poetic signifiers were assigned signifieds relevant on the socio-political plane' (1995: 249).

In *Prison Songs*, poems appear sharper. To show this, suffice it to look at a few stanzas from Soltanpour's long poem 'Spring 1972', dedicated to his comrade and PFG co-founder Puyan:

Spring 1972

Do not pass through our land
this year
O, Spring
with your flowers and stamen!
. . .
The claws of the spring
are still bloody
on the melting snow from the Winter of 1972

O, Spring!
Do not light up your red flowers
in the people's homes.
Hold your branches and leaves
in the blood of my brothers
so that the red flower's Spring
shakes the shoulders of mourners
with uncontrollable sob.
. . .

Salute to you, my mourning mother,
O, you mourning Spring!
Thirteen flowers upon the sunrise
thirteen brothers upon Chitgar
ninety-one soldiers
thirteen red, singing mouths
one-hundred and eighty-two rounds
thirteen bending walls of flower.
(Soltanpour 2016: 64–5, 67)

This long poem contains clear references to Siahkal and the execution of the thirteen guerrillas at Chitgar shooting field. Other signifiers – spring, flower, sunrise, mourning, sobbing – aid the framing of the guerrilla insurgency. In *From the Abattoir* (mostly written in prison), with poems such as 'An Elegy for Torture', his poems become unambiguously declaratory:

In Pahlavi Prison

. . .

Calm down, O, my mother, calm down
Let the dawn appear
Let them at the dawn
tie me up to the pole
Let them fire
Let the star of firing
madly shoot through the galaxy of blood
and blood blazes
Let the garden of blood
be slashed
on the ground of the firing squad.
Let the seed of the bullet
grow like a forest in the blood's sun
and cry out
These seeds won't stay on the soil
Out of the heart of the soil, they flower like lightning
and travel over this plateau like thunder
It is blood and it stays.
(Soltanpour, n.d.: 33–4)

Clearly, the poem deploys the usual tropes of political poetry, accentuated by the preferred symbolism of guerrilla poetry (forest, flowers, thunder) and intensifies it with reference to the militants' bloody battles (firing squad, bullet and a lot of blood), as if the existing symbolism still lacked in expression. Compared to many of his earlier poems, this one is angrier, bloodier and as directly pugnacious as it can get. I have shown through my thirty-year poetic history that poetry issues verdicts about actualities and unveils possibilities. *In such possibilities, life imitates art.* Our poetic verdicts lead us to the openness in which a new world becomes possible. Shamlu is the master of this. And yet in this poem, typical of Soltanpour's later poetry, there is virtually no room for imagining a new world. Not only does it lack openness, *this poem imposes closure on our imagination*. The right measure of verdict and openness is disturbed by the poet's declaratory intervention. This poem remains so context-specific that it can only have a really short shelf-life. The community of deliberate inferences is shunned altogether, no room is left for interpretation. The poem is intended for the militant practitioner, and not for the public at large: it does not invite; it only affirms. That is why, to quote Yousef, 'Said [Soltanpour's] poetry, despite others' claims, is being erased from memory' (quoted in Shams-Langarudi 1991c: 531). Soltanpour's poetry embodied the concerns of Shamlu and Barahani after the Khusheh Poetry Festival about *she'r* becoming *sho'ar*, although to this day no one can state where the boundary actually lies. After all, one person's poetry is another's slogan because poetry is essentially a personal experience. And this is a paradox.

The guerrilla poetry extended into the guerrillas' poetry. Members and supporters of PFG did write poetry to celebrate their cause and honour their fallen comrades. In a way, they were heirs to Soltanpour, but through him also to the entire modern tradition of political poetry that began with Yushij. Here is possibly the most famous PFG poem about the group's challenges and casualties during its first year. Published and distributed with PFG insignia, and made famous by a musically enthralling cassette-tape production, the long *Karnameh-ye Khun* (*Chronicles of Blood*) is an epic poem written by Mansour Khaksar (1939–2010), although it was never released under his name. Here is a passage:

> The year nineteen seventy-one
> the year of blood and bullet
> the year when defeat and victory
> joy and sorrow
> were interlocked
> like two bright and dark braids.
> The year when spite
> ruined the smiles on faces
> when on the ruined smiles
> hope and joy bloomed abruptly.
> The year when the great bell of blood sounded
> and storm blossomed.

The depiction of the life-and-death battle between the Fadai militants, who had initiated urban guerrilla warfare in Iran ahead of later militants, and Iranian security in these opening lines is far more poetic than Soltanpour's last poem. It reveals a collective walk on a precarious thread. The poem then portrays the distinct battles of the PFG in epic iteration – Siahkal, bank hold-ups, street shootouts, military court proceedings, imprisonments, tortures and executions – sections that are chained together with the refrain, 'The year when the great bell of blood sounded / and storm blossomed', giving the reader of this long poem room for breath. Despite its length (440 lines, 18 sections), this is energised, fast verse. It concludes by depicting Fadaiyan love and dedication:

> Salute, salute you great bell of blood
> Salute, you martyred comrades
> who devastated yourselves
> to re-create your people.
> Salute, you flames of love for the people
> that glowed in your eyes.
> Salute, you bloody stars
> Salute, you growing stems of storm
> Salute, you People's Fadai Guerrillas
> Salute, you toiling masses of Iran.
> (Anon. 2013)

The poem's epic narration ends with a declaratory tone which, while remaining cautious not to yield to 'slogan', surrounds concrete referents to PFG with symbolic imagery. Just like the PFG militants in 1971, the poem also risks walking on the fine thread that separates *she'r* from *sho'ar* but does not surrender to *sho'ar*, thus retaining its poetics.

But that is not always the case with guerrilla poetry. As mentioned, many individual Fadai Guerrillas came from cultural backgrounds. Thus, it is not surprising to see that soon after 1971 guerrilla poetry generated the guerrillas' poetry: members of the PFG wrote their own poetry and fiction, especially in prison. At this time something else also happened: guerrilla/Siahkal poetry was staggeringly and invariably male-dominated and its dominant voice was clearly masculine. In the PFG ranks many women wrote poetry, songs and fiction, but their efforts were not showcased in the male-dominated culture of resistance. Aside from Ashraf Dehqani (1949–) whose prison memoir, *Epic of Resistance* (1974), after his escape from Qasr Prison in 1973 became an underground 'bestseller', Marzieh Ahmadi-Osku'i (1935–74), Ghazal (Paridokht) Ayati (1951–77), Roqiyyeh Daneshgari and Sediqeh Serafat were among the PFG members or prisoners with published poems or fiction (underground in the 1970s) and performed song lyrics after 1979. Perhaps the most celebrated of these women is Ahmadi-Osku'i, whose posthumous *Memoirs of a Comrade* (1974), in Persian and Azeri, showcases a talent whose artistic refinement was cut short by her tragic death. Most of her poems fall within the poetry with distinct references to 'Fadai', and as such are close to what Barahani would call 'slogan'. But an acute awareness of her femininity informs most of her poems: she does not submit to the dominant masculine image of the guerrilla. Her poetic personages are women, and not generic women either, but toiling, exploited and abused, down-trodden women – the woman she identifies as having come from abject conditions in Azerbaijan:

Pride

I'm a mother,
I'm a sister,
I'm a devout spouse
I'm a woman,
a woman from the dead parishes of the South,
a woman who from the beginning,
has run over the scorching grounds
of all plateaus
    with bare feet.

This woman is a real, working woman, not a idealised figment of masculine fantasy:

I'm a woman,
a worker whose hands
turn the giant machinery of the factory,
and everyday,
the teeth of the cog,

shred her abilities before her eyes,
a woman out of whose essence of life,
the blood-thirsty corpse gets fatter,
and whose ruined blood
increases the investor's profits,
a woman with no equivalent
in that shameful dictionary of yours.
[A woman] whose hands can't be white,
> or her figures delicate,
> > or her skin soft,
> > > or her hair fragranced.

And because she is a working woman, she is capable of fighting for her future –
she takes her agency in her own hands:

I'm a woman,
a woman with no equivalent
in that shameful dictionary of yours.
A woman in whose chest lies a heart
that is full of putrefied wounds
> of rage.
A woman in whose eyes
> there shines
> > the colourful reflections of freedom's bullets.
A woman whose hands are trained
> by her labour
> > to hold a gun.
(Ahmadi-Osku'i 1974: 166–9)

This existentially-felt poem arises from the poet's understanding her agency
through her experience. The poem's aesthetics are intertwined with its feminine imagery. Perhaps for this very reason, Ahmadi-Osku'i is not keen on
using the (male-propagated) symbolism that informs much of guerrilla/
Siahkal poetry. When she tries to exceed her personal self-discovery and
poetise about the universal fighter of liberation, however, we see an entirely
different picture:

Proletariat

My grandfather was a slave,
my father a serf
and I am a worker.
My grandfather rose up, he was crucified.
My father fought back, he was killed by the guillotine.
I am a fighter too, they put me in prison.
They loaded their guns and called my name.
Proletariat!
Charge:
Armed struggle against international imperialism
and in defence of the toiling masses of the world.
They kneeled and aimed
waited for number 3 and fired.
Sentenced to death!
(Ahmadi-Osku'i 1974: 192)

An inescapable poetics permeates this verse, especially in the first six lines (a poetic depiction of class struggle in Marxist historical materialism), and yet, in my judgement, the poem fails to visualise the poetic essence of the struggle.

We all know that language is a matter of convention created by a community of speakers, as Saussure has shown long ago, and poetic lexis is not an exception. For the early 1970s community of zealous students and intellectuals, militant symbolism was indeed poetic. Paradoxically, though, the success of guerrilla and Siahkal poetry in constructing new historically-specific signifier-signified pairs became its own undoing. When we all agree that, for example, the mountain signifies the unconquerable militant determination, the river refers to finding meaning in life in its flow towards the utopia of the sea, the swamp becomes the place where the blissful dramas of life stagnate, the star represents our ideals, the jungle stands for the protective thicket of the rebels, and the tulip denotes the gone-by soul that had tried to reach the star, this is precisely when symbolism crumbles. The *figurative becomes literal* and the guerrilla poetry becomes increasingly naked, as in many of Soltanpour's poems in this period.

Why do symbols deliver? They potentially deliver us to an alternative (unreal) world, beyond the existing reality, and thus shape our existential comportment and commitment. When symbols become fixed, they fasten us to one (unreal) reality only. This fixity diminishes the poetics of poetry, but is this not exactly what the militants wanted: that everyone be affixed to this (not-yet) alternative reality?

Nevertheless, the power of symbols lies in their nimble significations, despite our agential attempts at tethering them to our political purposes. Among the poets of this generation, Goleserkhi remained unwaveringly poetic:

An Unnamed Poem

Landed on your chest
our enemy's deep, fatal wound
but,
      O, you tall cypress, you didn't fall
      dying standing – such is your way
in you, the songs of dagger and blood
in you, the migrant birds
in you, the chant of victory
so bright your eyes
           have never been.
With your blood,
    Tupkaneh square
       will awaken
          in the people's rage.
From the other side of Tupkhaneh
the people will pour
       to this side.
Bread and hunger
     will be equally shared.
O you standing cypress
it's your death that creates.
Our enemy erects walls.
These decent and beleaguered passers-by
don't know your name, these shabby-worn passers-by.
And this is unfortunate, but

the day the masses learn about it
                    every single drop of your blood will become an altar.
The masses,
will chant
        in every patriotic ballad
                        your great name.
Your name, the flag of Iran.
The Caspian [Sea] lives on by your name.
(Golesorkhi 1995: 38–40)

Tupkhaneh Square in central Tehran divides the city into the poor south and the middle-class and rich north, and the author stands on the northern side ('this side'), but by virtue of his sacrifice, the south-dwellers will one day awaken and pour into his side, and this is when 'bread and hunger / will be equally shared': a true depiction of the militants, who mostly came from educated, middle-class backgrounds but who fight for the underprivileged. The poem succeeds without availing itself of much symbolism. And this is precisely why this specific poem became popular. In a way, what we are witnessing in this poem and in that of Ahmadi-Osku'i is the *ends* – both as *limitation* and *terminal point* – of guerrilla (or Siahkal) poetry and its claim to a particular set of symbols. Just as poetry had anticipated the coming of the elusive guerrillas or the heroic liberator as early as the 1950s, so did this *end*, in its dual meaning, of a particular poetic symbolism anticipate in advance, by the mid-1970s, the upcoming demise of this genre of poetry and the movement with which it identified. The generation that created and sanctioned this poetic style came of age: the PFG leadership was lost in security raids and the student and intellectual support for militantism began to dwindle by 1976 (Vahabzadeh 2010: 56). The 'end' of guerrilla and Siahkal poetry, as the wisdom of hindsight illuminates, anticipated the end of the years of steel and blood.

The Goethe Poetry Festival of 1977, featuring fiery speeches and poems, including those of Akhavan-Sales, Soltanpour, Kasra'i, Kushabadi, Kho'i and Sa'edi, a powerful cultural precursor to the 1979 Revolution that influenced younger people by positively sanctioning open dissent, marks also the end of an era of poetic resistance that had started with the Khusheh Poetry Festival of 1968. The literary commitment that had won the day in 1968 reached its zenith in 1977 before its decline in terms of novelty, energy and reach. And that is another story.

Poetry is mysterious. More so when it is lived.

Conclusions: The Magic of Literary Existence

A movement was anticipated by the late 1960s. It was in the air, but unreal until the Siahkal operation and the subsequent myth around it concretised this movement. A list of 120 poems or songs written by prominent poets, songwriters and PFG members, and specifically in relation to the Fadai movement, has already been diligently compiled (Mohammadpour 2014). As discussed in Chapter 1, this is how the event works: it appears and imposes a rupture. In and by itself, the event has no essence that qualifies it as 'event'. Simultaneous moods of despair and hope mobilised a new generation of defiant and radical activists to appear on the scene and create a public discourse around the event. *Due to its privileged place in Iranian culture and thinking, poetry was the first and greatest ally of this radically, defiant movement. Poetry was a defiant movement in its own right.* What George Katsiaficas observes about the 1960s in general fully applies to Iran: 'The new radicalism demanded a simultaneous transformation of politics, economy, and *culture*, of social structure and *individual subject*' (1987: 36; my emphasis). The guerrillas emerged to finally embody a poetic litany.

This extensive chapter shows how poetic possibility rendered intelligible and desirable the particular iteration of a perilous journey of militant activism. Persian poetry has a privileged place in Iranian and Persian culture and collective thought. The Persian language is poetic as Persian poetry has the ability to change the syntactical structure of language and still make perfect sense. Classical poetry (in particular Rumi's) is rich in this regard, and so is New Poetry. Note these immortal lines by Shamlu, *ma bi chera zendeganim / anan beh chera marg-e khod agahanand*, which seriously defy translation. Poetry, I believe, is the *urtext* of Persian literature. In our study of the relationship between the militant action of the 1970s and the arts, poetry plays a significant and central role: it both anticipated the guerrilla movement ahead of its time and celebrated and glorified it, at times hagiographising the self-sacrificing ('fadai') militant. This observation reveals the dialectics of the arts and political action, that which, I argue, led to life imitating art in this period. No other art form in Iran quite enjoys this privileged position.

I call the relationship between art and action (life) 'dialectical' because there is transcendence attached to this opposition. Life begets art, begets life, begets art, but always at a 'higher' level.

Through social history, literary history, phenomenology and literary theory, this chapter has laid the theoretical foundations for other art forms and also narrated the process that led to guerrilla and Siahkal poetry from literary existence to cultural existence to collective intelligibility. I told the story of the articulation of a generation's experiences that no ideology can express. *Only poetry can.*

This chapter has offered a thirty-year poetic history from Nimaic political poetry and its enriched symbolism in the 1940s to the guerrilla and Siahkal poetry in the 1970s that largely seized the collective poetic imagination. I submitted, in relatively rich detail, the importance of sanctioned significations and linguistic stability in political poetry. With its initial advent in the late 1960s – in particular around the Khusheh Poetry Festival – guerrilla poetry was accused of devolving into 'slogan' – a sign of significatory stability. The debate was epistemological and aesthetic: there is no clear-cut distinction between *she'r* and *sho'ar* that remains valid regardless of historical context and the emerging and changing communities of deliberate inferences. I showed that guerrilla and Siahkal poetry indeed returned to the gist of Nima's symbolism: that in order for the poetic symbol to be meaningful, it must have relative stability, or, stated differently, the symbol must intervene between imagery and reality in a reasonably steady way. *Our story was one of transition from symbolic fixity (of signs) to their unfixity through suggestion back to new fixity.* By the time the Goethe Poetry Festival took place, the debate over the epistemological and aesthetic markers had become moot, albeit never settled. With some negligence we can view the popularity of guerrilla poetry as situated within the pincers of the two aforementioned poetry festivals, between 1968, the peak of political repression, and 1977, the time of the regime's economic and political crisis leading up to the 1979 Revolution. Eerily, guerrilla activity was also at its zenith between 1971 and 1976.

Linguistically, guerrilla poetry was achieved through the substitution of certain signifieds under a select number of signifiers. It created a codified language by substituting symbols within the binarism inherited from the (Nimaic) Night Poetry. The symbolism that clearly situated a defiant poem on the right side of the irreconcilable binary across the allegorical political divide – as in the political literature of the guerrillas – was constructed around 'people' or *khalq*, which originates with Yushij, as opposed to the 'enemies of the people' or *zedd-e khalq*, a key theoretical concept of militants (see Jazani 1978: 29, 161; Jazani 1976f: 159, 164; Vahabzadeh 2010: 93). This binary stood at the foundation of the principle of intelligibility of this political and poetic discourse. Other naturalistic symbols (jungle, star, river, mountain and others) or political ones (blood, bullet, weapon and others) are organised around this key opposition. As such, aside from its style, or perhaps precisely because of it, the guerrilla and Siahkal poetry represents a collective and participatory achievement of the poet, the (politically-minded) reader, and state censorship!

In addition to significantly contributing to a culture of protest in the aftermath of Siahkal, the guerrilla and Siahkal poetry successfully created a contemporary, material and tangible epic: this poetry rendered the guerrillas larger than life. It had a *metonymic* effect. Confronted by a regime of censorship that harshly repressed freedom of expression, the artistic and poetic community yearned for acts of political rebellion in which they would poetically dwell. The Siahkal operation thus became the watershed moment for a culture that celebrated the heroism of the elusive, omnipresent and immortal freedom-fighters. With the gift of this historic referent (Siahkal, the PFG), poetry captured a whole generation's imagination: *what might have been too ideological or too dangerous to be experienced first-hand by thousands of Iranian dissidents was rendered poetically graspable and desirable.* Indeed, Iranian militants of the 1970s owed their post-revolutionary popularity to the artistic creativity around their hallowed presence. Poetry overcame the brutality of everyday guerrilla life. In fact, poetry literally created poetic justice, to use a cliché. Poetry's mimesis, as Derrida has shown in a different context, created a 'reality-effect' (Derrida 1981: 206). Due to this 'reality-effect', poetry reached the audience that political statements could not. The 'imagined' world of dissident poetry became the lived experience of a generation, and writing guerrilla/Siahkal poetry was transformed into a rebellious act: while the militants fought with their guns and bombs, the poets campaigned through their subversive symbolism. In this process, an 'interpretive community' (Karimi-Hakkak 1995: 250) sanctioned a specific reading that functioned as the alphabet of literary defiance. This community was formed around the idea of 'literary commitment' to social issues that functioned both as decisive and divisive: it was decisive because it mobilised poets and literati around the cause of freedom and against repression and censorship through their writings, and it was divisive because it tended to marginalise the genres and schools of poetry that found political commitment extraneous to the art itself. Interestingly, this very commitment invited the unsettled debate about what constitutes *she'r* as opposed to *sho'ar*.

Reading poetry symbolically in a (politically) sanctioned way was then transformed into a political act: a particular community of deliberate inferences was formed. Paradoxically, as the symbolism of guerrilla poetry became ever more fixed, this community dissipated because of the poetry's success: now everyone, friend and foe, was able to decode guerrilla poetry. The symbolic poetry of defiance was deployed by the poet and interpreted by readers in an intentional and collaborative manner, just as these poems were identified by censorship and security forces. If the guerrilla was committed to fight the regime with her machine gun, the poet was equally committed to fight repression through his poetry. Writing guerrilla poetry, then, turned out to be a perilous occupation, on account of which many poets – Golesorkhi, Yousef, Soltanpour, Mirzazadeh, among others – ended up in prison.

Poetry then became supplemented by militant activity. My reading of Jazani's theory of 'armed propaganda' shows its merits here. The triangular effects of an armed operation – communications, metonymic and political – find equivalents in poetry. But what poetry adds to the former is that poetry *valorises and mystifies* these effects, releasing the militant action from time and place and committing it to poetic ersatz beyond particular temporality and spatiality. As such, where armed propaganda remains limited in its reach, poetry succeeds in universalising it. In order for militants to stay fighting and representing hope for change, the poet must render them universal fighters. With Siahkal, the PFG and other militants after it, the event that poetry had anticipated found its concrete, historic referent, and now poetry – previously pure imagination – became lived. Now it was for poetry to create poetic images of the concrete referent. We come full circle:

<table>
<tr><td>Poetic anticipation of heroic freedom-fighter</td><td>⇒</td><td>Concrete emergence of fighter, now a referent</td><td>⇒</td><td>Poetic universalisation of fighter – beyond referent</td></tr>
</table>

The triangular effect of armed struggle is that which, socially, politically and culturally, connects poetry and politics in the 1970s Iranian Gestalt of a young, rebellious generation.

In the years of repression and political impasse, poetic imagination succeeded in rendering militant opposition intelligible, even desirable. Like a spark whose glow leaves a disproportionately wider and more enduring impression on the eye in absolute darkness, the guerrillas' operations left embellished impressions on Iranian dissident consciousness, evoking tangibly real embodiments of age-old fables of heroism. And it was this impression, which was in large part the achievement of the particular poetry, as the key component of protest culture, that reigned over an era of Iranian poetic life in the 1970s.

3

CHANTED DEFIANCE: SINGING A CULTURE OF RESISTANCE

You can't have a revolution without songs.

(banner at President-Elect Salvador Allende rally, 1970)

The last young man arrived too
and the first young man addressed him:
repeat thirteen times
that you're awake,
so that I tell you
yes, grab your knapsack
and write on the petals of a poppy
thirteen times anew
one can always arrive
right at the time of harvest.

. . .

Repeat thirteen times
there's no blood of Judas in my body
so that I tell you, it's enough
just to grab your knapsack
and your walking stick too
and brother
rise up!

Shahyar Ghanbari (2012)

If poetry was the prophetic voice that artistically anticipated and valorised militant resistance more than a decade before Siahkal, it was the protest songs that, in the 1970s, popularised poetic depictions of the existential dilemma of living under dictatorship. Unlike poetry's anticipative tone, 'protest songs' represent the 'delayed effect' of the guerrilla movement. Aside from passionate lovers yearning to express themselves through poems, poetry is, *stricto sensu*, typically and historically the art of literati, students and the educated classes, the art of seekers who are able to get away from the mundane and delve instead into poetic imagination and its envisioned world. Clearly, there is an organic relationship between poetry and music: both entail rhythms and are as ancient as human collectives; even today's free-verse poetry often contains a certain (internal) rhythm that threads the words in ideational harmony. In songs, the music enhances – in a way, appropriates, accentuates and externalises – the internal, phonological rhythms of the verse. Aided by the soul-grabbing power of music, songs take poetic words to the public, often in the course of the mundane lives of people, reaching deep inside their feelings and lifting them to the musically sung ideas. Moreover, music is so innate to the human mind that anyone without (or with) musical knowledge can hum or whistle a tune upon hearing it, often only right after the first time of hearing. Braided with the tune, lyrics become musically invigorated and thus remembered. Songs are the greatest mnemonic arts.

The Siahkal 'resurgence' and the advent of the PFG and other militants corresponded with the emergence of Iran's New Song-Writing (*taraneh sara'i-ye Novin*) movement that introduced modern protest song to Iranian culture. In fact, belonging to the same generation as the militants, some key artists associated with New Song-Writing not only celebrated the guerrillas and their cause, they contributed to the artistic iteration of the profound angst of their generation – the social anxiety that was graver than the militants could grasp and articulate through their ideological and political lenses. This chapter shows that while it emerged almost synchronously with the rise of urban guerrilla resistance, the protest song has outlived the guerrillas, to become a component of Persian musical culture to this day.

Persian contains both formal language and colloquial utterances, and the differences between them can at times be significant. Songs have the capacity to bring poetry, written in formal to colloquial language. Even Persian verbs show the overlap: 'Poetry's links to spoken, chanted, and sung performance are manifest in the Persian language: one term for composing poetry is *she'r goftan*, literally "to speak a poem," while the verb *sorudan* refers both to composing poetry and to singing, and the verb *khandan* means "to sing" as well as "to read"' (Hemmasi 2013: 59). As such, songs represent a significant means of communicating feelings in Iranian culture.

The theoretical components pertaining to poetry submitted in Chapter 2 also apply here, since lyrics and songs are subject to the same analytical approaches as is poetry – albeit with the added factor of music. This chapter offers the history and transformations of song-writing before showcasing and analysing the key protest songs of the 1970s.

From *Tasnif* to *Taraneh*

No phenomenon just erupts into existence, and the Iranian protest song is no exception. A phenomenologist always looks into the origins of that which makes its appearance to consciousness – what Edmund Husserl called *Urstiftung* or the primal (or original) establishment (or foundation). As is known, crafting songs to convey political messages in modern Iran goes back to the Constitutional Revolution (Siamdoust 2017: 3): a historic junction at which a political movement overdetermined the development of music, rendering the latter more relevant to changing public sensibilities. A similar process also took place in the 1970s. By the time the first political *chansons* reached the public, the traditional music or *musiqi-ye sonnati-ye Irani* had already undergone interesting changes. This music is based on *radifs* or particular arrangements of melodies and 'is regarded as a quintessential Persian heritage. In this musical system, there are twelve principal modal categories, which are divided into seven *dastgahs* (loosely, [musical] "modes") and five *avazes* (loosely, "lesser modes"), not to be confused with "avaz" in its definition as free-metered vocals within Persian classical music' (Siamdoust 2017: 20). The traditional music was generally for the elite (Jannatie-Ataie 2007), and the ordinary people had their own loosely constructed (and often poorly-worded) folksongs, known as *tasnif*, ballad or rhythmic songs. 'In the words of the historian of music Ruhollah Khaleqi, a *tasnif* is a "short song always accompanied by lyrics, which may treat events and happenings of the day, sometimes in a critical light"' (Siamdoust 2017: 43). Traditionally sung by street singers and self-taught bands or in brothels and opium houses, these folksongs were produced for laypersons, and the words reflected the everyday realities of the vastly illiterate nineteenth-century people. In contrast, the traditional musical system relied heavily on classical Persian poetry, in particular, *ghazal* (lyrical poem or sonnet) and *ruba'i* (quatrain), and it did not have the capacity, in the nineteenth century, to adapt to new ideas because of its consumption by the ruling and upper classes, who were not interested in social change.

The talented Ali Akbar Khan Shirazi (1843–1906), better known as Sheyda, created the modern Persian *tasnif* or song or *chanson*, having left behind some of the most memorable *tasnifs* (like '*Bot-e Chin*' or 'The Chinese Idol'; lyrics also by Sheyda), still popular today, that brought well-constructed rhythmic music together with imaginative and elegantly-worded *chanson d'amour*. As the constitutional movement progressed, the constitutionalist poet Abolqasem Aref Qazvini (1880–1933) used Sheyda's *tasnif* innovations, thus composing *tasnifs* with political verses. His famous song 'Az Khoon-e Javan-e Vatan Laleh Damideh' or 'Out of the Blood of My Homeland Young Tulips Have Grown' (1907) is regarded as Iran's first 'protest song' (Azizi 2007). It was also Aref who held Iran's first modern concerts: taking music out of the private milieu of elite or wedding parties, he gave it an openly social existence. For lyrics intended to have an impact on public consciousness, it was necessary for music to re-emerge as a publicly performed art. Out of one of the first modern democratic revolutions in the world, as is well-known, there emerged the dictatorship of Reza Shah Pahlavi (1878–1944; reign: 1925–41). Incidentally, the last 'protest song' appeared at the beginning of Reza Shah's reign but soon after it was banned and occulted until a couple of decades later. 'Morgh-e Sahar' ('The Morning Bird') – one of the most enduring Persian protest songs – was composed in Mahur *dastgah* by maestro Morteza (Mordechai) Neydavud (1279–1369) with its lyrics written by poet-laureate Mohammad Taqi Bahar in 1927. But when the song was performed for the first time, the name of its lyricist was withheld for fear of Reza Shah's reprisal. It was first sung by the female vocalist Ms Iran Al-Dowleh at a private garden party; a later version of it sung by Moluk Zarrabi (Moluk Farshforush Kashani; 1907–99) was recorded on Polyphone (Parvin 2007). In a profoundly allegorical way, Bahar reflects in his lyrics on the turbulent years of the constitutional revolution, from the civil war to the return of autocracy, to famine, misery and Reza Shah's coup – in short, the loss of a people's collective dreams:

> O Morning bird, begin moaning
> freshen up my burning sorrow
> break apart and turn upside-down
> this cage with [your] flaming sigh
> O wing-tied nightingale, come out of the corner of this cage,
> [and] sing the tune of freedom of humankind
> And with your breath enflame
> the expanse of this earth's mass [*khak-e tudeh*]
> The oppressor's tyranny, the hunter's cruelty
> have brought my nest to ruins
> O God, O heavens, O nature
> take our dark night to sunrise
> It's the onset of the spring, flowers blooming
> [and] dew is raining from the cloud of my eyes
> Just like my heart, this cage is suffocating and dark
> O my flaming sigh throw fire at this cage
> O nature's hand don't pick the flower of my life
> look toward the lover's side, O blossoming flower, and do it more
> O loving-hearted bird make the story of separation shorter, much shorter.

The lyrics' rhythm is a derivation from the classical metrics group of *rajaz*. The allegorical nature of this song allows for multiple interpretations across different lived realities of oppressed Iranians in the past century. But one thing remains constant: the song captures the time of collective despair when the horizon of change seems dim. The injured, loving and mourning morning bird witnesses the plights of a nation (with all its diverse beliefs: God, heavens, nature), that suffers not from lack of action or imagination, but from overwhelming tyranny. Hinging on the nightingale/morning bird, the lyrics' fresh 'political' symbolism, whose ambivalence does not immediately provoke the authorities and certainly not without a stretch of interpretation, holds together such long-existing metaphors as 'night' and 'sunrise' to convey its message and mood. Capturing the rich and powerful beginning of protest songs, 'The Morning Bird' heralds the original watershed of a thriving culture of vocalised resistance in the decades to come.

The modern *tasnif* continued to flourish during the reign of Reza Shah, however: now it was in the hands of professional musicians and trained male but also aspiring female vocalists, including the phenomenal Qamarolmoluk Vaziri (1905–59). Soon, *tasnifs* were performed in the popular cabarets located in the famous entertainment district of Lalehzar Street in Tehran (although performances in these cabarets were largely banal and uncreative) and recorded on Polyphone records: the business and technological aspects are important for understanding how music becomes commercially viable, thereby financially supporting the crew and artists. *Tasnif* got a boost with the establishment of the country's first state-run radio station, Radio Tehran, in 1940. As radio programmes expanded in the next decades, so did the music industry. Obviously, though, political *chansons* could not exist under Reza Shah. By this time, Aref Qazvini had made a name for himself as a dissident artist with many political songs. Once the voice of the revolution, he died in solitude and poverty (see Malek 2014: 3–4), and with his death the political song was eclipsed until its surprising return in the 1950s.

The Allies' occupation of Iran in 1941 forced Reza Shah to abdicate in favour of his young son Mohammad Reza Shah. The 1941–53 period witnessed an era of social, political and cultural opening: political parties, labour unions, women's and minorities associations and newspapers and magazines flourished – a period terminated by the 1953 coup. The Shah returned to absolute power with a heavy hand. Interestingly, in the twelve-year relaxed period no political song of significance is noticeable. In the years following the coup, two songs 'dominated' radio programmes and the record market. One of them was the hit song 'Bu-ye Ju-ye Mulian' ('Fragrance of Mulian Creek'), composed by maestro Ruhollah Khaleqi, that is said to have been commissioned by the government for broadcast on Radio Tehran. It was arranged for full orchestra and sung by top vocalists Marzieh (Khadijeh Ashraf-al-Sadat Mortezai, 1924–2010) and Gholam Hossein Banan (1911–85) (Monfaredzadeh 2017: 658). The song used a famous *qasideh* by a pioneer of classical Persian poetry, Abu-Abdullah Ja'far, better known as Rudaki (859–941 CE), a court poet and harp player who lived during the Samanid Empire (819–999 CE). He wrote this poem and sang it to Amir Abu-Nasr Samani, successfully persuading the king to return to Bukhara from his long sojourn in Harat. This particular song literally celebrates the return of Mohammad Reza Shah to power, as the last lines of the poem clearly indicate: 'the king is a cedar tree and Bukhara an orchard // the cedar tree always returns to the orchard // the king is the moon and Bukhara the sky / the moon always returns to the sky.'

The other post-coup hit song was a love song that became a symbol of mourning and loss in the eyes of the people, especially after the execution of members of the clandestine Tudeh Party Officers Organisation in autumn 1954: the words of 'Mara Bebus' or 'Kiss Me' were taken from a poem by pro-Mosaddeq Heydar Reqabi (1931–87; pen name Haleh) and Majid Vafadar (1912–75) wrote its tune (Monfaredzadeh 2017: 658). Reqabi had published his poetry collection titled *Aseman-e Ashk* (*The Sky of Tears*) in 1950. But a more dominant narrative holds that Reqabi actually gave the lyrics to Vafadar before leaving Iran to escape persecution because of his political activities (Hosayni Dehkordi and EIr 2000). The song was first sung by Parvaneh and adopted as the soundtrack of a movie called *Etteham* (*Accusation*) in 1956 (dir. Shapour Yasami), but it failed to attract attention. In 1957, the National Radio commissioned its rearrangement. Based on Vafadar's tune, the immortal version was arranged by maestro Parviz Yahaqqi (Sadiqi Parsi; 1935–2006), who played the violin, with Moshir Homayoun Shahrdar (1885–1969) on piano and Hassan Golnaraghi (1921–93) on vocals. Apparently, the famous version was recorded without the knowledge of the artists (Hosayni Dehkordi and EIr 2000). The song's broadcast was roughly coincidental with the execution of the pro-Tudeh officers, which contributed to the common and enduring misconception that the song mourned the officers (Khoshnam 2017: 641–2). The poem itself is *not political*. Only by a collective stretch of imagination can it be so regarded. Thus, 'the only widely popular song from this period is a heartfelt, passionate ballad titled "*Mara bebus*" (Kiss Me), characteristic of "political songs" under repressive conditions in that at first, it hardly sounds political at all' (Siamdoust 2017: 57). This is a song of separation in a turbulent turn of life, with the added heroism of the protagonist that connotes a 'political' message. It was only rendered political because people wished to read into it a political message in the post-coup era of despair:

Kiss me, kiss me, for the last time
may God protect you as I walk toward my destiny
Our Spring is passed, the past is passed, I am searching for destiny

Amidst the storm, allegiant with the boatmen
disregarding one's life one must pass through the storms
at midnights I've vowed with my beloved (*yaram*)
to set alight a fire in the mountains
In the dark night, I'll travel and pass through the dark path
Now look, my flower, don't shed tears of sorrow for me

O Beautiful girl, I am your guest tonight and will be staying with you
so that you rest your lips on mine
O Beautiful girl, the spark in your gaze and your innocent eyes
will set alight my night.

The original poem exceeds the sung parts (above). At this time (1950s) Nima's political symbolism (night, mourning) had already made inroads into collective poetic-political imagination, at the very least within literary circles. Tropes, symbols and metaphors are collective achievements, being subject to the historical community's tacit or explicit agreements on signifier–signified pairs, as Saussure teaches, without regard for the linguistic sign's referent. At this time, therefore, other metaphors (as in the lyrics) – storm, mountains, destiny – perhaps were not yet quite 'politicised'; nonetheless, these words were tethered to the aforementioned Nimaic symbolism. This process allows for the transposition of the romantic poem into a loving expression of a defeated fighter, *thanks to the context*. Accordingly, I submit, the political interpretation of the song is owed to Nimaic poetry – a point confirmed by the new generation of song-writers as well (Jannatie-Ataie 2011).

Recall Schürmann in Chapter 2: as soon as I speak of the pine trees around the lake, immediacy is lost. Reading this song as a political one also leads to permanent loss of immediacy: say, its actual impression on the movie-goers when it was sung by Parvaneh in *Accusation*. It is now almost impossible to *experience* it simply as a romantic poem (reminiscent of Karo's lyrics) about lovers' parting ways because of unkind times. Reading this *chanson* politically has become apodictic today. Anyway, the political interpretation and popularity of the song did not escape the authorities: to counteract it, the National Radio reportedly commissioned another version of the tune with different lyrics and more lavish orchestral performance to erase the memory of 'Mara Bebus' (Monfaredzadeh 2017: 658). Nonetheless, 'with *Mara Bebus* . . . symbols and allegory entered Iranian song-writing and stayed on' (Khoshnam 2017: 642).

Two more observations: 'Kiss Me' was a *tasnif* written in the traditional Avaz Isfahan musical mode, although the tune might have been borrowed from a Greek folk song and modified (Kharrazy 2020). It is not, however, performed using traditional instruments (tar, tonbak or kamancheh). Violin and piano were used instead. As such, with a captivating and slow 4/4 time signature that follows a faster prelude on the piano that then just keeps the beat, this *tasnif* leaves a different impression sound-wise; in fact, it sounds somewhat modern. Golnaraghi's fantastic and precise vocals merge with the beat (Kharrazy 2020). In this song love and separation (denotation) and politics (deliberate communal inference) sit beautifully together. The braiding of romantic love and political struggle render 'Kiss Me' a unique protest song, in contrast to the 1970s protest songs where romantic love is largely absent: an effect of guerrilla warfare.

The growing music industry in the 1950s–60s gradually explored Western music: jazz, pop, rock 'n' roll, and above all gypsy jazz (especially Russian and Greek folksongs). Slowly and steadily, non-traditional tunes emerged, gradually training the public's ears to like 'Western' music. The 1960s accelerated this process. 'This [new] music continued to take in Eastern (including Indian, Arabic, and Turkish) influences, but trends and sounds coming from the increasingly internationalizing force of the rock and pop music scene in the West were tipping the music in that direction.' This music had found its niche too. 'This more "modern" or "cosmopolitan" type of pop music was increasingly performed in the top cabarets like Bakara, Mayamey (Miami), and Moulin Rouge, and had taken over radio and television programs' (Siamdoust 2017: 46). Already by the 1950s, Iranian pop had brought about its own celebrities: 'There were . . . famous male artists, such as Viguen [Derderian, 1929–2003; Karo's brother], whose moniker was "The Sultan of Jazz" (until not long ago, and among older Iranians to this day, "jazz" is used to mean simply "pop") and who was among the first to introduce the guitar into Iranian music in the [early] nineteen-fifties; and slightly later, Aref [Arefkia; 1940–], the "Golden Throat" who often sang sentimental pieces of romance with opera style vocals' (Siamdoust 2017: 45–6). In this process, pop music gradually became accepted, growing over *tasnif* and making inroads both in terms of the music industry and in radio broadcasts (Breyley 2010). Viguen's invitation to Radio Tehran and his early-1950s memorable love songs like 'Mahtab' ('Moonlight') and 'Raqib' ('Rival') pushed pop music into the public taste. An entire generation of Iranian children in the 1960s and 1970s went to sleep listening to his mesmerising 'Lullaby', sung softly along with a gentle guitar tune, following the popular radio programme *Nocturnal Story*, every night. Written by Viguen's brother Karo, the lyrics were movingly 'modern': 'sing a lullaby, my little bird / the world is a fable / every nocturnal moan of this sad guitar / is the tear of a thousand nest-less little birds.' Imagine being the (urban) child who falls asleep with these magical words that *suggest* the sadness of living in an unjust world. 'Viguen represents an important period in the social transformation . . . In those years, Viguen whispered fresh words in his songs. In the age of tar and kamancheh, the photo of Viguen and his guitar was for our people a new and unbelievable image' (Jannatie-Ataie, quoted in Yunansian 2013).

The popularity of this new style enabled a culturally significant shift in song-writing: while *tasnif* continued its course and was promoted by radio programmes such as *Golha* (Flowers), with its Western and pop rhythms, melodies and beats, *taraneh* became popular especially with the younger generation. *Taraneh* allowed for greater freedom in choosing the words denoting contemporary or modern imagery. As times changed, *tasnif* revealed its limitations in the selection of lyrics. Almost all *tasnifs* were worded with the classical style of poetry and thus traditional imagery. In traditional song-writing, the lyrics from classical forms like *masnavi*, *ghazal* and *dobeiti* were primarily written or selected so they would fit a certain melodic style. Thus, the poetic imagery was basically classical, using age-old tropes like nightingale, flower, cedar tree, spring, new moon or thirsty lips (Mohammadian-Omriyan and Torki 2015: 105, 106–10). *Taraneh* changed as it parted ways with *dastgahs*. Younger song-writers used *chahar-pareh* and *masnavi* as primary poetic forms. They also broke with traditional scanning and rhythm as they saw fit (Mohammadian-Omriyan and Torki 2015: 115, 117), thus breaking away from the traditional understanding of poetry and lyrics.

While *tasnif* supported protest songs, however precariously and disjointedly, for about half a century, it was *taraneh* or modern song-writing that had the expressive aptitude needed to reflect the revolutionary generation's *weltanschauung* that bred militant resistance. At risk of jumping ahead of my argument, parallel song-writing styles defined the 1960s and 1970s musical stage. Traditional song-writers and poets like Mohammad Hassan (Rahi) Mo'ayyeri (1909–68), Seyed-Esma'il Navab Safa (1924–2005), Rahim Mo'ini Kermanshahi (1922–2015), Bizhan Taraqi (1929–2009), Touraj Negahban (1932–99) and Parviz Vakili (1932–84) were part of the music industry that gradually by the mid-1960s developed to include the new song-writers like Iraj Jannatie-Ataie (1946-), Ardalan Sarfaraz (1950–), Shahyar Ghanbari (1950–) and Zoya Zakariyan (1950–) (Mohammadian-Omriyan and Torki 2015: 103). The first group, however, had already emerged as the standard-bearers of *taraneh*-writing (Jannatie-Ataie 2005: 26). The generational difference is therefore meaningful for our study. The two generations of song-writers targeted different (but overlapping) markets and both were supported by state-run radio and television. Additionally, after 1953 poets also experimented with folklore, recycling folk metaphors or appropriating folk stories to express their existential angst and *suggest* political messages in rhythmically mnemonic ways that lent themselves to music at a time when pop music was still in its infancy. Examples include Shamlu's 'Pariya' ('The Fairies', 1953; sung by Dariush in 1972), 'Baroon' ('Rain', 1954), 'Ye Shab-e Mahtab' ('A Moonlit Night', 1954; sung by Farhad in the 1970s), 'Raz' ('Secret', 1955), 'Dokhtara-ye Naneh Darya' ('Mother Sea's Daughters', 1959) and Farrokhzad's 'Beh Ali Goft Madarash Ruzi' ('Said to Ali His Mother One Day', 1964) (Azizi 2007).

Some regard *taraneh* as contrasting with *tasnif* (as a legacy of Qajar music) by rightly emphasising the infrastructural elements, including the establishment of the National Radio (1940), which promoted and contributed to professionalising composition, song-writing and singing, as well as modernising music (Mohammadian-Omriyan and Torki 2015). The point is taken; however, I argue, one cannot view *tasnif* and *taraneh* as mutually exclusive, as 'traditional' versus 'modern' song. Elements of *tasnif*, in particular its imagery or metaphors (blood, tulip, mountain, storm, among others) were teleported into *taraneh* and functioned as constants. In fact, there were many instances of reciprocal relations between the adherents of the two schools. After *taraneh* promoters and artists were confident about the marketability of their style; they even began incorporating traditional instruments (tar, santur or tonbak) and even *dastgahs* into pop music, producing some creative Iranian pop-fusion music.

By the time Iran began its decade of rapid development in the 1960s, and with the expansion of universities and the middle class, pop music reached new popularity. By now, commercial, portable turntables had become available and affordable, sitting in many urban homes right next to the radio and television. This in turn gave a boost to the recording industry and caused less dependence on state-run radio and television when it came to musical preferences. Importantly, records could now be imported, or copied by record producers, and sold on the Iranian market as a lucrative business. American blues and rock music and French *chansons* found their way into the aesthetic tastes of young musicians and song-writers, leaving a lasting impact. Iranian musicians generally took the beats or rhythms they had borrowed from other folk or pop music, changed them and mixed them with the vernacular melodies that Iranians loved. The 6/8 time signature (colloquially called *shesh-o-hasht*) proved to be the most popular: it was rhythmic, danceable and invigorating, thus allowing a lot of happy love songs to define Persian pop. In contrast to *tasnif*, *taraneh* allowed for lyrics describing everyday objects, relationships, themes and expressions – in short, lived experiences – thus allowing people to *immediately* relate to the song instead of going through the interpretive mediation required to decode the tropes and signifiers of classical Persian poetry that *tasnif* generally presented. This is a significant turn. The artistic movement called the New Song-Writing was not possible without Iranian pop music, which generally followed the musical preferences of young Iranians. The pioneers of pop or folk music included Viguen, Jamshid Sheybani (1922–2009), Mohammad Nouri (1929–2010) and Manouchehr Sakha'i (1935–2011) (Khoshnam 2017: 642). One must also mention the Black Cats, Iran's first pop music band, founded in Tehran circa 1961 by Shahbal Shabpareh (1941–), that played in Kuchini (Italian *cucini*: 'you cook') restaurant – a unique establishment, founded by the veteran actress Vida Qahremani (1937–2018) and her husband. Qahremani brought to the Iranian cinema its first on-screen kiss (with Nasser Malekmoti'i in a 1945 movie), breaking a taboo. The restaurant had a dance floor (called *dansing*, also new) where young women and men would dance to Western hits of the day as well as a gallery called Mond (French *monde*: 'world') that featured the arts of younger artists. Kuchini featured the pop music of the Black Cats band, whose members became prominent pop figures in the 1970s and later: Shahram Shabpareh (1947–), Hassan Shama'izadeh (1943–) and, above all, the incomparable vocalist Farhad Mehrad (1943–2002). As a child, Farhad had learned music on his own and had spent around a year in the UK. Upon return to Iran, he performed American and English songs and was invited to join the Black Cats in 1965. Singing English (and later Russian) songs had a clear impact on his future as a vocalist of memorable Persian songs. That explains why Farhad's vocals involve precise scanning and narrative singing and almost no phrasing. Some of the memorable songs of these pioneers must be credited with training the ears of the populace to enjoy pop music. Soon, in Tehran, 'several beat, psychedelic and garage rock bands were formed. This was an alternative scene, much smaller than the mainstream scene' (Breyley 2010: 222). Behind these popular singers were (at time anonymous) cohorts of musicians, song-writers and arrangers. '*Taraneh* is a multi-arts phenomenon. [It] is not the product of a single person's or artist's creativity, especially in our country where often the poet, the musician, and the singer were not and are not one person' (Jannaite-Ataie 2007). '*Taraneh* is a simplified (*sahl-o-momtane'*) poem and its linguistic structure is rooted in the people's everyday conversations. In traditional song, there are not many instances of such devices and most of the tropes in these songs are of the same kinds of tropes found in [classical] poetry. But in new songs, using popular idioms and expressions constitutes a key characteristic of the song' (Mohammadian-Omriyan and Torki 2015: 119). I must point out that throughout the twentieth century there were also the songs popular with the mostly uneducated masses of the lower classes and the 'tough-guy' (*dashmashty* or *jaheli*) subculture – a genre with its own vocalists, industry and cabarets in Lalehzar Street. Although never entirely detached, *taraneh sarai-ye novin* departed from *taraneh-ye rasmi* (or 'official song-writing'), which relied mostly on classical poetry and classical understanding of lyrics and thus on a particular aesthetics and imagination that did not reflect the experience of Iranian youth of the 1960s. For the younger generation, *taraneh* must have reflected the specific issues of their day and have reported their concerns to the world (Jannatie-Ataie 2013a). Adhering to international musical standards, the 1960s *taraneh sarai* also departed from this genre of *musiqi-e ammi* or *mardomi* ('people's music') and its superficial pop music (Azizi 2007). One factor in the growth of the modern *taraneh sarai* was the rise of the educated class and its expectations regarding songs. *Indeed, musical preferences have class character.* As Iran moved through the 1960s, modern song-writing grew as its support by the music industry augmented. Strangely, the growth of the private music industry through pop song-writing is due to the fact that in the 1950s colloquial language was not allowed in songs broadcast by National Radio; the latter required formal language in the lyrics (Mohammadian-Omriyan and Torki 2015: 110–11). That policy gradually changed in the 1960s as pop music became widespread, but clearly the industry was ahead of cultural policymakers.

Speaking of infrastructure and industry, it so happened that the New Song-Writing emerged out of a music production studio named Tanin ('Echo'). It was founded in 1969, providing a venue where *taraneh* could break new grounds. From Tanin there emerged fresh pop music and pop singers as well as protest songs. Tanin was founded by musicians and lyricists, including the lyricist Touraj Negahban and the composers Parviz Atabaki (1936–2008) and Babak Afshar (1934–). Ardalan Sarfaraz positively confirms that without Tanin the New Song-Writing would not have happened (Sarfaraz 2006). Top established artists such as the pioneer pop musician Parviz Maghsadi (1938–2009) and the lyricist Parviz Vakili (1932–84) were also active with Tanin (see Jannatie-Ataie 2010a). What a unique opportunity it was for younger, aspiring artists to be associated with these masters, and this is exactly what happened. The vocalists Farhad Mehrad, Dariush Eghbali (1950–) and Googoosh (Fa'eqeh Atashin; 1951–), soon to be Iran's pop diva, the song-writers Jannatie-Ataie, Sarfaraz and Ghanbari and the composers Esfandiar Monfaredzadeh (1941–), Varoujan Hakhbandian (1936–77) and Babak Bayat (1946–2006) also had their careers kickstarted through Tanin Studio (Khoshnam 2017: 644). A new movement's advent is always embodied by its key protagonists. In the late 1960s, as Jannatie-Ataie recalls, there were many composers who wrote melodies but not many song-writers. Some wrote classical lyrics that did not fit *taraneh* melodies. So, there was an opportunity for young song-writers who wrote specifically for *taraneh* (2011). Tanin Studio changed this trend, creating the milieu for collaborative music by young, aspiring artists. Many memorable songs from the late 1960s through to the 1970s emerged from the artists associated with Tanin.

The New Song-writing Movement

With the evolution of *taraneh* in the 1950s–60s Iran – through its fusion with pop music that in our case was influenced both by Western (European, North American) and Eastern (Russian, Turkish, Balkan and Armenian folk music, Arabesque melodies, gypsy jazz) (see Hemmasi 2013: 60–1) – and growth of the industry that sustained and marketed such music, an artistic movement called the 'New Song-Writing' (*taraneh-sarai-ye novin*) emerged. Thus, modern song cannot be regarded as an autochthonous phenomenon; on the contrary, it reflects Iran's fascinating cosmopolitan culture in the 1960s.

In turn, New Song-Writing bred protest songs (*taraneh-ye mo'tarez*). To be accurate, though, while New Song-Writing has established itself as a genre that continues to this day and has protest song as its subset, they socially emerged simultaneously. To zero in on its protagonists whose vision and style supplied its particular genric characteristics: it is commonly held that New Song-Writing is the brainchild of three lyricists, Jannatie-Ataie, Ghanbari, Sarfaraz – who brought together lyrical love and critical social commentary wrapped in graspable metaphors and tropes – as well as four musicians, Varoujan, Bayat, Monfaredzadeh and Farid Zoland (1955–) – whose musical talents proved to have organic connections with the new lyrics (Azizi 2007; Jannatie-Ataie 2011). In the astute words of an observer, 'It was known that Iranians wanted rebellion and protest to be soft to the ear (*gushnavaz*)' (Khoshnam 2017: 642).

The New Song-Writing rescued Persian pop from obsolete, banal and repetitive expressions. Let me reiterate that by the late 1960s the lyrics were no longer secondary to the tune. In fact, lyricists would now take their songs to their favourite musicians and work with them collaboratively (Jannatie-Ataie 2005: 38–9). Let me elaborate: Monfaredzadeh was childhood friends with director Massoud Kimiai (1941–) who asked him to write the soundtrack for his film *Qeisar* (1969) – a box-office hit and a cult film. Upon completion of the *Qeisar* soundtrack, Monfaredzadeh left for Munich, Germany, in April 1969 to study music. He returned to Tehran in April 1970 to receive an award for his *Qeisar* soundtrack at the Sepas Film Festival and decided to stay (Monfaredzadeh 2017: 663–4). After *Qeisar*, he became a coveted composer (Darolshafai 2012). Then, Kimiai asked him to write another soundtrack for his upcoming movie *Reza Motori* (1970), also a hit, starring the iconic

Behrouz (Khalil) Vossoughi (1938–). Monfaredzadeh wrote the melody, and with Ghanbari's captivating lyrics 'Mard-e Tanha' ('The Lonesome Man') was born. This was a creative moment for Monfaredzadeh as he brilliantly juxtaposed traditional melodies with Western and classical music with a simple but impressive arrangement. Farhad's vocal represents a narrator's voice and does not have much phrasing (Kharrazy 2020). The movie won two Sepas Film Festival awards (1970): best actor in the leading role, Vossoughi, and best original soundtrack, Monfaredzadeh.

Let us momentarily diverge: Ghanbari had spent his youth in Europe and returned to Iran with the memory of the revolutionary uprisings of 1968. In 1970, he wrote the lyrics 'Qesseh-ye Do Mahi' ('The Tale of Two Fish'). With music by Babak Afshar, arrangement by Varoujan, and sung by eighteen-year-old Googoosh, this sad, allegorically rich and suggestive song about a fish's mourning and reminiscing about her love who was taken by a seagull, and her awaiting the same inescapable fate, was a hit and established Ghanbari as a sought-after lyricist. 'After us it is the other couples' turns / it's the day of the ugly deaths of other hearts / . . ./ I don't want to be alone / be a fish in the sea / from now on, I like / to be in fables.' This is a song about a milieu where love, plain and simple, is oppressed. Sarfaraz regards 'The Tale of Two Fish' as having launched the New Song-Writing. Released as single on a 45-rpm seven-inch record in March 1971 (almost coincidental with Siahkal), it sold hugely.

Back to our discussion. Monfaredzadeh was looking for a distinct voice to sing 'The Lonely Man'. Admittedly, Monfaredzadeh (2008, 2014) was intentional about his choice of voices (preferring Farhad and Googoosh). He wanted new voices for his new music. This is when he crossed paths with Farhad, who was initially reluctant to sing for a movie but was eventually persuaded. Farhad was a spiritual and reclusive artist who between 1971 and 1979 only sang eleven songs, seven of them in collaboration with Monfaredzadeh (Darolshafai 2012). This is a significant moment: three faces of Iran's protest music converged to create a most memorable song for an unambiguously non-political film (about a smart burglar who is betrayed and dies at the end). In this case, Monfaredzadeh wrote music to Ghanbari's words. Ghanbari's magical expressions and tropes, Monfaredzadeh's stylish music, sung with Farhad's ethereal and emotional voice, rendered the song explosive. The song was produced as a top-seller record single, presenting Farhad to the public, making him a superstar. Adding mystique to the song, the dissidents of the time interpreted that 'The Lonely Man' alluded to Samad Behrangi's tragic death (believed to be a SAVAK conspiracy) – a man who stood 'tall like a mountain' and whose life was 'short like a sleep' (Parand 2012a):

The Lonely Man

With a soundless voice
tall like a mountain
short like a sleep
there was a man, a man.
With poor hands
deprived eyes
fatigued legs
there was a man, a man.

The night, with its black coffin
sat in his eyes
the star grew dark
and fell on the ground.
Not even his shadow
had ever stood behind him
he was sad and fatigued
the loneliest of all.

With thirsty lips
he did not reach
the picture of a spring to see
a drop, drop, drop of water, drop of water.
In the pulseless night
this way, that way
he fell to hear
the sound, sound, sound of a step, sound of a step.

Do the lyrics sound like a soundtrack written for a crime movie? Aside from Vossoughi's splendid acting and a coherent script by Kimiai (see Chapter 5), the movie relates no social or political message. The song's reference to this forlorn man, of course, connects it to the movie's protagonist and his dying alone. But the referentiality of the song stops there. The image of a man so lonely that not even his shadow stands behind him, when sung with the assertive vocals of Farhad and his articulate scanning of words, can be politically suggestive: this man could be the political activist of this day, right before the Siahkal operation. And yet this is not an anthem: the lyrics' *existential tone* sounds like an elegy for a man in the pulseless night of political repression. Amazingly, the lonely man did not reach the spring to see the drop of water and fell before he could hear the 'sound of a step': in retrospect, the step of clandestinely advancing (Siahkal) guerrillas just a few months later. Ghanbari's anticipation is uncanny, as were the anticipative poems of Shamlu and Farrokhzad (Chapter 2). Ghanbari's brilliance resides in his deployment of new symbolism: his metaphors and tropes are not extracted from the available, generous arsenal of post-Nimaic tropology. The night is 'pulseless', like a 'black coffin', and the man is 'tall as a mountain' and 'short as a sleep'. The reader can appreciate how fresh this imagery is. New Song-Writing changed the nature of simile (Mohammadian-Omriyan and Torki 2015: 121–3). This may generate disagreements, but I argue that 'The Lonely Man' marks the watershed moment in Iran's protest song.

These new songs deploy new metaphors, tropes and symbols, releasing them into the public subconscious, thus delivering poetry's post-Nimaic symbolism from the realm of the intellectuals and literati to public culture. 'Words such as "night, story, crying, body, soil, exile, voice, shadow, death, leaving, mirror, wall, name, shouting, blood, belief, solitude, stranger, wound, fear, sob, sunset, jungle" are counted in this order as the most frequently echoed words used in these songs and [these words] accompany [a] specific ideological load' (Mohammadian-Omriyan and Torki 2015: 116). These words, among many others, suggest a political message primed with an existential angst.

What connects 'The Tale of Two Fish' and 'The Lonely Man', as suggested, is a certain *existential* undertone, an expression of *collective anxiety*, in the lyrics. Indeed, one of the arch-characteristics of the New Song-Writing — which reflects the mood of the young at the turn of the 1960s to the 1970s, a mood that also fed this generation's turn to militant opposition — is the inseparable presence in the lyrics of streaks of pessimism, fatalism, even nihilism, and at times, a resignation to the oppressive conditions. Even love songs of this genre are not exempt from this (see Mohammadian-Omriyan and Torki 2015: 126). This feature is indeed what is 'new' about the New Song-Writing: unlike the naive and banal love songs of dominant popular music, the new songs reflect how these composers and lyricists alike – representing educated young people – pondered and reflected on their social conditions: profoundly concerned about the conditions of their homeland and finding themselves socially and intellectually detached from the masses (just like the guerrillas), and making efforts to 'educate' them through their art. So, the tripartite effects of armed propaganda – communications, metonymic and political – are present in the New Song-Writing Movement, albeit unwittingly. The New Song-Writing was not purely driven by commercial interests – at least not for its trailblazers. The ambient events in society grew over the song-writing process. Neither *tasnif* nor commercial pop *taraneh* had the musical and lyrical capacity to echo society's rapid and painful transmutations. This is how song-writing felt the need for a different process: now, composers would seek out the lyrics that would reflect the greater, collective need for expression and write melodies on them (Jannatie-Ataie 2011). As Monfaredzadeh puts it, 'That is why as . . . the producer, I would seek out the poem and made it into a [song's] lyrics' (2008).

Music is the most popular of all arts. Jannatie-Ataie declares that because seeing and hearing are easier than reading, songs are the most popular and influential of the arts (Jannatie-Ataie 2007). 'Furthermore, and this is quite important, among the arts, music is the most inclusive and salient communal discursive space, because . . . it is present in most Iranians' lives in multiple forms and forums, and unlike theatre or film, can be consumed while other life activities are going on. Music is also more affordable' (Siamdoust 2017: 19). Music could be listened to at home and at work, and later, with cassette tapes, everywhere and even while driving, and nowadays it is totally portable.

The seeds of Iran's protest songs, therefore, go back to the late 1960s' new genre of songs and a growing music industry. *Deeply concerned about their thraldom to state censorship and repression, the artist-protagonists of the*

New Song-Writing challenged the status quo through both poetic symbolism (at times convoluted) and media expansion, and they found the soundtrack as a most valuable medium through which to communicate their ideas to society before this avenue was blocked by the state. But just like poetry, society needed the *event* for chanted expressions of defiance to surface. Siahkal provided the wished-for event and highly politicised songs; 1971 proved to be the year of protest music (Darolshafai 2012), and Farhad and Dariush emerged as its principal voices. Unbeknownst to the PFG, there was already a cohort of musical artists prepared to promote the cause of the militants through the music of defiance. Censorship's grip on Iranian arts was only tightened after Siahkal. That is when protest song came up with the most creative ways of challenging the state and voicing the concerns of a generation.

Protest Songs: Semiological Guerrilla Warfare

The 1960s were, *inter alia*, the decade of protest songs worldwide. Among the most internationally renowned protest singers were Bob Dylan and Joan Baez in the United States. *Just like the worldwide urban guerrilla movements, the protest song was part of a global movement of a generation yearning to bring about meaningful change.* Protest songs primed cultures, especially youth cultures, for critical engagement with the status quo in a world torn by revolutions, and by student, women's, civil rights and liberation movements on the one hand, and imperialist wars and military juntas on the other.

Just as protest song has been a global movement, so were 'new song' movements across the world. Thus, Iran's New Song-Writing – although coming from its vernacular roots musically and lyrically and its specific global influences – was also not unique to Iran either. The case in point is *La Nueva Canción* or the 'new song' movement (a.k.a. *trova* or *canto*) in Latin America. It originates with songs in the 1950s and 1960s in the southern tip of Latin America with hybrid music consisting of Andean and European instruments and melodies with politicised lyrics that referred to imperialism, social movements, poverty, democracy and so forth in the face of brutal military dictatorships. The US-backed coup that deposed the democratically elected President Salvador Allende in Chile in 1973 also resulted in transforming one of the most famous faces of *La Nueva Canción,*

Victor Jara (1932–73), into one of Chile's greatest revolutionary martyrs. Unlike its Iranian counterpart, Latin American protest music (particularly in its birthplace in Chile, Argentina and Uruguay) has been the subject of extended studies (see Chornik 2018; Morris 1986), and this is partly due to its extended reach, unlike the Iranian case.

The original protest song movement in Iran was a subset of the New Song-Writing, but the former cannot be thought without the latter. As young poets and lyricists, the protagonists of protest songs were impressed by this global trend, feeling the urge to radically rethink the potential of song-writing for their generation, one that emerged from a rising middle class and increased urbanisation and industrialisation of the country, that produced a different experience for this generation than the one captured in the previous generation's artistic imagery (Jannatie-Ataie 2005: 62; 2013a; 2013b). The Siahkal operation *inadvertently* catalysed the protest song movement. To be clear, there are two interrelated phenomena here: *taraneh-ye novin* was a movement that cultivated within it political, *protest songs*. The latter is a subset of the former, just as the former is the latter's artistic condition of possibility. Interpreting history from this particular angle, what happened after February 1971 was that challenging the US-backed state by the PFG and other militants was translated into the *taraneh-ye novin*'s challenging the censorship intended to force a politically conformist culture. The confrontation of protest song writing and censorship in the 1970s, however painful, stands out as a fascinating cultural and linguistic phenomenon. It was possible for poetry to 'bypass' censorship when the poet would pocket a copy of his about-to-be-censored poetry collection from the print shop and duplicate and distribute copies 'illegally' among his peers (as did Kushabadi). University students were more than happy to stencil-copy handwritten versions of entire books, as I did also. But to circumvent censorship thus was out of question for songs in the age of radio, cinema and records (before cassette tape). Besides, unlike poets, who always had a bills-paying job in some capacity (sometimes in government ministries), song-writers, singers and composers mostly made a living out of their collaborative art. As such, protest song-writers ended up putting out a fierce 'semiological guerrilla warfare', to borrow a marvellous term from Umberto Eco (1986), against state censorship. From the communications point of view, the new song actualised the possibility of a diverging field of message, of a branching-off from both traditional and pop song, and thus, readers experienced a sort of freedom in interpreting the lyrics and music in an unsanctioned way. In Eco's words (in a different context), 'For the receiver of the message seems to have a residual freedom: the freedom to read it in a *different* way' (1986: 138; original emphasis). *Censorship, the media henchman of a repressive state, was set up to repress not just this or that metaphor and the 'politically incorrect' interpretations of it. More radically, censorship was instituted to ban difference. And the defiant generation of the 1970s aimed at winning the right to be different.* In a dialectical fashion, the 'protest' element in the songs was indeed the consequence of censorship. Jannaite-Ataie claims that protest song in a repressive country would not be a *protest* song in a democratic society (2011). I am very hesitant to fully endorse his observation: in America, with its exemplary freedom of speech, we still have protest poetry and song: Allen Ginsberg, Jack Kerouac (and Dylan and Baez) are cases in point. Nevertheless, these new artists turned out to be superbly adept at it. They believed that 'society was ready for a different view in songs and lyrics', and 'new songs and lyrics could prepare society . . . teach it solidarity, teach it love, even teach it fighting. Songs play a very sensitive role in our society' (Eghbali 2011). They also strongly adhered to style and the artistic merit of their work. As the famous vocalist Dariush Eghbali (2017) reflects, 'Our view was different from [the then dominant] previous music. Our music was to protest in the language of love, not in the language of rage (*khashm*), not in the language of agitating (*tahiij kardan*) people, not in the language of picking up arms. I was shocked seeing that I lived in a country where people do not see what is going on behind the curtain.' The statement clearly reflects the social and political commitments of singers, song-writers and composers: their abhorrence of repression and yearning for freedom.

Broadcasting music from state-run radio required the songs that were to be broadcast to be approved by the Music Board (*Showra-ye Musiqi*). Obviously, then, any song with hints of political message would not be cleared for public broadcast. The alternative would be commercial records. But gradually SAVAK became aware of the defiant potential of songs on records and tried to shut down the recording studios. In fact, the performers and singers were required to present their lyrics bearing the stamp of approval by the Music Board to the recording studio. Through these obstacles the state continued not only to censor but also to harass artists (Eghbali 2011; Jannatie-Ataie 2005: 28). As committed semiological guerrillas, the artists did their best to get through censorship and still steadfastly announce their political commentary through their words. So, when it became harder to just release record singles, protest song-writing switched to the soundtrack, something already tried by Monfaredzadeh due to his friendship with Kimiai. Thanks to censorship, *song-writing itself had become a guerrilla warfare of striking and hiding!* At this time, the movie was screened by a particular bureau called the Council of Lyrics and Melody (*Shora-ye She'r va Taraneh*; see Hemmasi 2013: 79, n. 13) and the soundtrack was regarded as only a component of it. At this time, if a song was not intended for radio or television broadcast, it did not need to be cleared by the above screening process. This loophole served protest songs until 1974 when this avenue was eventually blocked and recording studios were no longer allowed to record a song without the approval of the song by the Ministry of Culture and Arts (Darolshafai 2012; Eghbali 2017; Jannatie-Ataie 2005: 45; Monfaredzadeh 2014; 2017: 672). Furthermore, to tighten the grip, a SAVAK agent would be sent to studios to review and compare the recorded material with the officially approved song, and only then would he allow the studio to release the recorded song to its owner (Monfaredzadeh 2017: 672). These complexities require from us nimble methods – a combination of social history, literary hermeneutics and discourse analysis to go through shining moments in this battle of linguistic signs. To stay with the thesis of this book, I will engage from this point onward with the specific songs in which the connection between protest songs and militant action in the 1970s is implied.

Friday (1971)

'Jom'eh' ('Friday') registers the first protest song in (proclaimed) reaction to Siahkal and the subsequent expedited trial and execution of the thirteen in March 1971. Originally, Monfaredzadeh wanted to write a song about the gloom and ennui of Friday evenings (Friday is the last day of the week, and equivalent to the Western Sunday), but the 'taboo-smashing Siahkal' had impressed him. 'I thought I could support this movement through a song', he reflects, '[one that was sung] with a solid and distinct voice, like Farhad's' (2017: 665). His preference was to choose poems or lyrics first and then make music for them (Monfaredzadeh 2017: 667), so he invited Ghanbari to write the lyrics. Monfaredzadeh narrates the rest:

> It was a Friday evening. To write the lyrics Shahyar Ghanbari came to my house. I spoke to him about how sad Friday evenings were . . . He said he had experienced the bitterness. This is how he wrote the lyrics on that meeting and I too wrote the melody with love. We gifted this song to the film, *Khodahafez Rafiq* made by our comrade . . . Amir Naderi. 'Jom'eh' was never broadcast from the state radio. But a few weeks after its distribution as a record in stores, when I heard that on Friday evenings the conscript soldiers were singing the song on board army buses that were taking them back to the barracks, I felt happy and hopeful. I had hit the target. 'Jom'eh' was a protest [song], [something] not of the state-sponsored kind of art material, and it had been popularly acclaimed, especially by youth. (2017: 665)

Monfaredzadeh cleverly took advantage of the loophole (not screening the soundtrack) (2017: 666). 'Friday' became the soundtrack of *Khodahafez Rafiq* (*Goodbye Friend*, 1971) directed by Amir Naderi (1946–). The film starred Saeed Rad and was about a burglar who betrays his accomplices and dies at the end. Despite its many flaws, the film is considered one of the first movies representing Iran's New Wave Cinema. Farhad lent his memorable voice, articulate scanning of the words and emotional performance to this song, rendering it a hit song, and Shahbal Shabpareh played the drums. To ensure that the song reaches greater audience, Monfaredzadeh had it recorded also with Googoosh's voice (released later) and even planned to have it sung by the popular singer Ne'matollah Aghasi (Azmudeh; 1939–2005). When, in the autumn of 1971, the single was released, it purportedly became a bestseller, reportedly outselling Aghasi's popular song 'Ameneh' (Darolshafai 2012; Malek 2014: 12) – a claim I find hard to believe, having witnessed the latter's popularity at the time. The song's simple and beautiful rhythm is slow, and it opens with drums, choir and a shaker that sounds somewhat cacophonous. Farhad's distinct vocals also sound slightly detached from the music (Kharrazy 2020). The song certainly suggests a gloomy ambiance, but one that is permeated with ennui and melancholy that sounded through the overdone shakers and percussion:

Friday

In the wet frame of these windows,
I see a picture of the sad Friday.
How black is this mourning attire on its body,
I see in its eyes heavy clouds.
From the black cloud drops blood,
on Fridays blood drops instead of rain.
I cannot breathe, Fridays don't end,
I wish I would close my eyes, but I'm unable to.
From the black cloud drops blood,
on Fridays blood drops instead of rain.
Friday has lived for a thousand years,
on Fridays sadness roams wildly (*bidad mikoneh*),
one gets tired of oneself,
and shouts through lips wide shut:
from the black cloud drops blood,
on Fridays blood drops instead of rain.
Friday is the day of departure, the season of letting go (*del kandan*).
And stabs me in the back, the one who is my companion.
From the black cloud drops blood,
on Fridays blood drops instead of rain.

By its creators' admission, this is a song about Siahkal – a first public artistic reaction to the event. In fact, Ghanbari does have a moving poem about Siahkal, dedicated to the thirteen executed guerrillas, some lines of which appear on the epigraph to this chapter. Monfaredzadeh was admittedly a PFG supporter, and through his friend Kho'i he had met Puyan. For him, the PFG was protesting the very conditions that he was objecting to, but through different means (Monfaredzadeh 2014). However, it is hard to connect the words to the event hermeneutically. The referentiality of Siahkal is well hidden within the lyrics' forest of words, just like the well-trained guerrillas. No wonder the song escaped SAVAK and became a bestseller. This is at the time when the newly-founded PFG was engaged in life-and-death battles with state security (1971–2). It is intentionally, I argue, distanced from the event. Frequent allusion to the tedium and emptiness of Fridays fills the song with a sense of being trapped in an unending Friday of life ('a thousand years'). On the 45-rpm record, under the title, there is a curious phrase: 'Dedicated to you as every weekday is a Friday for you'. It was meant to accentuate the feel the artists wished to convey. Furthermore, the refrain, 'from the black cloud drops blood, / on Fridays blood drops instead of rain', sung by Farhad compellingly, stands out as probably the sole political allusion to repression. To the politically-conscious of the time this line might have *suggested* Siahkal, but for us fifty years later it does not. That refrain, once interpreted in a particular way and attached to the event, guides us to interpret other tropes and signifiers in a political manner: mourning attire; 'shouts through lips wide shut'; and not being able to 'close my eyes' to what is happening around me. At times, then, *the context and lived experience of the community determine the process of signification – one that is achieved through a lateral and collective intentional interpretation. Sometimes suggestion works more effectively than denotation.* All one needs is a community of interpreters: at least one account holds that, amazingly, the young people who listened to 'Jom'eh' in the early 1970s already knew the song was *intended* for Siahkal (see Hemmasi 2013: 63). *Suggestion produces intentional listening.* Regarding protest songs under censorship, the community of deliberate inferences plays an even more pivotal role: it interprets the art not just for the art enthusiasts but also for the layperson in the street.

The Fairies (1972)

Shamlu's 'Pariya' ('The Fairies', 1953) has been enthusiastically celebrated by scholars (Ghanoonparvar 1984: 129–47; Hemmasi 2013; Karimi-Hakkak 1977). It was called 'a landmark in modern Persian poetry. In it dance, song, music and poetry merge, while the deceptively simple and childish story becomes the vessel containing a far-reaching allegory' and 'the prophesy of an imminent revolution' (Karimi-Hakkak 1977: 204–5; see Ghanoonparvar 1984: 131). 'The Fairies' is dated 1953, the year of the coup, and was published in *Fresh Air* (*Hava-ye Tazeh*; 1956). It was composed in the tradition of Persian *matal*: rhymed and rhythmic short folk fables orally transferred down the generations.

In short, 'The Fairies' is narrated in 'rhythmic appeal and musical quality' (Ghanoonparvar 1984: 130) from the viewpoint of a tall horseman on a white horse who encounters three weeping fairies outside the 'town of captive slaves', the jingle-jangle sound of whose chains can be heard. Trying to cheer them, he heralds that the 'ding dang of the slaves' shedding their chains' can now be heard. The fairies continue weeping, making the horseman's announcement about ending injustices of the world futile. To shake them out of their state, he touches them and is stunned in witnessing that the fairies are actually sorcerers: one becomes a jug of wine, the other a sea, and the last one a mountain. He drinks the wine, travels across the sea to the other side and reaches the peak of the mountain, thus quashing the sorcerers' magic. The people are now liberated: 'Since the people aroused / life became ours.' It is interesting to see that none of the poem's praisers cared to point out its narrative inconsistency: the narrative connection of the fairies to enslavement of people is at best *implied* in the simultaneity of the deliverance of the slaves and the destruction of the fairy-appearing sorcerers by the liberator. The poem's structure is also disjointed and only held together through refrains that nonetheless cannot compensate for the lack of consistency. There is certainly a 'didactic message' (Ghanoonparvar 1984: 144) to the poem. It is celebrated, as an added value, for its significance in 'bringing together the literary and the common modes of speech' (Karimi-Hakkak 1977: 204) and was apparently a successful case of this, although I am not sure how one measures significance and success when one declares: 'The success of "The Fairies" stunned even the poet himself, who for twenty years had insistently discounted its importance' (Karimi-Hakkak 1977: 205). Such statements reveal how the intelligentsia simply regard the 'people' as an extension of themselves and the world as the perimeter of their own worldview. Laypersons did not read Shamlu; they read Karo.

Yet, in April–May 1972, nineteen-year-old Dariush put a melody using the traditional Dashti *dastgah* on his abridged version of 'Pariya' (cutting down the 180-line poem into a 29-line lyric). 'This melody was then arranged by Parviz Maghsadi for an ensemble of Western instruments, including strings, woodwinds, electric bass, and trap set, and recorded for Bibiyan's Apollon label in Tehran' (Hemmasi, 2013: 68). It was later arranged by Abdi (Abdolreza) Yamini (1953–2009) (see Hemmasi 2013: 67; Mohammadi 2016: 239). Musically, although Dariush has delivered decent vocals, the song sounds more like traditional music, even reminiscent of Shi'i *rowseh* (Kharrazy 2020), which might explain some of the intellectuals' fascination with it – it is a sad, melancholic song:

The Fairies

Once upon a time
Under the blue dome of the heavens
Naked in a sliver of twilight
Sat three Fairies
Sobbing, they cried
Like the clouds of spring
They wept, the Fairies
From the horizon, jingling
Came the sounds of chains
From behind, inside the turret
A night wailing was heard
'Fairies, are you hungry?
Fairies, are you thirsty?
Fairies, are you tired?
Are you birds with bound wings?
Dear Fairies,
What happened that you weep so?
In this distant desert
Don't you wish it would snow?'
Our world was not a fable
There was no hidden message
Our world is very clear
Anyone who wants to understand it, can
Our world has thorns
Its deserts have snakes
Everyone wants a piece of it
Its heart is known to everyone
Our world is great
Whether you like it or not, that's the way it is.
(trans. Farzaneh Hemmasi and Mohammad Hemmasi; Hemmasi 2013: 84)

The fairy-seeming sorcerers in Shamlu re-emerge as grief-stricken fairies in the song, as if they weep for the existing state of the world. In contrast to Shamlu's version, Dariush's lyrics refers to no liberator, no emancipation, just a folkish *matal* about the oppressive conditions of life: the world is what it is, like it or not. And yet, while the published version of Shamlu's poem was sold in bookstores, 'the sung *"Pariya"* . . . was banned by the state as soon as it was recorded' (Hemmasi 2013: 58). Reportedly, Dariush was subsequently banned from the television variety show *Shesh-o-Hasht* ('Six-Eight') (Mohammadi 2016: 239). Upon submitting the song to the Council of Lyrics and Melody, SAVAK officials declared that it could not be distributed and called in producer Manuchehr Bibiyan (1933–) and Dariush to question them about their hidden motives. Fortunately, copies of the song had already been out and were now in circulation. So SAVAK agents asked for an alternative version with new words (Hemmasi 2013: 69). In Dariush's recollection: 'Pariya' 'was already recorded and people were passing it along . . . When I sang *"Pariya,"* it was just based on a poem that only one layer of society knew about. After my song, the rest of the society muttered it as well' (Dariush as quoted in Hemmasi 2013: 70). Dariush regards the 'The Fairies' as a formative experience, 'as the first time he realised *the political potential of his music*, an understanding he considers to guide his current work as a singer of "social-political" (*siyasi-ejtema'i*) songs' (Hemmasi 2013: 68).

As mentioned, the revolutionary spirit of Shamlu's *matal* was replaced by a sense of resignation ('that's the way it is') in the song. But I argue, as SAVAK's reaction attests, this resignation is quite sobering and alerting. Bibiyan recalls the SAVAK agent's remarks that confirm my observation: 'Don't you know that when *"Pariya"* is sung, people will start interpreting it? [People] will give it to children to sing in their classes – *"Pariya,* are you hungry? Are you thirsty?"' (Bibiyan as quoted in Hemmasi 2013: 70).

The adventures of the song prove that *songs can go where poetry cannot* – attesting to the potentially huge social impact of protest songs. Given the 'communicative efficacy of popular music and poetry under conditions of political repression', '[m]ass mediation and high levels of circulation are two critical factors in popular music's dissemination of politics to various publics' (Hemmasi 2013: 58). I disagree with the observation that SAVAK's sensitivity in this case is due to 'its popular music form [and] disambiguated and publicised meanings, creating a more directly oppositional text than the original poem' (Hemmasi 2013: 58). In fact, I am surprised not to see 'disambiguation' in the original poem, which has denotative signifiers like 'slave', 'the people's city', 'oppression' and, of course, '*khalq*' (people), a revealing signifier of Marxist political jargon. Dariush's lyrics in fact heavily sanitised Shamlu's poem (only keeping the word 'chain'). I infer that SAVAK's sensitivity towards this song is an outcome of the *Siahkal effect*. 'The Fairies' trails 'Friday', and by this time everyone, above all SAVAK, knows the political intentions behind 'Friday'. SAVAK decided to be proactive in this case, I submit, knowing that while Shamlu's poems are for intellectuals (and intellectuals by and large have names and addresses and can be paid surprise visits), the song is for the masses who enjoy anonymity, and that anonymity is the source of nightmare for all states, but particularly the security apparatus of a repressive regime.

The sung version of 'The Fairies' outlasted the regime that had banned it and remains a popular Dariush *taraneh*. Its operatic version in English, created by Sheyda Gharachedaghi, went on stage in Toronto in 1989 and was recently released as an audio CD. It is the first opera written by a female Iranian composer and was banned in Iran because it contained a female lead vocalist (Akbarzadeh 2020). The song is now exilic.

Jungle (1973)

According to its lyricist, the Iranian protest song began with 'Jangal' ('Jungle') (Jannatie-Ataie 2005: 44), although Sarafarz and I believe the protest song precedes Siahkal and begins with 'The Tale of Two Fish' or 'The Lonely Man'. Young Jannatie-Ataie had begun writing lyrics in the mid-1960s. He had also recited poetry at the Khusheh Poetry Festival and then decided to switch to *taraneh* so he would speak of the angst of his generation (Jannatie-Ataie 2005: 38). His collaboration with Parviz Maghsadi established him as a visionary lyricist. With its rich, captivating keyboard, guitar and drums, the undying 1965 love song 'Gol-e Sorkh' ('Red Rose') was sung by the incomparable Viguen. 'The red rose that you gave me / withered in the silence of my home / the fire of love and affection / grew dim in the autumn of my chest' (I will return to this song!).

Created through the collaboration of Jannatie-Ataie with his childhood friend and composer Babak Bayat (Jannatie-Ataie 2005: 60–1; Khoshnam 2017: 644) and Dariush, 'Jungle' was indeed about the Siahkal guerrillas (Eghbali 2017). As Dariush reminisces, 'I acquired political awareness besides these dear ones' (Eghbali 2017). Interestingly, Jannatie-Ataie rejects that he 'intentionally' wrote the lyrics about the Fadai guerrillas. He explains:

> Their [the wanted guerrillas'] images [Chapter 1] were printed and posted in the streets, [as security forces] were looking for their comrades ... The ordinary people in the streets were full of sadness and rage [about it]. It wasn't possible for you to live in the city and love the people, your child, your father, your lover, and not feel how imposing this atmosphere was. People cried [for the executed militants]. It was a new experience. Radio and television had spoken of them [the guerrillas], and the entire society was entangled with this issue. As a member of that society, I too realised that there was an event that surrounded me and didn't let go of me. (Jannatie-Ataie 2010b)

In other words, his lyrics were born of a collective sense of being choked. And this was a shared feeling. Jannatie-Ataie (2013a) is very clear about this song being not actually a political statement about Siahkal but his *impression of*, and empathy with, the militants trapped between hostile military and the frightened peasants they had fought to liberate. According to Dariush, 'When Iraj described "Jungle" [to me], I already knew what had happened in Siahkal. [The soundtracks for the film] *Ali Konkuri* [*Konkur Exam Ali*, 1973] was also interpreted in this way for me and I sang them knowingly' (Eghbali 2011). But perhaps the humble comportment of the Siahkal guerrillas towards the villagers was even more gripping, 'the fact that some villagers had helped police to capture the militants but the guerrillas did not hurt them. These things seethed in me and I wrote that song' (Jannatie-Ataie 2005: 44–5). He refers to the incident when, in trying to rescue their apprehended comrade, three guerrillas, including commander Safai-Farahani, were captured by frightened villagers who tied them up and tortured them for several hours before the gendarmes arrived and took away the prisoners. Out of their love of the people and against every rule of guerrilla warfare, these armed militants had decided not to hurt these men – a remarkable show of humanity. Jannatie-Ataie explains how he came up with this particular song:

I did not write this [song] because we were supposed to be in their [the guer-rillas'] place in Siahkal and being attacked from behind by police forces and attacked from the front by the villagers who had been told that these [guerrillas] had come to kidnap [their] women and children. This was the feeling that not only I but also other artists had in that period . . . Clearly, we got impressions from the important and propagated events in society. (Jannatie-Ataie 2010b)

Soon a popular song among intellectuals, 'Jungle' offered a clean and beautiful melody presented through a straightforward arrangement and clear recording. Dariush delivered one of his best vocals as he sang the lyrics in fidelity to the mood of the words (Kharrazy 2020). The sounds of the instruments – flute, strings, cymbal and snare drum, all played softly – merge, causing the tune to flow like water. The flute track, in particular, brilliantly sways the music and harmonises beautifully with Dariush's vocals.

Thanks to censorship, 'Jungle' could only be released as a soundtrack, and it landed on the 1973 film *Khorshid dar Mordab* (*The Sun in the Swamp*), written and directed by M. Saffar. Although top actors Saeed Rad, Fakhri Khorvash and Mohammad Ali Keshavarz starred in it, this is a filmfarsi (see Chapter 5) production that exploits the themes of honour sororicide and the demise of the supercilious culprit that define this genre. The story takes place in the lush jungles of Gilan where a bizarre, isolated family shelter a murderer who gets killed at the end after sleeping with the family's young daughter. Since the film makes frequent but irrelevant references to the jungle's myster-ies, a song about a desperado fighting his foes in the jungle seems fitting:

Jungle

Behind me, behind me is inferno
in front of me, in front of me, the abattoir of man.

The spirit of the black forest
with the hand of its branches
is taking my spirit away.
As soon as I pause for a moment
the owls whisper in each others' ears
that the wounded leopard is dying.

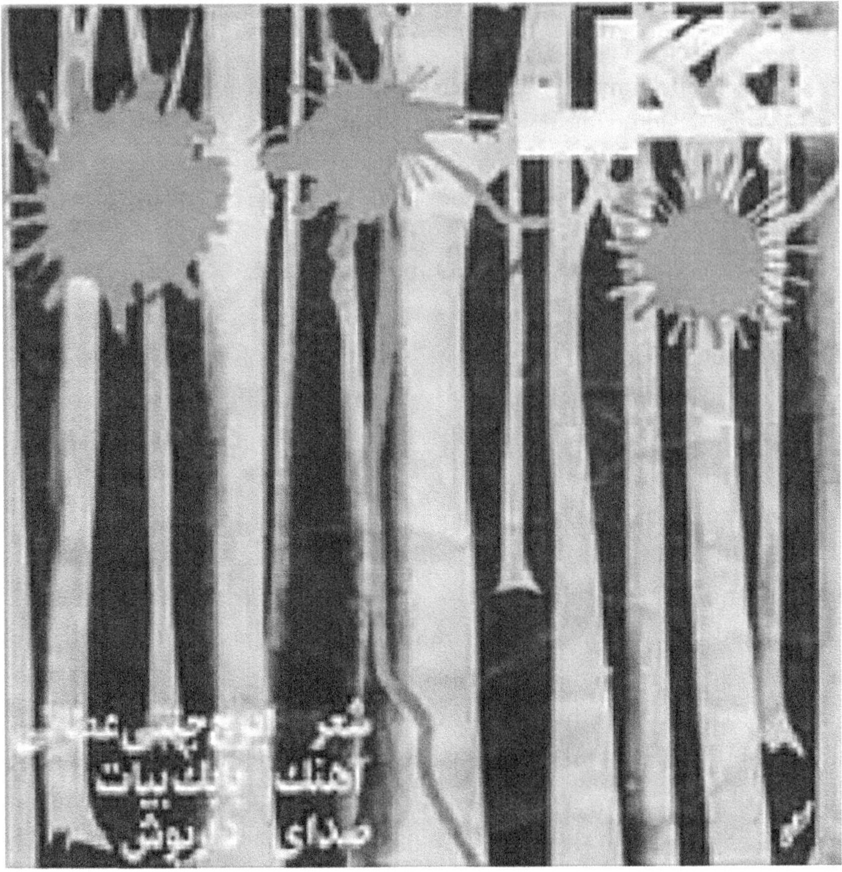

Figures 3.1 (above) and 3.2 (opposite) Jacket covers of the record single 'Jungle' (1973). Three blood splatters on the front and back represent the three artists, as if shot. The front cover shows thirteen tree trunks accentuated against a silhouette of the jungle's nocturnal background – a reference to the execution of the thirteen Siahkal guerrillas. The jacket provides unmistakable cues towards interpreting the lyrics.

There are no other ways for taking
the mourning stand (*hejleh*) of my decay
is the old jungle.
The heart of the humble moon
is captured by the noose of the branches
and I see its twilight.
The dread of going in my body

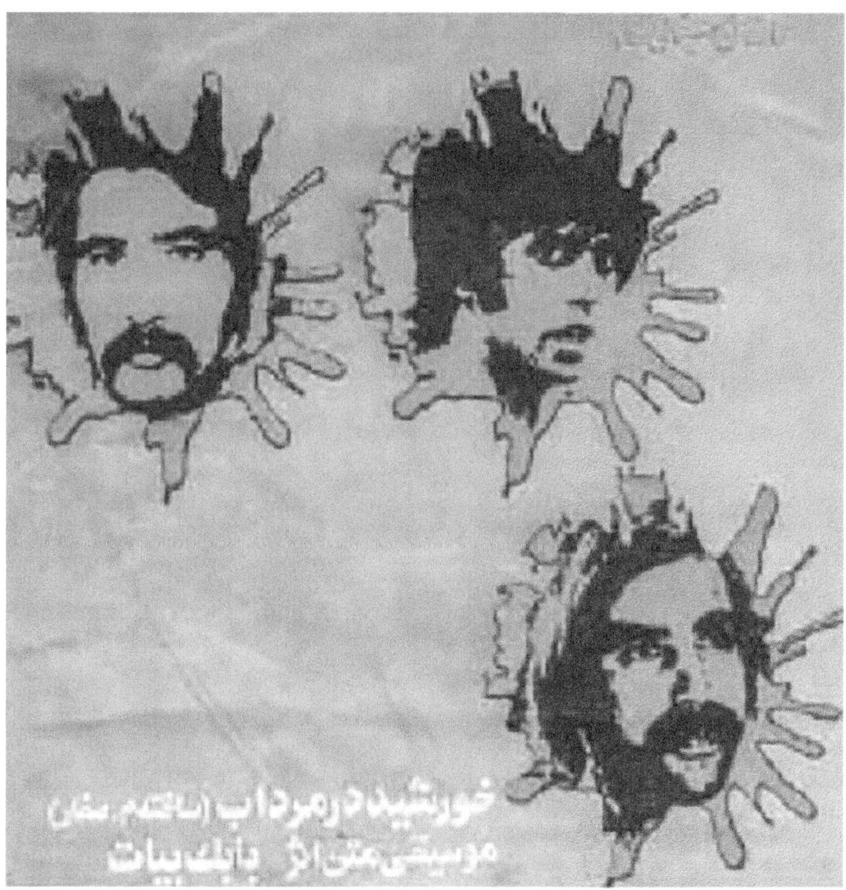

the fright of staying in my heart
and I dream of returning.
In every step
and in every moment
I see the shadow of my enemy.

Authorial intent, for us fifty years later, allows for seeing the reference to Siahkal or at least finding this a political *chanson*. But I strongly doubt whether the audience of that filmfarsi or the record would have been able to connect the two. The music's slow rhythm and the soft flow of the flute and violin certainly invite reflection on the carefully chosen words of the lyricist. Caught in the pincer of an inferno and an abattoir (the refrain

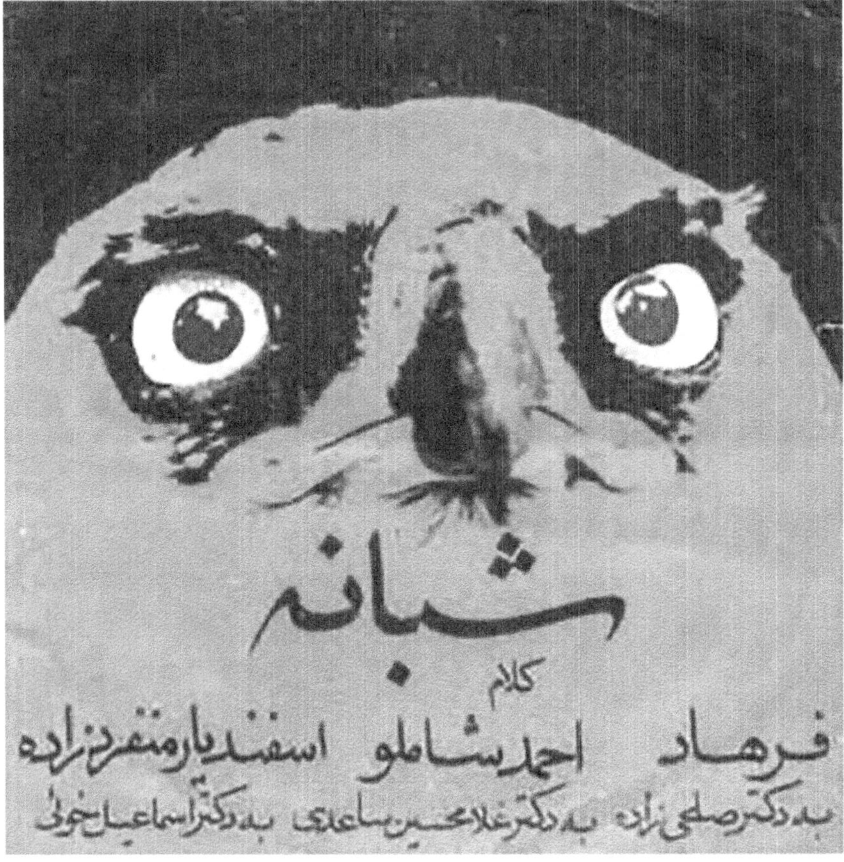

Figures 3.3 (above) and 3.4 (opposite) The explosive jacket cover of the record single 'Shabaneh' (1973) based on images provided by Massoud Massoumi (Monfaredzadeh 2017: 669). Seeing in the dark with exceptional clarity, accentuated with a red overlay against a black background, the owl projects a slanted and piercing gaze towards the top right of the viewer, as if solemnly fixed on a person standing behind and above the viewer's shoulders, surveilling her activity. The nocturnal bird clearly represents the night. (Black and red are anarchist colours, although I doubt that was intended here.) On the back cover, the three artists (from left: Monfaredzadeh, Shamlu, and Farhad) appear lined up on a slot machine right above a triple seven: jackpot. At the top, the second coin from the right shows the Shah's profile bowing down to the American flag on the left. If the song itself had left any ambiguity about its message, the bold jacket artwork certainly clarified it! Not surprisingly, the jacket was banned as soon as the record hit the market.

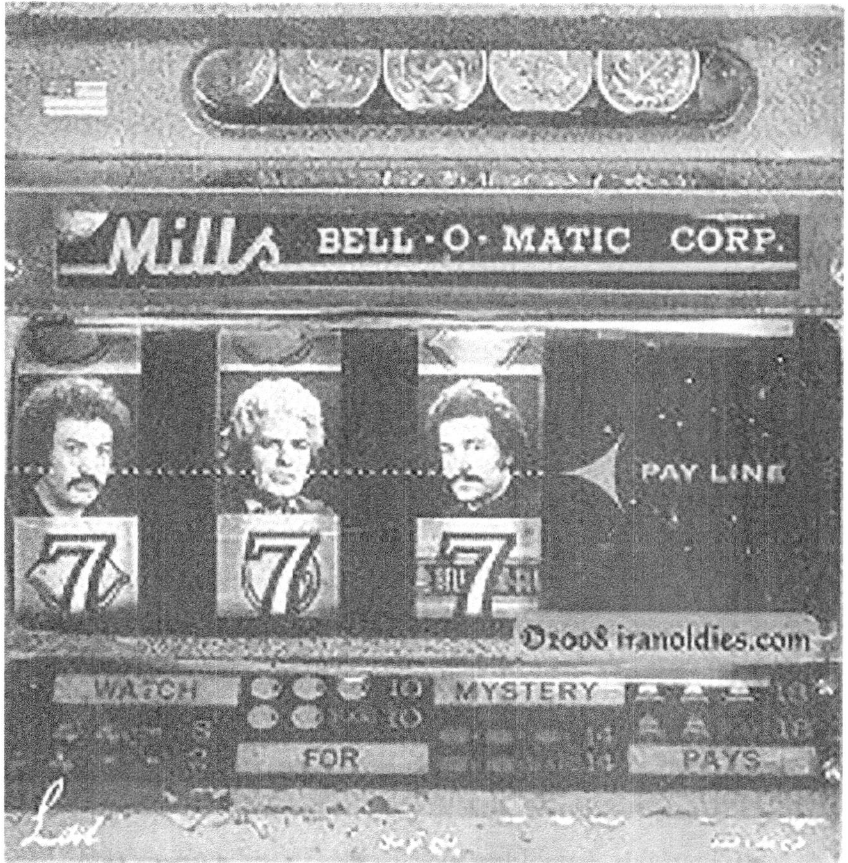

that repeats three times), the wounded leopard (the guerrillas) is about to die, and now I am brought to the choice of leaving or staying, both equally frightening: this is indeed an existential choice of a generation that Jannatie-Ataie beautifully captures, in a society where in every step I see my enemy's shadow. By this time, 'jungle' was already a metaphor known to censorship. Other signifiers (enemy, noose, fear) are self-explanatory. New signifiers such as '*hejleh*' (mirrored stands that are erected to announce a young person's death), owl and the moon create an eerie ambiance while offering new metaphors. Miraculously, the song gets away with censorship and becomes a record.

To make matters more interesting, the record jacket artwork turns out to be equally explosive (Figures 3.1 and 3.2). The song's significatory connotations are skilfully linked to the referentiality of jacket images, directing the interpretation of the audience to the extra-poetic intentions of its creators, allowing the attentive listener to decode the coded message within a larger social discourse. *At times, the non-linguistic sign stands out, especially under censorship, to fix the concealed discursive suggestions to the event,* revealing that there is no 'outside-text' (Derrida). This is how *suggestion* becomes *denotation.* Only one person is needed to decode this reference, and then it would go viral, only to expose the artists to security forces.

Shabaneh (1973)

In 1973, as guerrilla warfare had begun to gain greater momentum and popularity, arguably the most iconic, explosive and vividly 'political' of all protest songs hit the music market, although it was not connected to the militant movement. With its clear message and rich music and soundscape, this record seems as if all previous protest songs were dress rehearsals for this one. Its captivating jacket artwork, designed by the multi-talented Monfaredzadeh, was in and of itself a work of art (Figures 3.3 and 3.4). It sold an astonishing 10,000 45-rpm record singles (Darolshafai 2012) despite the fact that it was priced almost twice as high as other record singles (50 Rls versus 30 Rls). Its price caused Monfaredzadeh to be summoned to the Guilds Chamber (*Otaq-e Asnaf,* the central price regulation bureau) and told that the sale of the record was banned due to the unjustified price mark-up. It turned out that SAVAK had exploited the cost of the record to take it off the market (Monfaredzadeh 2017: 669–70). But why?

I have already discussed *shabaneh* or the 'night(ly) poem' subgenre (Chapter 2) championed by Shamlu. Monfaredzadeh chose one of Shamlu's old *shabaneh* poems. Referring to his love of the movies and collaboration with Kimiai, Monfaredzadeh admittedly regards himself as an 'image music-composer': an image would give him the feel of the tune he wished to compose. So, he arrived at *taraneh* through a soundtrack. That is why, in composing music, he always searched for specific poetry as a guide (Monfaredzadeh 2014). 'Shabaneh' is the best example of his approach. Recorded in Bell Studio in Tehran, the song is completely imaginative. With 'Shabaneh', Monfaredzadeh's music is at its peak: he creates a hauntingly memorable soundscape.

The original poem, dated 1961, was published in Shamlu's *Moments and Always* (1962) and dedicated to Gohar Morad (Gholam Hossein Sa'edi):

Shabaneh

The alleys are narrow, shops closed,
the houses are dark, roofs collapsing.
Tar and kamancheh have fallen silent,
the dead are taken from alley to alley.
Look! Our dead don't seem dead,
they don't even resemble a dead candle.
They're like a lantern that's out
not because it's out of oil, there is still a lot of oil in it.
People, I'm tired of it all,
I've no hope for good and no complaints of evil.
Though I'm not distanced from others,
I've got nothing to do with this bunch.
(Shamlu 2010: 446–8)

My English translation cannot deliver the natural, everyday speech in this poem, written in colloquial Tehrani dialect in which people use a lot of contraction in uttering words. Farhad's firm scanning of the words, sung exactly on note, accentuates the utterance. The sung part of the music is braced between two impressive soundscapes that set the ambiance. Here Monfaredzadeh uses sound effects (rarely used before) in a serious fashion. The music begins with slow drums accompanied by the (inferred) sound of a horse-drawn hearse, dogs barking and belled sheep bleating, before these sounds fade into fast, military-rhythm rimshots that then fall silent so we hear jackals (or wolves) howling yonder while people whisper an unrecognisable buzz (in Persian, *pech-pech*, the sound of 'p' and 'ch' blended together; *pechpech kardan* also means 'to whisper'; the buzzing men happened to be there in Bell Studio and joined in to produce this sound effect). The *pech-pech* was meant to suggest a place where people have to whisper in each other's ears due to fear of security surveillance. Then the musical instruments appear to a slow and simple melody and the key melody is accompanied by a human whistle (Kharrazy 2020). Drums, bass guitar, flute, and what sounds like a comb instrument (or 'comb saxophone': covering the teeth of a comb with parchment or plastic and buzzing through it by sticking the lips into it), take over the rhythm. In the middle of the song, after 'there is still a lot of oil in it', the hooting of an owl appears. In particular passages, back-up male vocalists echo and support Farhad's vocals. Here, again, Farhad appears as a narrator instead of a singer. The music ends with lyrics fading with the first two lines repeating, and the slow drums return, only to fade into the sound of morning birds chirping and a rooster crowing.

The music, in short, is haunting and dark, although at the end it musically diverges from Shamlu's resigned poetic impression. Shamlu wants to have 'nothing to do with this bunch', suggesting that our intellectual has lost hope in good; however, the song ends with the good news of daylight, in contrast to its beginning with the night's encroachment and its subsequent domination as represented by the owl's hooting. In sum, Monfaredzadeh re-imagines Shamlu's poem as a rural experience. As a teenager I listened to this song endlessly on our nifty portable Topaz record-player, while staring back at the owl. I remember that people 'heard' the inaudible whisper to utter 'SAVAK' – a stretch of imagination that Monfaredzadeh rejects (2014).

The poem expresses the dismay of intellectuals living in the post-1953 era. It describes a dying society where all is falling stagnant, silent and dark, as if the dust of death is spread over the land. There stand out for listeners the lines referring to the lantern and oil: I recall that everyone understood that these lines referred to Iran's petro-dollars, in spite of which the country still suffered from serious economic and societal discrepancies. So, the lantern, a metaphor of knowledge, is out not because it lacks fuel but because there is political intent in the lantern's being out, *suggesting* deliberate deprivation of the masses in a country whose ruling class holds the extravagant Persopolis festivals to celebrate monarchy.

'Shabaneh' is indeed the most political song of the New Song-Writing movement in the 1970s. It represents a case of brilliant appropriation and re-interpretation of poetry by the composer that proves the power of music. Shortly after this song, Monfaredzadeh was arrested in relation to a different case.

Today, one experiences a paradox in listening to this song after forty years of the repressive and corrupt Islamic Republic: 'Shabaneh' is indeed a depiction of Iranian society in 2020. Is this because the song offered an exaggerated depiction of the social and political atmosphere of mid-1970s Iran? Or is it because the song will live on as long as there is repression in the country? Or is it because symbols outlive artistic intentions?

The Fine Scent of Wheat (1974)

Though certainly not the most controversial protest song, 'Bu-ye Khub-e Gandom' undoubtedly proved to be the most consequential. It reflects, above all else, the intellectuals' commiseration with the poor – an effect of the polarisation of Iranian society not just economically but also discursively, an awareness raised by the revolutionary literature of the 'guerrilla period' and built upon the growing sentiment of distrust towards the Shah's developmental plans. Six months in the making in Bell Studio, it was reportedly originally intended as a soundtrack. The single's release, it is claimed, was coincided with the Asian Games tournament hosted in Tehran (1–16 September 1974) (Tabatabai 2014), but this is not entirely accurate (see below). Reportedly, its jacket collaged two contrasting images of ruinous abodes in southern Tehran and a mansion in the city's north (Malek 2014: 15; Mohammadi 2016: 284). Dariush sang this richly metaphoric song, written by Ghanbari for the music by Varoujan. Musically, Varoujan created a beautiful, soft and melancholic introduction that continues with steady tonality through the song. Dariush delivered an emotional vocal, although his voice reveals a nasal problem when he sings high notes (Kharrazy 2020):

The Fine Scent of Wheat

The scent of wheat mine, all I have yours
a palm-size field mine, what I grow yours
I'm a plagued inhabitant of this eastern tribe
you're the glassy traveller of *shahr-e farang* [Europe/West]
My skin is made of the night, your skin of red velvet
my garment is my clothing's blisters, yours a leopard's hide
You think of a jungle of steel and skyscrapers
I think of a room your size to sleep in
My body is my soil, your body the wheat's stem
our bodies are the most thirsty, thirsty for a drop of water

Your city *shahr-e farang*, its people cashmere-robed,
my city the city of prayers, its domes covered with gold
Your body like an axe, my body a hard root
the pulse of a heart's picture remains on the tree
I should not be singing elegy for my body's soil
you are a visitor after all, I'm the blood in the veins of this soil
My body doesn't like to be injured by your hand
so I shout along with whoever is here or is not
The scent of wheat mine, all I have mine
a palm-sized ground mine, what I grow mine

The song's narrator is clearly in dialogue with an absent interlocutor whom he represents and distorts. These references would make better sense if we knew the movie's storyline. This never-made movie, written by Fereidoun Goleh (1940–2005), reportedly entailed a love story between a Western woman and an Iranian man (Jannatie-Ataie 2005: 48). In any case, the poem clearly indicates that the silenced interlocutor is a foreigner, a 'glassy traveller of *shahr-e farang*' ('glassy' possibly refers to pale skin, and if so, a figment of Middle Eastern man's objectification of European woman; here Frantz Fanon in *Black Skin, White Masks* comes in handy!), who, wearing 'a leopard's hide', allegedly thinks of the 'jungle of steel and skyscrapers'. The narrator, by contrast, is an underprivileged man from the peasant class in the vicinity of a religious city 'of prayers' with golden domes (Qom? Mashhad?); like 'a hard root', he is one with the soil of his palm-size field, that is 'thirsty for a drop of water'. He is the 'blood in the veins of this soil' because his toil gives life to the barren land, but he is threatened by this 'visitor' whose body is 'like an axe' and ready to injure the narrator. Once these contrasting images are put together, the entire *taraneh* is effortlessly decoded. Unlike other protest songs reviewed here, this song is fairly easy to interpret politically, and anyone can do it too! It represents the firm stance that the country's exploited peasants, representing *khalq* and by extension colonised people, take against foreign domination. The song begins with a piercing image of the status quo's injustice – 'the scent of wheat mine, all I have yours' – but ends with declaratory revolutionary justice: 'the scent of wheat mine, all I have mine'.

However short-lived, the urban guerrilla movement achieved something significant: it polarised society across antagonistic lines. It was almost impossible for Iranians in the 1970s to be neutral about the state of their country. One had to take a stance for or against the Shah and his foreign supporters. Galvanised through the anti-imperialist and anti-dictatorship discourse they vehemently propagated, the PFG nonetheless could not topple the regime through its perceived but unrealised mass movement; however, the Fadaiyan created a pyschological polarity that prepared the Iranian collective psyche for eventually participating in the 1979 Revolution (Vahabzadeh 2010: 246). From the lyrics, I surmise that the script hinged on a failed love story and the separation of the lovers due to external forces greater than their purported power of mutual love. The traveller in this poem is thus rendered only an ersatz of foreigners, one that is discursively positioned within a number of decodable metaphors so that the narrator can easily dismiss her through his constructed binary. But *every binary, à la* Derrida, *is a hierarchy*, precisely because of which, I infer, the dismissal of the foreign agent leads to liberation and justice in the last two stanzas. Accordingly, *the song provides a unique discursive-poetic field for the self-assertion of the Iranian anti-colonial subject. This song belongs to the discourse of national liberation.*

Whether it was because of the song's clear message, or the security's sensitivity about the upcoming Asian Games and the international focus on Iran, or both, security officials decided to descend on the song's creators and other figures of the New Song-Writing. Dariush, Ghanbari and Jannetie-Ataie were arrested. Sarfaraz, Zoland and others were taken in for questioning (Jannatie-Ataie 2005: 29; Malek 2014: 15). Jannatie-Ataie recalls that his place was raided as if the officers intended to arrest armed militants (Jannatie-Ataie 2005: 29). Jannatie-Ataie was released a few weeks later and sent for mandatory military service (Jannatie-Ataie 2005: 66–7). The story of the arrest and imprisonment of Dariush, now a popular singer among the youth, is illuminating. Though initially reluctant to go, he was lured into the residence of the actor Behrooz Behnezhad (1949–). On his way, he reminisces, 'I felt I was choking in this city. There was a sad atmosphere and I wanted to escape from this city.' A few minutes after his arrival at Behnezhad's, SAVAK agents broke the door down and stormed into the apartment 'as if they wanted to arrest the guerrillas'. He was taken to the notorious Evin prison where he was told he had been arrested for insulting the Shah. SAVAK had checked his bank account and pressed him to explain why, as a popular and successful artist, he did not have substantial sums in his account. The interrogators wanted him to confess that he had given sums to the guerrillas. He was interrogated about his 'objectives' and if he was a 'saboteur' (*kharabkar*, today's 'terrorist'). He was repeatedly asked the 'guerrilla question': 'are you following the guerrillas?' (Eghbali 2011). He was also asked about the books he had read and his contacts (Eghbali 2017). Meanwhile, the newspapers reported that he was charged for possession of narcotics (hashish and opium), printing a photograph of the dishevelled, dirty and slender Dariush in front of drug paraphernalia, trying to represent him as a common criminal. But he was clearly imprisoned because of 'Bu-ye Khub-e Gandom' (Eghbali 2011). 'I was not political', he reflects, but 'Evin Prison was for me a university [that taught me] where I was really living! After prison, I developed an interest about social and political issues' (Eghbali 2017). Dariush was not subjected to physical torture, but about a week into his arrest, he was taken to a shooting field at 2 a.m. and tied to a post for execution. The agents kept him tied up for half an hour and then said they had just had a phone call stating that the execution that day had been cancelled (Eghbali 2017). Dariush was arrested on 28 August 1974 (a month prior to Asian Games) and released on 21 March 1975 (less than eight months later) without being charged, and he recalls that he spent six months in solitary (Eghbali 2017; see also Jannatie-Ataie 2005: 66–7). Dariush further reflects on the psychological impact of imprisonment:

> In prison I learned where I was living: in a place where one is imprisoned for a poem, for a song. The good moments of being in the studio were taken away from me, and now whenever I want to record I have to go to the studio several times to get in touch with the feel of the song and express it. I noticed that before going to jail, I would just go to the studio and stand in front of the microphone and sing the song with the image I had constructed for me. (Eghbali 2011)

The condition for his release (in spring 1975) was singing a song to praise the Shah. His friends Bayat and Jannatie-Ataie rushed to save him, composing the songs 'Talayedar' ('Flagbearer', 1974) and 'Rasul-e Rastakhiz' ('Prophet of

Resurrection', 1974). Poorly recorded and sung by Dariush, these were broadcast on national television (Eghbali 2017) but quickly sank into oblivion.

Obviously, these arrests were not just because of the one song. SAVAK was clearly targeting the protagonists of protest songs and wanted to threaten these cultural figures. What is interesting is that Dariush was briefly arrested again in 1975 for signing a song, by Sarfaraz and the composer Fariborz Lachini (1949–), named 'Matarsak' ('Scarecrow'), which can be regarded as a protest song. This was a song about a lover's disillusionment with her fake loved one, hence the word 'scarecrow'. Of course, there are a few fairly suggestive lines in this song: 'but this isn't your fault that we are all scarecrows / feverish, blind, deaf and dumb, we are all servants to the scarecrow.' SAVAK accused Dariush and others suggesting that by 'scarecrow' they meant the Shah. Semiological guerrilla warfare at its best! The song only got clearance for production when the work *matarsak* was changed to *arusak* (doll) and sung by someone else (Eghbali 2017).

Under dictatorships, nimble tropes and elusive signifiers can cause health hazards!

1974: The Censorship Strikes Back

Censorship had conditioned the lyrics that belonged to the New Song-Writing. The semiological guerrilla warfare was at its height by 1974. By now, censorship had mastered the art of decoding language. As Jannatie-Ataie argues, metaphor had become the source of endless suspicion because now censorship assigned specific signifieds to signifiers such that the latter could no longer be metaphors, which by definition contain multiple meanings. The signifier 'night' could no longer mean night *literally*; in the eyes of state censorship 'night' *actually* and always was meant *figuratively*, and its metaphorical and allegorical meanings were fixed. Interestingly, by now both censorship and the New Song-Writing aficionados were 'trained' to interpret the lyrics *only* metaphorically (2005: 28). This collective, *deliberate* interpretation, an outcome of censorship, created a community of listeners for whom the word 'night' never simply referred to the earth's rotation and 'red rose' (or 'red flower', *gol-e sorkh*) had become a proper name, the last name of Khosrow Golesorkhi. Censorship became so ridiculously strict that certain words (night, red flower, dagger) were banned from appearing in songs (Jannatie-Ataie 2005: 52).

In any case, by 1974 the state closed the soundtrack screening loophole. New regulations (mentioned above) made it almost impossible for protest songs to be recorded (Monfaredzadeh 2014). From this point onwards, the 'protest' elements in songs became much subtler and suggestive and created by artists other than the usual suspects of the New Song-Writing, although the artists were steadfast in pushing their work through an exhaustive process of 'negotiating' with censorship, and a few exceptions aside, the heyday of protest song was over until 1978, the year of the Revolution. By 1974–5, guerrilla activity was at its height and attracting greater attention, thanks to the student movement. The sung messages that resonated significantly with the younger generation and reached a much wider audience than any political tract or communiqué had already played an 'educational' role for the people in general, raising awareness about the social and political conditions of their homeland beyond state propaganda. The power of the medium of music proved untameable.

The Ashi Mashi Little Sparrow (1975)

A soundtrack as well, this old folk fable from Kazerun in Fars Province was adapted by Monfaredzadeh for the most outstanding 'guerrilla film' in the history of Iranian cinema: *Gavaznha* (*The Deer*), directed by Kimiai (see Chapter 5). *Gonjeshkak-e Ashi Mashi* is a *matal* in the dialect of Kazerun. The origins of the version used by Monfaredzadeh remain apocryphal, as are all the stories about the rhymed fable ever since the movie's screening. According to Monfaredzadeh, 'Gavaznha was the peak of protest cinema until then. The . . . helplessness of the people in *Gavaznha* was my guide to select a *matal* from folk culture that, as a child, my mother sang in my ears. *Matals* . . . are rhythmic words but without music. I chose *Gonjeshkak-e Ashi Mashi* and composed a music for it' (Monfaredzadeh 2017: 672–3). This means that Monfaredzadeh chose his own version of the *matal*.

There is very little information on this fable, except for one two-page exposé in *Ketab-e Hafteh* (1961), a weekly magazine that Shamlu and Mohsen Hashtroodi (1908–76) edited. This is where Shamlu decided to publish this fable, originally written by the Kazerun native Hassan Hatami (1935–2016), but in doing so he unprofessionally and unjustifiably edited it into a colloquial Persian iteration, thus killing the original Kazeruni dialect (although retaining the lines). Hatami did not approve of Shamlu's misappropriation. In any case, this version is significantly different from the sung version. Hatami's version narrates the story of a sparrow which, having trusted people of different guilds and social statuses – baker, old woman, bride and governor (*hakem*) – is time and again tricked by them and in response retaliates by stealing that which is dear to each. At the end, the governor warned the sparrow not to come back: 'ashi-mashi little sparrow! / don't you sit on our rooftop / it'll rain and you'll be wet / it'll snow and you'll become a snowball / you'll fall in the paint pond (*howz-e naqqashi*)' (Hatami 1961: 120–1). This part also appears in the sung version. In Hatami's original version, the sparrow steals a drum and sings 'The governor is incompetent' (*hakem 'orzeh nadareh*) before soaring high in the sky. Monfaredzadeh's version adds these lines to the preceding:

who'll catch you? the lackey
who'll kill you? the butcher
who'll cook you? the chef
who'll eat you? the governor.

In this version, the sparrow is victimised, in contrast to the original in which it survives. I did not find reliable sources to confirm this, but it is claimed that '*ashi mashi*' means 'don't sit with the shah' (*mashi* as contracted '*maneshin*' or 'don't sit'; Shamlu *speculates* that '*ashi mashi*' means the colour of mung bean soup!). But considering the sensitivity surrounding the film, and himself, Monfaredzadeh changes the last word: 'I self-censored out of fear and changed "*hakembashi*" [governor] in the original *matal* into "*hakimbashi*" [physician]' (Monfaredzadeh 2017: 673). Possibly one of the best works of Monfaredzadeh, the melody brings together Western orchestration with an Iranian musical mood (Kharrazy 2020). It was originally sung by the opera singer Pari Zangeneh (Parirokh Shahyalani; 1939–) and this version appeared at the film's start. However, Zangeneh's vocals do not accord with this song, and detract from it (Kharrazy 2020). This song required a solid and aggressive vocalist: some years later, Farhad sang the song and registered it as one of his own.

Artistically, the choice of a folksong for the soundtrack of a political film could have been inspired by the circumstances surrounding 'The Fairies' and the ability of reconstructed folk tales to deliver political messages. But there is a personal reason: Monfaredzadeh was released from prison, after nine months (September 1973–May 1974), in relation to the case involving a dozen writers and intellectuals whose prominent figures were Golesorkhi and Daneshian (Monfaredzadeh 2017: 670; see Chapter 2). But he was only marginally connected with this group (Samakar 2001: 168) and thus got away without a prison term. It was the first day of filming *Gavaznha*. SAVAK had forced him to commit in writing that he would inform SAVAK if any militant contacted him. He felt isolated and preferred old friends not to approach him. That is why the *matal* that his mother sang to him made sense: 'don't sit on my rooftop', because it will have consequences (Monfaredzadeh 2014).

As I said, though, this is not a political *taraneh* by any measure; yet in 1974 'Ashi Mashi Little Sparrow' – an old folk tale about injustices in the world – was rendered 'political' by virtue of *association*, by virtue of its discursive *attachment* to the film, in short and, more importantly, by being *deliberately positioned* within a *context* that situates, organises and renders a message by pinning it to an existing discursive terrain. This is evidence that protest song in Iran, unlike the majority of political poetry, was powered by *suggestion* – by stating something without stating it.

Poppy (1974–6)

The execution of Golesorkhi and Daneshian on 18 February 1974 left a deep scar on the conscience of intellectuals. Their trial and death proved beyond doubt that, to quote Golesorkhi in his defence statement, 'political charges in Iran do not need proof and documentation', and completely innocent intellectuals like Golesorkhi and Daneshian could be charged, tortured and murdered by the state. We have already seen the poetic responses to their execution. After Golesorkhi's death, Zoland and Sarfaraz decided to dedicate a song to his memory. They composed the song that was titled and started with the word *Gol-e Sorkh* ('red flower' or 'red rose'), but the Council of Lyrics and Melody did not issue a release permit for it. It is crucial to note that after Golesorkhi's death, the word *gol-e sorkh* had become banned. As Jannatie-Ataie observes, if he had written his song for Viguen's hit, 'Gol-e Sorkh', in 1974 instead of 1965, it would have been banned! Upon the artists' insistence, it took them a year of negotiating with the Council and making changes to the lyrics before the song was cleared. '*Gol-e Sorkh*' was replaced with '*shaqayeq*' or 'poppy', and prison (*zendan*) with greenhouse (*golkhaneh*), among other changes. Finally, the permit was issued, and the song was arranged by Andranik Asaturian (1941–2014), sung by Dariush and released in 1976 (Jannatie-Ataie 2005: 47; Malek 2014: 16; Mohammadi 2016: 327). This slow-paced (and difficult to translate) song is clearly an elegy. It became popular, and the hearsay surrounding its referent (Golesorkhi) made it a protest song – one that had defied even the strictest censorship:

Poppy

My heart is in pain like yours, O Poppy, my eyes are oceans of rain, O Poppy!
Severing ties feels like dying, but falling in love is so easy, O Poppy!
O Poppy, my pain goes beyond reckoning because I'm not hurt by strangers
The one who's got my blood on his hands isn't away from me longer than a sigh
O Poppy, O Poppy, O Poppy! You forever-loving flower!

O Poppy, I'm so lonely here, because no one's falling in love here
The grief for his sad love feels like mountains, but my ruined heart feels like glass
O Poppy you were the last lover, you died and love died after you
You were taken at last by mirage, love and regret to the greenhouses of forsaking

We ran, ran, and ran to the story-filled nights
Our paths were tied by fate but in the end we left each other
O Poppy your place was not in a vase, nor in tales, but in the meadow of God
Now what you've left behind is that you're the prince of all lovers

This is a heartfelt, loving elegy, lamenting the loss of a singular life. Please read 'poppy' as '*gol-e sorkh*' and 'greenhouse' as 'prison' to better experience how moving this song really feels. Golesorkhi was friends with many artists, so 'severing ties' (*del boridan*) with him felt 'like dying' to them, while 'falling in love' with this symbol of noble dignity was 'so easy', O Red Flower! Musically, 'Poppy' uses traditional music for its simple harmony, and although the opening, with cymbal, strings, flute, and then drums is impressive, the tune could use better arrangement; for one thing, the drum work could be softer (Kharrazy 2020). The song was released about two years after Golesorkhi's death, in the year the security apparatus finally descended upon the PFG, killing its legendary leader Hamid Ashraf in June 1976, pushing the group to the verge of annihilation. Hesitant and shaken, the PFG returned via the survivors of security raids, but the guerrilla period that had shaped Iran's political life since 1971 was now practically gone.

'Poppy', in this context of decline of militant resistance, reminded Iranians of so many bright young men and women who could not tolerate existence under repressive conditions: some souls picked up weapons to assert that they were alive, some spicked up words.

Shabaneh-2 (1978)

After producing 'Shabaneh' in 1973, Monfaredzadeh returned to Shamlu's poetry and came up with 'Shabaneh-2', a song he was not able to produce until 1978, and on the unfortunate occasion of the massacre of anti-Shah protestors in Jaleh Square in Tehran on 8 September 1978 by the army, a day known as the Black Friday. The massacre was a turning point: after this day the preceding protest movement was transformed into a revolutionary movement that in February 1979 led to the downfall of the monarchy. On the basis of previous experiences of protest songs in appropriating *matal*-like lyrics to convey political imagination ('The Fairies' and 'Ashi Mashi Little Sparrow'), Monfaredzadeh chose another 'Shabaneh' from *Fresh Air* (1958). Dated 1954, this poem was written in prison when Shamlu was arrested after the coup (Shamlu 1958: 147–51; 2010: 184–7). This is a long folkish rhyme (62 lines) in four verses, and is a modern *matal* with a *mélange* of folk imagery (night, moon, bucolic setting) and personages (fairy, Uncle Yadegar) and modern (politicised) signifiers (street, martyr, blood). The first two verses of the poem charmingly depict the parables of a fairy emerging from the desert to bathe in the spring, followed by the willow tree trying to reach the sky to pick a star, and these two sections do not seem narratively connected to the last two and their political overtone, except through the starting refrain to the first three verses: 'on a moonlit night / the moon comes to my dream / and she takes me . . .' In each of the three verses the moon takes 'me' to a different place. Here are the last two sections of the poem that are relevant to our discussion:

Shabaneh-2

On a moonlit night, the moon comes to my dream
and out of prison she takes me like a moth

she takes me where in the dark night
till morning, holding lanterns of blood,
the martyrs of our town announce until sunrise
in the streets and at the squares
      'Uncle Yadegar! O avenging man!
      Are you drunk or sober? Asleep or awake?'

We are drunk and sober
O martyrs of our town,
we are asleep and awake
O martyrs of our town!
One night at last the moon will emerge,
from behind the mountain and over the valley
and will pass smiling
above this square

Sung by the incomparable Farhad, and given his emphatic scanning and inscription in which every word of the poem comes to life with vivid weight, this 'folk' song leaves no doubt about its political overtone. Mind you: the poem was selected in 1973 but its *revolutionary* relevance, by virtue of its *pronounced* connection with and dedication to the Jaleh Square tragedy, in which hundreds of protesters were killed and injured, only came to life in 1978. In other words, this is a case of social and political *overdetermination* of the literary work, a phenomenon that had not left protest song and New Song-Writing ever since their inception. The song entered the age of the cassette tape, a medium with an easy duplication function, and that helped the song's popularity. At this time, termites of crisis were obstinately eating into the pillars of the regime's power. The state had diminishing resources with which to enforce censorship at this time. Protest song had won at last!

The Weather Is Pleasant (1979)

While in prison, Monfaredzadeh had spent forty days in a cell with Daneshian (Monfaredzadeh 2017: 670–1). Political prisoners oftentimes sang songs and anthems in their cells. Daneshian was formerly a rural elementary school teacher and had created a song that he taught to his class and sang to himself when taking a stroll in rural areas (Salehi 2003: 218).

The lyrics of this song were popularly attributed to him, which is incorrect. The poem 'Sorud-e Bahar' ('Spring's Anthem'), dedicated to Patrice Émery Lumumba (1925–61), leader of the liberation movement of the Congo and the first Prime Minister of independent Congo, was written by Dr Abdollah Behzadi on the occasion of Lumumba's killing by mutineers supported by former coloniser Belgium. Behzadi's poem was published in *Siah-o-Sepid* (*Black & White*) magazine in March 1961 (Salehi 2003: 217). Daneshian had taken a few stanzas of it and made them into a song that was titled by its first line. In prison Monfaredzadeh learned the song and its melody (Samakar 2001: 164). On the eve of the Revolution, to commemorate his comrade, Monfaredzadeh arranged and recorded the song in haste. Rehearsals took place in his home and he played all the four instruments on the music. This was a 'choir' song, sung by seven of Daneshian's friends including Monfaredzadeh himself. It was recorded on Sunday 18 February 1979 on the fifth anniversary of the execution of Daneshian and Golesorkhi, and taken to the now liberated national television on the same night. It was immediately broadcast by national television and became a revolutionary hit:

The Weather Is Pleasant

The weather is pleasant, the flower budded out of the earth
on her return the swallow sang the melody of hope
blood is now flowing in the veins of the vegetation
the blessed spring arrives with coquetry

To our family, our friends and our intimate comrades
to the raging men who are fighting
to all those who reveal through their pens
the decline of our time in the eyes of the world's inhabitants
may your spring be blessed

and may the chains of servitude, may the loads of poverty and ignorance
all over the world and in every shape
be torn apart and disappearing

The regime that had murdered Daneshian and imprisoned Monfaredzadeh was no more. Censorship was gone, and the shared hope was that Iran would never see days like the 1970s again. No one new that dark clouds were gathering over the country and soon the repressive days of the 1970s would appear only as a light version of what was ahead. But this protest song, that celebrated the raging women and men of weapon and of word, keeping hope alive and promising a new world without servitude, poverty and ignorance, captured the nation's imagination at the daybreak of the world's last classical, popular revolution.

Other Songs

The history, significance and contributions of the New Song-Writing movement require an independent study. The focus of this research necessitated studying only some key protest songs. However, noteworthy in the 1970–5 period arc scvcral songs with a protest character. The protest song did not die during the hiatus imposed by censorship (1975–8); it gingerly shifted to a different style and new vocalists. After 1975, protest song and New Song-Writing certainly experienced a setback, but they appeared here and there just like a gentle undertow.

Thus, protest songs and the New Song-Writing can also be studied *thematically*. Lamenting the conditions of the country and the younger generation's angst runs through many protest songs in the early 1970s. This theme – *a house that is no longer a home* – appears in many protest songs of this period. After 'Jungle', Jannatie-Ataie and Bayat created 'Home' ('Khuhen'). First sung by the emerging singer Sattar (Abdolhossein Sattarpour; 1949), the song did not receive broadcasting approval. This slow-tempo, sad song speaks of a house (country) destroyed by a deluge (coup?), a house in ruins that reminds the narrator of its past love-filled life: 'my home, this ruinous home, brings a thousand memories to me / my home, this dark home, what memories it evokes in me.' The version sung by Dariush in 1973 stayed in the public memory (Khoshnam 2017: 644; Mohammadi 2016: 228). In the moving song 'Cul-de-sac' ('Bonbast'), Jannatie-Ataie, Bayat and Dariush teamed up again to create a similar but now hopeful message, suggesting that working in concert can overcome the barriers to freedom: 'in the midst of all these connected, twirling alleys /

our old alley is a cul-de-sac.' This is where we have grown up and are coming of age, but at the end of this dead-end alley is a mud wall that stands 'between us and the great river that like being itself is always flowing'. With the river's roaming sound always in our ears and its image in our dreams, we must not submit to despair. 'Take my weary hand / so that we destroy the wall / one day, any day, sooner or later / we will reach that great river.' The signifier 'river' in these songs is a 'Behrangi effect', the impact of his famous *The Little Black Fish* (Chapter 4), after which the symbol 'river' as flowing change ('like being itself') seriously entered the dissident discourse and resonated with the young, who regarded their existing conditions as stagnant. Finally, Jannatie-Ataie, Monfaredzadeh and Farhad offered the rich and impressive 'Roof' ('Saqf', 1977): 'I'm thinking of a roof / a seamless roof / a solid roof / sturdier than steel / a roof that clothes our fears / and is our garment in the cold of the night / . . ./ under this roof I speak to you of flowers, of night and stars / I speak of you and wanting you and I speak of you all over again.' Sadly, this is just the narrator's dream. There is no shelter here: 'alas, alas, our roof is the cloud's body in the sky / a horizon's infinity is our shortest distance.' The New Song-Writing represents the anxieties of a generation that wishes to feel *free at home*, a basic human desire denied by a hubristic state that was run by the younger generation's unresponsive parents.

The stories of other songs containing the protest element are fascinating. Let us attend to a few, as protest songs would go viral in this period (Eghbali 2017), when the protest element increasingly went beyond the usual suspects. Ramesh (Azar Mohebi Tehrani, 1946–2020) was one of the most versatile and avant-garde vocalists, dancers and actresses of pre-revolutionary Iran, with a charming panache, who sang 600 songs in fifteen years of her singing career before she chose silence in exile, and was certainly an unpolitical vocalist. In 1972, she sang 'You're the Rain, You're the Sun' with lyrics by Mina Asadi (1943–) and music by Monfaredzadeh. Asadi had written the lyrics in memory of PFG founder and members respectively, the brothers Abbas and Asaddollah Meftahi, after their execution in 1972 (Amrai 2020). The song is identifiably lyrical but with a few notable lines: 'you can, if you want, raise hell / you can free the exhausted doves from cages / you can expose, expose the fiend of the night.' Ramesh did not stop there. Earlier, I spoke of the metaphor 'river'. Written by Mohammad-Ali Bahmani (1942–), the song 'Rivers' ('Rudkhunehha') was inspired by Behrangi's *The Little Black Fish* that was a banned book at this time. Young Sadeq Nojuki (1950–) composed its pop music with a fast tempo, and Ramesh invigorated it with her heartfelt vocals (see Mohammadi 2016: 338; see Chapter 4).

The protagonists behind protest songs proved equally creative in challenging state censorship. By 1974, as mentioned, the state took the upper hand in this semiological warfare by shutting down all access to broadcast and marketing. To many, that was the end of *taraneh-ye mo'tarez*: Jannatie-Ataie believes that *taraneh* reached its 'golden peak' between 1966 and 1979 (2005: 24), a period that interestingly overlaps with the height of his own career. I hope I have shown that songs can be banned but the nimble magic of language cannot. Moreover, new generations emerge with their own cultural and artistic sensibilities that outlive certain musical preferences and tastes. This is why protest songs continued during the post-revolutionary 'Spring of Freedom', and then, with the fully-fledged social, cultural and political repression after 1981, protest song and most of its original protagonists migrated into exile. Some artists like Dariush continued with what they did best. Others grew silent. Exile is cruel, especially for artists. Protest song, however, is not reducible to its first protagonists. With or without the New Song-Writing elements and its originators, protest music lived on, allowing a weary and demoralised nation to keep breathing in the present dark and long night of its collective existence. Masters of traditional music such as Mohammad Reza Shajarian (1940–2020) and Shahram Nazeri (1950–) used traditional music and classical poetry to criticise existing conditions and advise hope in the 1980s and 1990s. Brilliantly, by mostly dwelling in classical poetry, they deployed tropes and metaphors that would pass through state censorship. This time allowed for a new generation of talented musicians and vocalists from diverse backgrounds, trainings and world-views to come of age and take over the protest song: rock and gypsy-jazz singer and musician Arash Sobhani (1971–) and his Kiosk band, hip-hop artist and vocalist Soroush Lashkari (1984–), a.k.a. Hichkas (Nobody), hip-hop producer and vocalist Bahram Nouraei (1988–), multilingual Persian-Swedish alternative band Abjeez (Safoura and Melody Safavi), world-musician and vocalist Mohsen Namjoo (1976–), to name a few. When asked about the *raison d'être* of the New Wave music, lyricist Ardalan Sarfaraz replied that it was perhaps because we were new people touching our old wounds (Sarfaraz 2006). Every generation since his own, indeed, has been touching their old wounds.

The PFG and Protest Songs

The literary origins of PFG activists, and in particular their love of poetry as the source of liberatory imagination, was discussed in Chapter 1, and Chapter 2 showed the significant (at the time uncanny) contribution of poetry in anticipating and then supporting 'the event' of Siahkal and the subsequent guerrilla activism. Given this context, one might expect Fadaiyan to appreciate protest songs, if not the New Song-Writing movement. Surprisingly, they did not. Fadaiyan were generally dogmatic in their cultural views and judged the new songs by their form and within their commercial setting, as if following Al-Ahmad's idea of *gharbzadegi* (westoxication). The Iranian Left in general advocated such prejudice towards popular arts. According to Jannatie-Ataie, the leftists condemned the 'new song' as a Western import, in contrast to the cultural products of the workers' movements or socialist countries. He reminisces that leaders of leftist groups advised their membership to listen to classical and traditional musical genres instead of modern pop music (2007). My experience in the ranks of the post-revolutionary pro-OIPFG student movement confirms this. We *unofficially* were advised to value traditional music (like Shajarian) or even older popular songs (like Banan, Marzieh) instead of the New Song-Writing genre. We were unofficially also encouraged to explore and listen to the music of the Soviet Union, in particular the Azeri and Tajiki variations, as a kind of cultural education of the Left. Pop music and its figures were regarded as *jelf* (gaudy), *mobtazal* (banal) and petit-bourgeois, while its opposites were praised as being *sangin* (weighty) and *kargari* ('workerly'). Anything but folk songs and dance was seriously frowned upon, and dancing to pop songs was deemed carnal! Interestingly, most leftist activists I knew loved New-Song Writing songs and their famous figures, now banned (Googoosh, Dariush, Farhad or Fereidoun Foroughi); in fact, we all listened to the pop songs of Viguen, Sakha'i, Shabpareh, Ramesh, and many others. And yet everyone succumbed to this foolishly normative subculture that encouraged dishonesty. What is most surprising analytically is to understand why Fadaiyan did not see that poems and lyrics are identical twins and that it is the music that takes the message of lyrics to the larger public beyond the middle class and intellectuals who read poetry.

That said, here we have an interesting case of PFG activists themselves taking the initiative to create popular songs. Of course, here I am bracketing out the official PFG 'anthems' and songs. I have already spoken about 'The Weather Is Pleasant'. While in prison, Said Soltanpour was instrumental in creating a few songs that were destined to outlive the PFG and permeate Iran's cultural memory, just like the New Song-Writing's protest songs. While the details of how the most popular album of the Left in post-revolutionary Iran originated in prison remain obscure, it is known that after being released from prison, pro-PFG university student Davood Ardalan (a.k.a. Davood Sharareh) travelled to Washington, DC some time in the autumn of 1978, where he met Mehrdad Baran (Ranjbaran), who was studying music and played the cello. Having in mind an album that, he hoped, would challenge the increasingly religious overtone in the revolutionary discourse, he composed the music or arranged the existing tunes for these songs and added a few more. Some of these songs actually came with existing melody that Ardalan had memorised in prison. Baran was a member of the pro-PFG student group in DC. Once the music was ready, he recruited a few comrades and created the choir of around fourteen women and men to sing along with Ardalan's tenor voice. With a lead vocalist, a small choir, cello (Baran), piano (his brother Behzad Baran) and percussion Baran recorded the songs in November 1978 in a music studio of the Catholic University of Washington, DC, where Baran studied for a Master's degree in Music. The recording took seven days and admittedly was not without technical flaws. Baran explains some of these flaws in a fascinating way (Baran 2018). He also attributes the appeal of these songs partly to their raw character (Baran 2018).

The album was a rushed production because the idea was to promote the Fadaiyan's values and actions within a revolutionary movement that was flowing ever so strongly (see Baran 2017a, 2017b, 2018). Upon completion, Ardalan took the cassette tape of this album, now called *Shararehha-ye Aftab* (*The Rays of Sunlight*), back to Iran where it was duplicated, reportedly having sold 2.3 million copies during the 'Spring of Freedom'. This version did not contain the credits: the names of the poets, composer, musicians and singers were irrelevant at the time (although by virtue of singing in the OIPFG rallies, Ardalan alone became a Fadaiyan celebrity): what was important was the message (Baran 2018). The original album did not even appear bearing any Fadai insignia, and registered as its producer the 'Burgeoning (*balandeh*) Art and Literature' ('serving the New Revolutionary Movement of Iran and solidarity of peoples'). The OIPFG leadership was culturally too

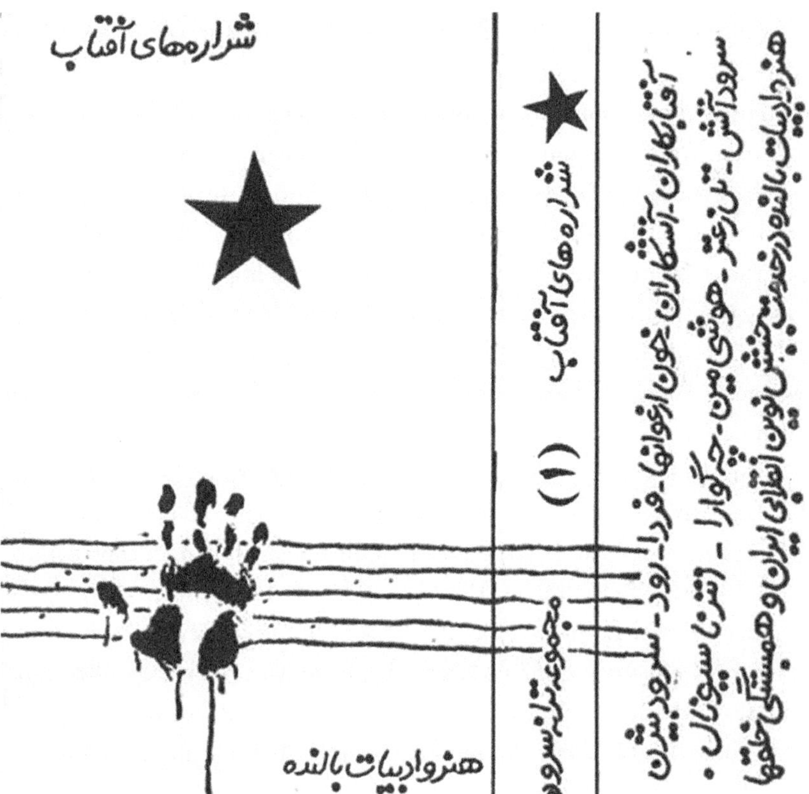

Figure 3.5 The original and simple cassette-tape jacket of the album *The Rays of Sunlight* (1978). A bloody handprint on the musical staff under a star signifies the 'Fadai' character of the songs. The title is strangely accompanied by the subtitle: 'Collection of Song-Anthems'. Side A offered the seven songs produced by Baran and his comrades. Side B contained four English songs ('Tal al-Zaatar', 'Ho Chi Minh', 'Che Guevara', 'International'), along with a Persian translation and recitation by Ardalan.

sclerotic to appreciate the very subculture the Fadaiyan had unwittingly created through their struggles since Siahkal. The Fadai supporters were ahead of their leaders.

The original titles of several of the seven songs were changed in future reproductions: 'Sun-Planters' (or 'Jungle's Sun-Planters', a.k.a. 'Winter's Come to an End', dedicated to the Siahkal guerrillas), 'Fire-Planters', 'Blood of Judas Tree', 'Tomorrow' (or 'Mina's Flower', dedicated to the young Marxist Mina Rafi'i who was killed in a shootout by police), 'River', 'Anthem for Bijan' (a.k.a. 'The Silk of Twilight', dedicated to Bijan Jazani), 'Anthem for Fire' (or 'My Iran', dedicated to the post-coup revolutionaries). The lyrics of these songs are popularly attributed to Soltanpour, but we do know that the lyrics of 'Anthem for Bijan' (which is no anthem at all!) were definitely written by Siagozar Berelian and those of 'Sun-Planters' are attributed to Seyed-Ali Salehi (1955–) (Parand 2012b). As mentioned, some songs were based on existing tunes available to the prisoners ('Sun-Planters' uses the Armenian song 'Sari Sirun Yar' or 'My Beautiful Mountain Love', and 'Blood of Judas Tree' is based on an adapted folksong of Lorestan sung by Manuchehr Homayunpur [1924–2006]). Baran wrote brilliant melodies for the rest.

Discursively, these songs dwelled precisely in the field of metaphors and tropes established through Nimaic and post-Nimaic poetry as well as the New Song-Writing. The fact that Soltanpour, a poet of the 'guerrilla poetry', wrote most of them reveals the connection. These songs are certainly kin to the lyrics of protest songs. This is how 'Sun-Planters' opens: 'The winter's come to an end / the spring is blossoming / the red flower of the sun appeared again and the night's become a fugitive / the mountains are tulip-fields / and the tulips are awake / they are planting the sun in the mountain one flower at the time / In the mountains / his heart is awake / he's bringing / a gun, flowers and wheat / in his chest, my love, he holds a jungle of stars.'

While these songs deploy the well-known signifiers like night, blood, flower, star, fire, dawn and mountain (among others), they make quite explicit use of such fairly straightforward signifiers as people (*khalq*), violence (*qahr*), hatred (*kineh*), gun (*tofang*) and, above all, Siahkal and Fadai – denotative signifiers and proper nouns that are no longer tropes or metaphors: these signifiers forced the poet's intentions in constructing meaning and closed off possible diverging interpretations. And this is how 'Anthem for Bijan' opens:

'On the silk of the dawn / sunlight rose from blood / and to every star / reached a flame from its [sun's] red / bullets rain so that from the river of fire and blood / there appears the good news of the masses' morn.'

As mentioned, by definition these are songs that discursively and aesthetically belong to the reservoir of modern Persian poetry and song-writing. They quite perceivably could have been sung by Dariush, Googoosh or Foroughi. And yet, amazingly, the album is called '*majmu'eh-ye taraneh-sorudha*' or 'a collection of song-anthems'. Song-anthem is an invented term that aims to hide the anxieties of leftist artists about the 'petit-bourgeois' character of pop songs, while paradoxically these very artists in fact had created, well, pop songs. In the parlance of the leftist activists of the time, apparently, the added qualifier 'anthem' (*sorud*) was meant to distinguish 'political songs' from non-political ones, and this reports a deep and meaningless prejudice. Indeed, Soltanpour and other pro-Fadai artists had realised the social power of the song and wanted to contribute to it in their own way.

These songs, as is known, grew widely, and into the cultural memory of post-revolutionary generations. 'At the presidential candidate Mir-Hossein Mousavi's largest campaign event, on 23 May 2009 in Azadi Stadium, "Aftabkaran" . . . a song with communist connotations, was revived' (Siamdoust 2017: 18). Although this re-appropriation smacked of opportunism, it registered the song in the collective consciousness of an entirely new generation. Other artists offered their renditions of these popular songs, in particular 'Sun-Planters'. Now an established conductor based in Paris, on 6 June 2013 and as a part of the Silk Road concert, Baran presented, along with the Bahar Choir (Arash Fouladvand, conductor) and *Orchestre Philharmonique de Paris Est*, the majestic orchestral and choir version of 'River' and 'Blood of Judas Tree'. Just like the songs associated with New Song-Writing, these songs also proved to be timeless and immortal.

The song 'Blood of Judas Tree' entered Iran's musical culture at the time of a historic change. But here I invite readers to ponder its opening lines at our own particular historic moment (summer of 2021), during one of the darkest and most suffocating nights of Iranian history, when Iranians *en masse* are suffering under a decaying, brutal dictatorship. May these words by Soltanpour, in the manner of the 1950s and 1960s poetry, *anticipate* another historic change that will bring the people of Iran freedom and justice:

It's set the meadow ablaze, in this night of our homeland, the blood of
  Judas trees,
O exhilarating hail, set ablaze from shore to shore until sunrise,
as rests a storm in the blood of the weary and broken-hearted,
see the humans of future and contemplate your time, the storm is rising.
Set this cage ablaze, release the birds and the messengers,
so that the smile of freedom and the grapes of joy will grow with the sunrise.

Conclusions: Suggestion, Overdetermination and Existential Protest

Protest music of the 1970s was the outcome of the convergence of three
streams: increased commercialisation of songs that created a stable niche
for artists, the New Song-Writing movement and its creatively re-imagining
of the power of song, and the new directions in pop and modern music.
Note that this process is economically hardly imaginable without increased
industrialisation and urbanisation, the rise of the new middle class, and the
expansion of universities and higher learning institutions. In a way, just like
Fadaiyan and other militants, the dissident artists associated with protest song
emerged as the dialectical negation of the conditions that had begotten them.
In short, *Iran's repressive development of the 1960s created the conditions of possibility of them both*. This socio-political observation has literary implications.

A certain 'elective affinity' brought together the militant and cultural
resistances, the latter case entailing the semiological struggle of the New
Song-Writing against rampant censorship. In light of the Siahkal 'event'
and its subsequent 'mythic' status in dissident discourse, Persian pop song
found new directions in voicing the profound concerns of a generation
caught between the state-propagated image of 'good life' and the country's
harsh realities: inequalities, poverty, repression and alienation. Both the
militants and protest songs were the progeny of the particular socio-political
period of 'repressive development'. The militants picked up arms. And
the New Song-Writing artists? *Their weapon was their words*. Back to my
expanded theory of 'armed propaganda': the protest song spread political
messages in a *certain post-Siahkal direction* by deploying signifiers, metaphors and allegories, and thus politicised pop songs and the imagination
of younger aficionados of pop music. So much so that even non-political
songs (like 'Tale of Two Fish' or 'Ashi Mashi Little Sparrow') could be

interpreted as political messages beyond the wildest dreams of either the PFG or the guerrilla poetry.

Like poetry, protest song operated on copious symbolism and profuse metaphors. The same community of deliberate inferences reconvened on the deployment of these literary devices. But unlike poetry that had begotten Siahkal and guerrilla poetry as a genre, the protest song managed to retain its 'autonomy'. Yet the latter managed to be socially awakening due to the power of music, its socially wider reach and, thus, its greater impact on society compared to poetry. The protest song expanded the list of 'forbidden' words that were increasingly banned by censorship, which forced the lyricists, armed with literary devices, to 'fight a door-to-door guerrilla battle' (Eco 1986: 143). The lyricists' social commentary constantly transgressed the state-sanctioned discursive boundaries and was constantly pushed back by censorship. This is the essence of literature: the power of polysemy allows for multiple meanings. In our context, the *literal* is to be fought over, negotiated and 'settled' between artists and censorship while the *figurative* reaches attentive ears. The real battle, however, was fought on the constantly shifting boundary between the literal and the figurative, the said and the suggested, an osmotic lining which no state, no community, no human can ever stabilise because language itself is fluid.

True, the real-time battle is fought between the institutions of repression and artistic creativity. But it would be remiss of us to reduce this to a political battle of conflicting agents, since the battlefield itself was not their own. *That which calls the antagonists to fight is linguistic and resides in the language itself*: it pertains to 'the unfixity of the relation between signifier and signified and the process of overdetermination by which a particular word condenses around itself a plurality of meanings' (Laclau 2005: 22). Any word, insofar as it has the potential to connote a meaning – metaphor, trope, symbol, allegory – contains the capacity to rip the meaning from one context or discourse to another. This is the power of *suggestion*: to tear the signifiers from their shared, pop-song meanings is to *suggest*, even by extra-linguistic intimations (hearsay, jacket covers, the soundtrack of a political film), that they contain words that do not 'mean' what they mean! Suggestion is at work even for those songs with 'attributed' 'protest' character ('Cul-de-sac' or 'Ashi Mashi Little Sparrow') or for the intentional 'political' decoding of complex layers of signification

('Friday'). *Suggestion produces intentional listening* by pointing out the unfixity between signifier and signified, thus *transposing* signifieds within the lyrics into a different discourse. Paradoxically, therefore, intentional listening is never intentional. It is semiotic and structural. But how exactly does that *transposition* work? Through *overdetermination*. In our case, this is achieved by Siahkal: the subsequent 'myth' around it and the Fadai movement that originates with it (Vahabzadeh, 2021) *overdetermined artistic creativity*, tethering the signifier–signified pairs unto a specific, politically-charged fixity (when the 'scarecrow' *suggests* the Shah!) and then communalised this fixity through marketing these songs like any other pop song. So, the constant battle over the metaphors was in fact over controlling the overdetermination and under-determination of the linguistic sign – a battle that permanently blurs the distinction between literal and figurative. In this process, 'immediacy is lost' (Schürmann): we cannot go back to a truly fresh reading of these songs and experience, say, the signifier 'night' simply as night. As historical subjects residing in language, we can only live in a mediated world. And there is a liberating aspect to this process: this is how the artists and the younger generation try to exercise the right to think, write, sing and all the while be *different*. The most matter-of-fact reality of this period was that *being different* was denied to citizens due to the state's ideological self-fascination. In fighting state censorship and supporting the freedom-fighters of their time, these 'cultural guerrillas' (Eco 1986: 143), the artists associated with protest song fought back against state-propagated ideology and its *imposed* notion of 'good life' (a paradox) through the weapon available to them: the word itself.

And as already suggested, this fight was a profoundly existential one.

4

STARK REALISMS, ALLUSIVE IMAGINARIES: SHORT FICTION AND REBELLION

The glow-worm said: Comrade rabbit I always try to illuminate the lightless gatherings of others, illuminate the jungle, although some animals ridicule me and say, '. . . you try in vain to illuminate the jungle with your meagre light.' The rabbit said: these are older folks' words. We say, 'every light, however small, is still radiance.'

Samad Behrangi, 'Olduz and the Speaking Doll' (1967)

Death can easily descend upon me right at this moment. As long as I live, I should not be inviting death. Of course, when I face death at some point, and I will, it doesn't matter. What matters is what effect my life and death will have upon the lives of others.

Samad Behrangi, *The Little Black Fish* (1968)

Modern Persian poetry and fiction emerged contemporaneously, capturing the revolutionary-literary Zeitgeist of early twentieth-century Iran. Several contemporaries of Yushij – namely, Sadeq Hedayat (1903–51), Sadeq Chubak (1916–98) and Bozorg Alavi (1904–97) – founded modern fiction, although it originates with Mohammad Ali Jamalzadeh (1892–1997) and his *Yeki Bud Yeki Nabud* (*Once Upon a Time*, 1921). As mentioned, Yushij was intrigued by the advent of modern fiction – a literary movement he found braided with his New Poetry. In a letter, he posthumously praised Hedayat, the author of *The Blind Owl* (India, 1937; Iran, 1941), a rare, compelling and surrealist oeuvre and the hallmark of the modern Persian novel, 'the one who isn't alive now', as 'the exceptional virtuoso [*borumand-tarin*] I have seen in the realm of writing . . . among all my friends' (Yushij, as quoted in Ariyanpour 1995: 599).

The 'guerrilla period' in Iran was short-lived – from 1971 until 1976 (with the death of Ashraf). The PFG and other militants experienced the same flow and ebb between the pincers of these two turning points. After 1976, the urban guerrilla movement proved unsustainable by the activists who had hoped their zealous dedication would ignite the pent-up ire of the populace into a mass uprising. The student movement, the backbone of militant resistance, also pragmatically shifted towards long-term democratic methods (Vahabzadeh 2010: 56). In comparison to poetry and songs, fiction had a curious place: while certain works of fiction did have 'protest' elements in them, by and large fiction remained somewhat detached from militant *action*; one can find only a few works in the 1960s and 1970s that can be conceptually and narratively connected to militantism. This can partly be attributed to the fact that the creative process of fiction-writing takes much longer that the flashing bursts of poetry or lyrics. Novels were too slow to emerge to have a public impact in the context of the swift courses of events that defined the 'guerrilla period', and that is why I have excluded the novel from this study, although some key novels of this period will be briefly referenced here. If anything, militant activism only had a delayed influence on fiction. In his appraisal of the reflection of armed struggle in literature, contemporary fiction-writer and former PFG member Nassim Khaksar (1944–) surveys the works of fiction that capture the guerrilla reality, showing that these works had been almost entirely written years, at times decades, after the 'guerrilla period' (Khaksar, 2017). Fiction involving the militant's image, therefore, surfaced only after militantism had already rushed through its brief lifespan. This is amazing: we do not have 'guerrilla fiction', unlike poetry and songs. Furthermore, with the exception of a handful who came from literary backgrounds (for instance, the Tabriz circle of PFG), the young militants were too busy and too zealous to have dedicated time to reading novels amid their demanding university programmes and (semi-underground) activist life prior to 1971. Accordingly, it is no wonder that poetry became this generation's preferred literary expression. Yet, and this is a *notable paradox*, there was a particular corpus of short fiction that can be universally credited to have motivated militant activists – the works of Samad Behrangi, the single most important fiction-writer of this generation. No other fiction writer's impact on militant Marxists (or others) measures up to that of Behrangi, this chapter's focus. His work weighs so heavy in this context that other works of short fiction, viewed from my particular angle, had become relevant to the militants because of these works' direct or oblique intimations towards what Behrangi had already achieved before the Siahkal operation.

To appreciate Behrangi's contribution, this chapter takes the counter-intuitive route: it begins with his works and only then situates his literary origins within contemporary fiction. The reader, I hope, will appreciate this hermeneutic strategy.

Samad Behrangi: Nexus of Fiction and Action

Posthumously regarded as the 'Maxim Gorky of Iran' (Jahangiri 2012: 338), Samad was born in Tabriz in 1939 into a working-class family, one of six children. Details of his life have been chronicled by his younger brother Asad (Behrangi 2000), although his memoirs lack precision in documenting several significant details. Old enough to have a lived memory of the 1953 coup in a pro-Mosaddeq family (Behrangi 2000: 67–78), Samad graduated from Tabriz [Elementary] Teacher's Training College (*Danesh-sara-ye Moqadamati*) in 1957 and became a rural teacher in Azerbaijan. In 1962, while working as a teacher, he enrolled on the English Language and Literature program (the 'Night Program' intended for working adults) at Tabriz University. By the late 1950s, Behrangi had befriended like-minded young Azeris, soon to be cultural figures, including the translator and editor Gholam-Hossein Farnoud (1940–2019), the historian and translator Rahim Ra'isnia (1940–), the translator and author Behruz Dehqani, and Kazem Sa'adati (1940–71) – the latter two died, respectively, under torture and by committing suicide as Fadai guerrillas. Behruz's sister, Ashraf (1948–), was also arrested in 1971 but escaped from Qasr Prison in March 1973 and attained celebrity status among dissidents after publishing her interrogation memoirs. Behrangi and Dehqani had found each other in the

College (Behrangi 2000: 173–86). These intellectuals converged through their cultural approach to fighting injustices that they had experienced as Azeris who were banned from publishing in their mother tongue and as young men from working-class backgrounds. They constituted the impetus of the 'Tabriz Circle' that had a lasting impact on showcasing the rich Azerbaijani culture for Persian speakers. Behrangi, Dehqani and Farnud published *Adineh*, the Friday Literary Supplement of the Tabriz newspaper *Mahd-e Azadi*. Publishing seventeen issues (between 23 September 1965 and 9 September 1966) before it was shut down by the authorities, the Supplement bonded these young Azeri literati with dissident intellectuals in Tehran: Shamlu, Al-Ahmad, and fellow Azeri Sa'edi. Of foreign writers, *Adineh* presented translations of Langston Hughes, Sean O'Casey, Franz Kafka, Bertolt Brecht, Maxim Gorky, Aziz Nesin, Ernest Hemingway and André Breton. Farrokhzad, Nima, Sa'edi, Dariush Ashuri, Mohammad Hoquqi, Manouchehr Atashi, Bijan Jalali and the editorial group (presenting translations of Azerbaijani folk fictions or English sources) also appeared in the Supplement. Revolutionary, historical figures like Kuchek Khan, Sattar Khan and Hassan Sabbah (leader of Hashashin, Order of Assassins, 1090–1275) surfaced in these pages too. Notable was an issue dedicated to Tabriz's role in the Constitutional Revolution, interestingly, with an elegy for the constitutionalist militant (known as '*fadai*') Abbas-Aqa Tabrizi, who had assassinated Qajar vizier Atabak Azam in 1907. Behrangi also published on the role of Azerbaijan in the Constitutional Revolution in *Adineh*, a piece that was later published independently (Behrang, n.d.). Aspiring young Azeris like the poet and future Fadai guerrilla Ali-Reza Nabdel (pen name Okhtay) debuted in *Adineh* (see also Behrangi 2000: 111–20). In short, *Adineh* indicates the critical, 'culturalist' approach of Azerbaijani intellectuals who were clearly *not* Azerbaijani nationalists (a reaction to Persian-speaking chauvinists) but were interested in forging collaborative relations with other dissidents. Nabdel (1977) captured this philosophy circa 1970 in his treatise *Azerbaijan and the National Question*. He rejects the (ethno-)nationalistic approaches of Azerbaijani and Kurdish autonomists to the liberation of minorities during and after the Second World War (or *jonbesh-e melli*, 'nationalist movement') and instead emphasises an intra-Iranian approach (or *jonbesh-e sarasari*, 'all-encompassing movement') that advocates egalitarian and democratic relations within the Iranian diversity through decolonisation. The PFG was the product of the *jonbesh-e sarasari* philosophy. While clearly identifying this mostly Persian periodical as an Azerbaijani publication, *Adineh* clearly had a liberationist and internationalist tendency, and that did not escape SAVAK. Dehqani mostly published translations. Behrangi published Azerbaijani folk tales in Persian within several books, partly in collaboration with Dehqani (see Behrangi 2000: 173–86; Dehqani 2005). Behrangi also translated Shamlu, Farrokhzad and others into Azeri (Hanson 1983: 3) and wrote a significant instructional book called *Alefba* (*Alphabet*) to teach Persian to Azerbaijani first-graders who knew no Persian coming to school – a book that has reportedly been destroyed by the author.

Between 1957 and his untimely death at the age of 29 in 1968, Behrangi taught in the villages of Azerbaijan, where he witnessed first-hand the poverty-stricken rural life. He began to seriously question the American educational methods (Dewey method) imposed by Tehrani, middle-class, Western-educated policymakers and taught on teacher-training programmes. For a provincial rural teacher teaching in Persian to non-Persian-speaking children, these methods could not have been more alienating. Daringly, Behrangi launched a devastating critique of Iran's pedagogical methods in *Investigations into the Educational Problems of Iran* (1965, published by a small Tabriz publisher; a short, friendly review of it, published in *Adineh* no. 2 [30 September 1965, pp. 2, 4], gave it publicity). He refutes the applicability of predominantly American pedagogical and psychological books propagated in Iran. These books are written, he argued, for educating American children who 'eat a complete meal at least once a day and their parents subscribe to at least one of the many newspapers and magazines published in their country' (Behrangi 1970: 5). 'I was first introduced to these books in Tabriz Teacher's Training College. There the ideas of John Dewey were presented as the descended words [of God] and expected to be accepted without question' (Behrangi 1970: 8). He heavily reflects on his experience as a rural teacher to show the bureaucratically infertile, uncreative and shallow approach to education. As a pioneer in critical pedagogy in Iran, Behrangi points out the class essence of education, arguing that pedagogical cookbooks designed by Ivy League scholars in the Global North do not work for the global periphery. Note that he is writing in the 1960s, as the Shah's White Revolution reforms were changing the fabric of society towards the industrialisation of a country that was now enjoying a constant flow of petro-dollars feeding a large rentier state. Part anecdote and recollection, part critical analysis with deriding humour, not only does *Investigations* berate the functionaries behind curricular development, it equally scorns the illiterate or semi-literate older generation caught in their obsolete beliefs and superstitious worlds. More importantly perhaps, Behrangi condemns his peers: the teachers. They 'are slackers. The easier the better. Anything that calls for responsibility, is new and profound, goes against instincts or beyond the circle of what they had seen, heard or known is [regarded as] useless. It is disposable. At the very least one must not pursue [such ideas]. The objective is a happy family. And if the scanty (*chenderqaz!*) monthly salary is not enough, well let's start a life on monthly payments' (Beharngi 1970: 113). This is a critique of the parasitic, inefficient and unproductive middle class within an enormous bureaucracy that was supposedly created to advance Iran towards being an industrial power. Reading these lines, one is reminded of Al-Ahmad's devastating criticism of Iran's shallow development in *Westoxication* (1962). The ideas and the prose of *Investigations* reveal family resemblances with Al-Ahmad's work. Just like Al-Ahmad, Behrangi points at a social and bureaucratic epidemy (Hanson 1983: 4) that permeates the country's educators. In any case, his *Investigations* further brought this young Azeri literato to Al-Ahmad's attention and forged 'an affectionate personal relationship' between the two, including mutual visits in Tehran and Tabriz, as is clear in Al-Ahmad's recollections in the special issue of *Arash* magazine (Hanson 1983: 3–4). Al-Ahmad confirms that *Investigations* brought him to Behrangi (Al-Ahmad 1968: 8). In any case, although written in accessible prose so it would reach a wider audience instead of being a rigorous critical treatise, young Behrangi's *Investigations* must be regarded as a pathbreaker in the critical pedagogy of the Global South, connected to a growing tradition that led to the influential *Pedagogy of the Oppressed* (1968 in Portuguese, 1970 in English) by the Brazilian educator Paulo Freire. Samad's critical stance caused him trouble with the Ministry of Education. Later in 1964, he was suspended from his teaching position for about six months for having in 1963 published a poetry collection in the Azeri language (Behrangi 2000: 91–4).

In the 1960s, aside from *Investigations*, *Adineh* and Azeri folk tales, Behrangi also began writing and publishing short fiction. As an elementary school teacher, he had found his audience. Although he must be credited as the key figure of children's literature in Iran, his allegorical works of fiction go beyond 'children's stories'. Not only is the designation 'children's stories' a misnomer, it reflects a Western epistemological bias that Iranian intellectuals had contracted through their uncritical importation of Western knowledge. This is a problem of categorisation and expectation. Behrangi's short stories are no more 'children's stories' than are Leo Tolstoy's fables and folk tales – allegorical stories containing age-old wisdom (Tolstoy 1962). 'Behrangi's corpus of fiction – short stories often referred to as children's stories in the West, but really timeless folk tales meant for child and adult alike – is deeply rooted in his village teaching experiences and his love for Azeri folk culture' (Hanson 1983: 2). Indeed, his folkish fables, especially the earlier ones where humans and animals interact and magically enter the worlds of one another, are deeply rooted in the Iranian tradition of storytelling, although his work clearly demonstrates not only modern but also exceptionally conflictual motifs. Behrangi published a number of short story books in the 1960s that culminated in his oeuvre *The Little Black Fish* (1968), published shortly before his untimely death in a drowning accident.

Speaking of conflictual motifs, Behrangi did defend his work as 'children's literature', which indicates that he had accepted the categorisation of his fiction, but with a proviso: against the Western, liberal view that children's stories should contain moral lessons, timeless maxims and an escape to innocence – the 'Christian morals' (Behrangi 2017b: 8), in the tradition of Hans Christian Andersen – he argued for a different children's literature, one that reflects the harsh realities of Iranian majority outside the purview of the urban middle class: 'Shouldn't we tell the child that in your country there are children that don't see the colour of meat or even cheese for months or years?' Then, he submits, 'the time has passed for limiting the children's literature to advise and suggest dry and irrefutable maxims . . . whose general and final outcome is to keep children unaware of the great and critical and crucial issues in their living environment' (Behrangi 2017b: 5; orig. 1968). The context helps us appreciate his vision. Iran's 'children's literature' (*adabiyyat-e kudakan*) was founded by the pioneer educator, founder of the first kindergarten and the first school for hearing-impaired children in Tabriz, Jabbar Baghcheh-ban (1885–1966). It was, however, Mehdi Ha'eri-Yazdi (1921–2009) whose fiction, since the 1950s, defined Iran's 'children's literature': inspired by the ancient tradition of storytelling, he reworked many key classical fables, Rumi's allegorical tales and Quranic stories into modern children's stories. His stories were compiled in the multi-volume bestseller series *Good Fables for Good Children*, which won him not only UNESCO recognition and many national prizes, but also the acclamation 'Father of Children's Literature in Iran'.

Other authors in this genre in this period, Ahmad Reza Ahmadi, Nassim Khaksar and Nader Ebrahimi (1936–2008), might have been successful or prolific, but they did not attain Hae'ri-Yazdi's status and certainly did not nearly relate to Behrangi's conception of 'children's literature' as a medium for cultivating social awareness and courage to challenge the status quo. Thus, Behrangi's ideas must be viewed within the contrasting context of Ha'eri-Yazdi's moral education or the predominantly escapist literature of other writers. Behrangi concludes:

> Now it is time to attend to two issues in the children's literature . . . The first point: the children's literature must be a bridge between the colourful world of unawareness (*bikhabari*), dreams and sweet fantasies [on one the hand] and the dark and conscious (*agah*) world, submerged in the bitter, painful and obstinate realities of the social environment of the grownups [on the other]. The child must cross this bridge and reach the dark world of grownups fully aware (*agahaneh*), armed (*mosallah*) and with a lantern in her hand . . .
>
> The synopsis and second point, the child must be given a precise world-view (*jahanbini*) and a measure (*me'yar*) with which she can evaluate different moral and social issues in the ever-changing social conditions and situation. (Behrangi 2017b: 7–8)

These ideas define his children's fiction. Deprivation, conflict, violence and inequality, as well as young people challenging their superstitious and oppressive parents, all appear in his works. Clearly, Behrangi's stories aim to *socially* educate children rather entertain them. Back to my point regarding the epistemological problem of categorisation: considering his lines, can we still read Behrangi's fiction as 'children's literature'?

Behrangi had created, by late 1950s, a circle in Tabriz with his close comrades, Dehqani and Sa'adati, to which they also gradually recruited, among others, young Nabdel and Manaf Falaki, the latter being a rug-weaver child-worker and a student of Behrangi. He and his friends were active in student and teacher activism. All four men died in the ranks of PFG in 1971–2. Notably, Behrangi was active in the teachers' strike of 1961 in Tabriz (Behrangi 2000: 81–6). He also participated in the funeral procession of Takhti in Tehran, which was turned into a protest rally. He was also distantly involved in the 1967 student strike in Tabriz (Behrangi 2000: 194), with Faraj Sarkuhi (1947–) being a key activist from Behrangi's circle in that strike (Farahati 1991: 143). Predictably, these activities brought him under security attention. He frequented the circles and homes of dissident writers and intellectuals in the 1960s. This is how Behrangi forged a friendship with Puyan. It was Puyan who had reportedly coined 'Iran's Maxim Gorky is on his way' in referencing Behrangi, the one who 'writes foundational books' (quoted in Behrangi 2000: 172). Although not firmly asserted, it is also colloquially stated that Behrangi and Puyan had met, possibly more than once, in Farrokhzad's residence or in her presence, and that she recorded their discussions in her poem 'Conquest of the Garden' in *Another Birth*: 'Everyone's afraid / everyone's afraid, but you and I / joined the lamp and water and mirror / and did not fear.' This opening leads to her supposed meeting with the two men: 'and on that strange, conquering mountain / we asked young eagles / what's to be done?' (Farrokhzad 1993: 384–5). Since *Another Birth* was published in 1963, these meetings must have taken place in the early 1960s at the time of Bahrangi's activity in the teachers' movement and during the semi-relaxed political conditions of 1960–3. Puyan and Behrangi had subsequently met in Tabriz, and Behrangi would then give his Tabriz friends underground literature (Behrangi 2000: 172–3). According to Farahati, after Behrangi's death Dehqani created a certain 'university group' consisting of several students and affiliates of the Tabriz Circle with the intention of 'subverting the regime through armed struggle' (2006: 193). To that end, they began organising themselves in disciplined fashion by excluding friends they found unfit for the struggle (Farahati 1991: 195). Puyan knew Behrangi but not his comrades, although he knew of the Tabriz Circle. So, after Samad's death, Puyan took a risky trip to Tabriz's Shams bookstore, frequented by Behrangi and his comrades, and he miraculously succeeded in connecting with Dehqani (Hamidian 2004: 30–1). Indeed, the Tabriz Circle must be regarded as a founding group of the PFG.

Behrangi's death was received by Tehran intellectual circles, above all Al-Ahmad and Sa'edi, in a (constructed) shroud of mystery. A leftist friend (and future PFG member), the veterinarian doctor and military officer Hamzeh Farahati, was accompanying Behrangi to the border River Aras in the Arasbaran region when they decided to swim in the river on the hot day of 31 August 1968. Not knowing how to swim and caught in the unpredictable currents of the river, Behrangi called out to his friend before disappearing in the water, and the efforts of Farahati, who desperately swam in the currents to save him, were futile (Farahati 2006: 157–8). According to Asad Behrangi, who reached the scene a couple of days later, Samad's body was recovered a few days after the accident, five kilometres away from the original drowning spot (Behrangi 2000: 226–7; see Behrooz 2000: 45). Interestingly, Asad always insisted on the conspiracy theory, despite the fact the he knew the truth. In any case, Farahati's presence invoked the suspicion of the military authorities: security agents searched his home and found, among other things, an English copy of *Das Kapital*. He tried to kill himself using a hammer (Al-Ahmad reports it was a cone-sugar mini-axe [Al-Ahmad 1968: 7]) on the spot but failed and was arrested, taken to a military hospital and then to interrogation by military counter-intelligence, before being released and going back to work a few weeks later. In 1970, Farahati was arrested in relation to his connection to an underground group led by Dr Houshang Azami (1936–76) and ended up in prison until winter 1971. He was imprisoned again in 1974 in connection with the PFG until his release in March 1978 (Farahati 2006: 159–66, 223, 233–7, 266).

The untimely death of a twenty-nine-year-old, known leftist writer in a drowning accident would certainly be surprising, in particular when at the time of death Behrangi was in the company of a 'mysterious' military offi-cer (Farahati 2006: 167), and these components of the incident generously fed the imagination of dissident intellectuals who needed a martyr for the movement that had not yet emerged. Accordingly, this was a unique oppor-tunity not to be missed. Al-Ahmad, Sa'edi and other dissidents had already had their dress rehearsal about nine months earlier (in January 1968) when they had spread (false) rumours that attributed to a SAVAK conspiracy the death by suicide of Takhti, who was pro-National Front though not politically active. Tens of thousands marching in his funeral procession in Tehran turned it into a protest rally, chanting: 'Workers know this, toilers know this: Takhti has become a martyr' (Behrangi 2000: 261). As mentioned, Behrangi had attended Takhti's funeral and his forty-day memorial (Behrangi 2000: 260–1). In this case, as Farahati was imprisoned and thus nowhere to be seen, the circumstances surrounding Behrangi's fatal drowning cultivated another conspiracy theory. A special issue of *Arash* magazine, dedicated to Behrangi, served to officiate this conspiracy theory simply by casting doubt over his death (see below). SAVAK inadvertently played a role in feeding the conspiracy idea, too. Asad Behrangi reports that while he was away on the banks of the River Aras searching for his brother's body, 'SAVAK agents had come to Samad's home and made a mess of everything, broke his desk, sifted through his letters, interrogated those present at home and had taken a few books and notes with them' (Behrangi 2000: 229). Also, Asad reports deep cavities on Samad's thigh and leg. In any case, after Gendarmerie officers processed the case on the spot, Samad's body reached Tabriz to a huge, waiting crowd who had come to honour their teacher. His funeral, held in a mosque, also witnessed a large crowd. In Tehran, the nascent Iranian Writers Association held a well-attended memorial for Behrangi that Asad and Sa'adati attended (Behrangi 2000: 229). In all likelihood, Asad must have reported to Al-Ahmad and others the searching of Samad's home by the authorities and the status of Samad's body, statements that must have also nurtured the conspiracy theory.

Martyr of a Future Movement

Behrangi was a dissident intellectual fairly typical of 1960s Iran: educated, leftist, anti-tradition, secular, liberationist, and a cultural worker. There is no doubt that he would have contributed immensely to the militant movement that was launched over two years after his death – a movement that owes its existence, in part, to Behrangi's intellectual legacy. And yet, in exactly what capacity he would have taken part in the militant movement remains a matter of speculation. After all, by 1971, the Tabriz Circle had contained two diverging streams: those who joined the PFG (Dehqani, Nabdel, Sa'adati,

Falaki and several others recruited by them, including Roqiyyeh Daneshgari and Ashraf Dehqani) and those who, like Al-Ahmad and Sa'edi, believed in long-term cultural impact (Raisnia and Farnoud) (Farahati 2006: 192) but offered unwavering moral support for the movement. The ghostly *a-venir* movement that somehow constantly made its appearance in literature and in small sparks, but clearly was not yet on the ground, nonetheless needed a martyr. And a Special Issue of *Arash* magazine (no. 18, dated November 1968) – dedicated to Samad Behrangi's legacy, and on whose cover Behruz Golzari's iconic artistic image of Behrangi appeared – served precisely that purpose. *Arash* presented the myth of Samad's death by SAVAK, a claim that became oral history, again, through *the literary device of suggestion.*

The issue of *Arash* brought together elegiac notes, analyses and memoirs of comrades to celebrate Behrangi's well-deserved though hitherto overlooked literary status. A detailed, and fascinating, discourse analysis of this issue of *Arash* goes beyond this book's focus, but I offer a brief weaving together of the elements that conjured the myth through literary devices, producing a social construct.

The issue opens with a brief statement of the then newly-founded Iranian Writers Association (dated 11 September 1968) which refers only to the 'untimely death' (*marg-e nabehengam*) of Behrangi but speaks of nothing else aside from a eulogy. The volume proceeds with Eslam Kazemiyyeh's editorial that casts doubt on the drowning: 'The news is that Samad Behrangi, teacher of Azerbaijan villages, had gone to swim in the River Aras and because he did not know how to swim' (Kazemiyyeh 1968: 3). Here is the literary *suggestion*, and to augment its impact, the sentence is intentionally left incomplete. A few lines later, Kazemiyyeh vaguely references Sa'edi as if Sa'edi had related to him: 'But at the end, we did not find out why Samad died' (Kazemiyyeh 1968: 4). Step by step, the suggestion more assertively leads away from accidental drowning. 'They said Samad did not know how to swim and has stepped in the section of the river where water is rushing and rapid and submerged there. This is not a reasonable statement' (Kazemiyyeh 1968: 4). But here he needs to kill a parallel rumour: Aras is a border river, so Kazemiyyeh expressly rejects the idea that Behrangi had the intention to cross the border illegally to the Soviet Union (1968: 4), as if he were escaping from prosecution. What

Kazemiyyeh leaves as a suggestion, Al-Ahmad moors to the shores of certainty by deploying his distinctly personal prose, in this case the funeral of and mourning for his elder brother, to *make* his narrative believable. Using endearing terms and calling him his 'brother', Al-Ahmad states that Samad had drowned near Khoda Afarin village, which is wrong (Behrangi 2000: 227), and perhaps this particular location was the one he had visited in the summer when water levels were low, and he had no other visual reference. Khoda Afarin is 30 kilometres away from where Samad had drowned. But this 'mistake' serves him well. He offers memories of his young friend Samad to arrive at these lines: 'But this? Samad is dead? [He] for whom we had fathomed so many aspirations' (Al-Ahmad 1968: 7)? What aspirations (*arezuha*)? These are still preparatory narratives to smoothly tether the reader into Al-Ahmad's dismissing suicide. So, his narrative *supplements* Kazemiyyeh's myth-busting to narrow down the speculations into two: accident or conspiracy. But accidental death is implicitly shelved too. So, Al-Ahmad reveals that Behrangi had gone swimming with a friend who 'was a young officer' (1968: 7–8) only to strike with a question: 'Have they gotten rid of him?' (Al-Ahmad 1968: 7). Who are 'they'? He then goes back to personal memories and wraps up by referring to two mythological young men *killed* in Ferdowsi's *Shahnameh*: 'in [censored] environments, it is always like this. They kill Siavushs and Sohrabs' (Al-Ahmad 1968: 11). If no other suggestion works, parallelism with mythology will. Al-Ahmad later confessed in a letter to Mansour Owji that he had made up the story (see Al-Ahmad's letter in Farahati 2006: 189). The line-up would not be complete without Sa'edi, who appears next (after a poem): he begins with the statement that appears in the epigraph to this chapter. 'Samad Behrangi has no date of birth or date of death', declares Sa'edi. 'His death is as unbelievable as his life was, and his life was so merged in excitement that it resembled a fable (*afsaneh*)' (1968: 15). Then he creates *relations of equivalence* between key leftist notions to situate Behrangi politically: 'He knew hunger; he knew poverty; he knew disease and saw injustice (*zolm*)' (Sa'edi 1968: 16). His literary trick casts doubt over 'death', not to deny that Behrangi was dead but to suggest that his was not simply a 'death'. He hysterically declares, 'It's a lie. Don't believe it. Samad isn't dead. Samad's alive. Samad's alive. Samad's alive' (1968: 107). In this eulogy, though,

Sa'edi made a statement that in decades to come captured the essence of Behrangi's life: '*His masterpiece was his life*. He was always busy learning and teaching' (1968: 107).

The foundations for the myth have now been laid. Behrangi's friend Farnoud wrote a fiery essay to contrast Samad's stories (their particular genre) with the bourgeois-moralistic children's stories of Hans Christian Andersen (1968: 60). As if he would anticipate the incomparable future impact of Behrangi on the generation that manned armed struggle, Farnoud prophetically concludes his article by a blazing statement: 'Now we must await another little black fish who would repeat his cry in our suffocating space: "I want to kill the seagull and bring peace to the fish"' (Farnud 1968: 60). Another notable contribution was that of Puyan, under the pen name Ali Kabiri, as he had at this time begun, with Ahmadzadeh and Meftahi, to organise the nucleus of an underground group that later became the PFG. Puyan tries to be abstract and philosophical, but his piece did not serve the subject well, except for one revelation. 'We have chosen "to be" but have thought much less about "how to be"', Puyan averred. 'Knowing "how to be" arises from awareness (*agahi*) of "why to be." And those who believe in their knowledge (*agahi*) know how to be' (Kabiri 1968: 63). He connects this knowledge to 'evolution', but stresses that the 'prospect of a society devoid of inequalities always attracted Samad' (Kabiri 1968: 63). Then, as if he were reflecting on his generation's experience, Puyan declares that Behrangi 'was of the small group [of people] who connected reading to seeing and experiencing'. Therefore, 'although he died a poor man, he left a legacy for his friends that offers a signpost at every step' (Kabiri 1968: 64). This *legacy* went beyond anybody's imagination. *What amazes us about these words of the PFG co-founder is the way Puyan exposed his intent to appropriate the works of his comrade Behrangi for the movement he had envisaged.* True, Behrangi's works were the single item of literature most influential on the first generation of PFG activists, but these particular words offer a glimpse of how that influence was *intentionally constructed* by PFG activists.

The rest of the 112-page Special Issue of *Arash* consists of memories of Samad by not only friends but, more importantly, some of his rural students, as well as excerpts from his writings and, last but not least, poetry dedicated to him, including a poem by Okhtay (Nabdel). The issue also features an interpretive article by Manouchehr Hezarkhani, to which I will return. But let us note that it is here that Behrangi posthumously receives the highest commendation when Hazarkhani calls him *'honarmand-e khalq'* or 'the people's artist' (1968: 17).

Still, situating Behrangi in his particular historical context would not be complete without Shamlu's 1972 remarks that provide the crux of this loss. 'What makes Samad's death bitter is the loss of a unique individual' (Shamlu 1978: 28). *A unique individual*: if there were any doubts about Behrangi's uniqueness in terms of his tremendous influence on the militants (which makes him the dominant figure of this chapter, too!), Shamlu's wisdom pinpoints his literary standing with incredible accuracy. 'Samad was the amazing face of *commitment* . . . the giant of commitment! The *monster of commitment*', he heralds. '*For commitment is a dragon that guards the most precious treasure of the world: a treasure called freedom and the right of nations to live on*' (1978: 29; my emphasis). Chapter 2 has already presented the debates around literary commitment. I submit that Shamlu, as a supporter of the militant opposition, appropriately grasped the tremendous role of this humble, rural teacher in his particular historic nexus: his literary commitment aimed at safeguarding *freedom* and *liberation* – that is, the spirit of *national liberation* in the world and in Iran. *The writers guard freedom; the militants fight for liberation*: they are comrades-in-arms. Behrangi held the two together. If Golesorkhi was the poet and the martyr of the movement, Behrangi was its teacher and visionary. And that leads Shamlu to his conclusion: 'Samad was one head of this monster [of commitment]. And I wish . . . I wish this monster had a thousand heads, thousands of heads' (Shamlu 1978: 29).

Fiction in the 1960s

To appreciate Behrangi's works of fiction, we need to situate them in the context of fiction in this period (the 1960s up until 1979). This was the time of Sa'edi, Bahram Sadeqi (1936–84), Ahmad Mahmoud (1931–2002), Houshang Golshiri (1938–2000), Mahmoud Dowlatabadi (1940–), Ebrahim Golestan (1922–) and Simin Daneshvar (1921–2012). These writers stand out in a cohort of wonderful writers of the 1960s – arguably Iran's most creative decade in the twentieth century. With the post-White Revolution rapid modernisation – urbanisation, increased public and higher education, a growing industrial working class and the creation of a huge bureaucracy that employed millions – fiction turned to reflect the chimeric world-views and anxieties of a nascent, urban middle class from heterogeneous cultural backgrounds living in a world of proximities they could not quite comprehend, a class that was nonetheless showcased in a distilled and monolithic fashion in the national media as a sign of progress. Fiction also depicted the other Iran: the one that was veiled in the mass media and left out of development, the rural and provincial Iran shrouded in lethargic, age-old superstitions and cruel yet accepted customs. The state's cultural policies promoted a shallow, westernised lifestyle, the subject of Al-Ahmad's sharp criticism in *Westoxica-tion*. After all, this was a regime obsessed with ballooned-up superficialities like vacation plans and consumer goods: 'To the day when every Iranian owns a Paykan' (Iran's first manufactured car in 1967), then-Premier Amir-Abbas Hoveyda (1919–79) famously said. The state-promoted culture was met in different forms in the fiction of defiance of this period. 'In all progressive intellectual tendencies, one notices attempts at promoting [native] culture and resistance to the cultural policies of the state' (Abedini 1990: 14). At the same time, the critical view of westernisation fed its opposite discourse of the 'return to self' by Al-Ahmad and Ali Shari'ati (1933–77) – a trend that expanded rapidly.

In the works of Mahmoud and Sa'edi, notably, the rural Iran makes its serious advent, but the countryfolk in their works speak their vernacular Persian, not the literary Persian that dominated fiction at this time. Mahmoud's social realism brings to forth the 'other Iran' in its harsh, crushing and unjust circumstances, often drawing on the 'political' element in the narrative, either implicitly, as in the short stories in *Strangers and the Native Boy* (1974a), or explicitly as in *The Neighbours* (1974b; orig. 1966). Many of Mahmoud's narratives in this period – in particular 'The Native Boy' and *The Neighbours* – make explicit reference to the political atmosphere of the 1950s and implicitly to the Tudeh Party. In this realist genre, Mahmoud Dowlatabadi stands out as a steadfast and prolific novelist and screenplay writer, the creator of the ten-volume *Kaleydar* (1979–84), the most voluminous novel in the Persian language, with a striking genric family resemblance to the socialist realist novels of the Soviet novelist Mikhail

Sholokhov (recipient of 1965 Nobel Prize for Literature), especially his *And Quiet Flows the Don* (1934). Dowlatabadi's stories centre on the challenges of rural life, often in his homeland of Khorasan Province. His novels, *The Legend of Baba Sobhan* (1968; adopted by Kimiai in his film *The Soil* [*Khak*, 1973]), *Aqil, Aqil* (1972) and *Soleiman's Migration* (1973) all narrate the cruelties of rural life, with the latter title focusing on the oppression of, and daily violence against, rural women by men. Also subscribing to this genre is Ali-Ashraf Darvishian (1941–2017).

Sa'edi's peculiar 'surrealism', as Hassan Abedini calls it (1990: 112–13), compellingly depicts the rural inhabitants in their milieux in such a way as to highlight how – caught in the quicksand of oppressive beliefs and exploitative relations that nonetheless are meaningful to their daily survival – profoundly alienated they are, both internally and externally. Sa'edi imaginatively enriches his narratives with strange apparitions, unexpected turns of events and unlikely happenings, thus undermining reality by extending the real situation into the realm of human psychic fancy – the way the inhabitants of a particular Gestalt *see* their world of spirits with powers beyond intervention by the narrator. As a doctor of psychiatry, Sa'edi was fascinated by rural Iran's mental disorders and superstitious hallucinations; he used his trips to Khuzestan and Azerbaijan to create memorable works, notable among them 'magical realist' works, *The Mourners of Bayal* (1991; orig. 1964) and *Fear and Trembling* (1998; orig. 1968). These works reflect the countryside's backwardness, overshadowed by the state-propagated over-representation of (affluent) cities (Abedini 1990: 113). Though not concerned with rural Iran, and in fact reflecting on the urban life of (mostly) the intelligentsia, Bahram Sadeqi also brilliantly collapses the distinction between real and unreal in his works. Associated with the School of Isfahan in the 1960s, Sadeqi's fiction reveals the decadence of urban life. His masterpiece novella, *Malakut* (*Realm of Spirits*, 1974), reflects his philosophy of life seen through the eyes of a possessed man, and the narrative oscillates between real and unreal, but the latter never stands out as such. This is the *literature of anxiety*, a deep cultural angst – a lasting legacy of Sadeq Hedayat. This is a deeply rooted cultural anxiety that the works of Sa'edi and Sadeqi reveal, and it is reflected through insecure, paranoid and mortified individuals who take this anxiety with them through rapid and westernised development. Theirs are stories of distorted modernisation through which the individual is suspended in the void between modern rationality and traditional phantasms, trying to cope. In short, they reveal, the modern Iran has failed to create new citizens.

This anxiety informs the novels of Golshiri, co-founder of the School of Isfahan and the Iranian Writers Association. Written within the period of our study and highly acclaimed (to the extent that the director Bahman Farmanara [1942–] made a movie adaptation of it in 1974), Golshiri's immortal novel, *Prince Ehtejab* (1969), portrays the irreversible decline of the old, despotic khanate and imperial order, as narrated through the painful memories of a Qajar prince. His remembrances appear between reality and hallucinations pertaining to murderous self-righteousness of the rulers and their prevalent sexual desires and impotence, all attesting to a civilisational decline that is entangled in repetition compulsion (Freud) and does not lead to any meaningful and promising future. Golestan expresses similar concerns in his novels and novellas in this period, the most creative of his writing career. Many of his works in this period were actually published after 1979. Golestan is also a filmmaker who wrote his own screenplays, notably *Mudbrick and Mirror* (1964), a film that presents the depth of alienation of the urban working poor, the people rapid development had displaced. A member of the Tudeh Party in his youth who resigned in protest against party corruption, Golestan published the allegorical *Secrets of the Genie Valley Treasures* (1974), also made into a film he directed (1974), to deride the shallow modernisation of the Pahlavi era. A simple country man accidentally finds ancient treasures buried outside his village and finds an antiques-seller in the city through whom to illegally sell his loot. His wealth dramatically changes his relationships in the village as his newly-found status, expressed through his financial expenditure, rises. He begins to order others around, buys silly, flashy objects and builds a fancy-looking but poorly built house, before his house crumbles and people abandon him (Golestan, 2002). Once decoded, this story anticipates the declining fate of Iran's rentier state and the *nouveau riche* class.

Simin Daneshvar emerged as the Queen of Persian fiction with her *Savushun* (1969) – a bestseller novel estimated to have sold half a million copies (by 2016) in a country where a book's usual print-run is five hundred to a thousand copies. Its realist-symbolic narrative unfolds through the point of view of the protagonist Zari, on whom the story hinges: a well-off, landowning family living during the Second World War invasion of Iran by the Allies, struggling with the local governor's despotism and complex relationships with other families around them, each from a particular social group. The conflict of Zari, who believes in gradual change, with the active politics of her anti-colonial, nationalist husband, Yusof, who challenges the status quo and finally dies for his ideals, constitutes the narrative's dynamics and reflects the tension between two tendencies in modern Iran: reforms or revolution. Attention to detail is admirable in this novel. The realist narrative indeed contains a political symbolism that the reader can only appreciate (see Abedinin 1990: 76–82).

A significant exception to this trend is Chubak's *Tangsir* (1963), his first novel, which depicts a real character named Zayer Mohammad in a town near the southern port city of Bushehr who singlehandedly revolted against corrupt financiers and authorities in his town, killing three men before vanishing without trace, thus becoming a regional legend. Clearly promoting 'hope and resistance' (Abedini 1990: 47) and representing Chubak's *naturalisme*, the novel celebrated the power of the individual in challenging a complex system of power. This work, however, became mired in debates between critics who called it inflated and without proper structure and those who admired it (Abedini 1990: 45). The novel's popularisation of the idea of armed resistance against injustice was only shown a decade later, in the 'guerrilla period', in a movie based on the novel that amplified its message (Chapter 5). As an honorary mention, I am inclined to cite Parviz Zahedi's 'Forty Stairs' (1967), a stylistically typical story of the 'School of the South' (*adabiyyat-e jonub*), as a rare and overlooked potential instance of the 'guerrilla fiction' genre that was never born: a tribal armed uprising in Khuzestan against the state is depicted through the narrative of a rural vendor's son who accompanies his aging father on his three-day foot trip to these tribal territories, now militarised. This is happening during Reza Shah's reign and his policy of forced relocation and settlement of migrant tribes: 'The government wants to uproot them' (Zahedi 1967: 18). So, the tribal Khan's fighting back – which happens in the distance though the shots are clearly heard – is judicious. Enjoying the unrivalled hospitality of a tribal family in their camp, the vendor decides to forgo the monies he was owed and return. On the way back, they help an injured officer to the next gendarmerie post where they learn that the Khan has been lured into a trap and killed in Chel Pellekan (forty stairs) passage.

I cannot offer an exhaustive survey here, but these key authors and works represent the context of fiction in the 1960s, the decade of creative imagination and novel genres. But clearly, none of these brilliant works and authors (and many others), many of whom were known dissidents, either had any influence on or anticipated the gestating militant opposition, or even allegorically depicted the younger dissidents' concerns. These outstanding novels, novellas and short stories reveal primarily the *intellectuals'* preoccupation with Pahlavi modernisation and concomitant cultural anxieties of transition, genuine concerns that are nonetheless too lethargic to create hope for change or inspire vanguard feats. In its reporting of Iran's post-reforms social conditions and intellectual quandaries, a subtle sense of *resignation* dominates the literature of this period, as *this genre of fiction seizes upon abundant socially-critical depiction but offers meagre-to-non-existent politically suggestive imagination.*

In this period, though, foreign novels addressed the lack of vernacular socialist novels. Searching for 'political novels' brought many dissidents to translations of *Pane e Vino* (1936) by Ignazio Silone, *The Grapes of Wrath* (1939) by John Steinbeck, *For Whom the Bell Tolls* (1940) by Ernest Hemingway and *Spartacus* by Howard Fast (1951) – to name a few popular ones.

Against this background, and given his vision of 'children's revolution' as a medium of *emancipatory imagination*, we can now better grasp and properly appreciate Behrangi's innovations in fiction as a gateway to the then imminent militant struggle.

Birth of a Genre

Behrangi's writing career is indebted to his collaborative research and publication, with Dehqani, of Azerbaijani folk tales, a project they began in the late 1950s and continued in the 1960s and published in several magazines (their collection, *The Fables of Azerbaijan*, was published posthumously in 1975). By the mid-1960s, Behrangi had already developed a style of 'children's' stories that had identifiable resemblances with the Azerbaijani folk tales in terms of narrative structure. I am inclined to call this, *à la* Roland Barthes, *homology* – that is, similarity of sequence with different content (1977: 83–4). From the Azerbaijani folk tales Behrangi borrows the magical (and childish) realm between real and 'nonreal', and with that, the mysterious and concealed portal that links the two worlds: the oppressive world of humans with its countless tentacles that pull the children protagonists into abjection and the free and wise world of trees, birds and animals, the friends of children. One only needs to read his renderings of Turkic tales like 'Crazy Dumrul' (*Deli Dumrul*, an ancient Turkmen legend that is told on the medieval Turkmen migratory route from Turkmenistan to Azerbaijan to Turkey), 'Talkhun' (April 1961; first published in Shamlu's *Ketab-e Hafteh* [no. 88, 18 August 1963] and then in *Talkhun and Other Stories* [1969]), 'The Fable of Care' ('Afsaneh-ye Mohabbat', 1967), 'The Pigeon-Keeping Bald Man' ('Kachal-e Kaftarbaz',1966; pub. 1967) and 'The Old Woman and Her Golden Chick' (1968). In these stories, humans enter the non-human or magical worlds, and as the loyal friends of oppressed humans, animals converse with and help humans to alleviate their hardship. The famous tale 'Koroghlu and Hamzeh the Bald' (dated summer 1968) showcases the legend of Koroghlu (literally, 'son of a blind person') and his 'liberation army' of women and men who campaigned against the tyrant Hassan Pasha (c. the Safavid era). In his army, women and men are equal, wealth is shared and there is no hierarchy of status. Commander Koroghlu is subject to harsh criticisms for his failures by his comrades, including his beloved warrior-wife, Negar. The story, and especially the rebels' bastion, Chenlibel, sounds like the campaign of Babak Khorramdin (798–838 CE), with his emblematic mountain-top castle near the town of Ahar in East Azerbaijan Province, who stood up to the invading Muslim Arabs where Azerbaijan is today.

Encouraged by his professional relationships with Tehran-based dissident writers and intellectuals who helped him publish his stories and articles in magazines, by the mid-1960s Behrangi had been so prolific that he had developed quite a writing portfolio for himself. Being a rural elementary teacher, Behrangi had found his audience, but there is more to this: in all his stories, Behrangi depicts the grown-ups, the adults, as oppressive, malicious, superstitious, inert, inept, and the defenders of the status quo. In contrast, the children, and their non-human friends, are freedom-loving, benevolent, kind, capable, and seekers of another, better, world. 'All the protagonists in Behrangi's works deny the status quo and search for a life different [from] the conventional life' (Abedini 1990: 148). To proceed with the central theme of this book, I need to treat the corpus of Behrangi's fiction within one particular discourse, but I will interpret *The Little Black Fish* separately, due to its impact on the PFG.

The most memorable protagonist of Behrangi's children's literature is a little rural girl named Olduz ('star' in Azeri Turkish). *Olduz and the Crows* was written in 1965 and published in 1968 (in 1980 Marzieh Boroumand directed a play based on it in Tehran's Te'atr-e Shahr). *Olduz and the Speaking Doll* is dated autumn 1967, but it is actually a prequel to *The Crows*, and I review them in the order of the narratives. *The Speaking Doll* opens with Olduz telling the children-readers, in a prelude to Behrangi's story, that she met Mr Behrangi in her village school when she was ten years old after she had returned to village to live with her mother (Behrangi 2017b). In the story, Olduz's father has divorced her mother, and now Olduz lives in a town with her naive father and cruel stepmother who wants Olduz out of her home. She endures daily mistreatment at home, and once is even tortured for a confession by her stepmother. So, she often seeks refuge in the storage room in solitude and occasionally spends time with her friend Yashar, who is a rug-weaver and whose mother periodically does housework for Olduz's family. Olduz is about five years old when her giant doll, made by her mother out of old rags, begins speaking, ending her loneliness. At this moment, a vengeful magic makes its appearance in her home, one that constantly punishes the stepmother for her cruelties: when her stepmother forces her husband to kill and cook Olduz's cow friend, the meat tastes and smell horrible, and they give it away to Yashar's family, but to them and Olduz the meat tastes like honey. Then we see the nocturnal trip of three pigeons, which turn out to be the two children and the doll! As they fly over the rivers, meadows and mountains, they realise how vast the world is. They reach a jungle where, upon turning back into humans and doll again, the two deprived kids are majestically entertained and served by animals and a band of friendly dolls and their elder Sara. Interestingly, the animals call each other *rafiq* or 'comrade'. The conversation in the epigraph of this chapter, widely quoted by leftist revolutionaries, takes place in the party (Behrangi 2017b: 104) and is the highlight of this story – an intimation of Behrangi's political views: *the activist is the one who lights a lantern in the dark.* The metaphor is captivating, given the context of the post-coup period. Anyway, the pigeons' frequenting of Olduz's home baffles the stepmother, who, suspecting Olduz's involvement with them, beats up Olduz before fire ants come to her rescue, attacking the vile woman. Finally, having overheard Olduz's talking with her doll, the malicious stepmother burns the doll (Behrangi 2017b: 132–3), leaving the little girl in deep grief. An allegorical figure of Iran's forsaken young, abandoned to their evil and naive parents who are too numb, wicked or incapable of experiencing the enchanted beckoning of another world, Olduz continues to endure hardships in her home-prison.

Our adorable Olduz re-appears with her new friends, the crows, in the next story. Bored and lonely, she befriends Mama Crow (*naneh kalagheh*), who wonders why she is not playing. Realising that after her doll was gone and Yashar was working Olduz had no friends, Mama Crow plays with her. When asked why she steals soap (crows love eating soap), Mama Crow replies, 'As long as everyone just works for himself, theft will stay with us' (Behrangi 2017b: 15). She further explains that if she can provide for her family, she will not need to steal (Behrangi 2017b: 33). While Mama Crow patiently answers Olduz's questions and tells 'the reason for everything' (Behrangi 2017b: 23), the stepmother only orders her around; she never reasons with her. The stepmother finally captures and kills Mama Crow and smacks Olduz so hard that she falls unconscious and recovers only after a long time. Soon, Olduz is visited by Mama Crow's son, who gives her a few of his feathers. Only kind and pure children can speak to crows (Behrangi 2017b: 54). Together, Olduz, Yashar and the crow stage a scene to spook the adults, or in Behrangi's words, 'wise children troll ignorant parents' (Behrangi 2017b: 45). A harsh winter descends upon the town, and a child, Yashar's friend, freezes to death overnight at home. The stepmother gives birth to a baby, who dies a week later. The crow suggests that Olduz should escape and live with the crows and Grandma Crow shows them how, praising them: 'I like you. You're very different from your parents. Good for you! But you're still young and inexperienced. You must learn a lot and think better' (Behrangi 2017b: 63). On the day of the great escape, when a flock of crows shows up at Yashar's place with a net to carry the children with them, Olduz turns out to be locked up by her parents. In an exciting rescue mission aided by Yashar's mother, Olduz breaks free while the crows gang up on her parents. 'They went to the town of crows. They went to a place better than that of "dad." They went to a place where there was no "step-mother"' (Behrangi 2017b: 75). Once safe, they all pay tribute to Mama Crow and her son who were killed for helping Olduz. 'Long live those children who never forget their deceased and martyred friends' (Behrangi 2017b: 77). Just like Koroghlu's bastion, the town of crows is on a mountain-top – possibly a reference to Babak Khoramdin's castle.

Behrangi's *One Pear, A Thousand Pears* (summer 1968) breaks new grounds in surrealism, in that the pear tree is the narrator – a brilliant literary move hardly seen in anthropocentric Persian literature. The pear tree tells the fascinating story of its germinating, growth, blossoming and fruiting, as well as its going through the seasons and reproducing. Driven by a sense of justice, she intentionally *refuses* to fruit unless the village's deprived children can have her juicy pears but not the landowner, forcing a mystery upon the gardener, who takes every measure to remedy her condition, even thinking of felling the tree, but to no avail. Two boys, Pulad and Saheb Ali, who had planted the pear tree on the landlord's property, debate whether the fruit is theirs or not. 'Saheb Ali said: "He [the landlord] can't do shit. The land belongs to he who works it. The piece of land where we planted our tree is ours." Pulad found courage in himself and said: "Yes, it's ours. If he [the landlord] does shit, we will set his garden ablaze"' (Behrangi 2017b: 268). The statement could not be more socialist! *One Pear, A Thousand Pears* is the story of defiance and justice: the pear tree's refusal to fruit even by endangering her life (reminding us of hunger-strikers) unless her fruits reach poor children. The children understand that they have agency and envision the possibility of stepping up their action against the landlord. The latter, interestingly, is absent: but his absent presence drives the entire story. He is the one who has set up and manages the entire system – an allegory of the Shah – but through his agents, who themselves are close to being slaves to this system. The symbolism could not be more suggestive. Again, the young boys are the ones who can imagine ways of acting outside the system. The story delivers its message magically: here Behrangi succeeds in 'maintain[ing] the narrative in the difficult boundary between reality and imagination' (Abedini 1990: 147).

Behrangi's 'children's stories' reach new heights with *Twenty-Four Hours in Sleep and Wakefulness* (summer 1968). The story of migrant children in Tehran who work at odd jobs, panhandle or become street vendors, it is told from the point of view of Latif, a village boy whose father is a street vendor. *Twenty-Four Hours* opens with a depiction of the street life of Latif and his friends, boys his age. Latif befriends a huge stuffed camel behind the toy store's window. The camel cares for Latif and takes him away from his harsh life to the party of toy animals held in a villa in chic and clean northern Tehran. Here, Behrangi's political education reaches its height when he talks about class differences. Latif has never seen the other Tehran and is bewildered by what he sees. 'The camel laughed and said: "You're right Latif jan. Tehran has two sections . . . South and north: the south is filled with smog and dirt and dust but the north is clean . . . The south is the district of penniless and hungry people and the north is the district of [the] rich and affluent"' (Behrangi 2017b: 291–2). The toy animals admire Latif's loyalty to the camel, lamenting that the rich kids quickly get bored with their toys and abandon them. These dreamscapes create questions in Latif's mind. But his father's response to his question about inequality clearly captures Behrangi's view of the older generation. 'I . . . said: "Being rich is a good thing, dad, isn't it? One can eat whatever one wants and have whatever one wants, isn't it, dad?" My father said: "Don't be ungrateful, boy. God knows well who to make rich and who to make poor"' (Behrangi 2017b: 296). But that is hardly convincing. Latif's realisation that his poverty has no reason but class inequality first stirs hateful vengeance in him. As he looks at his dirty and untidy self reflected in a store window, his feeling of shame quickly turns to hatred towards the three clean and tidy boys next to him. 'I wanted to smash the three rich kids' brains', he immediately thinks. But then he wonders, 'Was it their fault that I live like this?' (Behrangi 2017b: 300). When the store owner shoos him away, he rages and throws a stone at the store window, smashing it into a thousand pieces (Behrangi 2017b: 301). He destroys what he cannot have. Finally, when one day he notices that a rich girl, calling her father 'Papa', gets out of a fancy car, walks into the toy store and buys his camel friend, Latif begs them not to buy it. He weeps out loud and the story ends as he thinks, 'I wish the submachinegun behind the store window were mine' (Behrangi 2017b: 308). Unlike the three previous works I reviewed, *Twenty-Four Hours* holds together the stark contrast between reality and fantasy but leaves no ambiguity in suggesting solutions. The *apparent* layer of signification in the story's closing statement suggests Latif's envious fury stemming from deprivation, a banal *ressentiment* in Nietzschean fashion.

A sub-machine gun, after all, destroys; it does not create. But there is revealed before the phenomenological gaze a deeper layer of signification: with the toy camel gone, Latif's deprivation is intensified, as this already poor boy is now also deprived of his gateway to a dream-world, a world of fantasy where pain and suffering stop. *The sub-machine gun therefore destroys the world that destroys dreams.* And this is the existentially revolutionary meaning, I argue, that informs Behrangi's *weltanschauung*. It is *Twenty-Four Hours*, I submit, not *The Little Black Fish*, that speaks of the ultimate verdict of Behrangi about his country.

These stories depict how children's experience of poverty and cruelty under an inescapable order, imposed and safeguarded by their parents, urges them to desert their reality. While Behrangi consistently characterises the older generation as superstitious, malevolent, simple-minded and violent, he also shows them caught in oppressive conditions they can neither leave behind nor even fathom going beyond. This is an aging generation entangled in the harsh realities of life, but Behrangi does not pity them. On the contrary: he scorns and condemns them for their passive submission, their becoming selfish to make life easier and taking out their anger on their young. This is a resigned and insipid generation, blameworthy for its lack of imagination or vigour. The younger generation, by contrast, is capable of imagining another world. *The children are too young to have internalised the hegemonic effect of reality.* A rural elementary teacher can see this clearly in the fresh minds of his students. In breaking away from their oppressive reality, the children enter worlds of 'fantasy', and in these worlds, they find friends they never believed they had. This world can only be a 'fantasy' if our culturally sanctioned epistemological yardstick is the 'reality' every adult has sheepishly internalised. Once we remove reality (and realism) as the measure of actual and possible, the dream-world stands out as the allegory of an entirely new world. In fact, those things an adult calls 'fantasy' in these stories are indeed alternative realities. In the sagas of Olduz, the world of the jungle is an egalitarian world; the speaking doll is her guide to another order of things; and the crows are the ultimate dedicated revolutionaries. The toys that Latif befriends complain about rich kids because they want to befriend poor children whose friendship is genuine and lasting, uncontaminated by the fetishism of the affluent classes. The caring pear tree asserts her agency, acting against injustices that agonise her by endangering her very own survival. Fighting injustice needs sacrifice: the greatest expression of love. And who, other than the pear tree, understands injustice? The two boys, not the old gardener. This is the world of fantasy, but it can only be revealed to the young ones who do not submit to their conditions. In imagining, they discover that *a better world is possible.* All power to imagination!

Is it still a matter of speculation how Behrangi would have reacted to the foundation of the PFG?

On Behrangi's Trail

In his extensive heartfelt tribute to Behrangi on the first anniversary of his death, Darvishian (1969) sanctioned a revolutionary reading of Samad. Already before his untimely death, Behrangi had influenced passionate and dedicated social-justice-oriented young teachers from the provinces. Darvishian was a young rural teacher from the Kurdish town of Kermanshah who was born into a poverty-stricken working-class family. His trips to Tehran brought him the friendship of Al-Ahmad, in whose home he met Behrangi, who was only two years his senior, but Darvishian held him in high regard (Jeyhun 2017) and began his career as a writer of fiction. A prolific writer, he also collected and published Kurdish folk tales and multi-volume Iranian fables. Reflecting the backwardness, misery and ignorance of the rural and urban poor and the injustices they suffered, his writings were soon banned and he was imprisoned several times.

Between 1971 and 1979, he spent a total of six years in prison (Jeyhun 2017), in part for his first published collection of short stories, *Az In Velayat* (*From This Village*; orig. 1973), a book that won him quite a reputation among leftist dissidents. Darvishian's fiction in this period depicts, at times from a child's viewpoint, stark class contrasts and cruelties of deprivation. This is a collection of twelve stories (from the 1960s) that captures the abject conditions of those Pahlavi modernisation had left behind. In 'Doesn't Have' ('Nadarad'), for instance, a rural teacher reminisces about hearing his star student Niaz Ali Nadarad dying of illness when the newspaper page covering the broken glass on the window shows a title, 'Healthcare for All' (Darvishian 1977: 7). In 'Wolf', a rural teacher is stalked by a wolf when walking at night in snow to get Samad's books to the village (Darvishian 1977: 49–52). The people in his stories are superstitious, greedy, mean and manipulative but toiling to death at all times, and they are such simply because of their poverty. His stark realism speaks for itself without the author's verdict. The same realism appears in his *Abshuran* (orig. 1974), twelve related stories about the neighbourhood in Kermanshah, next to the creek in the book's title, where the protagonist Ashraf (probably the author) speaks of the realities through his experience as a child in a poor family (Darvishian 1979b). His novella *When Will You Return, My Dear Brother?* (1979a) is also told by a child narrating the raiding of their meagre home in the middle of the night by security agents and the arrest of his activist brother who is also the family's breadwinner. This is one of the more interesting works of Darvishian in this period, with a memorable conversation like this: 'Then, the sweaty agent took me to a corner and softly asked, "Tell me, does your brother ever talk about Lenin?" I replied, "We have Vaseline at home . . . but my brother never bought us Lenin"' (1979a: 17). In another novella, *The Wall Newspaper of Our School* (orig. 1975), a boy narrates memories of his first year of high school, his challenges, defeats and victories in the face of an autocratic school principal (Darvishian 1978). Abedini's remarks about *Abshuran* in fact apply to most of Darvishian's fiction in this period:

> In these stories the reader does not arrive at new discoveries about life, for the writer treats reality as a case that is discovered once and for all and requires no further search. As a matter of fact, in order to magnify deprivation, he takes only the most obvious manifestation of poverty – bread deprivation. Lacking attention to cultural poverty and the roots of ignorance, banality and desperation cause his portrayal of a reality that is more simplified than the reality that every conscious human witnesses in everyday life. (Abedini 1990: 150–1)

Darvishian's style of fiction is Behranigi-esque but the content is not. Behrangi's impact on Darvishian's fiction is clear but one-sided. Imagination is noticeably lacking in his work. He once said, 'For me, writing was a protest, a response to the unjust and unequal environment of our lives' (Darvishian, quoted in Jeyhun 2017). Protest, not vision. His works in this period entailed both realist fiction and children's stories. But his children's stories are only a faint reminder of Behrangi's work. Darvishian is unable to transcend what he sees, unlike Behrangi, and thus stands only as witness, not a visionary. So, he remains primarily a reporter, not an author, in many of his works.

The works of Mansour Yaquti (1949–), also born in the Province of Kermanshahan, and his nakedly realist style, bring him close to the genre Darvishian employed. He was also a rural teacher, but as a part of the Literacy Corps (the programme through which high school graduates would serve their mandatory two-year military service as elementary school teachers in remote areas) before he was hired as a teacher and continued to teach in rural Kurdish areas of his province. He was imprisoned twice under the Shah and fired after the Revolution, spent five years in prison, and worked as labourer, night watchman and building caretaker, all the while continuing with his writing. Though not analytical, Yaquti's notes (1978) on the challenges the rural teachers faced, his criticism of the education system and the teachers' vicious and abusive treatment of students trails Behrangi's treatise on education. His fictionalised lived experiences constitute the bulk of his work. *My Childhood* (1972) contains six connected stories narrated from the first-person point of view of a teenager. These are (over-dramatised) stories, in the realist genre, of rural poverty, hunger, deprivation and village-to-city migration that offer no possibility of transcending their conditions. A similar mood dominates *With the Children of Our Village* (1974). Possibly one of Yaquti's best works of the 1970s, the novella *Pajush* (1978), presenting through an omniscient point of view, opens with the teenage protagonist Abdul looking for food in the trash. He has quit school and lives in an abject abode with his father being a heroin addict and his mother burdened with managing the family. Themes of poverty and gendered violence run through the story. In searching for work, Abdul first becomes a kebab shop hand before his old boss turns out to be paedophile who tries to sexually molest him. In revenge Abdul leaves, stealing his cash and spending it on his family. Next, he becomes a helping hand in an entrails kebab shop. Within a couple of days his boss tries to rape him, and in the altercation that follows Abdul kills him and flees. Then we see Abdul in juvenile prison, apparently for stealing his former boss's money, where he meets Ebrahim, a former print shop worker and book reader. They continue to meet after their release, and Abdul joins Ebrahim's reading circle. The story ends with an interesting twist: Abdul's revolutionary training is aborted when he is identified and arrested for murder. Over all, Yaquti's other works in this period are similar in style and narrative, indeed 'repetitive' (Abedini 1990: 151). The force of conditions seems absolute, the obstacles insurmountable. Yaquti is the narrator of being trapped in abject misery.

It is interesting to note that when Behrangi narrates poverty, as in *24 Hours* or 'The Beet-Seller Boy' (November 1967; the story of a poor boy, his student, whose hard work pays off), he always leaves the future open: his protagonists either see a way out (the sub-machine gun in *24 Hours*) or overcome their condition ('The Beet-Seller Boy'). Behrangi's characters are capable of agency. That is not so much the case in Darvishian and Yaquti. In their zeal to portray the counter-image to the regime's modernisation, these authors simply focused on the miseries of those left behind without giving the poor meaningful agency. By implication, the poor they portray can only wait for a liberator, but this can *only obliquely* connect Darvishian's and Yaquti's naked realism to the guerrilla period. They are heirs to Behrangi mostly in their teaching the spite arising from class-based deprivation, although an intellectual claimed that 'the loathing (*nefrat*) that Behrangi teaches the children . . . is a human loathing' (Hezarkhani 1968: 24). Stylistically, basic literary devices (simile, metaphor, suggestion) are noticeably absent from their works. Interestingly, their reporter-style realism made their easily accessible and quickly-read works popular among the leftist opposition.

Story of a Story

Written in 1967 and published in 1968 (a few weeks before his death), *The Little Black Fish* represents Behrangi's (children's) fiction at its peak: undoubtedly the most important artistic piece of the guerrilla period, a book that positions Behrangi as the single most influential writer with measurable impact on the PFG. I reiterate with greater confidence my earlier appraisal that 'Behrangi did not live to see the influence of . . . *The Little Black Fish*, which became Fadaiyan's unofficial manifesto – a book that is believed to have attracted more militants to the Fadai movement than any of the PFG or Marxist texts' (Vahabzadeh 2010: 134).

As it was banned some time after its publication, the book itself became a much-coveted cultural object. Its publication process is a fascinating story in itself. Reportedly, Behrangi had given the story to Sirus Tahbaz (1939–98), editor of *Arash* magazine, hoping he would publish it. Tahbaz did not find it publishable in its present form. Some time after the Centre for the Intellectual Cultivation of Children and Youth was founded in 1965, Tahbaz suggested Behrangi's manuscript to Firuz Shirvanlu (1938–88), who was in charge of the Centre's publication bureau. Shirvanlu was a Maoist activist in England with the Confederation of Iranian Students-National Union (CISNU). He had returned to Iran in 1962 along with Parviz Nikkhah and other comrades to start a revolution. Upon return, he joined Franklin Press in Tehran but was arrested along with his comrades after the assassination attempt against the Shah in Marmar Palace on 10 April 1965 by the Imperial Guard soldier Reza Shamsabadi (1943–65). While it is greatly doubtful that Kikkhah and others were involved, members of the group were charged and received prison terms. Shirvanlu was released in November 1966. Upon release, he established his advertising company Negareh, recruiting young, aspiring artists, including the future internationally renowned filmmaker Abbas Kiarostami (1940–2016), the poet Ahmad-Reza Ahmadi, the graphist and illustrator Farshid Mesghali (1943–), the writer and playwright Farideh Farjam (1934–) and the illustrator and graphist Nikzad Nojumi (1941–). This is when he was invited to the Centre and appointed publications manager (Mirzai 2019). Given Shirvanlu's background, he received Behrangi's manuscript enthusiastically but also agreed with Tahbaz that it was not ready for publication. He appointed Farideh Farjam and M. Azad (Mahmoud Moshref Azad Tehrani; 1933–2005) to work with Behrangi and develop a publishable version – a process that took about a month. The published version is dated winter 1968. As a children's story, it needed illustration, the commission going to twenty-six-year-old Farshid Mesghali, whose amazingly vibrant linocut images won him the First Graphic Prize of the Sixth International Children Books Fair in Bologna, Italy (1968) and the Honorary Diploma of Bratislava Biannual, Czechoslovakia (1968) (Bassiri 2018: 771, n. 9; Mesghali 2015; Mesghali 2016). Shirvanlu had reportedly expressed to Asad Behrangi that he was very happy about his role in the publication of *The Little Black Fish* (2000: 127). The Centre published the book with a print-run of 5,000 copies and it immediately sold out: the hardback priced at 70 rials, the paperback at 35. Later, the Centre also published this book as a double 45-rmp record – something unusual for that time and featured in the Introduction to this book (Behrangi 2000: 123).

The Little Black Fish: Longevity of Allegory

Using a frame narrative structure, *The Little Black Fish* opens at bedtime when grandma fish tells the story of a little black fish to her 12,000 little grandchildren: the little black fish lived with his mother, swimming up and down a brook every day along with other fish. His abrupt declaration one morning to his mother of his decision to leave and discover where the brook leads astonishes her and their neighbours, who intervene, ridicule and threaten him. They speak of a snail who had asked similar questions and been slain by them. The black fish says goodbye to his friends, who swim him to the end of the brook, thanking him for 'waking us from our rabbit's nap', calling him a 'knowledgeable and courageous friend' (Behrangi 2017d: 8). After swimming down a waterfall, he finds himself in a pond among narcissistic tadpoles, who ridicule his appearance and think their pond is the entire world. Further on, he realises that he is in a creek now and runs into a crab who hunts frogs for food and tries to lure and eat him, but the crab is struck dead by a passing shepherd boy. Soon, the black fish meets a gecko on the shore and asks him about the dangers ahead: the pelican, swordfish and seagull. The gecko tells him that only the first lives nearby, and gives him a small dagger, made from a thorn, that he makes for the brave passing fishes so that they can tear the pelican's pouch and escape, if captured. Thrilled by the news that others have also travelled this path, the little fish learns that they have already formed a group and pull the fisherman's net to the bottom of the sea and release trapped fishes. He then runs into a gazelle wounded by a hunter, watches turtles basking in the sun, enjoys partridges' calls, and is mesmerised by the scent of grass.

Soon he finds himself in a flock of tiny fishes, who inform him he is now in the river and are surprised to hear of his intent to travel to the sea. They, too, want to go to the sea, they confess, but are afraid of the pelican. At night, the black fish has a fascinating conversation with the moon, who tells him the world is too vast for him to see it all, but encourages him to continue on his journey. In the morning, he leaves, along with a bunch of unsure tiny fishes who still fear the pelican. He tells them, 'You think too much . . . Once we are on our way, we'll shed our fears' (Behrangi 2017d: 18). Before long, they find themselves in the pelican's pouch. The tiny fishes plead with the pelican to release them, blaming the little black fish. The pelican asks them to kill the little fish if they want to be released. The black fish threatens them with his dagger, telling them it is a subterfuge: they agree that the black fish should play dead to see if the pelican releases the tiny fishes, but the pelican immediately swallows the tiny fishes despite their service. The black fish then cuts through the pelican's pouch with his dagger and escapes.

Just after he luckily escapes an attack by a swordfish, he meets a group of fishes who welcome the little black fish to the sea. They call each other 'comrade' (*rafiq*). Thrilled to join them and fight the fisherman, he asks them for time to explore around. But soon he finds himself in the gull's beak. He plays dead and escapes, but is captured again and swallowed immediately. In the gull's dark stomach, he encounters another fish. The little black fish begins wriggling, and when the seagull opens his mouth to laugh, his fish companion escapes. He pulls out his dagger, and the flying seagull suddenly twists his body in pain before falling in the water and drowning. And the little black fish was never seen again.

It was late: the old grandma fish says goodnight. 'Eleven-thousand nine-hundred ninety-nine little fishes said "goodnight" and fell asleep. Grandma also fell asleep, but a little red fish could not sleep, no matter how she tried. All night, she was thinking of the sea' (Behrangi 2017d: 28).

Already heralded as early as 1968 as a story that is 'not for entertaining but for educating' (Hezarkhani 1968: 18), *The Little Black Fish* was received enthusiastically by dissident intellectuals. Manouchehr Hezarkhani's *foundational* reading of it in 'The Worldview of the Little Black Fish' (in the Special Issue of *Arash*) as a *political allegory* set the tone for future interpretations of the story, in particular the PFG members, thus wresting it away from the children's literature genre and fixing it as a political and liberationist manifesto. Reviews like his must have inadvertently contributed to the book's being banned in 1973. Hezarkhani decodes the story in such a way that it is now almost impossible to encode it afresh, unless one changes the narrative (see below). As an extension of metaphor, allegory dwells almost entirely in the symbolic as it produces fixed signification by unpairing the existing signifier–signified pair: the signifier is connected to a signified that has almost no referential connection to the signifier within the community of speakers. In short, allegory offers an at-hand meaning but points at something other than that. Relying mostly on personification, 'allegory involves a continuous parallel between two (or more) levels of meaning in a story, so that its persons and events correspond to their equivalents in a system of ideas or a chain of events external to the tale' (Jahangiri 2012: 337). Thus, as with every other symbol, allegory arises from *differential signification*. Since no narrative is by essence allegorical, allegory is an attribute of society, of dominant readings in particular times and places that supersede them, and it is thus a collective achievement, one that is rendered and promoted by the community of deliberate inferences. It might be the author's intent to write allegorically: one is reminded of the classical narrative poem *Mouse and Cat*, by Ubayd Zakani (d. 1370), a brilliant satirical work exposing the hypocrisy of religion and power in medieval Persia. In our case, Behrangi clearly intended to write an allegory. But unless the allegorical reading is sanctioned by deliberate inferences and promoted as such, it will not gain that status.

Our particular fish signifies a *difference*: his simple intention of breaking away from the daily routine, a question instilled in him by the slain snail (an unlikely friendship), to find the end of the brook is received and condemned by older fish, his mother and their neighbours, as a *rebellious act*, a specific reaction that intensifies his determination to leave. If these neighbours were just meaninglessly there up to this point, they now become obnoxious and intolerable. The 'clash of the two generations' (Hezarkhani 1968: 19) is best expressed when the neighbours regard the protagonist's zeal for exploration as juvenile impulse. These older folk are lethargic adherents of obsolete beliefs and meaningless routines: protectors of the status quo. They can be dangerous: they even threaten to kill the black fish, just as they had murdered the snail (Behrangi 2017d: 6). Driven by banal ignorance, these ordinary folks can easily turn into a murderous mob to preserve their way of life. *In normative societies, mere difference can be a life hazard.* Behrangi smashes the myth of 'older and wiser' further on: in the pond, the mama frog challenges the little black fish by saying 'I've lived long enough to know that the entire world is this pond' (Behrangi 2017d: 10), to which the black fish replies, 'If you lived a hundred of these lives, you'd still be an ignorant and desperate frog' (Behrangi 2017d: 10).

Our protagonist's friends in the brook are as curious as he is, but they lack the courage to embark on this perilous journey. They represent the silent moral supporters of the movement, gaining awareness but unwilling to walk any further, preferring a safe life, however tedious. A story of the 1960s, the decade of the Shah's unrestrained police state, *The Little Black Fish* must do away with the psychology of fear (Hezarkhani 1968: 26). This does not mean becoming heroically fearless, but having the courage to take just the next step in the journey *despite* our fear. That is what the little fish does, and as such, Behrangi's protagonist is not really 'heroic'; he is the curious one who has the courage to take the next step. Each step leads to the next, and having learned there are indeed others who have travelled this path, the little black fish grows eager to join them in the sea. By the time he reaches the river, his reputation begins to spread: 'a little black fish who has come from afar and wants to find out the end of the river and has no fear of the pelican' (Behrangi 2017d: 16).

The funniest characters in the story, the narcissistic tadpoles, are said to represent 'quasi-intellectual petite-bourgeoisie' (Hezarkhani 1968: 23), but I think this is quite a stretch, as the tadpoles express no sign of intellect. In fact, it is their stupidity that makes them hilarious. They represent the new middle-class state employees, happy in their small pond of monthly salaries, mortgage payments and banal amusements, incapable of critical reflection. They are literally immature (being tadpoles), but even when they mature they will end up becoming their ugly mama frog, who is still mentally immature!

On his journey, the black fish encounters two kinds of people: the likes of the crab, the common criminal type, and opportunists who take advantage of and hurt unsuspecting others. The hunter (having injured the gazelle) belongs to this category, too. Others, like the gecko, are wise and willing guides. It is the gecko who informs the black fish about the dangers ahead, and that others have created a group in the sea to challenge the fisherman. The gecko teaches him the *power of collective action*: 'Because they work together, once the fisherman throws his net, they enter it and pull the net together to the bottom of the sea' (Behrangi 2017d: 14). Aware of the dangers ahead, the gecko gives the black fish a *weapon for self-defence*. The moon provides spiritual comfort and empathy. But then there are the malicious pelican, swordfish, and seagull, powerful predators who threaten all fish: they live in a different world from the fish (two of them birds, the other a fish with a 'sword') in the sense that they and fish have no common ground. These represent predatory functionaries of security apparatuses who capture all those exposed to them by virtue of their having left their assigned domains of existence. Each has a jurisdiction, according to the gecko: swordfish and seagull in the sea, the pelican around the corner (Behrangi 2017d: 12–13). The pelican, in particular, represents state security: sly and equipped with a jail (pouch), he interrogates his captives, planting fear in them, threatening and pushing them to betray their friends. That is the trap the little fishes fall into, but they are not rewarded for their co-operation; in fact, they are killed, while the little black fish manages a jailbreak, thanks to his dagger. In the gull's stomach, he is not just trying to save this other fish: 'I want to kill the gull, so that other fish will be in peace' (Behrangi 2017d: 26). He achieves that by sacrificing himself – a *fadai* (self-sacrificing) action par excellence.

This is a story, *inter alia*, about collective action. The fisherman represents those engaged in the exploitation of others (capitalism, implicitly). It can be only challenged by the collective action of those exploited. Behrangi hails resistance to exploitation and the repression that sustains it as a heroic action, and 'he only regards one as hero when one is in action' (Hezarkhani 1968: 29). The dagger does not challenge repression: it is a means of self-defence. Thus, the claim that *The Little Black Fish* is about 'armed struggle' (Bassiri 2018: 701) is a misunderstanding. The story suggests that Behrangi believed that in order to arrive at popular collective action it was necessary for activists to be capable of self-defence. This is not quite the same thing as supporting armed struggle. Challenging the status quo, which begins with the simple question of what lies beyond one's home, one will run into many dangers, repression above all. Self-defence becomes necessary. A reading of this story as indicating that a 'small but resistant group with their differences to ignorant multitude, although small in number, can have [a] hazardous and enduring effect in creating social metamorphosis through not [being] deceived by the ruling class deceptions' (Jahangiri 2012: 342) is true when we emphasise that the group of fish in the sea work together as emergent collective actors.

In *The Little Black Fish*, Behrangi deploys the metaphor of the *journey* as searching, travelling and arriving. A new metaphor for this generation perhaps, but in fact one of the oldest in the allegories of classical Persian literature. Since Ferdowsi's masterpiece, *Shahnameh* (1010 CE), the metaphor of the journey, the odyssey of self-exploration and the acquiring of wisdom, has attained an exalted place in literature. Attar's monumental *The Conference of the Birds*

(1177 CE) hinges on the allegorical, perilous saga of arriving at truth – a theme dominating Sufism and Persian mysticism. Attar offers an archetypal work by disclosing how the journey leads to self-consciousness and self-realisation. *The Little Black Fish* dwells in this rich tradition working through the Persian collective subconscious; however, what this 'children's story' did was to *deploy the metaphor of the journey – as a way of seeking out not only the truth but also one's inner powers to attain it – to an entirely new generation, in the late 1960s, as this generation was intent upon a perilous journey of its own. In short,* The Little Black Fish *rendered such a radical excursion, and by extension armed struggle, intelligible and desirable.*

Behrangi drowned in a river soon after the book's publication. As a rural teacher who travelled a lot and learned on the way, he died a death that symbolically invoked his last story. I find this truly uncanny.

The Little Black Fish Redux: An Existential Analysis

The little black fish is the epitome and embodiment of *difference and defiance par excellence*. He does not just challenge oppressors; he also defies the everydayness (*ruzmarregi*) and averageness of fellow 'citizens' in his community and throughout his saga. Thus, I argue, the story has yet a deeper layer of meaning concealed to interpreters and scholars: the existential layer. Going beyond the conventional readings afforded to *The Little Black Fish*, here I attempt an analysis intended to reveal the *existential structure* that informs the emerging and expanding *weltanschauung* of the little black fish, by dwelling on Martin Heidegger's *Being and Time* (1996; orig. 1926), without its esoterism or complications, and in light of my recent philosophical work (Vahabzadeh 2019a). By deploying a number of key concepts of existential analysis, I will shed new light on the *anxieties* of many defiant little red fish like Behrangi and the PFG founders.

Humans are all born in a place and at a time not of their choosing. As such, humans are geographically, culturally and linguistically predetermined and conditioned. It is through 'thrownness' (*Geworfenheit*) that the 'world' (*Welt*) discloses itself to us and how we experience the 'facticity' of being-there (*da-sein*) in this particular time and place. So, it is not possible for any human *not* to be in a 'world' at any given time, although our worlds shift. This reveals itself, depending on our conditions, through de-worldedness and re-worldedness (Vahabzadeh 2019a). Phenomenologically, 'world' has a specific meaning: *Welt* means all that which is as such, a specific set of relations. The story begins with our protagonist questioning his particular thrownness in the brook and in the midst of other fish, his mother included, that live in the matter-of-factness of their world. These constitute the 'public', the anonymous 'they' (*das Man*) characterised by their averageness and assimilative attitude. Their concern for being is not owned by them, so to speak. In their 'fallenness' (*Verfallenheit*), as a mode of being-in-the-world, 'the they' fall to a world as naturally pre-given, as how things are. In their publicness, 'the they' interpret the world in a certain way that does not go beyond its (presumed) *facticity*. Averageness takes away individuality. The little black fish's decision to explore what lies beyond the brook is not only resisted by neighbours, it triggers in them a profound anxiety about the loss of the familiar, matter-of-fact world, so much so that they even threaten to slay the little fish, as they had the snail. We can see how in averageness and the communal interpretation of the world in a certain fashion a people can effortlessly slip into the (murderous, fascistic) mob. This is partly because, to diverge from Heidegger momentarily, our protagonist's *question* is so radical, it *inevitably* renders the presumed *universality* of the world of this flock of fish *particular*, thus shifting the epistemological grounds. As I have suggested elsewhere, Siahkal took place on a different *ground* from that of the idea of 'good life' under the Shah (Vahabzadeh 2021). Back to our existential discussion: the black fish finds the narcissistic tadpoles ridiculous as 'the they' who enjoy their 'idle talk'. They cannot supersede their averageness and in fact insist on it. In his quest for discovery, the little black fish does not see the limits of the brook as a border, a closure, that retains his world intact. On the contrary, he views what is beyond the *boundary* as the beginning of other potential worlds without fully understanding it. In Heidegger's words, 'A boundary is not that at which something stops but, as the Greeks recognised, the boundary is that from which something *begins its presencing*' (Heidegger 1975: 154; original emphasis). Presencing (*anwesen*) captures the dynamic disclosedness of being in time–being's possibilities. Our fish regards the end of the brook not as a limit but as an invitation to the frontier's beyond, where, he later realises, his own potentialities may flourish. This is due to the unfinished or unsettled character of the fact of thrownness: my being-there is determined

(I cannot change the conditions of my birth) but not determining (I can grow out of it, because of it). The little fish's decision to explore other waters is conditioned by the others' insistence on staying within their everyday averageness. His being-in-the-world comes with a 'projection' (*Entwurf*): he does not know where he is going or what lies ahead, but he is willing to *throw* himself into the possibilities lying ahead, in contrast to his neighbours or the tadpoles, who are in denial of other worlds, as expressed in his neighbour's claim 'The world is here where we are, and life is what we have' (Behrangi 2017d: 4) – Behrangi's allusion to the rising middle class of state employees in this period, the alienated '*das Man*'. In short, our protagonist's being-there (*da-sein*) is now genuinely being delivered to the 'there' – to his potentials. This potential, being other than what he is, supersedes averageness but still remains *unthematised*.

It all starts when the matter-of-factness of the world is encountered as a limitation of the 'there' of being-there. 'The little black fish still does not know what he wants but he knows he does not want the present conditions' (Hezarkhani 1968: 21). The anxiety of going up and down the stream all their life until one dies, the feeling of entrapment, reflects itself in finding everyday activity (as 'busy-ness') to be tedious. 'No mother', he declares, 'I'm tired of these errands' (Behrangi 2017d: 3). At the moment of departure, the black fish's curiosity opens a limited horizon: finding out the end of the brook. 'For months I've been thinking about where the end of the brook is' (Behrangi 2017d: 2). Gazing into the boundary of his world in turn invites curiosity about what lies beyond. The first appears as a reasonable point of departure, whereas the latter remains obscure. This is precisely the *presencing* of possibilities. Halfway through the journey, the little fish still searches for the end of the creek until the gecko tells him about the sea and others like him who have now created a group: this makes his goal clearer.

The end of the brook takes him to the pond and thence to the creek, whose end delivers him to the river and then to the sea. The world expands as each outer limit appears as a place for sojourn and reflection. As he enters the pond, creek, river and sea, he meets different species of fish, the frog and the gecko, and learns more about *their* worlds and the worlds beyond his reach – he sees an injured gazelle, talks to the moon, hears the partridges and smells fragrant grass. He realises that while his world will forever remain the water-world, there are other worlds out there. His fighting the pelican and escaping from the swordfish give him new perspectives about life's essential precarity when one exceeds averageness. The world *as such* appears to him in its potential richness, and the further he travels, the more he learns. This indicates *the relativity of knowledge to our current position*. He begins with an intuition: 'You might think someone has taught me these things, but know that I've been thinking about these for a long time' (Behrangi 2017d: 3). Then, a certain *thematisation* emerges from his journey. Being alerted to the dangers in the way and in the sea, his aim now becomes joining other fish *like him* and challenging the fisherman. This is one in many possibilities: the one he *projects*. We come full circle: from thrownness to projection. Once one discovers the richness of the 'there' in one's *da-sein*, when one's being-there becomes *authentic*, then the road *must* be travelled, however concealed the future. This is why he states to the little fishes, 'You think too much . . . Once we are on our way, we'll shed our fears' (Behrangi 2017d: 18). *Life is essentially practical*; humans are not driven to our potentials because of theoretical concerns. The decision to join other fish in the sea, despite the dangers, reflects the care for joining those with a similar experience and a shared *world*, as *a particular communal relationship of contemporaries unified in their projection*, of those who wish to challenge the tyrannical fisherman and liberate other fish.

The 'there' of being-there remains theoretically infinite but *da-sein* is practically finite. Recall that the little fish did not want to grow old and die swimming the daily errands. This would be the anonymous perishing of 'the they'. Yet, in the journey through which his *da-sein* grasps its ownmost, he embraces his *mortality as a part of his projection*. 'We are all born of our mothers for death', said Ferdowsi in *Shahnameh*. 'Death can easily descend upon me right at this moment . . . What matters is what effect my life and death will have upon the lives of others' (Behrangi 2017d: 23–4). Here mortality appears as the *authentic* potentiality of *da-sein*. In light of his *da-sein* being in its ownmost through this projection, now death appears as a meaningful endpoint of his *da-sein*'s possibility. *Da-sein*'s being-towards-death shows its existential *anxiety* for its possibilities. 'Higher than actuality stands *possibility*' (Heidegger 1996: 34; original emphasis). This is no ordinary anxiety. It is a deep existential concern about *da-sein*'s authenticity.

My existential analysis of *The Little Black Fish* speaks to the profound anxiety of the rebellious generation of the 1960s–70s in their search for authentic *da-sein*: its anxiety of surpassing the averageness of the growing, alienated middle class ('the they'). Seeking to enter another world through action, this generation abandons the tedium and injustice that comes with Pahlavi modernisation. Latif's sub-machine gun epitomises rebellion as a boundary that, once travelled, will take one to the point of no return. These days, I hear liberal-minded 'intellectuals' bemoaning the lives of promising, talented young women and men who were killed in the ranks of militants. Such laments reflect averageness: the militant's death is an authentic, final act of her potentiality. The alternative would be to stay within the existential cocoon in a world of gnawing averageness.

It was this existential impasse that beseeched this generation to break the silence through the roars of their weapons.

Beyond the Rebellious Generation

The Little Black Fish has spread culturally and globally beyond its author's imagination, that of the younger people or the activist generation whom it inspired. Its personal and collective influences are referenced in several autobiographies or non-fiction works in English (Bassiri 2018: 708). It has also been translated into English, Italian, French, Turkish, Japanese and Mandarin. Prior to 1979, 'Behrangi's story had been translated more than any other modern Iranian story and was hailed as a major revolutionary and literary work' (Bassiri 2018: 710). All major works of Behrangi have been published in Turkish, and *Küçük Kara Balık* has been positively received in Turkey: it is one of the favourite books of the Istanbul mayor, Ekrem İmamoğlu, who distributed free copies of the book among voters in his election campaign in 2019 (Shabani 2019) and also recommended it, among other books, for reading during the COVID-19 lockdown. A comparative study probes the English re-translations of the book – six in all including one by CISNU (Bassiri 2018). Every translation is inevitably an appropriation, but in some cases the translator significantly departs from the original – killing in effect its rich allegories. The most significant trajectory is to re-encode the story for a liberal, Western audience, emphasising the element of the celebration of difference and eliminating the fight for a better life. Driven by marketing, the most recent re-translation, by Azita Rassi (Tiny Owl, UK, 2015), rewrites parts of it, 'minimises the armed struggle, and the idea that rebellion is the solution' (Bassiri 2018: 701). It offers a hygienic and diluted 'remake' for entertainment, violating Behrangi's intentions and his views on children's literature. Betraying the story in a self-orientalising way, this particular translation shamelessly refashions the story without its message of vision, persistence and change, robbing the little black fish of his agency and presenting him as a victim. One is not inspired by the little fish but feels sorry for him in this version. The spirit of a generation with incredible dreams and interminable synergy is thus scaphised in this so-called translation.

Regarding the story's influence on popular music and culture, let me showcase a couple of highlights. As already discussed (Chapter 3), the popular and talented (and non-political) singer Ramesh sang one of her most popular love songs, 'Rivers', in the mid-1970s, after Behrangi's book had been banned, and in its lyrics (by Mohammad-Ali Bahmani) she popularised the metaphor of 'river' as journey, this time with a mystical twist in its 'Rivers, O rivers, I too want to be on my way / To reach the sea and become a fish'. These lines suggest that being a fish is not a given, and 'becoming' a fish, an individual, is posed as an accomplishment gained through daring treks. What Iranian officials banned returned to popular culture in a different medium – an indication of Behrangi's rich impact. Several Persian and Turkish songs have been dedicated to Behrangi. Among them there stand out Babak Bayat's 'Behrang's Garden' ('Bagh-e Behrang'; lyricist and release date unknown) and 'Samad' (1981) by Siagozar Berelian (lyrics and music). A testament to the longevity of this masterpiece, in 2016, Googoosh sang 'The Little Black Fish' (Abbas Hazheer's lyrics and Babak Amini's music) as a tribute to Samad Behrangi on a mellow pop rhythm. The lyrics, expressing nostalgia for the bygone age of audacious travellers, emphasise journey and danger, making textual references to Behrangi's story: 'so you write a poem of journey's substance / so that we shed our fears and be on our way / in single files to the borderless boundary of danger.' 'Do something so we become travellers to the sea / the way of little black fish is to accept adventure / his is the story of smashing the night's awe and embracing our wishes.'

Allegories live on despite adversities of the banal and the average: from the dungeon of the seagull's stomach, the chutzpah of the little black fish continues to spark inspiration.

The Little Black Fish and the PFG

Our heroic little fish stands out indeed as the very first Fadai. I have previously submitted that this 'children's story' attracted more young people to the PFG than any Marxist text (2010: 134). What I argued there I reiterate here with greater confidence. Behrangi did in fact produce a work that removed the collective-psychological impediments of the restless generation of future militants: his work nullified the state-propagated *psychology of fear*; it promoted the idea that one finds the correct path *only by taking the first step*; the story showed the power of *collective action* by a small group of dedicated individuals; and finally, it properly contextualised the question of *survival or death* in political action under a repressive regime. Behrangi's was the first work to achieve this complex task, and he chose the genre of allegorical fiction to spread the message in 1968.

The other, equally important, work that achieved similar objectives was Puyan's polemic pamphlet *The Necessity of Armed Struggle and the Refutation of the Survival Theory*, published anonymously and distributed clandestinely in spring 1970 (Vahabzadeh 2010: 134–8). Offering a summary of his group's discussions, Puyan argues that the regime's apparent invincibility is a product of the dissidents' resignation and endless waiting for semi-relaxed conditions. Here is where he makes references to *The Little Black Fish*: 'We are not like fish [swimming] in the sea of popular support, but more like little and scattered fishes surrounded by alligators and seagulls' (Puyan 1979: 4). The metaphor is already at work in the political works of the PFG. If Behrangi provided the rebellious generation of the 1960s with vision and zeal, thus *rendering armed resistance intelligible and desirable aesthetically*, Puyan *reasoned* in its favour. And allusions to Behrangi's powerful character do not end with Puyan. Five years later, reflecting on its *decision* to launch an urban guerrilla movement, the PFG still regards Behrangi's work as its *original and foundational moment*:

> But presumably the political impasse that all the dissident groups had reached in the 1960s must have also impacted the progressive and active circle of these comrades [the Tabriz branch of then future PFG], and it did, except the impasse did not pacify them. On the contrary, the way out of the impasse was shown in the book, *The Little Black Fish*, by comrade Samad. The book . . . showed the necessity for the vanguard's armed struggle and disregarding one's life and being a *fadai* [self-sacrificial]. (*Nabard-e Khalq* 1975: 108)

The allegory of *The Little Black Fish* fitted perfectly with a defiant generation preparing to embark on the militant path. But, to reaffirm my argument, the story's connection to the PFG was mediated by the association of Behrangi's comrades in the Tabriz branch of PFG and by Behrangi's friendship with Puyan. It must have been Puyan, Dehqani and others who promoted Samad's story as a precursor to their movement's literature before this literature even emerged. I do know – and I personally have been also a part of this process of guided political education half a generation later – that the first step in being recruited into closed political groups was to undergo months of education that entailed reading revolutionary novels, novellas and poetry and discussing them with one's contact, before one is deemed qualified for joining the group. Without a doubt, *Puyan must have played an instrumental role in promoting* this book by assigning it to potential comrades in the early stages of recruitment to the Ahmadzadeh–Puyan–Meftahi group that co-founded the PFG. An original PFG member confirms that this book depicts the cultural presentation of the PFG's guerrilla movement (Hamidian 2004: 56). In short, aside from its merits and its fit, *The Little Black Fish* was promoted by certain activists as the unofficial manifesto of the PFG.

Soon, the book gained an extraordinary status beyond the PFG. In 1971, three years after Behrangi's death, leftist students at the University of Tehran held a festival in honour of Behrangi and featured *The Little Black Fish*. The book also attained a significant place in the student opposition abroad, namely in CISNU, which, as mentioned, translated it and other works by Behrangi into English (Bassiri 2018: 695; Hanson 1983: 7). This trend proved unstoppable. Whatever Behrangi's personal political choices might have been, *he was now inexorably a part of this movement*. No wonder, then, that the book, published by the state-sponsored Centre for the Intellectual Cultivation of Children and Youth, was banned in 1973.

Conclusions: Star (Olduz), Fish and Sub-machine Gun

Behrangi's works and visions constituted the *modus operandi* of the militant generation. He contrived a unique body of 'children's literature' akin to magical realism that reached its most committed audience among defiant young people by late 1960s. Who would have thought that one of Iran's most resilient militants, the uncompromising and steadfast enemies of the status quo, and the obdurate critics of their parents' generation, were in fact influenced and led to their years of lead and blood by a 'children's story'?

Behrangi himself had an organic connection to this generation, and as a result his literary oeuvres and (projected) politics cannot be partitioned. We saw in this chapter that his fiction had hardly any parallels within the literary works of this period, which means that as a pioneer of socially inspirational fiction, he stands out as an exception to his contemporary counterparts. Indeed, hindsight reveals that the fiction-writing community were slower than poets and song-writers in responding to the urban guerrilla movement. In Behrangi's works, real and unreal criss-cross, and this encouraged the future revolutionaries to brazenly *imagine deep*. Also, Behrangi's life as a committed teacher and secret revolutionary, and his untimely death (with the stories surrounding it), become a part of his literature. If Jazani was the unwitting intellectual father of Siahkal, and via that, obliquely, the PFG, Behrangi was the PFG's moral and intellectual elder brother.

Returning to the insights of my interpretation of Jazani's theory, here we can see how Behrangi's fiction relates most directly to the triangular effects of armed propaganda, communications effect, metonymic effect and political effect – in particular, the latter two. Language is essentially symbolic. Behrangi's work is deeply allegorical. The *allegory constitutes a second layer of the symbolic* and can be accessed only after the symbolic is decoded. A symbol does not announce itself as symbolic, unless the speaker announces it. In allegory, it is an intentional decoding that unlocks the second symbolic layer. As such, most often, unlike the symbolic which always remains nimble, the allegorical stays firm in its decoded state. As a symbolic pioneer in terms of militant discourse, Behrangi's fiction thus contributed to the metonymic effect of the future movement and its political message, once again through a historic *suggestion* shared by a rising community of restless rebels.

The *hermeneutic key* is to read Behrangi's works not as individual stories but as a corpus. This approach allows us to read his stories as the various moments within one interrelated narrative. Now we can see how the principles of future armed struggle are nestled in different venues within his fiction: the dreams of Olduz and her friendship with magically-powered animals who teach her the ability to escape her harsh reality, the little black fish's quest for finding curious and rebellious others and, through that, finding

himself as an agent of change, and Latif's wish at the lowest point of humiliation to have the toy sub-machine gun. These principles were to be extracted
later by the zealous activists who were willing to receive their revolutionary *weltanschauung* and beliefs from their indigenous narrative rather than
through convoluted and stifling Marxist texts that arrived in the Persian
language through unsophisticated (even erroneous) translations. As such,
Behrangi's fiction did not just anticipate the advent of militant opposition;
his fiction invited the guerrillas.

5

REBELS ON THE SILVER SCREEN: HOW MOVIES LIMNED ACTION

When you left, I didn't know who had left. Now that you've returned, I know who has returned.

Massoud Kimiai, *The Deer* (1974)

One cannot stay indifferent. You wanted to stay neutral but got involved anyways.

Khosrow Sinai, *Long Live!* (1980)

Since Mozaffar al-Dinn Shah Qajar brought the first cinematograph to Iran in 1900 for exclusive elite entertainment, its subsequent early entrance into the public arena rendered cinema, in time, a far-reaching cultural medium, almost unrivalled. Ever since, cinema has lent itself to the unending waves of emerging and original filmmakers who found in this artistic medium a unique opportunity for visual expression and experimentation, representing and imagining. From the first Iranian (silent) film *Abi and Rabi* (1930; dir. Ovanes Ohanians) and the first talkie *The Lor Girl* (1933; dir. Ardeshir Irani; produced in India) onwards, the Iranian movie industry has seen growing commercial success, despite ebbs and flows due mainly to its competition with imported films, particularly in the 1960s and 1970s. Also, filmmakers have created world-class movies that have consistently attained for Iranian cinema an international reputation (Dabashi 2001; Naficy 2011b; Sadr 2006). Upon settling in society, predictably, cinema (and later television) was denounced and boycotted by the clerics and their followers in traditional classes and among the uneducated masses, but the magic of the silver screen fashioned massive attraction, so much so that it practically anulled the reactionaries' contempt. So, the introduction and popularity of moving pictures in Iran equalled a cultural revolution. As Iran modernised institutionally and socially during Pahlavi rule, 'film began to make real inroads into cultural life' (Sadr 2006: 15).

Not surprisingly, cinema's entry into public culture gave birth to twins: artistic creativity and state censorship. Ever since the state under Reza Shah imposed the first rules on cinema, filmmaking has continuously been confronted by the intrusive regulation of artistic creativity. Between 1921 and 1939, regulation of the movies, including imported films, took place under the auspices of City Hall and the Political Bureau of the Ministry of Interior. The 1950 Cinema and Educational Institutions Bylaws mandated films to receive a 'screening permit' before a public showing. Among its many prohibitions, this bylaw banned films that showed 'revolution, or instigating a revolt' and 'prison break', as well as nudity, ideological propaganda, and opposition to constitutional monarchy. In 1965, a new Bylaw of Film and Slides was ratified, and in 1968, a fifteen-member committee of professionals (artists, lawyers, psychologists, etc., serving three-year terms) was set up for screening the movies (Mehrabi 1992: 521–5). In 1968, new Regulations Pertaining to Stage Shows and Screening License were also ratified (see OMCP, 2000a: 1012–14). That said, in many cases in the 1970s, SAVAK intervened in the process, in its attempt to curb the artistic impact of the pro-militants in public. We should be mindful of a significant difference here: in this period, poetry and fiction were really hard to censor as avid readers would simply duplicate banned books and distribute them. With the advent of the cassette tape in Iran (late 1960s) banned music was duplicated even more effortlessly and quickly than textual arts. Cinema and theatre depended on expensive, stage infrastructure, and in the case of movies significant investment in production, post-production and distribution. A banned film would have caused its investing studio considerable financial loss, not to mention that a cinema screening a film or a theatre staging a play could simply be ordered to shut down immediately. Consequently, one could imagine that Iranian cinema suffered the most in the grinding stones of censorship.

With its tremendous impact on everyday life, as well as its polarising effect, the guerrilla movement could not but inspire filmmakers. In fact, between the sympathetic stories and eyewitness accounts widely whispered about the guerrillas' daily battles with security and their courage in their engagements, on the one hand, and the daily newspapers' front-page headlines announcing the victories of security forces and casualties of *kharabkaran* (literally, 'saboteurs') and terrorists with their pictures printed to serve the state's psychological warfare, on the other, pictographic imaginations abounded. It was as if a lived and living movie were being screened simultaneously on the streets, in the headlines and subsequently in the people's imaginations – and yet with no unified plot. The *metonymic effect* of armed action could not be clearer. Even the PFG leaders had recognised this effect, and it appeared in Jazani's reflections on how three years of sustained armed struggle had created fables and legends in praise of the militants (Jazani 1978: 78), although the masses, he observes,

> have not yet risen to materially support them [the guerrillas], but in the past three years they have been attentive to their affairs. By conveying the news and propagating hundreds of rumours, the people have made the regime desperate. Every fallen guerrilla has left behind heroic legends. Following the attack on the Siahkal post and even after the execution of the thirteen, the jungles were filled with guerrillas. After the execution of Farsiu and announcing rewards for the nine fugitive guerrillas people made fun of the regime by making dozens of jokes. After his martyrdom, Puyan came back to life repeatedly. In his street battles (*jang-o-gorizha*) Saffari [Ashtiani] found superhuman abilities and before his martyrdom he had single-handedly fought the enemy for hours. Mehrnush [Ebrahimi] jumped from one rooftop to another with her submachinegun, gunning down the enemy's agents. [Ahmad] Zeybarom revived our national fables of chivalrousness and humanity (*javanmardi va ensandusti*). These are positive signs of the people's sympathy towards, and interest in, armed struggle. A people who always found themselves at a loss, now see an agent confronting their enemy, the one who does not take death seriously and . . . fights to the last breath for justice. (Jazani 1978: 78)

Cinematic imagination brightly radiates from this passage. And it is no wonder: Jazani ran an advertising agency before his arrest. And yet Jazani is only narrating what had been whispered among the public and in dissident circles. I have had the privilege of hearing such whispers in my teenage ears – words I could only hear, but had learned, and deeply internalised since childhood, so that such words I could not speak or retell. This is how dissident filmmakers were inspired by guerrilla warfare, and given the costly nature of filmmaking, one needed only a few films (as opposed to volumes of poetry or dozens of songs) to get the message across. These films did not offer artistic propagations of the militants' ideologies or even their causes. Instead, and more profoundly, the filmmakers stood out as the expressionist painters of the militants' selfless deeds and heroic deaths in stark brushstrokes on moving pictures on the movie theatre's silver screen. *Larger than life.*

A Quick Detour: Dissident Theatre

Iranian stage show (*namayesh*) has an ancient history (Beizai 1965), a subject beyond this study. Iranian theatre, rapidly modernising in the 1940s and 1950s into a popular cultural medium, supplied the growing movie industry with talented stage actors. As a medium, theatre also played a role in offering plays with political messages – including foreign plays by Shakespeare and Brecht as well as those of Sa'edi. However, like cinema, theatre relies on an infrastructure that can be tightly regulated by the state, and that is why it offered very limited protest elements in this period. At a time when television had not yet permeated homes, theatre thrived as a popular medium purely for entertainment – namely, in Tehran (Lalehzar) and Isfahan – that presented often comic skits about popular subjects. Politically conscious theatre, by contrast, only reached the educated publics and did not have the wide reach of poetry, music, or even movies.

Educated and artistic theatre is epitomised by Anahita Theatre, founded in 1958 by Mostafa and Mahin Osku'i, trainees of the prominent pro-Tudeh Party playwright Abdolhossein Nushin (1907–71), founder of Iran's modern theatre. They staged *Othello* in 1958, as well as other intellectual-oriented stage productions until Anahita went bankrupt in 1964 (Azarkolah 2017: 696, n. 2). In the 1960s, theatre lent itself to social critique, but to a limited extent due to regulations. Prominent among critical stage shows was the 1965 stage production of Sa'edi's *The Varzil Club-Wielders*, dealing with the Shah's land reform, directed by Ja'far Vali (1933–2016) and starring Ali Nassirian.

Among these the brilliant musical *The Tale of a Town* (*Shahr-e Qesseh*) stands out. It was written and directed by Bijan Mofid (1935–84) and was originally a long radio drama in 1966, about a town of animals, their competitive and exploitative mutual relationships, critical commentaries about a rapidly changing society in which individuals feel alienated, and the reactionary role of tradition and the Shi'i clerics. A reflection of society in the 1960s. The play then went into stage production and landed on several stages up until 1968. It turned out to be one of the best-attended staged productions of contemporary Iranian theatre. As one might expect, its longevity was partly due to the state security's clearance.

Founded in 1968 on an initiative by Nasser Rahmaninejad, the Iranian Theatre Association (*Anjoman-e Te'atr-e Iran*) was envisaged as offering socially conscious theatre and challenging censorship. In the 1970s, the Association staged many productions, mostly by European playwrights of leftist and critical inclinations. The audience for these plays, predictably, was university students and intellectuals, and the Association's works came under severe scrutiny by the security forces. To understand my claim about how theatre was subjected to the harshest censorship, let us recall *The Teachers* (*Amuzgaran*), written by Mohsen Yalfani (1941–), directed by Soltanpour and staged in 1970. The story takes place within a room in the shared accommodation of seven single high-school teachers and their friends. The entire play consists of their conversations: each of these men understands teaching differently. The play reflects the hegemonic ideas of society and signs of resignation to the status quo. The show was stopped by SAVAK after ten nights and both Yalfani and Soltanpour were arrested. Yalfani was released three months later but banned from publishing his works. After Siahkal and PFG and OIPM foundations and activism, defiant theatre moved towards more directly confrontational, albeit symbolically expressed, themes. In 1972, arguably the first 'religious play', *Once Again, Abuzar* (*Bar-e Digar Abuzar*), written by Reza Daneshvar (1947–2015), was staged in the iconic Hosseiniyeh Ershad lecture hall where Ali Shari'ati regularly delivered his fiery speeches (Azarkolah 2017: 700). Yalfani and Soltanpour collaborated on Brecht's *The Visions of Simone Machard* in 1972 (Azarkolah 2017: 700). Yalfani was arrested again in 1974 during the rehearsals for Maxim Gorky's *The Petty Bourgeois* (a Theatre Association production). This time, he received a four-year prison term. In fact, key figures of the Theatre Association, most of whom were supporters of the PFG, were arrested in 1974 and received prison terms (Azarkolah 2017: 702). Insofar as conditions allowed them, defiant theatre artists staged a number of Brecht plays, as well as other plays with political themes. Besieged by austere censorship, however, theatre in the 'guerrilla period' was barred from delivering original works by dissident playwrights. This snapshot shows that with its many key figures prosecuted and imprisoned, defiant theatre suffered arguably the most severe and disproportionate repression – a condition that was only exacerbated by the specific dependence of this cultural medium on stage production by the authorities, as well as by the imposing cost of stage production, which made dissident theatre a risky business.

Reeling into the Sixties

The movie industry in Iran came through the 1940s and 1950s as commercially profitable: confronted by state sponsorship and a lack of professionals but inspired by popular (imported and dubbed) Indian films, the investors favoured a quick return on their cash and financed cheaply-made domestic films around popular themes that entertained the growing number of mostly uneducated or poorly educated cinema-goers in urban areas, thus disregarding artistic values or production quality. At times, stage actresses and actors were recruited to play in these films, and these are the artists who contributed to future internationally-acclaimed films. Given the religious prohibition on film, especially in its earlier decades, it is not surprising that 'Iranian cinema proper . . . [was] piloted by various social minorities. The Armenians, the Jews, and the Zoroastrians, most of them Iranians of deep nationalist proclivities and yet outside the domination of Islamic authority, were principally responsible for introducing cinema to the public from the remissive corners of its cultural inhabitations' (Dabashi 2001: 13).

Meanwhile, though, the industry simultaneously succeeded in producing popular actors without prior training who guaranteed commercial profitability and in time rose to become producers and investors as well. In the 1950s and 1960s, Nasser Malek Moti'i (1930–2018), Mohammad-Ali Fardin (1931–2000) and Reza Beik Imanverdi (1936–2003) reached unrivalled popularity (and wealth), representing a commercially profitable but artistically barren and curious style known as filmfarsi. Despite the different movie plots in which they starred, many characters that these actors (and others emulating them) embodied soon converged to typify a certain hyper-masculine figure that grew rampant in filmfarsi, permeating, in part, even artistic cinema. Commodification of the movies, like elsewhere, was the prime objective of this industry. To make a complex history short, Abdul-Hossein Sepanta (1907–69), who had written and acted in *The Lor Girl*, played a key role in movie production. Other notable producers and film-makers of this period included Esma'il Kushan (1917–81), Farrokh Ghaffari (1922–2006) and Samuel Khachikian (1923–2001), who founded studios and produced commercial films in the subjects that were not only popular, but also pointedly and intentionally lacked the slightest allusions to social and political issues (see Fadavi 2017: 675–8; Mehrabi 1992; Naficy 2011a; 2011b). Dozens of films were made each year, and the movie theatres screened them along with greater numbers of dubbed imported films from Bollywood, Hollywood, Egypt, Italy, Turkey and elsewhere.

The Iranian film industry was always beleaguered by imported films that dominated the market. Bollywood films, Hollywood westerns and epic-histor-ical genre, Italian spaghetti western, comedies, and (edited) 'sexy films' (bor-dering on soft porn), as well as a few artistic productions ('*film-e festivali*' in common parlance), populated the increasing numbers of cinemas, especially in larger cities, and left practically little room for genuine vernacular cinematic experiments. A few exceptions aside (*The Deer* [below] or *Along the Night*, dir. Parviz Sayyad [1939–], starring Googoosh), only popular filmfarsi or com-edies like the Samad movies (dir. Sayyad) could be commercially lucrative and withstand the constant barrage of imported films (to which the Revolu-tion put an end). 'For two decades, Iranian cinema had been struggling to compete with foreign films through crowd-pleasing escapist fantasies' (Sadr 2006: 136; see Shahidani and Rostami 2019: 175). Domestic production declined, such that by 1976–7 newspapers anticipated the 'death of Iranian cinema' (Mehrabi 1992: 172; see Shahidani and Rostami 2019: 176). While filmmaking was in peril, the movie theatre industry was profitable, thanks to foreign films. According to the Ministry of Culture and Arts, of the 720 films that received a screening permit in 1975, only 67 were Iranian – under 11 per cent (Mehrabi 1992: 517). While funding some domestic productions, national television also heavily showed foreign films and TV series. In a sample week in July 1977, Channel 2 aired only foreign (American) films every day (Mehrabi 1992: 172, n. 3), and foreign TV series dominated domestic production in terms of popularity (Naficy 2011b: 69).

Speaking of popular cinema, in the 1950s the movies invented and produced a cultural trend that, in its development into a genre, semiologically permeated Iranian cinema in the years to come. This involved the cinematic construction of the hyper-masculine, uneducated and tough protagonist from the traditional down-trodden classes, with ambiguous social status, who is caught between conflicting loyalties in upholding honour by protecting a female relative, lover or mistress (somehow always in need of a masculine saviour!) in an exaggerated way that pushes him (often in seeking a personal vendetta) into conflict with dishonourable thugs, clashes with the law or both. Reminiscent of the way Hollywood created the (often lone) gun-slinging cowboy in the Wild West utilising specific aesthetic visual codes, this genre drew from the ancient but ubiquitous Iranian tradition of 'chivalry' – 'variously called *lutigari, javanmardi* or *fotovvat*' (Naficy 2011b: 266) – which has been undergoing rapid urbanisation that has rendered it a floating, and increasingly parasitic, subculture with no future in modern Iran. In Hamid Naficy's words, 'The numerous terms that Iranians have used to describe the toughs testify to the tensions and complexities of this duality in belief, value, and behaviour'. He continues:

> Many of the terms, such as lout (*lat*), ignorant thug (*jahel*), loafer (*velgard*), knife-wielder (*chaqu kesh*), bully (*qoldor*), and lumpen (*lompan*) are pejorative and critical of the toughs. Others, such as velvet hat wearer (*kolah makhmali*), slick brother (*dash mashti*), brave and generous [male] (*javanmard*), cunning trickster (*ayyar*), champion (*pahlevan*), dervish (*darvish*), and tough guy (*luti*) are either neutral or laudatory. (Naficy 2011b: 266–7)

This is how the *kolah makhmali* (literally: wearer of a black velvet chapeau) phenomenon, as a masculine aesthetic code, appeared in *Lat-e Javanmard* (*Generous Villain*, 1958; dir. Majid Mohseni), starring Malek Moti'i. This genre peaked in *Kolah Makhmali* (1962; dir. Esma'il Kushan) and dominated commercial cinema until the Revolution. It popularised the *lat*, 'a lumpen character feigning a degenerate version of chivalry' (Dabashi 2001: 40). The visual typification of this (socially dying) hyper-masculine protagonist, ironically, produced concrete outcomes. 'After its countless duplications in Iranian cinema, it grew into a particular style and behavioural type (*olgu-ye raftari*) and made many viewers to imitate it [in real life]' (Mehrabi 1992: 87). In short, by depicting this dying subculture, the movie industry helped its survival among uneducated movie enthusiasts. Likewise, in association with the preceding, popular movies also promoted a disastrous misogyny and sexual objectification of women: a woman was always either related to the man (mother, sister or loyal virgin) or was a prostitute, and in either case without agency or even meaningful presence, only an object of protection or desire or both. 'In contrast to poetry and literature of this period that were busy experimenting and flowering . . . cinema was at its lowest, struggling in the swamp of banal stories, impossible and fake loves, *namus*, rape, revenge and violence' (Fadavi 2017: 684).

French-educated Amir-Houshang Kavusi (1922–2013), who had returned to Iran in the early 1950s to be a part of the growing film industry, soon turned against it. 'Kavusi's directorial debut, *Seventeen Days to Execution* (*Hevdah Ruz Beh E'dam*, 1956), a detective story in which he used a subjective camera, did very badly both at the box office and with the critics' (Naficy 2011b: 152). Rising in the cinematic community as a staunch and razor-sharp critic, he coined the immortal and derisive term 'filmfarsi' to refer to the peculiar, aforementioned chimera of commodified cinema. Aiming at an alternative cinema, Kavusi founded CineClub Iran in spring 1955. Holding Iran's first international film festival in 1959, CineClub became an important hub for training future outstanding filmmakers and critics, including Bahram Beyzai (1938–), Hajir Darioush (1938–95) and Parviz Davaie (1935–) (Fadavi 2017: 678–9). Kavusi also founded *Honar va Sinema* (*Art and Cinema*) magazine in 1961. For him, filmfarsi designated 'a cinematic product based on rushed story, unsupported heroification (*qahremansazi*) without cinematic or dramatic justification . . . dancing and singing (without connection to the narrative), lack of cause-and-effect, unreal loves, pure agitation, and abusing the element of accident for patching up the events and their outcomes instead of a logical approach' (Ali Shirazi as quoted in Fadavi 2017: 679). As Kavusi reflects, he noticed that 'the viewer of vernacular films is "conditioned" by such [filmfarsi] filmmakers, which means that in "vicious circle" a certain cinematic exchange takes place. The filmmaker feeds the viewer worthless melodramas scented with love and sacrifice and deception and remorse alongside useless songs, and the trained (*dastamuz*) viewer also seeks such films' (Kavusi 1989: 165). In this state, cinema reached the 1960s – the decade of artistic experimentation.

Already by the late 1950s, Iranian cinema showed sclerotic signs of awakening to the immense potentials of cinematic depiction, in great part thanks to Italian neorealism, in particular *Bicycle Thieves (Ladri di biciclette*, 1948; dir. Vittorio de Sica). At this time, though, these were few and far between. Notably going against the grain was the neorealist *Jonub-e Shahr (South of the City*, 1958), directed by Farrokh Ghaffari (co-written with Jalal Moghaddam [1929–96]) and starring the stage actress Fakhri Khorvash (1928–), a prominent actress in the years following. One of the few films in which the main character is a woman with visible agency to overcome her conditions, and shot in the immiserated quarters of poor, working-class southern Tehran, the film utilised genric tropes of filmfarsi (velvet hats, café dancers and performers ad nauseam) that were largely superfluous to the narrative structure. But it also deployed a frame narrative, related from the oppressed female protagonist's point of view (which was quite remarkable for this era). After the death of her husband, Effat (Khorvash) is forced to work in a cabaret in the city's rough south, where she meets Farhad (Farhang Amiri), but she is also pursued by grocery market boss Asghar (Abdol-Ali Homayoun), which leads to conflict between the two men. Farhad and Effat, however, forge a true love and rise above their conditions and into a middle-class life. The film offers an implicit critique of patriarchal and machismo culture by exposing the victimisation of women outside of familial relations in a rapidly urbanising society that transforms traditional family networks. Asghar clearly represents the knife-wielding, pro-monarchy *lat* and Tehran's central grocery market boss, Tayyab Haj Rezai (1911–63; executed by military court), who helped the Shah's return through the 1953 coup. Revealing the poverty, violence and ignorance that dominated Tehran's south, the film was denied a screening permit because the post-coup government was sensitive about 'protecting its own public projection of Iran as modern and prosperous. The offending scenes of poverty were removed, as well as references to executions. When the film opened in six cinemas, spectators received it enthusiastically, before the police banned it five days later' (Naficy 2011b: 188). The controversy surrounding the film's being so quickly banned caused Ghaffari to meet with the Prime Minister, the Minister of Interior and the head of SAVAK, who found the film as playing into the hands of the Soviet threat (Naficy 2011b: 189). It was banned for three years until its mutilated version was finally approved for public screening. Certainly not a prominent film, *South of the City* nonetheless proved that Iranian neorealism could depart from filmfarsi.

I have already spoken about the *literature of anxiety* (Chapter 4). A similar anxiety permeates Iranian cinema at this time. By the 1960s, there were sure signs of two parallel cinemas emerging: commercial filmfarsi and the New Wave (Naficy 2011b: xxiii) and this decade witnessed a surge in critically acclaimed films. Ghaffari made another neorealist film, *Shab-e Quzi* (*Night of the Hunchback*, 1964; also co-written with Moghaddam), reportedly based on a *One Thousand and One Nights* tale, making a marked departure from filmfarsi and its tropes. It entails a more accurate account of the contrasting conditions of the different classes in Iran (Mehrabi 1992: 108–10). This multi-actor movie, whose events take place in the course of one night, is lauded as 'a progenitor of the new wave, [and] was one of the first movies to inscribe a sense of generalised fear, one that extended beyond the frame to point to social fears' (Naficy 2011b: 358). However, the film builds on a dark humour that permeates the narrative: following a private party, the hunchback of a cheap entertainment band dies, choking on his food. His body becomes a burden and a source of anxiety: throughout the night, his bandmates first dump the body at the house of a neighbour, who then tries to do the same, and so on, and thus the corpse changes unwanted hands. No one dares call the cops because they each have something to hide, but the police finally discover the body. In the transference of the annoying corpse, the film reels through the diverging realities of different classes. The characters all hold secrets that can bring them up against the law: a society that hides anxieties under the skin of the night. While each character has his or her own fears, they are somehow united by a general anxiety. Intentionally avoiding the conspicuous visual cues of filmfarsi, *Night of the Hunchback* can be regarded as the beginning of New Wave cinema in Iran.

This unending social anxiety – ubiquitous yet ineffable – informs Iranian modernity and characterises the New Wave. As society rapidly and authoritatively forces its way away from *Gemeinschaft* and into a perplexing *Gesellschaft*, each person's societal location becomes a source of alienation and fear.

If, in *Night of the Hunchback*, it was the dead performer's corpse that aroused it, in *Mudbrick and Mirror* (1964), an existentialist film (Naficy 2011b: 360) written and directed by Ebrahim Golestan (1922–), it was the abrupt arrival of an infant, abandoned by her mother in a black chador (a walk-on part played by Forough Farrokhzad) at night on the back seat of Hashem's taxi, that becomes the source of anxiety. This film deserves applause for exposing best the fear of urban places: its 'mise-en-scène – abandoned buildings, high walls, steep staircases that lead to mysterious dark places, night scenes, Kafkaesque offices in the Ministry of Justice, strange characters, and the repeated discussion between Hashem and Taji of walls, fear and hatred of darkness, and worry about' (Naficy 2011b: 359). Following a futile search for the woman to whom to return the baby, and after the officer in the police station advises him to take the abandoned baby to the state orphanage the next day, Hashem (Zakaria Hashemi) takes the infant to his girlfriend Taji (Taji Ahmadi), a café waitress, who then develops motherly affections for the little girl, passionately intending to adopt her. She means to secure her loving but unstable relationship with Hashem by this adoption. At the Ministry of Justice, where the acquiescing Hashem intends to apply for adoption, he is discouraged from doing so and instead leaves the baby to the orphanage. Outraged, Taji rushes to the orphanage but eventually leaves, getting confused facing so many abandoned children in rows of cold, inhumane cribs and in various states of being, from joy to fear to mental illness – a metaphor for forced, faceless modernity and what these babies are expected to become: functionaries of a soulless, compartmentalised system (against which the 1970s militants revolted). This image is contrasted with the TV store nearby, where Hashem pauses, showing on many TV screens behind the store window the poet/intellectual who speaks of empathy and commitment: empty words. The movie ends with a woman in a black chador taking a taxi and leaving. Golestan's first long feature, the film was made over a long period due to a number of setbacks (Mehrabi 1992: 112–13). The café conversations between various characters reveal individuals who, despite their differences, share experiences of uprootedness. These very adults, with their peculiar personalities, are *suggested* in the images of the orphan children at the end of the film. This is uncanny. The dialogues between Taji and Hashem are also rich and suggestive, encapsulating Golestan's critical social commentary.

What brought international interest in Iran's New Wave cinema was indeed *The Cow* (*Gav*, 1969), directed by Dariush Mehrjui (1939–), based on a section of Sa'edi's novel, *The Mourners of Bayal* (1964), with a screenplay co-written by Mehrjui and Sa'edi. *The Cow* launched Iran's fully-fledged New Wave. Mehrjui 'achieved for Iranian cinema what no one before him had been able to do: give character and direction, articulate its potential and bringing it to global attention' (Dabashi 2001: 43). While on the UCLA cinema programme, Mehrjui was disappointed by the curriculum and instead graduated with a philosophy degree in 1964, and this explains the deeper philosophical component of the film: the identification of human and animal. A 'turning point' in Iranian cinema indeed (Mehrabi 1992: 126), this film did not initially receive a screening permit because it had mercilessly depicted the immiserated peasants of rural Iran – an image the state refused to project after the Shah's trumpeted land reform. Only after Mehrjui screened the film at the Venice Film Festival, where it received praise, did the Government allow its public screening, by having Mehrjui add a note to opening credits that the story goes back to the pre-land reform era!

The Cow takes place in a poor, remote village in arid countryside, portrayed through stark, black-and-white cinematography. The villagers all share an anxiety about the malicious inhabitants of a neighbouring village (Bolur), the Boluris, who pose a threat by reportedly damaging or stealing their meagre subsistence. At times, three Boluris appear in the horizon. The Boluris represent, as in previous films, the *outsider* who brings fear and anxiety. The villager Masht Hassan (brilliantly played by Ezatollah Entezami, 1924–2018) depends on his pregnant cow as a source of livelihood but is also deeply attached to her, to the point of loving her dearly, talking to her affectionately, hugging and kissing her tenderly and repeatedly. One day, when Masht Hassan is away working as a farmhand elsewhere, his beloved cow dies. Her death coincides with three Boluri thieves' nocturnal visit to the village. Knowing the extent of Masht Hassan's attachment to the cow and worrying about his reaction, his fellow villagers, in particular Masht Eslam (splendidly acted by Ali Nassirian, 1935–), decide to bury the cow and tell him the cow had escaped. Upon his return, Masht Hassan does not believe their story but waits for his cow's return nonetheless. Gradually, he begins acting like his cow, staying in the barn and grazing on dry feed, declaring calmly to the astonished fellow villagers, 'I am not Masht Hassan, I am Masht Hassan's cow.' After reasoning with him fails and an exorcising ritual proves futile, three villagers try to take him to the city to treat his madness, but the trip, on foot, is not possible unless they treat Masht Hassan like an animal. In pouring rain, Masht Hassan falls in a ditch and dies, just like his cow.

I think the claim that the identification of Masht Hassan and the cow represents the Sufi philosophy of the unity of lover and loved, reportedly declared by Mehrjui (Naficy 2011b: 338, 340), ignores the narrative's potential interpretation: Masht Hassan's condition indicates metamorphosis and reincarnation, underlying animistic beliefs that came to Persia with the Mongol invasion and have been concealed under the surface of Islamic beliefs. It is fear of the possibility of being reincarnated as an animal that makes the villagers treat Masht Hassan like an animal after his madness. In one of his rare positive reviews, Houshang Kavusi compared the identification of man and animal in *The Cow* to that of man and bicycle in *Bicycle Thieves* (Kavusi as quoted in Mehrabi 1992: 129–30), but Mehrjui's connection is reciprocal and intimate (Naficy 2011b: 339–40). All in all, 'Poverty in *The Cow* was not depicted as dignified or innocent. It was shown as ugly, bitter and desperate' (Sadr 2006: 131). *The Cow* remains a rare crown jewel of Iranian cinema – the epitome of New Wave that prepared Iranian film enthusiasts for new cinematic literacy.

In *The Cow*, too, we witness the presence of intruders, arrivants or strangers as the sources of anxiety and fear that run deep in the Iranian social psyche. This idea reappears, time and again, in both artistic and commercial films in the years to come, as in, among the best pictures, *Mrs. Ahu's Husband* (1968; dir. Davud Molapur, based on a novel by Ali-Mohammad Afghani [1925–]), *The Stranger and the Fog* (1975; dir. Beyzai), *Cul-de-Sac* (1978; dir. Sayyad) and *Bashu, the Little Stranger* (1985; dir. Beyzai). This list is incomplete. The common denominator of this cinematic motif is that community and individuals fall in line with the presence of the arrivant, and events go on a different direction, but mostly without the possibility of salvation.

In terms of our focus, some imported films promoted rebellion on the silver screen and still passed through censorship. *Viva Zapata!* (1952; dir. Elia Kazan; screenplay by John Steinbeck; starring Marlon Brando and Anthony Quinn) depicts the theme of the Mexican Revolution of 1910, and it immediately caught the attention of Iranian dissidents. Details of its screenings in Iran remain unclear, as there are no sources. It is known that the film had limited movie theatre showings in the 1960s–70s. It was aired on National Television just before and right after the February 1979 Revolution. *Burn!* (1969; orig. *Queimada*; in Iran, *Sho'lehha-ye Atash*; dir. Gillo Pontecorvo; starring Marlon Brando) depicts the fictional story of the colonial intrigues of a British *agent provocateur* who exploits a slave revolt against the Portuguese colonisers so that Britain can take over the fictional Caribbean island of Queimada. BB Cinema in Tehran screened the film on 21 July 1972 for forty-one nights; the film was also shown in other movie theatres across the country. Such films were enthusiastically received not only by university students and intellectuals but also by ordinary people, and provided the cinematic context for 'protest' films in the 1970s.

In sharp contrast to poetry, New Wave cinema in the 1960s had made no allusions to resistance: a handful of self-styled films in this decade tried to carve out an intellectual space for thinking and reflecting and to resist the lure of the box office that drove the film industry deep into the banal, repetitive, hyper-masculine and mostly misogynist filmfarsi. New Wave cinema continued in the 1970s with outstanding films that fall outside the scope of this study. What New Wave offered, though, was the possibility of a cinema for reflecting and thinking and for depicting life in its complexities and paradoxes. Soon after this particular cinematic style reached its zenith with *The Cow*, the Siahkal affair politicised Iranian cinema to some extent. Three key films in the 1970s can be regarded as having been artistically connected to the guerrilla period, to which we should turn now.

A Fadai Guerrilla in *The Deer*

Massoud Kimiai's black-and-white, neorealist *The Deer* not only represents the penultimate 'guerrilla film' in the 1971–9 period, it also stands out, due to the typicality of the story's main character, as a 'fadai' film. Kimiai's first feature-length film, *Come Stranger* (*Biganeh Bia*; 1968), starring superstar Behrouz Vossoughi (1938–) and with Monfaredzadeh's soundtrack, turned out to be a commercial flop. Monfaredzadeh (2014) relates that when he and Kimiai watched the film in a cinema, some in the audience mocked the characters out loud, whistled and even left. In this poetic story, Farangis (Marina Mater; 1942–) has a love affair with well-off young musician Mahmoud

(Farrokh Sajedi; 1942–2018) and becomes pregnant, but, fearful of commitment, Mahmoud leaves her. Amir-Ahmad (Vossoughi), Mahmoud's rich, generous older brother, steps in and marries Farangis, giving her a comfortable life, and raising her son as his own. Returning from his studies abroad, Mahmoud pops up in Amir-Ahmad's estates and Farangis leaves with him. Amir-Ahmad makes no effort to keep her, respecting the love between them. The film's box-office failure proves the depths of corruption of the cinematic taste of movie-goers by filmfarsi: they hated the story of the westernised, upper-class and non-possessive gentleman who treats a woman as his equal and respects her wishes.

Kimiai's second film, *Qeisar* (1969), contrasted with his first both in terms of its box-office earnings and in its opposite narrative. Living in southern Tehran, Fati commits suicide after being raped by one of the Aq Mangol brothers, leaving a note. Her elder brother Farman (Malek Moti'i) is killed by the three Aq Mangol brothers when he confronts them. His younger brother Qeisar (Vossoughi) tracks down and kills the brothers one by one before he is captured by the police. Contra *Come Stranger*, *Qeisar* was a step backward in subject matter and the values it propagated: it was an honour vengeance film with no creative storyline, dwelling in the *kolah makhmali* genre of filmfarsi, with a relatively coherent structure and powerful acting by Vossoughi. Nothing stands out in this film; in fact, its shower murder scene seems like a cheap copy of the 1960 Alfred Hitchcock film *Psycho* (Fadavi 2017: 686). That *Qeisar* became a cult film reveals the degeneration of audience taste. It is therefore quite an exaggeration to claim that the movie 'might be regarded as a personal rebellion against the changed relations in society' (Fadavi 2017: 687).

Kimiai then made the popular film *Motorcycle-Rider Reza* (1970), about a thief: a theme popular with the audience. His artistic *Dash Akol* (1971) was based on a short story by Sadeq Hedayat, while *Baluch* (1972) presented an honour vengeance film involving criminals, another step backward. *Earth* (*Khak*; 1973) was based on the novel *The Legend of Baba Sobhan* by Mahmoud Dowlatabadi (1940–): its conflict-based narrative hinges on a European rural landowner (female, interestingly) who decides to retake a piece of land that had been rented to a peasant family for generations by sending local thugs. *Earth* clearly presented a criticism of rural social and class relations. Vossoughi starred in all three films. It is against this artistic background that Kimiai made *The Deer* (*Gavaznha*; 1975).

Without a doubt, *The Deer* stands out as the most clearly identifiable 'guerrilla film' of Iranian cinema. It leaves a lasting impression by depicting the 'guerrilla fighter', largely without allowing interpretive ambiguities, as the transformative figure of social relations and the embodiment of resoluteness and dedication. Due to its content, the movie immediately became controversial and attracted severe security scrutiny, such that 'in the Tehran Film Festival [held] in Rudaki Hall and Cinema Paramount, *Gavaznha* was only screened twice' (Monfaredzadeh 2017: 673). It was almost impossible to get a ticket for these screenings; the black-market ticket price was just unaffordable (Kimiai 2020). SAVAK banned the film right after that.

'What made the film [produced by the Misaqieh Film Studio] controversial and caused the spectators to read it politically was how Kimiai [had] coded it' (Naficy 2011b: 385), a film loaded with political codes that SAVAK did not miss. 'The film's opening title sequence, designed by [Abbas] Kiarostami [1940–2016], which juxtaposes close-ups of harsh and tangled barbed wires with delicate feathers and floating dandelion seed balls, makes visible the contrast between beauty and innocence, on the one hand, and ugliness and corruption, on the other' (Naficy 2011b: 384). As mentioned in Chapter 4, Pari Zangeneh sings the suggestive folksong 'The Ashi Mashi Little Sparrow', composed by Monfaredzadeh.

The film opens as a man with a briefcase steps out of a car, declaring that this would be the last time he would rob a bank with those in the car, and that he would send them their share. With an abdominal wound he tries to conceal, this man, Qodrat (Faramarz Gharibian [1941–] in his debut appearance), visits his old high school in Southern Tehran, asking about his friend, Seyyed Rasul (Vossoughi), from the school caretaker, Rasul's father. In disbelief, Qodrat (Persian/Arabic for 'force' or 'power') learns that the once bullish and imposing *mobser* (classroom leader) was now a heroin addict. He finds Seyyed dozing on and off behind a microphone in a booth of a Lalehzar theatre, working as the announcer. The two find each other with great joy. Realising Qodrat needs a place to hide, Seyyed takes him to his humble room where he lives with his girlfriend Fati (Nosrat Partovi [1937–]) in a large, traditional multi-family rental house occupied by several tenants of meagre means who are constantly harassed by the thuggish and insulting landlord because they default on their rents. Fati works as an actress in the same theatre and she is sexually harassed by a particular male co-performer, expecting Seyyed to punish him. Unable to confront an able-bodied man, Seyyed bribes the man to allow him to pretend-hit him in front of Fati. At home, through many conversations, Qodrat reveals his profound sadness in witnessing the withering of Seyyed, stating, 'when I saw you, my heart came out of my chest.' Qodrat encourages Seyyed to break away from his addiction and be the boisterous tough guy he used to be. 'You beg the man who put you in this misery to bring greater misery to you', Qodrat roars at Seyyed. 'Where is that white-handled, fitting Zanjan knife of yours?' And when Seyyed confronts Qodrat about the cash in his briefcase, Qodrat tells him that this money can free many people from their misery: 'this theft is different from becoming a heroin addict.' Under Qodrat's influence, Seyyed begins recovering his lost self-confidence: he first beats Fati's co-performer at the theatre (this time for real) and then hits the tyrannical landlord when he tries to evict a tenant, causing all the tenants to gang-beat him. He is arrested, but threatens the landlord in the police station that he will knife him once he is released unless he withdraws his complaint right away, which the landlord does. Events accelerate as the plot nears the climax. While Qodrat is recovering, thanks to the loving cares of Seyyed and Fati, the police pour into the house looking for a man, arresting a loud man who fights them, but he turns out to be a decoy for the wanted man. Frightened, young and sickly Mohammad (Parviz Fannizadeh; 1938–80), for whom the police had come, rushes into the room, seeing Qodrat with a weapon. Qodrat calms Mohammad, protecting him, until Seyyed helps him escape through the roof at night. Fati shows Qodrat's picture in the newspaper as a wanted man. This is when Qodrat gets into an argument with Seyyed, telling him, 'Aren't you supposed to strike them in the head when they strike you in the head?' Following the argument, Seyyed returns to his sadistic drug dealer and kills him. At night, Seyyed tells Qodrat: 'Whatever happens, we are in. You go and we'll follow', declaring he had killed the dealer. Qodrat trusts Seyyed and Fati to deliver the cash to an address. In the preceding discussions, Qodrat does say that the cash was not loot, but intended to change many peoples' lives. The cash delivery is made, but when Fati and

Seyyed return they find their home surrounded by disproportionate swarms of police (which suggests Qodrat is no ordinary armed robber) under the command of a man with civilian clothing (a SAVAK agent). Seyyed convinces the commander that he can persuade Qodrat to surrender. He uses the opportunity to join Qodrat inside, but gets shot. A gun battle ensues. Concerned for his friend, Qodrat asks Seyyed to surrender, only to hear: 'Looks like you don't get it. This is *my home*. I always wanted to kick the bucket the right way. This is a good way. I'm in. Dying by a bullet is better than dying in the alley or under a bridge [of an overdose]. I'm not giving up this lucky turn.' Qodrat looks at him fondly: 'You're always my *mobser* (leader).' The last shot is an exterior shot of the room blowing up from the inside. Seyyed redeems himself and dies an honourable death alongside the resolute militant. The guerrilla, too, dies alongside the immiserated man, representing the poor masses he wished to liberate (Figure 5.1).

Gharibian brilliantly played the solid and unyielding character that embodied perfectly a Communist, Fadai guerrilla. Clearly secular in his mannerisms, Qodrat is indeed powerful because of his faith in his ability to empower Seyyed – by implication the downtrodden – to rise above his abject conditions. Like the typical Communist intellectual of the 1970s, Qodrat has a noticeable black moustache, and wears glasses with thick, black rims through which his piercing eyes glow – eyes that project both love and rage. And like a Fadai guerrilla in his base (secret hideout), he never takes off his

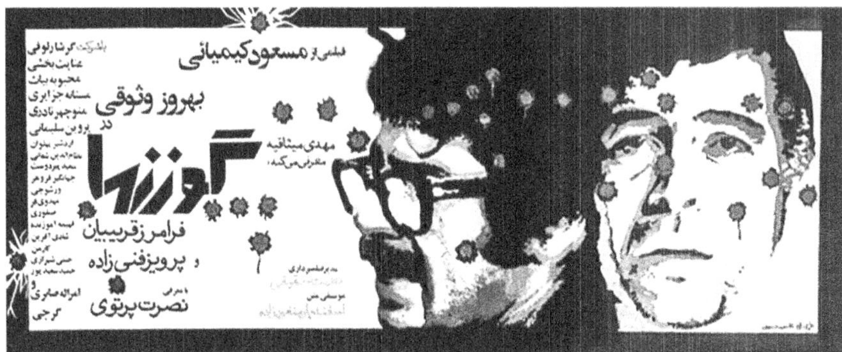

Figure 5.1 Cinema banner for *The Deer*. With the shots through the two protagonists' faces, the image leaves little doubt about what to expect.

boots, in sharp contrast to the Iranian custom of doing so. The film's abundant visual cues do not end there. Qodrat is fit and charismatic. He speaks eloquently. He is also an astute observer and never misses any detail – just like a trained underground militant. As evidenced by his conversation with fugitive Mohammad, he is able to garner the trust of others almost effortlessly. Moreover, Seyyed's facial expressions at times intentionally allude to Qeisar (Naficy 2011b: 385), foreshadowing his rebellion at the end. For his performance, Vossoughi received the best actor award at the Third Tehran International Film Festival in November 1974.

The film could not have been mistaken for anything else but a guerrilla movie (*film-e cheriki*). SAVAK called it that, and so did Princess Ashraf Pahlavi in a private screening where Vossoughi was also present (Naficy 2011b: 385–6). What the film achieved was to mirror, ironically, what every layman and intellectual knew already: that poverty, oppression and political violence were inseparable. *The Deer* was an ode to liberatory defiance that came to fruition through deep friendships and affective, beautiful male homosociality, in contrast to filmfarsi in which defiance is always lonely, vengeful, irrational and hyper-masculine. The male bonding (*dusti-ye mardaneh*) in *The Deer* was admittedly a reflection of Kimiai's own upbringing (Kimiai 2020). In contrast to filmfarsi's misogynist depiction of women as objects of protection (*namus*), sexual objects or both, Fati is a venerable, intellectual woman trapped in a social position clearly beneath her dignity and wisdom. Far from being a victim, she has agency and is capable of confronting her abusive co-worker on her own. The key characters of the narrative are organic to the social class they represent, and so is their speech. In short,

> *The Deer* posits a number of social issues that rested at the heart of 1970s Iran: political conflicts, armed struggle, police brutality, class division and drug addiction. The spatial coding of the film uses populist theatres and crowded poorhouses to portray a society on the verge of explosion. What connects all these fragmented issues is the nostalgic relationship between the two men . . . For those sensitive to the times they were living through, [Qodrat's] call to his friend could be read as an attempt to forge a united front between armed guerrillas and the marginal elements in society. (Sadr 2006: 142)

The claim that *The Deer* was inspired by Jazani's famous painting *Siahkal* (Fadavi 2017: 690) – which depicts in expressionist style a human figure with a deer's head carrying a light in a dark jungle (painted circa 1971 in Qom Prison) – is unfounded. Kimiai had no access to this painting at the time. He recollects that when he had been a school pupil his teacher had said that a buck has ugly but nimble legs that rush it away from danger, and beautiful antlers that sometimes get entangled in branches and trap it. How he associated this story with the film's narrative escapes me. What is certain is that he was impressed by armed struggle: it was actually Puyan's death that partly inspired the film. 'Puyan, Shah, SAVAK, prisoner . . . I cannot ignore these', Kimiai recollected decades later. 'You have to go through them to arrive at a truth whose judge you are yourself' (Kimiai 2020). *The Deer* was a work of redemption in more than one way: 'At that time they [the government] called any dissident (*mo'tarez*) *kharabkar* [literally, 'saboteur'; connotatively, 'terrorist']. This wasn't a good designation for the one who has a political conviction and implements it . . . [He] cannot be *kharabkar* . . . He deserved respect' (Kimiai 2020). More accurately,

> I found an officer that was the first to be present at the attack on Amir Parviz Puyan's (secret) house. He drew me the plan of the attack on Puyan's house and I set up the mise-en-scène of the last part of the film based on that. In fact, the last scene of *The Deer* was based on the plan to storm Puyan's house. Qodrat was perceived to appear close to Amir Parviz Puyan. And Faramarz [Gharibian] had understood [the character of] Qodrat really well. (Kimiai, quoted in Fadavi 2017: 690)

As mentioned, after the Festival screenings, SAVAK banned the film. Due to the controversy and widespread anecdotes surrounding the film, SAVAK decided to edit the film and then release it. First, Kimiai and Vossoughi were taken for interrogation and accused of intentionally making a 'guerrilla film'. Vossoughi was threatened with 'accidental' death (Naficy 2011b: 385). SAVAK put Kimiai under enormous pressure for *The Deer* (Monfaredzadeh 2015a), and the following year, its designated personnel frequented the Misaqieh studio and edited the film, despite Mehdi Misaqieh's arguing that he would prefer to can the film and accept the losses (Kimiai 2020). In the end, the ending was completely changed and re-filmed. In this stupid ending, clearly a mismatch with the rest of the film, Seyyed convinces Qodrat to surrender and the two promise to give up robbery and drugs and seek decent work after serving their sentences. When the modified version was finally released, *The Deer* was a box-office hit (Naficy 2011b: 386), earning 2.6 million tomans (roughly US$ 400,000) in 1975, the highest-earning film (Mehrabi 1992: 170). Interestingly, the audience already knew the ending had changed! The original version was finally released after the 1979 Revolution.

The Deer left a long-lasting impact on the visual memory of the guerrilla period. In 2020, a digitised and colourised version of the film appeared on YouTube – a testament to its longevity. The political interpretations of the film rightly situate it within a specific Gestalt, stressing the unification of dissident intellectuals and the masses they represented. Both Qodrat and Seyyed are redeemed in this story. As indicated by Seyyed's statement in the epigraph to this chapter, *Qodrat's return, in contrast to the* New Wave's *arriv-ant as a source of anxiety, is a messianic appearance. Thus,* The Deer *contains a messianic message of redemption: Seyyed, in joining Qodrat, redeems himself; Qodrat, in being joined by the masses – Seyyed – finds his battle justified. Their death together is a new beginning: it is the joining of the masses with the lone guerrillas – here, the reincarnation of Puyan, co-founder of the PFG.* The messianic moment, we know in retrospect, never arrived.

Sadly, *The Deer* was also burnt into the collective Iranian memory in an entirely different way, when during a screening in Rex Cinema in Abadan in the summer of 1978 a group of Islamist arsonists torched the cinema, killing 677 people.

Rebel with a Cause in *Tangsir*

Amir Naderi (1946–) debuted in Iranian cinema with *Goodbye Friend* (1971) – a (hyper-masculine) story about three friends who stage a sophisticated burglary of a jewellery shop, and then, driven by greed, betray each other. Naderi then made *Impasse* (1973) about a man who tries to leave the city after accidentally killing another man in a fight. Neither film stands out as artistic, and although intense anxiety dominates these films, the intended depiction of fear is largely lost in their filmfarsi-esque style, which reveals that Naderi had not yet developed his own visual signature. The popular action star Saeed Rad (1944–), acting in the leading role in both films, suggests that commercial success was a key factor. *Harmonica* (1973), however, brilliantly depicts the cruelty of social realities, captured in the relationships between a group of boys in a small southern town on the Persian Gulf. It allows Naderi, who was born in the southern port city of Abadan, to approximate a cinematic syntax of his own. In *Harmonica*, Abdollah gets a harmonica as a gift from his father. He uses his harmonica, a novelty in the village, to take advantage of other kids, above all Amiroo, who is obsessed with the harmonica and does anything to have a go with it, so much so that he is scorned for having become Abdollah's slave. The film ends with Amiroo throwing the harmonica in the sea, thus ending his abjection by terminating the object of desire.

With *Tangsir* (1973), made in colour and starring Vossoughi, Naderi turns to his native region once again. *Tangsir* won him a Sepas Film Festival award for best director (Pourshabanan and Pourshabanan 2018: 137), and the lack of scholarly attention to this film is odd. The film was adapted from the novel *Tangsir* (1963) by Sadeq Chubak. It trails previous New Wave movies based on adaptations from fiction, Mehrjui's *The Cow* and Kimiai's *Dash Akol* being prominent predecessors. As mentioned (Chapter 4), Chubak's novel was not received positively by critics. In fact, it received two quite damning reviews in *Thought and Art* (*Andisheh va Honar*) upon its publication, that criticised Chubak for formalism, elitism, failure to create the southern ambiance, and the characters' speaking unnaturally considering their level of education (Bahar 1363: 657–62; Vossoughi 1963: 662–6). But over a decade later, thanks to the *Siahkal effect*, *Tangsir* found a new meaning when a visual presentation of the novel appeared on the silver screen, amplifying Chubak's message of rebellion against injustice. The protagonist's confrontation with the four antagonists is influenced by armed struggle, and thus it has gained political significance. As is to be expected with an adaptation of this kind, Naderi's screenplay leaves out a number of themes in the novel, most importantly the colonial context of the British occupation of southern Iran in the late Qajar period and how the tyranny of local authorities and powerful merchants was connected to the country's disorder and the British occupiers' intrigues (Pourshabanan and Pourshabanan 2018: 140). In fact, the people of this region adjacent to Bushehr, including Tangestan and Dashtestan, had successfully revolted against Portuguese colonisers in the 1600s, just as they had fought British imperialism in the 1800s and early 1900s. The most memorable uprising against the British during the First World War in this region was that led by the constitutionalist Ra'is Ali Delvari (1882–1915). As with the Jangali movement, Iranians had a collective memory of Delvari's uprising, to the extent that Delvari's saga was depicted in the TV mini-series drama *Deliran-e Tangestan* (*Tangestan's Brave Men*; dir. Homayoun Shahnavaz [1936–2017]), which was broadcast in 1974–5. The significant omission of foreign occupation from the film, however, amplifies the effect of the protagonist's armed revolt against the local tyrants – a phenomenon resonating with the realities of Iran's 'guerrilla period'. Reinterpreting the story in this way was intentional, as Naderi proclaims: 'I have filtered the story of *Tangsir* through my own ideas, interpretations, perceptions and findings' (Naderi, as quoted in Pourshabanan and Pourshabanan 2018: 137). He adds, 'As a child, I had heard about Zar Mohammad's story and since then I felt like knowing him and liked him. What happened to him was conversant [i.e. familiar] to me' (Naderi, as quoted in Mehrabi 1992: 158). Like the novel, the film was not without controversy either: because Naderi focused on the characters in a social realist manner instead of attending to social conditions, some critics disapproved of the film, surprisingly likening it to a spaghetti western (Mehrabi 1992: 159), or simply a personal vendetta story. The film is neither.

The story takes place in Dovas, a suburban district of, and Tangsir, a county adjacent to, the port city of Bushehr on the Persian Gulf. A hard-working, family man, and a lover of his wife, Shahru, Zayer (or Zar) Mohammad was robbed of his life savings (of 1,000 tomans) by the co-conspiring elite of the town – Aqa Ali the *vakil* (lawyer or parliamentary deputy), Haj Abdolkarim the bazaar fabric seller, Sheikh Abutorab Borazjani the cleric or *molla*, and Abol Gondeh Rajab the middleman. Together, they have been swindling many working men out of their savings by promising them significant returns on their investments – returns that never materialised. A conflict between town-dwellers (*bandaries*) and rural people (Tangsirs) runs in the narrative's substrate. Mohammad is at times humiliated by fellow villagers for being helplessly victimised by this corrupt bunch who practically rule the town. Naderi beautifully and realistically depicts the abject conditions of the villagers, but also reveals how dignified and honourable the Tangsir people's lives are: Mohammad's wife and two children live in a shack (*kapar*) on basic subsistence, but they are not miserable. It has been two years since Mohammad had contracted his money out to the aforementioned people, and still every time he approaches any of them asking about his money (even though he asks them to just return 300 tomans) he is insulted and humiliated by them. He realises he has had enough. He announces, in the most politically suggestive statement of the film: 'What kind of a town is this? Its ruler is a thief, its lawyer [or deputy] is a thief, its Seyyed [Shi'i cleric] is a thief.' Local people sympathetically advise him to place his faith in a vague justice-to-come: 'God will punish them . . . on the day of Judgement', or 'Leave them to the naked blade of Hazrat Abbas' (Imam Hossein's younger step-brother, killed in the battle of Karbala, CE 680). But these comments anger Mohammad: 'What's wrong with me [fighting them]?' 'Even if I lose my neck, I'll get back what's rightfully mine.' Against the culture of submission, Zayer Mohammad enacts his agency.

He goes through a personal ritual before digging out his old rifle that has been buried in a palm farm. Then, in the morning, he kills Abdolkarim, Sheikh Abutorab and Aqa Ali. He is aided in part by their servants, who are sympathetic to Mohammad's cause. The news reaches the people, who gather in support, stating, 'Don't say Zar Mohammad. Say Shir [Lion] Mohammad!' The soldiers are deployed and people confront them. Mohammad the Lion kills the soldiers who shoot at the people. The military imposes a curfew. Mohammad seeks refuge in an Armenian's shop owned by the respected Baron Asator Arbab while the soldiers search the city. That Baron – an *outsider inside*, culturally and socially – unassumingly shelters a rebel – an *insider, now outside* the existing order – beautifully stands out. Baron's shop-hand, Esma'il (Fannizadeh), admires Mohammad and delivers his message to his family for a rendezvous. Esma'il tells him what he has heard in the alleyways: that Mohammad has killed ten soldiers, reminding him that 'the people will shred into pieces whoever gives you up!' Mohammad is now a legend and people speak of his having fought alongside Ra'is Ali Delvari. The people of Dovas revolt and attack soldiers. Upon his return, Esma'il is killed by soldiers. At night, Mohammad reaches the house of the town's respected cleric where Rajab is seeking refuge, dragging him out into the alley and executing him in front of the people, who have come out in support despite the curfew. In the meantime, a sympathetic soldier who serves in a company that searches Mohammad's family shack, in the mayhem when people revolt against the tyrannical commander, helps Shahru and her children flee to the rendezvous point. In his last public appearance, Mohammad the Lion gives his rifle to a man in the street and says to the rioting people, 'Take back what's rightfully yours!' He then disappears into the sea. The legend holds that he and his family were never seen again and lived their lives on the other side of the Persian Gulf.

Tangsir's cinematic style sets it apart from the mainstream genres of its time. It tells a popular story but in an aesthetically unique way. *Tangsir* revitalises the venerable tradition of revolt against injustice. The film does not offer a vengeance narrative. Rather, it promotes dignity and justice. As I said, Zayer Mohammad's family are poor but dignified, which implies that if people are left alone they can sustain themselves on meagre means, and it is the tyranny and greed of the powerful that disturbs the social order. Vossoughi's superb acting, in particular the resolute expression on his face, embodies the determination of Mohammad – just like a militant of the 1970s. In his campaign, Zayer Mohammad is confronted by the unholy alliance of religion, money and power. And this is why the movie is explosive.

While *The Deer* was the signature 'guerrilla film' of this time, according to the movie's foes and friends, it was *Tangsir* that captured the attention of the Fadai guerrillas. Perhaps the residual filmfarsi-esque elements present in *The Deer* still distanced politically-informed viewers from the film. The Fadai member Marzieh Tohidast Shafi', who had met Hamid Ashraf many times in her secret base, recounts that when Ashraf had learned about *Tangsir* he advised the comrades to go and see the film in groups of two. 'We looked at each other in disbelief. Can a guerrilla go to the movies? This was impractical for us, and in our minds, prohibited. But Hamid Ashraf believed that watching a good film and holding discussions about it is a good thing. In the discussion about the film I realised what a farsighted and dynamic person Hamid really was' (Tohidast Shafi' 2017: 276). It remains unknown whether the militants actually did manage to see the film. What is significant, though, is the fact that they had realised the *tripartite communications, metonymic and political effects* of the arts, however intuitively, when a rebel with a weapon appears on the silver screen and mobilises the masses towards justice.

Tangsir's message of revolt undertaken to protect one's dignity is clear, just like its depiction of the people's pent-up anger and frustration. This film is an example of an artistic oeuvre that is *overdetermined* by the political context – in particular, by the way literary and artistic social commitment sanctions a certain interpretation of the work that wrests the work away from the ambiguities that might lend themselves to possible readings that are not sanctioned by the community of deliberate inferences. As for *Tangsir*, it was the one movie that the guerrillas did not miss!

The Stone's Failed Journey

To be able to continue his work after *The Deer* and its subsequent issues (Monfaredzadeh 2015a; 2017: 673), Kimiai made a love-triangle film, *Ghazal* (1976), starring Gharibian (also distancing himself from *The Deer*), and the unmistakable filmfarsi actors Fardin and Pouri (Sediqeh) Banai (1940–). In *Ghazal*, two brothers fall in love with Ghazal, a prostitute, and eventually both kill her in order to retain their brotherhood. The film fails to reasonably depict the narrative's complex potentials. Next, though, Kimiai made another 'political' film, *Journey of the Stone* (*Safar-e Sang*; 1977), in colour, which became a commercial hit as it coincided with the initial events leading up to the Revolution. As with New Wave films, *Journey of the Stone* also dwells on the introduction of an unexpected arrivant (like *The Deer*), but this time not as a source of anxiety but as an agent of agitation and rebellion. Based on *Sang va Sorna*, a secular play by Behzad Farahani (1944–) (Monfaredzadeh 2015a; 2017: 673; Shahidani and Rostami 2019: 192), *Journey* portrays Mohammadabad, a village whose peasants are barred from running their own grain mill by the local landlord and his thugs; they are forced to pay half of their yield (or one fifth: the story mentions both!) as fees.

In this film, too, Kimiai was aided by his friend Monfaredzadeh, whose intervention won Kimiai an 800,000-toman grant from the Ministry of Culture and Arts based on a screenplay that had no religious component. The filming took forty-one days in the village of Ziyaran near Qazvin. Kimiai wishes to receive recognition by the post-revolutionary authorities for this film, and thus has not been forthcoming about *Journey*'s details. Present at the filming, however, Monfaredzadeh recollects that during the filming Kimiai was visited by (pro-Shari'ati) Mohammad-Ali Najafi and Seyed-Mohammad Beheshti, who spoke to him privately. The next day, Kimiai added the shrine scene and a heavy religious motif and discourse to the film. This surprising turn caused Monfaredzadeh to refuse to edit the film (as did Nasser Taqva'i) and compose its soundtrack (Monfaredzadeh 2015a; 2015b).

The film opens with a stranger (Saeed Rad) performing his prayers on a hill and witnessing the beating of a man who is chiselling away at a huge millstone by raiding horsemen. He rushes to his rescue and saves him, taking the injured man, Shir Ali, to his village, where no one is willing to help. A half-wit, Delavar, brain-damaged by the landlord's thugs twenty years earlier, guides him to the village's raging blacksmith (Hossein Gil; 1940–) who has lost his sons and son-in-law, Heydar, in the last stand-off with the landlord. His widowed daughter, Fatemeh (Giti Pashai Tehrani; 1940–95), is a strong and resolute woman. With no clear reason, the deeply religious stranger (called *ghorbati*, 'stranger'; his real name is never mentioned), who holds his prayer *mohr* in his armband and keeps referring to it throughout, cites religious dicta to encourage the blacksmith to stand up against oppression. 'The Quran on my arm signifies something', he cries; 'that God wants this [justice].' The smith's time-worn determination is suddenly rekindled with a *mélange* of vengeance and righteousness. 'This Beig (lord) belongs to the cruel clan. Every mill in this area is his.' Determined to move the millstone, they are joined by Zabih and Seyyed Yavar. The latter appears with green headgear and waistcloth and an Arabic sword (tropes signifying the legends of the martyred Third Shi'i Imam Hossein and his band). In conversations, it turns out that the stranger is a nomad who has left his tribe because they have lost their traditional ways. Meanwhile, the news reaches Beig, the landlord, who is crippled and an opium addict. In a verbal confrontation, the black-smith threatens the lord who tries to appease him, reminding him: 'Where is a place that has no lord? Is that possible?' The men embark on their quest. When Fatemeh insists on joining them, they acquiesce, after some (unneces-sarily patriarchal) remarks. They take their mules and stop on their way for prayer at the local shrine (*imamzadeh*), before resting at the home of Hey-dar's father, who opposes this lost cause, still hurt by his loss. The men leave Fatemeh here with Asiyeh (Farzaneh Ta'idi; 1945–2020), the late Heydar's sister, and reach the stone on the hills where they repel an attack by the lord's goons. They move the stone with extreme toil and peril to the shrine, where they are confronted by club-wielding fearful villagers. They know they can-not confront the people: 'We can stand off against Beig's men with our force but will be crushed by the people.' The peasants, though, simply yield after the (seeming) clergyman, Ja'far, lectures them that these are 'men of God' and have the 'strength of Imam Ali'. They call their enemy 'infidels' (*koffar*). At night, Ja'far is murdered by the lord's men. Vengeance now becomes a real force as the movement now has a martyr: 'A dead man whose wish is realised is alive!' The two women now join the group, as the blacksmith becomes the prayer leader, and they sing Ashura mourning chants (*noheh*), rhythmically beating their chests. With their extreme efforts (depicted with excessive exaggeration), the stone is finally taken to the village, the scene of their final confrontation with the armed headman of the lord's thugs and the people. After some verbal exchanges between the lord and the fellowship of the stone, once again, the stone-movers, now including the women, remind people of their religious duty to fight injustice with a hugely long, politically and metaphorically loaded lecture (as if speaking about the Shah):

> Sooner or later the people will understand that they are the greater lord. They will get there. Land is for the people. This lord is subservient to his own lord [God]. The lords are exerting their last strengths. We have brought you [the peasants] the millstone so that you will get enough wheat and flour, but he is taking a share of that. You are making allegiance to Yazid. If you stand up [against the landlord], you will [soon] hear the sound of your own mill.

The confrontation reaches its height when a couple of stone carriers are shot and the lord's headman is killed. For no apparent reason, the protagonists release the stone they had dedicated so much effort and sacrifice to bringing to the village. The round, heavy stone rolls down the hill and destroys the cruel landlord's house.

Journey borrows certain key elements from *The Deer* (the arrivant introducing action and change) and *Tangsir* (the idea of popular revolt). But it fails to cohere into a reasonable narrative. A comparison is illuminating. *Journey's* over-saturated deployment of Shi'i iconography and lexicon stands in contrast to *The Deer's* secular parlance. It also exaggerates the organic religious references in *Tangsir* in which religion is a matter of the protagonist's personal motivation and his socio-cultural bond with his community. Zayer Mohammad's religion is rich, meaningful and proactive, guiding his conscience. The religion presented in *Journey* is pretentious, hollow and reactionary – yelled through the mouths of angry, self-righteous men. *This shallow religion even fails to mobilise the peasants*; its only effect is to remove them as obstacles to this devoted band's intentions. If *The Deer* was literally a 'Fadai' film and *Tangsir* endorsed by Ashraf, *Journey* can only be attached to the world-views of dogmatic Islamists, not even *Mojahedin-e Khalq*.

These observations indicate an urban artist who understands neither religion nor rural realities and thus can only represent them through endless clichés. Everyone in the film acts according to the clichés attributed to them. The peasants are fearful and conservative. Women support the cause because their loved ones have been killed. The nomad is rebellious and subversive. Rad (the tough guy of filmfarsi) is an angry, belligerent, dogmatic and self-righteous man who yells a lot but with little substance. No character has any depth and they do not evolve through the narrative. Protagonists other than the stranger and the blacksmith are only tethered by them. The world is black-and-white in this colour film: the self-declared good stands up against radical evil. Much of the dialogues, spoken in phoney (supposedly generic rural) dialects, are threats and the rest either religious expressions or lamenting – the latter assigned mostly to Fatemeh and Asiyeh. There are no real dialogues and the 'conversations' are pretentious and mere *sho'ari* (slogans), mechanically uttered mottos (Mehrabi 1992: 183). The level of iteration and literacy does not fit the rural population's lack of education. Although Kimiai insisted on having two female actors play in this film (Monfaredzadeh 2015a), in the meagre screen time allocated to them the two women have no meaningful place in the narrative: in this hyper-masculine film, they are simply extensions of men, provoked into action by them, and otherwise left to lament. They have no agency or authenticity. Even worse is the relationship between the band of brothers: one cannot sense homosociality or camaraderie among them. These men are not fighters for justice but a bunch of dogmatic men driven by Nietzschean *ressentiment*, united for the uncreative destruction of the present order and too impotent to create a new one. With their showy Muslim attire, symbolism and anger, they visually remind contemporary viewers of the Salafi jihadists of *Da'esh* (ISIS)!

The stranger's arrival enjoys the visual signature of the lone gunslinger arriving in a dusty town, as seen in many westerns (Naficy 2011b: 427). His recruitment of local rebels reminds us of Akira Kurasawa's *Seven Samurai* (1954), except this time the stranger and others fail to mobilise the people. In fact, they are not even interested in that. The peasants are passive throughout: even in their two fleeting confrontations with the protagonists they remain feeble and stupefied. These intertextual visual cues do not add to the story. To compensate for his cardboard characters and shallow narrative and to cover up the clichés he generously utilises, Kimiai resorts to a patch-up quilt of allegories and symbolism. *Journey* is loaded with Shi'i iconography and rhetoric. The blacksmith who has lost sons, with his leather apron, is supposed to allegorically embody the mythic Kaveh the Blacksmith in Ferdowsi's *Shahnameh* (1010 CE) who revolted against cruel King Zahhak, slayer of his sons. The blending of the Persian (implicitly Zoroastrian) image of Kaveh with Shi'i symbolism (of Imam Hossein) exposes the Manichaean thinking of certain 1970s dissident artists who – unlike many leftist intellectuals (like Monfaredzadeh) – are *not* committed to a clear vision of emancipation. They ended up incapable of distinguishing between the ways of seculars and Islamists. That is why, in this particular case, Kimiai approaches ideas only through cliché. Our committed artist Kimiai, therefore, slips from substance to pretence: just as happened in poetry when dissident *she'r* bordered on *sho'ar* (Chapter 2). In short, the film's components are *inorganic* and patched-up. Religious iconography and lexicon are pretentious and shallow: the characters could have quoted Lenin or Mao and speak of 'revolutionary sacrifice' and the film would have still been the same: simplistic agitation. Always over-determined, symbols remain for ever nimble and even outside the power of their deployers. *Journey* tethers Kimiai's name without his specific style as in *Qeisar* and *The Deer*; it is a politicised version of his failed films like *Baluch*.

Screened in 1977, *Journey* proved to be profitable and was received very well by its audience (Mehrabi 1992: 183). In a way, the movie eerily anticipated the domination of Islamist agitators who derailed the general societal discontent that fuelled the 1979 Revolution. Kimiai enjoys this association and has been evoking it in his interviews to advance his post-revolutionary career. But this observation is only *ex post facto*. The first spark of the revolutionary movement was ignited by the (mass-attended) 10 Nights of Poetry hosted by the Goethe Institute in Tehran in October 1977 (Chapter 2) – a clearly secular, leftist event. In my judgement, it is unwarranted to conclude that the 'prayer scene, a "chest-beating" ceremony and the unsheathed sword adorning the background of the ritual represented a direct call for the synthesis of religious ardour with armed struggle' (Sadr 2006: 164). This film only signified the *degeneration* of armed struggle in the hands of the Islamists, at a time when both Fadaiyan and Mojahedin were nearly eradicated, and popular support for them was shrinking due to disillusionment with militantism. Why I claim this? *Journey* neither transforms the masses through the lone guerrilla's presence and action (*The Deer*) nor mobilises them in support of the lone rebel (*Tangsir*). If there is any association between the film and the Revolution's outcome it would have to be the fact that the self-righteous zealots of *Journey* could only destroy the master's bastion with regicidal gestures, as did the Islamic Republic, without actually building a new order driven by justice.

Had the Islamic Republic not crept up following 1979, *Journey of the Stone* would either have been remembered as nostalgia for a lost Islamist revolution or been the subject of derision by leftist and secular dissidents. The irony is, Iran's Islamists did win, but unlike the other two 'guerrilla films', today *Journey* appears so dated it is almost comical.

Protest Cinema

The seventies' cinematic protest was not limited to the aforementioned films. A few other films, too, offered the spirit of defiance in their own way. Of these, perhaps the most 'political' was Ebrahim Golestan's *Secrets of the Genie Valley Treasures* (*Asrar-e Ganj-e Darreh-ye Jenni*; 1972), a satirical and allegorical story of a poor peasant, Ali (Sayyad), who suddenly becomes rich when he accidentally unearths a buried treasure. The new-found money redefines the social relationships of this half-wit nobody who now enjoys the respect of his fellow countrymen and is able to order them around. He even divorces his rural wife and marries a city girl. Only city people are invited to his outlandishly extravagant wedding. His infatuation with showing off his wealth makes him hire engineers to build a flimsy but glittery modern house for him that resembles (circumcised) male genitalia and is ruined when the roadworkers blast a nearby hill. When that happens, everyone leaves him. In *Secrets*, Golestan issues his verdict about 'corruption and consumerism in 1970s Iran' (Sadr 2006: 155). Decoding the allegories might not have been easy for the average viewer, but the film clearly mocks the Shah (Reza Shah was a rank-and-file officer from rural Gilan who rose to the monarchy) and his found treasure of oil as well as Iran's shallow modernisation. It makes 'fun of the avarice and corruption of the newly rich, particularly the Shah' (Naficy 2011b: 380). In any case, this film was banned a couple of weeks after its only screening in Tehran. So it never had a public impact.

In *OK Mister* (1978), Parviz Kimiavi (1939–) depicts the untold side of Iran's neo-colonisation and criticises what Al-Ahmad had popularised as 'westoxication'. In this grotesque satire, William Knox D'Arcy (Farrokh Ghaffari) arrives at an Iranian village to drill for oil. The British entrepreneur D'Arcy (1849–1917) won state concession in 1901 to explore, extract and market petroleum in Persia. In *OK Mister*, facing the locals' indifference, D'Arcy brings his curious team of three, including a certain Cinderella, on a balloon. With Cinderella's charm, the villagers are literally 'netted' and quickly assimilated, speaking ridiculous English (this includes the sheep!), giving up water for coke, traditional attire for colourful tee-shirts and baseball caps, and local food for hamburgers. Meanwhile Cinderella falls in love with a mysterious local man who leaves her after nocturnal sex, making her force all male villagers to try the *giveh* (peasant footwear) he had left behind to find him, but to no avail. 'With oil came purchasing power.' Oil extraction flourishes, turning this sleepy village into literally a lake of plastic. Meanwhile, the archaeologist in D'Arcy's team loots ancient artefacts. Only a local old man (who reminds us of Khomeini) resists and gradually converts people back to the Persian language using the passcode 'soil, flower, wheat', creating a secret base. Finally, the villagers revolt, D'Arcy and his gang escape, but Cinderella finds her husky Prince Charming and stays. People take their village back, but it is beyond hope: they remain alienated, westernised peoples. *OK Mister* offers a caricature of shallow, imitative modernisation facilitated by petro-dollars and neocolonial intervention. Kimiavi's minimalist New Wave, as in his magnificent *P Like Pelican* (1972) and *The Mongols* (1973), works brilliantly in this critical postcolonial film, made in the early stages of the revolutionary movement that toppled the regime: he shows that once a people have been colonised they cannot go back to tradition. Hence, revolting against this system is civilisationally futile. The film is simultaneously a critique of the Shah's shallow westernisation, people's naive and voluntary assimilation, and traditionalist revolt (of the Islamists) that cannot bring back a people's lost authentic self. *OK Mister* is prophetic.

Although the span of our focus limits this study to 1979, there are two important films that relate to the 'guerrilla' effect but were produced after the Revolution. *From Cry to Assassination* (*Az Faryad ta Teror*, 1980) by Mansour Tehrani (1958–) depicts the story of three high school pals – Davud, Hossein, Reza – with shared experiences of poverty and classroom oppression. In response to their background each chooses a different path. The protagonist, Davud, searches for his pals and finds Hossein to be a junkie who later dies of an overdose in the streets. Davud finds a job as a military court general's driver and builds a decent life and marries. One day, he is kidnapped and taken to a safehouse where he meets his old pal Reza, a university graduate, who is now the head of a militant group. In response to the death sentence of their comrade, this group plans to assassinate the General. Reza exploits Davud's fraternal sentiments, and he agrees to co-operate. The assassination attempt is somehow intercepted by SAVAK and everyone involved, including Reza, Davud and the General, are killed. The narrative is certainly influenced by the PFG assassination of General Farsiu (1971), while the militants' mannerisms imply the OIPM. The film lacks depth, and yet it was banned within a month of its first public showing. Its soundtrack, 'Yar-e Dabestani-ye Man' ('My Elementary School Friend', originally sang by Fereidoun Foroughi, a protest song vocalist), became the anthem of Iran's student movement in the 2000s and of the Green Movement in 2009.

During the 'Spring of Freedom', Khosrow Sinai (1940–2020) wrote and directed *Long Live!* (*Zendehbad*, 1980) starring Sorayya Qasemi (1940–) and Mehdi Hashemi (1946–) and Sinai's young daughters. It won an award at the Karlovy Vary International Film Festival (in today's Czech Republic) in 1980 under *Viva!*. This is not a 'guerrilla film' but an in-depth exploration of the question of resistance. This engaging situation drama opens on a turbulent day of protest in Tehran in Fall 1978 as protesters are chased by soldiers and SAVAK agents, and are often shot in the streets. Mahmoud and his father scorn the protesters while his wife Manijeh defends them. An unexpected arrivant, a zealous protester, enters, seeking refuge in Mahmoud's home where he lives with Manijeh, their two daughters and his old father. The ordinary course of life changes dramatically with the stranger's abrupt arrival – a common New Wave theme once again. Mahmoud acquiesces to sheltering him, initially under pressure from Manijeh. In the dialogues between them, it is suggested that Mahmoud's father, a setar player, was arrested and his fingers broken under torture decades ago: he can no longer play his instrument. Mahmoud also suggests that twenty years earlier he had witnessed his comrades giving up their friends in prison, an experience that caused him to leave politics and seek peace in his family and professional life. This is the story of two generations of failed activism that culminates in the young refugee's revolutionary zeal. A *delayed guerrilla effect* appears in the film, when in reflecting on why he joined the revolutionaries – which he attributes to continued frustration at creating change in the country, which explains guerrilla warfare in Iran – the young refugee paraphrases *The Little Black Fish*: 'It's written in a book that one's life must have an impact on others' lives . . . Even one's death can have an impact on the lives of others.' A SAVAK agent identifies this house and enters. When he does not find the refugee, he mistreats Mahmoud's younger daughter. Meanwhile, Manijeh takes the refugee out of the hide-out in the attic. He attacks the agent and Mahmoud kills him. Mahmoud's father states to the corpse with contempt: 'You can't bully us in our own home.' Now they are left with a corpse. Mahmoud and Manijeh have grown fond of the young refugee now and try to disguise him and send him out. But the house is under surveillance by SAVAK agents, who shoot the refugee and then Mahmoud as soon as they step into the alley. The two generations – one that had given up politics and one still resolute – are united in their death. The life of the family is changed forever. In *Long Live!*, Manijeh, an educated woman and a wise wife and mother, has a meaningful impact on the unfolding of events – contrary to the previous 'guerrilla films'. She is the moral soul of the family: gentle, caring and influential. The dialogues are unpretentious, real, and so are the protagonists. The SAVAK agent is driven by both duty and personal hatred. Sinai's film has the dramatic elements of an absorbing and reasonable narrative, like *The Deer* and *Tangsir*, and he excels in character development. *Zendehbad* is an overlooked gem of Iranian cinema. One wishes for a Sinai 'guerrilla film'. The fact that those who rejected and scorned the protests initially and those who believed in it unite at the end is an indication of the 'guerrilla effect' – that the militants polarised society and that this spelled the downfall of the regime (Vahabzadeh 2010: 246).

Aside from the 'political' films, by the late 1970s a few films emerged which, similar to protest music, contained expressions of existential dissatisfaction with the status quo. A popular film in this genre was *The Scent of Wheat* (*Bu-ye Gandom*; 1977; dirs Amir Mojahed and Mohammad [Farzan] Delju), starring some of the youth icons of the time, the popular vocalists Ebi (Ebrahim Hamedi; 1949–) and Shahram Shabpareh, Aileen Viguen (Derderian; 1952–) and Delju (1954–). It narrates the story of three young male friends, one of them a drug addict, who, in trying to send a seriously ill young woman to Europe for treatment, meet their demise in the process. The film registers the mood of despair of the youth of this time (Mohammadi 2016: 352).

These films did not have an impact on the consciousness of Iranians in the 1970s: two were not publicly screened, and two were made after the Revolution. Let us note that if it were not for YouTube, films like *Secrets of the Genie Valley Treasures*, *OK Mister*, *From Cry to Assassination* and *Long Live!* would have been lost to obscurity.

Conclusions: Guerrillas and Filmmakers

Unlike Persian poetry, which prophetically anticipated the advent of the guerrillas, the cinematic depiction of the militants represented a 'delayed guerrilla effect'. This is, of course, quite understandable. Next to songs, cinema was the most popular artistic medium in the 1970s, and thus the one with the greatest impact. In comparison, though, the movies were not as accessible as songs because the film industry involved expensive production, which negatively impacted the number of 'political' films produced (as it entailed potential financial loss). Additionally, films required the infrastructure of movie theatres. Both of these infrastructural aspects allowed the state to regulate (and censor) the film industry to full effect, which led to the promotion of films on popular, emphatically non-political, narratives. In other words, these aspects allowed the state to have a *double control* over films: at the point of both production and screening. Poetry, fiction and songs (on cassette tapes) could be reproduced and distributed by individuals, but films could not be duplicated or shown outside of cinemas at this time. As a consequence, while theoretically the cinematic impressions of the 'guerrilla period' could have led to a greater number of films, it was practically infeasible to invest so much in a film that one almost certainly knew would be banned. Cinema is also distinct in other ways: poetry and fiction are words to be read; songs are rhythmic words to listen to and memorise. The movies on the silver screen provided a whole audio-visual experience enriched with a storyline. And yet, compared to poetry and fiction, movies and music enjoyed a wider audience: while appreciating poetry and fiction requires a certain level of education and literary interest, which made them popular among high school and university students (not to mention the educated classes), movies and music, in addition to their demographic constituency, reached widely out to the semi- or non-educated masses as well. This observation, therefore, necessitates another: *the effect of one film or one song on the political consciousness of the masses would potentially be greater than that of scores of poems or works of fiction.*

Iran's New Wave cinema introduced, among other things, the *existential anxiety* that permeated the Shah's shallow modernisation and the country's rapid, alienating and unsocialised urbanisation. By and large, artistic films of the 1960s and 1970s thematically entailed the figure of the stranger or arrivant whose unsummoned arrival would change the ordinary course of events and challenge the status quo, in response to which the story of many films unfolded. *Symbolically and literally, Siahkal also marked the abrupt advent of an arrivant – the justice-seeking and freedom-fighting guerrilla – who changed the ordinary course of repressive development, top-down modernisation and thus recent Iranian history.* As such, just like the arrivant of New Wave cinema (*The Cow, The Deer, Stranger and the Fog*, among others), Siahkal *overdetermined* the course of action in subsequent years, until urban guerrilla warfare lost its momentum circa 1976. Not surprisingly, it also overdetermined cinematic expression in both direct (*The Deer, Tangsir, Journey of the Stone, From Cry to Assassination*) and indirect ways (*OK Mister, Long Live!*). Just as Jazani had imagined the visually dramatic emergence of the guerrillas, cinema captured it on the silver screen, despite the commercial and security adversities that the filmmakers faced. Unbeknownst to them, the founder of a guerrilla movement and the artists of the film industry thus joined in vision. And just like the guerrillas fighting under impossible conditions, the filmmakers too risked so much to make the few dissident and political films of the 1970s under unbearable censorship.

Cinematic expression dwells between *suggestion* and *nomination*. It suggests, and the suggestion is overdetermined by the flammable political events that stood outside of the artistic medium. That is why, thanks to overdetermination by the culturally-constructed figure of an urban guerrilla, Qodrat, the penultimate Marxist guerrilla of Iranian cinema, *cannot* simply be a bank robber because everything about his manner is suggestive of the guerrillas and links him to an interpretive field that his character opens, which in turn puts a community of deliberate inferences in determinate interpretive action. Once this interpretive step is taken, cinematic expression *nominates* – literally, names – its subject. After decoding Qodrat, viewers would only expect the extraordinary from him. That is the 'guerrilla effect'. And this is how, in my interpretation of Jazani's theory of armed propaganda, through the metonymic, dissident cinema adjoins the communications and political effects of militant activism. Once the suggestion solidifies into the dominant interpretation, everyone is able to decode it. Once limned on the silver screen, the heroic and rebellious genie can no longer be taken back inside the repressive lamp.

CONCLUSIONS

ON ACTING AND THE ARTS,
A TRANSNATIONAL STORY

The story is now told: dissident arts and guerrilla action in 1970s Iran converged to create a culture of resistance against an autocracy. The Iranian case, as mentioned at the beginning of this book, was part of a *transnational phenomenon*: many artists of different talents and shades had artistically participated in depicting and supporting the movements for justice and freedom which they praised and in which they participated. In our case, the relationship between the arts and the militant movement was an 'elective affinity' growing organic, for a while, in a certain sense. On the one hand, the artists were worn out and exhausted by censorship and repression. They wished, as in poetry and fiction, for a tangible liberator and thus uncannily 'anticipated' it.

Still, they needed a *concrete* source of inspiration in political action that would prove they were not alone in their yearning for freedom. On the other hand, the guerrillas' originators, who could not stand the repression of the 1960s, took up arms, hoping that their sacrifices would mobilise the people. They mobilised not the masses but the artists, whose artistic defiance, ironically, the militants did not take seriously, although, paradoxically, the militants owed their metonymic presence and increased popularity in large part to the artists, who took the essence of their message of rebellion, in artistic expressions, to the populace. A new and *defiant weltanschauung* thus emerged and expanded.

Art-experience

The connection of dissident arts and militant action in Iran has been only sporadically acknowledged and documented. This book offers a systematic study, in relative detail, of how the cultural and social-psychological aspects of armed struggle, spearheaded by the PFG, propagated the image of the immortal self-sacrificing (the literal meaning of '*fadai*') fighter who embodied the everlasting struggle for justice in the face of an oppressive machine countless times stronger. I showed that Fadaiyan were unique among militants of the 1970s in that many of their originators rose from a cultural background, and among PFG members and supporters there were many poets, fiction writers, musicians, playwrights, stage artists and lyricists. They were surrounded by a larger cohort, of course. The militants owed their popularity to the contributions of dissident poets, lyricists, musicians, writers, stage artists and filmmakers *through their arts*. Militant resistance gained significant social and political presence because of the artistic representations of their fight for justice and freedom. This representation is curiously interesting: as militant action reached its zenith and guerrilla organisations were declining by 1975 – mainly due to the regime's security measures but also the gradual turning away of the student movement from militant methods – the arts still propagated the larger-than-life depiction of the militants, thus spreading the longevity of the image of the immortal militant.

I argue that the arts provided *political education* for the public: to be precise, artistic expressions constituted a cultural education with anti-dictatorship political content beyond the ideological positions, theoretical treatises and political pamphlets of the PFG and other militants – a *cultural education that artistically revealed the raison d'être of armed struggle and its proud and steadfast practitioners.* Attending to the works of art – poetry, fiction, movies, songs – and interpreting them through certain symbolism became a political act: a community was formed. The symbolic component of the work of art was deployed by the artists and interpreted by readers, listeners or viewers in an intentional manner founded on dissent and defiance. A community of deliberate inferences was thus formed as the beacon of interpretive acts informed by a specific set of symbols. Accordingly, the arts, poetry in particular, brought the guerrillas not only potential members to recruit, but more importantly, networks of anonymous supporters that sustained the movement. It was *the arts that rendered militant action intelligible, even desirable.*

For those who were attracted to militantism through the arts, in particular poetry, art had a different meaning from an object of pleasure and admiration: the arts provided them with an expanse of wandering, pondering and interpretation, as the arts revealed to these individuals the concealed possibility of *being different* in a normative society governed by unresponsive rulers – a society that was willing to sacrifice the *radically different* (as in the case of the little black fish), thus pushing those who refused that fate into militant *and* artistic defiance. I call the particular experience that links difference and possibility of a different world *art-experience*, an experience that goes beyond the arts itself. *Art-experience is not an experience of the arts, but the counter-hegemonic experience enabled by artistic expression.* It is indeed a *phenomenological* experience: an experience of that which has been hidden by the matter-of-factness of the received world, a life-altering experience that jolts one out of matter-of-fact life and puts one in touch with the existential void one has been living. In our particular case, art-experience dehegemonises the subject caught in banal everydayness, lethargic submissiveness and tacit (even active) political conformism that had been hegemonically propagated by the state's vision of a 'good life'. Once experience is mediated by a particular set of symbols, a corresponding universe is bound to emerge. Among the arts of defiance in Iran, poetry enjoys a privileged stance: the poetry of defiance 're-grounded' (Vahabzadeh 2007) experience. Art-experience carves out of the hegemonised subject a sober, critical actor and defiant agent of change. Unique and life-altering, art-experience constitutes the nucleus of the art of defiance. Art-experience simultaneously stands out as an existential experience of the thraldom of ennui and tedium and an experience of emerging out of it, refusing it, abandoning it. Indeed, art is action by other means. Defiant action, defiant thinking, defiant arts, therefore, register my proof that I stand resolute in being different. Radically.

All Power to Symbols

Everywhere we turn, we are surrounded by symbols because we have the capacity to speak and thus dwell in a world replete with potentially infinite but historically always already finite significations. Symbols, these 'plenary words' (Schürmann), mediate between us and reality. They are not the handiwork of artists; quite the contrary, the artist is at the mercy of the sign and its symbolic, metaphoric, tropic and allegoric variants. Far from being an act of volition in its formation, the community of deliberate inferences arises from the determinate symbolic universe that signification has made available at a certain point in history. This community is then endowed with the power to creatively advocate a new world of meaning. Aside from a personal choice in joining a certain symbolic universe, the artist has very little agency in symbolic matters and can only deploy symbolism within the possibilities of a system of signs. The artist, in other words, is subservient to the power of symbols and can embark on significatory paths already opened to the artist by the possibilities of the sign. In short, symbols dictate our action (Schürmann 1997b: 39). Symbolic universes rise and reign for a while before they cede to an inevitable process of exhaustion, although they never disappear. They remain in traces of past lived experiences of the symbolic world for our inquisitive gaze to probe them, often long after they have lost their historic significance. This book is an example of such an inquiry. The rise and fall of symbolic universes, or *symbolic regimes* to be accurate, cannot be explained through cause-and-effect. A phenomenological gaze into epochs that shape our collective lives and Gestalts allows us to see the dominance and withering of certain symbolic regimes in terms of the formation of a certain syntax of action and speech, informed by the changing realities and thus transforming horizons of our times.

Accordingly, in our specific context, although there have been numerous protagonists of the *arts of defiance* that this book names and reviews, these protagonists did not exactly 'plan' such defiance, and nor did the PFG or any other person with supposed agency. It is true, concrete individuals do make a choice in joining a certain side of a political conflict, especially in the bifurcated political ambiance of 1970s Iran (or of other authoritarian regimes). But before they partook in their agency, militants and artists alike were guided to the trailhead of resistance and defiance by identifying with and partaking in the paths already opened by symbols of rebellion that connect a certain defiant *weltanschauung* with a particular Gestalt of global resistance. Therefore, the true movement behind the rebellious 1970s has been an invisible one: that of symbols that translated and unified, through art-experience, the prior experiences of the rebels and artists into the convergence of militant action and defiant arts. Phenomenology allowed me to see the concealed within the apparent. Thanks to the sign's symbolic possibilities, symbolic defiance became possible before so many artists' names – those who resisted the political, social and significatory status quo – were identified with these possibilities.

If any symbolic universe has a lifespan, it means that the sign is inherently *unstable*. This is when, in the art and literary works that I have discussed in this book, the liberatory capacity of the sign, with its endless potentials, was pushed into fixity – a fixity without which taking a rebellious political and artistic stance would not have been possible. Unfixity is revealed through *suggestion* and fixity dwells in a particular convention of signs. The community of deliberate inferences engages in suggestion only to uphold the new symbolic as stable. That is why the arts that anticipated and supported the causes of the guerrillas dwelled in the fixity of symbols to the extent that the poetic image became so solidified that it could not be interpreted in any other way. In the case of guerrilla or Siahkal poetry significatory fixity became so rigid that this poetry ran the risk of becoming declaration (*sho'ar*) – that is, the terminal point of the nimble tropes and metaphors in the interest of fixity – instead of poetry (*she'r*): the single most important watershed of playful tropes and metaphors in the Persian language. The tendency towards fixity was especially true after Siahkal, as at this point poetry, fiction, film or song could no longer anticipate the advent of the freedom-fighter guerrillas imaginatively. The guerrillas were now here, as the human embodiments of the coveted and dreamt-of mythic liberator, and thus these arts, in particular poetry, had lost their prophetic voice and became affirmers of the rebellious, lived reality on the opposite side from the state's notion of a stable 'good life'.

The very unfixity that had enabled defiant art in the first place in allowing its uninhibited artistic-political imagination had now reached its end in this particular context. Stated differently, guerrilla activism after 1971 *overdetermined* and thus largely foreclosed on the potential openness of *suggestion* through determinate interpretations. To clarify this point, one can heed how in retrospect guerrilla or Siahkal poetry oscillated between *symbolically-mediated aesthetics*, on the one hand, and *immediate declarations aided by symbols*, on the other.

Interestingly, this fixity also helped state censorship to categorise and repress defiant literature or artworks. The 'region of language whose structure is determined by double meaning and mystery is the symbol' (Schürmann 1997a: 21). A symbol takes a common word and makes it uncommon, thus creating a *diremptive experience*: one expresses oneself through a common sign that appears as uncommon – when, for instance, 'scarecrow' is *overdetermined* to *suggest* 'the Shah'. In time, state censorship netted these symbols almost effortlessly and repressed them both by banning the work or forcing the 'editing' of it and by imprisoning the artist and writer. But the irony here is that the artists whose art of defiance was indeed founded on fixity, when confronted by the security apparatus, claimed unfixity in their defence. They *under-determined* the fixity, thus pushing it back to the field of *suggestion* – a brilliant move contra censorship in detaching the artwork from the artists, although it often did not work. Semiological guerrilla warfare par excellence.

Braided Semioses

Two modes of guerrilla warfare unfolded in 1970s Iran: the factual one was launched by the PFG, the OIPM and other militant Marxists and Muslims against the state and its repressive apparatus with the aim of liberating Iranian peoples; the semiological one, *à la* Echo, was launched by dissident cultural figures, poets, fiction writers, playwrights, songwriters and filmmakers against censorship, with the aim of acquiring freedom of expression. Although analytically useful, regarding the factual and semiological as separate, albeit interconnected, movements misses the point: they were not two distinct movements as the two were tightly *braided as one movement*. They both involved battles over linguistic and visual signs – metaphors, metonyms, tropes and symbols – in action and in the arts. Militant action and dissident arts are therefore braided together semiotically and symbolically.

Far from being a spectacular operation of measurable military significance, the audacious Siahkal operation was nonetheless profoundly symbolic. It embodied the Sorelian 'myth', one endowed with undeniable political semiosis. Just like the Sorelian 'myth', Siahkal invited activists and artists alike to leave the present and imagine a world different from the existing one, a world of social justice beyond the state-propagated and hegemonic notion of 'good life'. Expressed in Sorel's words, activists and artists contemplated framing 'a *future, in some indeterminate time*' (Sorel 2004: 124; original emphasis). The foundational counter-violence of Siahkal and the PFG thus prepared an entire generation for the necessary epistemological break with the existing, imposed violent order. The 'myth' is an organising principle of action precisely because of its semiotic and symbolic character.

It is precisely the symbolic character of political action that enabled me to re-interpret and develop Jazani's theory of 'armed propaganda' beyond its author's intentions and imagination. Unbeknownst to him, Jazani's theory did contain the unexplored and unthought triangular effects – communications, metonymic and political. It is due to the symbolic nature of political action that Jazani's 'armed propaganda' lends itself to applications in the social, literary and aesthetic fields beyond his own political aims or training. I strongly doubt anyone has hitherto interpreted any version of the concept of 'armed propaganda' – from its nineteenth-century French roots in the 'propaganda of the deed' to its twentieth-century versions in Vietnam and Cuba – in the way I proposed in this book. Jazani did in fact understand the symbolic meaning of guerrilla activity and its mythical endurance in collective imagery, as I have shown in his reference to the popular (and embellished) images of the guerrillas (Chapter 5).

I have given poetry a special status in this book. Borrowing from Michel Foucault, Persian poetry created a new savoir-faire in this period. This is because, in this age of national liberation (1960s–70s), it was defiant Persian poetry that intuitively understood the epoch's hermeneutical master-code that enabled the particular exegesis of the arts of defiance by Iranian artists who then poetically, but also politically, 'educated' the soon-to-emerge rebellious generation. We have already seen how poetry intimately embraced this period by anticipating, *poetically*, resistance in unambiguous terms at least a decade ahead of Siahkal and then by honouring and lamenting lost warriors and their legacy well beyond this period's de facto end. So much so that a certain political-poetic symbolism emerged in this period and stayed on, despite the fact that the guerrilla and Siahkal poetry genre that dwelled in it also withered away. I argued that poetry rendered the perilous militant opposition intelligible, even desirable. *Poetic possibility* is the condition of possibility of liberation.

Short fiction, as it turned out, was more particularistic than other art forms. Behrangi's fiction did not just anticipate the future militants. It *invited* militantism, and it did this in a fairly didactic way through the deployment of specific imagery contextualised within nearly inescapable and utterly abject human conditions. Perhaps it was this particular genre of fiction that managed to show with greater accuracy and urgency why it was imperative to engage in the Great Refusal.

The semiotics of action and arts thus converged, braided together, with the arts showcasing or accentuating one or more of the triangular effects of armed propaganda in any given artwork: this is especially true of the 'protest' song. Having released a cornucopia of metaphors and tropes, the protest songs of this period certainly amplified the communications effect of armed propaganda. In this, protest songs were akin to dissident poetry and guerrilla poetry. Because censorship hit songs hard, the sung tropes and intimations were at times convoluted and ambiguous and thus more often than not needed the intervention of a particular community of deliberate inferences to release allusions – through word of mouth (pun intended!) – in the *suggested* significatory and symbolic directions that would unlock the political message of the song. Being the most popular artistic expression at the time, protest songs served militants the best by taking the message of defiance to the masses, who would not otherwise read poetry or fiction but would constantly listen to their music. The protest song stands out among the arts of defiance in that it outlived the 'guerrilla period' and continued to be the voice of the younger generations and their *existential* concerns in the decades to come, while undergoing the sensibilities of the new generations. In relation to the militants, in contrast to poetry, protest songs of this period were more *impressionistic* in an unmediated way, and had been rather transiently touched by militant action.

To some extent, this is also true of cinematic expression. In fact, as Iranians were increasingly exposed to guerrilla activity and state repression, or in other words, as they were socialised into seeing the repressive nature of the state and the actions of selfless guerrillas by the mid-1970s, the cinematic expression, coming only later than that of the other art forms, managed to leave a deep impression on the people as it depicted the image of the defiant individual on the silver screen – larger than life. Indeed, songs and cinema indicate the *delayed effect* of guerrilla activism.

* * *

The movements of young militants and the artists in the 1960s and 1970s were braided in more than one way. They both staged a profound *existential protest* that constituted the substrate of their *defiance*: a protest against enforced residence under the barren, top-down, official and restrictive imagination of the country's self-fascinated rulers, politically resigned elders and the inept, if not unprincipled, political leaders of the legal opposition. This existential and generational protest reveals itself in every artistic expression and runs deeper than any ideology can capture. I have tried to go beyond the factual and show in this book that this existential protest unified an irreducibly diverse cohort of activists and artists around a certain epochal code whose signature expression was defiance.

I have written this book long after the end of that epoch of selfless rebellion, heroic resistance and committed defiance. Constructed not only through the militant resistance of dedicated young women and men but also by the earnest protagonists of a dissident culture and their poetry, fiction, songs and films, the rich symbolic universe of this period that is left for us to observe and appreciate constitutes the *foundations for the political sigillography of a particular age*. That age has come to an end. Yet, if at least some of us think we need to challenge the rampant global colonial, exploitative and oppressive realities of our age which are pushing our planet and its human and non-human inhabitants to the verge of ecological collapse, we may want to revisit the very history that is deemed concluded. One can always start afresh by returning to the legacies of previous generations. Existential protest and defiant imaginations seem like good places to start.

BIBLIOGRAPHY

Abedini, Hassan (1990) *Sad Sal Dastannevisi dar Iran, 2* [*One Hundred Years of Fiction Writing in Iran, Vol. 2*] (Tehran: Nashr-e Tondar).

Abrahamian, Ervand (1980) 'Structural Causes of the Iranian Revolution'. *MERIP Reports* 87 (May): 21–6.

Ahmadi, Hamid (2005) 'Sabeqeh-ye Estelahat-e "She'r-e Cheriki", "She'r-e Jangal", va "She'r-e Siahkal": Bahsi darbareh-ye "She'r-e Cheriki"' ['The Background of Terminologies, "Guerrilla Poetry", "Jungle Poetry", and "Siahkal Poetry": A Discussion on "Guerrilla Poetry"']. *Goharan* 7–8 (Spring–Summer): 52–72.

Ahmadi-Osku'i, Marzieh (1974) *Khaterati az Yek Rafiq* [*Memoirs of a Comrade*]. n.p.: OIPFG.

Ahmadzadeh, Massoud (1976) *Mobarezeh-ye mosallahaneh: ham estratezhi, ham taktik* [*Armed Struggle: Both Strategy and Tactics*] (Omeå, Sweden: Organization of Iranian Students).

Ajudani, Mashallah (2003) *Ya Marg ya Tajaddod: Daftari dar She'r va Adab-e Mashruteh* [*Death or Modernity: A Treatise on Constitutionalist Poetry and Literature*] (Tehran: Nashr-e Akhtaran).

Akbarzadeh, Pejman (2020) 'Opera-ye Pariya' ['The Fairies Opera']. *BBC Persian* (24 July 2020), https://www.bbc.com/persian/iran-features-53517802 (last accessed 30 August 2020).

Akhavan-Sales, Mehdi (1956) *Zemestan* [*The Winter*] (Tehran: Bozargmehr).

Akhavan-Sales, Mehdi (1990) *Bed'at-ha va Badaye' va 'Ata va Laqa-ye Nima Yushij* [*The Heresy, Innovations, and Aspects of Nima Yushij*] (rev. edn) (Tehran: Bozargmehr).

Al-Ahmad, Jalal (1962) 'Pirmard Chashm-e Ma Bud' ['The Old Man Was Our Eyes']. *Arash* 2 (January 1962): 65–75.

Al-Ahmad, Jalal (1968) 'Samad va Afsaneh-ye Avam' ['Samad and Popular Myth']. *Arash* 18 (November): 5–12.

Amrai, Hassan (2020) 'Marg-e Ramesh dar Ghorbat: Hamcho Ava-ye Nasim-e Parshekasteh' ['Ramesh's Death in Exile: Like the Call of a Broken-Feathered Breeze']. *Independent Farsi* (1 December), shorturl.at/dmtG7 (last accessed 11 December 2020).

Anon. [Mansour Khaksar] (2013) *Karnameh-ye Khun* [*Chronicles of Blood*]. Soundcloud track, https://soundcloud.com/amirmohsen/kaarnameh-khoon (last accessed 17 May 2021).

Anon. (1976a) 'Goruh-e Ahmadzadeh-Puyan-Meftahi pishahang-e jonbesh-e mosalahaneh-ye Iran' ['The Ahmadzadeh–Puyan–Meftahi Group: Vanguard of Armed Movement in Iran']. *19 Bahman-e Te'orik* 7 (June).

Anon. (1976b) 'Goruh-e Jazani-Zarifi pishtaz-e jonbesh-e mosalahaneh-ye Iran' ['The Jazani–Zarifi Group: The Vanguard of Armed Movement in Iran']. *19 Bahman-e Te'orik* 4 (April).

Anon. (n.d.) *Tarkhcheh-ye sazmanha-ye cheriki dar Iran* [*A History of the Guerrilla Organisations in Iran*] (n.p., no pub.).

Aqeli, Baqer (ed.) (1997) *Ruzshomar-e Tarikh-e Iran: az mashruteh ta enqelab-e eslami, Vol. 2* [*Chronicle of Iranian History: From the Constitutional Revolution to the Islamic Revolution, Vol. 2*] (Tehran: Nashr-e Goftar).

Arash (1968) no. 18 (November).

Arendt, Hannah (1970) *On Violence* (Orlando, FL: Harcourt).

Ariyanpour, Yahya (1988) *Az Saba ta Nima: tarikh-e 150 sal adab-e Farsi, Jeld-e Dovvom, Azadi . . . Tajaddod* [*From Saba to Nima: A 150-Year History of Persian Literature, Vol. 2, Freedom . . . Modernisation*] (Tehran: Entesharat Zavvar).

Ariyanpour, Yahya (1995) *Az Nima ta ruzgar-e ma: tarikh-e si sal adab-e Farsi* [*From Nima to Our Age: A Thirty-Year History of Persian Literature*] (Tehran: Entesharat Zavvar).

Ashraf, Hamid (1979) *Jam'bandi-ye seh saleh* [*The Three-Year Summation*] (Tehran: Gam).

Azarkolah, Hooman (2017) 'Sayeh-ye Jonbesh-e Chiriki bar Gostareh-ye Te'atre' ['The Shadow of the Guerrilla Movement on Theatre'], in T. Atabaki and N. Mohajer (eds) *Rahi Digar, 2* [*The Road Not Taken, Vol. 2*] (Berkeley, CA: Noghteh), pp. 695–707.

Azimi, Mohammad (1969) 'Yek Payam-e Amm' ['A General Announcement']. *Jahan-e Naw* 24(1) (March–April): 165–8.

Azizi, Hamid Reza (2007) 'Moruri bar Taranehsarai-ye Mo'aser Iran' ['A Review of Iran's Contemporary Song-writing'. *Gozaresh* 192 (October–November): 72–5.

Bahar, Shamim (1963) 'Yaddasht darbareh-ye *Tangsir*' ['Notes on *Tangsir*']. *Andisheh va Honar* 8: 657–62.

Baran, Mehrdad (2017a) 'Setareh Setizad o Shab Gorizad o Sobh-e Rowshan Ayad' ['The Star Will Fly Away, the Night Will Flee, and the Bright Morning Will Come']. *Kayhan London* (8 January), https://bit.ly/3hrjUQh (last accessed 12 September 2020).

Baran, Mehrdad (2017b) 'Sar Umad Zemestun Cheguneh Shekl Gereft?' ['How Was "Winter's Come to an End" Made?'] *Persian Dutch Network* (6 December), https://www.youtube.com/watch?v=m-CCu1XqCzI&ab_channel=PersianDutchNetwork (last accessed 13 September 2020).

Baran, Mehrdad (2018) *Sazandeh-ye Albom-e 'Shararehha-ye Aftab' Sokhan Miguyad.* YouTube video, 28 June, https://www.youtube.com/watch?time_continue=248&v=V-PahklGMOg&feature=emb_logo (last accessed 12 June 2020).

Bargu, Banu (2014) *Starve and Immolate: The Politics of Human Weapons* (New York: Columbia University Press).

Barthes, Roland (1977) *Image, Music, Text* (New York: Hill & Wang).

Bassiri, Kaveh (2018) 'Whatever Happened to The Little Black Fish?' *Iranian Studies* 51(5): 693–716. DOI: 10.1080/00210862.2018.1480358.

Bayat, Asef (2017) *Revolution without Revolutionaries: Making Sense of the Arab Spring* (Stanford, CA: Stanford University Press).

Behrangi, Asad (2000) *Baradaram Samad Behrangi: ravayat-e zendegi va marg-e ou* [*My Brother Samad Behrangi: A Report of His Life and Death*] (Tabriz: Nashr-e Behrangi).

Behrangi, Samad (n.d.) *Azerbaijan dar jonbesh-e mashruteh* [*Azerbaijan in the Constitutional Movement*] (Karlsruhe: CISNU).

Behrangi, Samad (1970) *Kandokav dar masa'el-e tarbiyati-ye Iran* [*Probing the Educational Issues of Iran*] (Tehran: Entesharat-e Bamdad).

Behrangi, Samad (2017a) *Majmu'eh-ye Kamel-e Qessehha* [*Complete Works of Fiction*] (Sweden: Alpha).

Behrangi, Samad (2017b) *Davazdah Ketab-e Qesseh* [*Twelve Books of Tales*], in Behrangi (2017a), *Complete Works of Fiction*.

Behrangi, Samad (2017c) *Talkhun va Noh Qesseh-ye Digar* [*Talkhun and Nine Other Tales*], in Behrangi (2017a), *Complete Works of Fiction*.

Behrangi, Samad (2017d) *Mahi Siah-e Kuchulu* [*The Little Black Fish*], in Behrangi (2017a), *Complete Works of Fiction*.

Behrooz, Maziar (2000) *Rebels with a Cause: The Failure of the Left in Iran* (London: I. B. Tauris).

Beizai, Bahram (1965) *Namayesh dar Iran* [*Performance in Iran*] (Tehran: Kavian).

Breyley, Gay (2010) 'Hope, Fear and Dance Dance Dance: Popular Music in 1960s Iran'. *Musicology Australia* 32(2): 203–26. DOI: 10.1080/08145857.2010.518354.

Chaqueri, Cosroe (1995) *The Soviet Socialist Republic of Iran, 1920–1921: Birth of the Trauma* (Pittsburgh, PA: Pittsburgh University Press).

Chaqueri, Cosroe (2002) *Az Eslam-e Enqelabi ta Gulag: Ash'ar-e Enqelabi-ye Lahouti, Hesabi, Ladbon, va Zarreh* [*From Revolutionary Islam to the Gulag: Revolutionary Poetry by Lahouti, Hesabi, Ladbon, and Zarreh*] (Tehran and Florence: Edition Antidote et Mazdak).

Che Guevara, Ernesto (1998) *Guerrilla Warfare* (Lincoln, NE: University of Nebraska Press).

Chornik, Katia (2018) 'Memories of Music in Political Detention in Chile Under Pinochet', *Journal of Latin American Cultural Studies*, 27(2): 157–73. DOI: 10.1080/13569325.2018.1450742.

Connerton, Paul (1989) *How Societies Remember* (New York: Cambridge University Press).

CSHD (Centre for Study of Historical Documents) (2004) *Chap dar Iran beh ravayat-e asnad-e SAVAK: Konfedrasion-e daneshjuyan-e Irani dar Orupa* [*The Left According to the SAVAK Documents: Confederation of Iranian Students in Europe*] (Tehran: Ministry of Information/CSHD).

Dabashi, Hamid (1985) 'The Poetics of Politics: Commitment in Modern Persian Literature'. *Iranian Studies* 18(2/4): 147–88.

Dabashi, Hamid (2001) *Close Up: Iranian Cinema, Past, Present, and Future* (London: Verso).

Daneshvar, Simin (1969) *Suvashun* (Tehran: Khawrazmi).

Darolshafai, Bahman (dir.) (2012) *Tamasha: Jom'eha-ye Farhad* [*Tamasha: Farhad's Fridays*]. *BBC Persian* video, https://www.youtube.com/watch?v=z2BiYXj5hZY (last accessed 14 July 2020).

Darvishian, Ali Ashraf (1969) 'Samad Javdaneh Shod' ['Samad Is Now Eternal']. *Jahan-e Naw* 24: 3 (July–August): 46–64.

Darvishian, Ali Ashraf (1977) *Az In Velayat* [*From This Country*] (New York: CISNU).

Darvishian, Ali Ashraf (1978) *Ruznameh-ye Divari-ye Madreseh-ye Ma* [*The Wall Newspaper of Our School*].

Darvishian, Ali Ashraf (1979a) *Key Barmigardi Dadash Jan?* [*When Will You Return, My Dear Brother?*] (Kermanshah: Asman).

Darvishian, Ali Ashraf (1979b) *Abshuran* (Tehran: Yar Mohammad).

Debray, Regis (1967) *Revolution in the Revolution? Armed Struggle and Political Struggle in Latin American* (New York: Monthly Press Review).

Dehqani, Behruz (ed. Yunes Orang Khadavi) (2005) *Man Marg ra Sorudi Kardam: Zendegi va Asar-e Behruz Dehqani* [*I Turned Death into an Anthem: Life and Works of Behruz Dehqani*] (Tehran: Baztab).

Deleuze, Gilles, and Félix Guattari (trans. D. Polan) (1986) *Kafka: Toward a Minor Literature* (Minneapolis: University of Minnesota Press).

Derrida, Jacques (trans. B. Johnson) (1981) *Dissemination* (Chicago: University of Chicago Press).

Ebrahim, Hadi (2018) Interview by Peyman Vahabzadeh (Chilliwack, Canada, 12 July).

Eco, Umberto (trans. W. Weaver) (1986) 'Towards a Semiological Guerrilla Warfare', in *Travels in Hyperreality: Essays* (New York: Harcourt), pp. 135–44.

Eghbali, Dariush (2011) 'Beh Ebarat-e Digar: Dariush Eghbali' ['In Other Words: Dariush Eghbali']. *BBC Persian* (20 December), https://www.youtube.com/watch?v=yrcH8rxUoF8&feature=youtu.be (last accessed 17 July 2020).

Eghbali, Dariush (2017) 'Beh Ebarat-e Digar: Dariush-Nagoftehha (Bakhsh-e Dovvom)' ['In Other Words: Dariush-Untold Story (Part 2)']. *BBC Persian* (28 March 2017), https://www.youtube.com/watch?v=KEHoUSEo_V8&feature=youtu.be (last accessed 17 July 2020).

Estedadi-Shad, Mehdi (2000) *Sha'ran va Pasokh-e Zamaneh* [*Poets and the Responses of Time*] (Spånga, Sweden: Baran).

Fadainia, Safar [Saeed Yousef] (n.d.) *She'r-e Jonbesh-e Novin: Enqelab-e Iran dar She'r-e Mo'aser* [*Poetry of the New Movement: Iranian Revolution in Contemporary Poetry*] (n.p., no pub.).

Fadavi, Hamid (2017) 'Sinema va Siahkal' ['Cinema and Siahkal'], in T. Atabaki and N. Mohajer (eds) *Rahi Digar, 2* [*The Road Not Taken, Vol. 2*] (Berkeley, CA: Noghteh), pp. 675–94.

Farahati, Hamzeh (1991) 'Qesseh-ye Raz-e Koshandeh-ye Aras' ['The Story of Aras's Deadly Mystery']. *Adineh* 67 (Feb.): 11–12.

Farahati, Hamzeh (2006) *Az An Salha . . . va Salha-ye Ba'd* [*Of Those Years . . . and the Years That Followed*] (Cologne: Forough).

Farnud, Gholam Hossein (1968) 'Mo'alem-e Mardom' ['The People's Teacher?']. *Arash* 18 (November): 57–60.

Farrokhzad, Forough (1993) *Divan-e Ash'ar-e Forough Farrokhzad* [*Collected Poems of Forough Farrokhzad*] (Tehran: Morvarid).

Gamari, Behrooz (2016) *Remembering Akbar: Inside the Iranian Revolution* (New York/London: OR).

Ghanbari, Shahyar (2012) '13, beh Delavaran-e Siahkal' ['13, to the Courageous Men of Siahkal']. *Ravi-ye Hekayat-e Baqi* (8 February), https://parand.se/?p=1286 (last accessed 8 September 2020).

Ghanoonparvar, M. R (1984) *Prophets of Doom: Literature as Socio-Political Phenomenon in Modern Iran* (Lanham, MD: University Press of America).

Giáp, Võ Nguyên (2014) *People's War, People's Army* (n.p.: MIA).

Golesorkhi, Khosrow (ed. Kaveh Goharin) (1994) *Ey Sarzamin-e Man* [*O My Homeland*] (Tehran: Negah).

Golesorkhi, Khosrow (ed. Majid Roshangar) (1995) *Bisheh-ye bidar: az majmu'eh she'r-ha va maqaleh-ye Khosrow Golesorkhi* [*The Wakeful Thicket: Selected Poems and Essays by Khosrow Golersorkhi*] (Tehran: Morvarid).

Golesorkhi, Khosrow (ed. Kaveh Goharin) (1996) *Dasti Miyan-e Deshneh va Del* [*A Hand Between Dagger and Heart*] (Tehran: Farahang-e Kavosh).

Golestan, Ebrahim (2002) *Asrar-e Ganj-e Darreh-ye Jenni* [*Secrets of the Genie Valley Treasures*] (Tehran: Baztab Negar).

Gott, Richard (2008) *Guerrilla Movements in Latin America* (New York: Seagull).

Gramsci, Antonio (1971) *Selections from the Prison Notebooks* (New York: International Publishers).

Hamidian, Naqi (2004) *Safar ba Balha-ye Arezu: Sheklgiri-ye Jonbesh-e Cheriki-ye Fadaiyan-e Khalq, Enqelab-e Bahman, va Sazman-e Fadaiyan-e Aksariyat* [*A Journey on the Wings of Dreams: the Formation of the Guerrilla Movement of People's Fadaiyan, the February (1979) Revolution, and the Organisation of Fadaiyan-Majority*] (Stockholm: no pub.).

Hanson, Brad (1983) 'The "Westoxication" of Iran: Depictions and Reactions of Behrangi, al-e Ahmad, and Shariati'. *International Journal of Middle East Studies* 15(1) (February): 1–23.

Hatami, Hassan (1961) 'Gonejeshkak-e Ashi Mashi: Matal-e Kazeruni' ['The Ashi Mashi Little Sparrow']. *Ketab-e Hafteh* 2 (15 October), 120–1.

Heidegger, Martin (1975) 'Building Dwelling Thinking', in *Poetry, Language, Thought* (New York: Harper Colophon), pp. 143–59.

Heidegger, Martin (trans. J. Stambaugh) (1996) *Being and Time* (Albany, NY: State University of New York Press).

Hemmasi, Farzaneh (2013) 'Intimating Dissent: Popular Song, Poetry, and Politics in Pre-Revolutionary Iran'. *Ethnomusicology* 57 (Winter): 57–87.

Hezarkhani, Manouchehr (1968) 'Jahanbini-ye Mahi Siah-e Kuchulu' ['The World-view of the Little Black Fish']. *Arash* 18 (November): 17–29.

Hobsbawm, E. J. (1963) *Primitive Rebels: Studies in Archaic Forms of Social Movement in the 19th and 20th Centuries* (Manchester: University of Manchester Press).

Hosayni Dehkordi, Morteza, and EIr (2000) 'Mara Bebus' ['Kiss Me']. *Encyclopedia Iranica*, https://www.iranicaonline.org/articles/mara-bebus (last accessed 8 August 2020).

ISNA (Islamic Republic News Agency) (2020) 'Nosrat Rahmani' (15 June), shorturl.at/ipC37 (last accessed 9 May 2021).

Jahangiri, Azam (2012) 'Political and Social Features of the Allegorical Short Story *Little Black Fish* Written by Iranian Writer, Samad Behrangi'. *International Journal of Basic and Applied Sciences* 1(4): 336–46.

Jahani Asl, Mohammad Nasser (2017) *Identity, Politics, Organization: A Historical Sociology of the Democratic Party of Iranian Kurdistan and the Kurdish Nationalist Movement.* Ph.D. dissertation, University of Victoria.

Jameson, Fredric (1988) *The Ideologies of Theory: Essays 1971–1986. Vol 2* (Minneapolis: University of Minnesota Press).

Jannatie-Ataie, Iraj (ed. Yaghma Golrouee) (2005) *Mara beh Khaneham Bebar!* [*Take Me Home!*] (Tehran: Darinush).

Jannatie-Ataie, Iraj (2007) 'Hokumat-e Ideolozhik-e Mazhabi Bazdarandeh-ye Afarinesh-e Honar' ['Ideological-Religious State: A Barrier to Artistic Creation']. *Asar*, http://www.asar.name/2007/04/blog-post_5560.html (last accessed 12 August 2020).

Jannatie-Ataie, Iraj (2010a) 'Az Aghaz-e Rah ta Tanin: Goftogu ba Iraj Jannatie Ataie-1' ['From the Beginning to Tanin: An Interview with Iraj Jannatie Ataie-1']. *Deutsche Welle Farsi* (29 November), https://p.dw.com/p/QKTU (last accessed 12 August 2020).

Jannatie-Ataie, Iraj (2010b) 'Bayan-e Eshq dar Jame'eh-ye Siah-e Sansur: Goftogu ba Iraj Jannatie Ataie-2' ['From the Beginning to Tanin: An Interview with Iraj Jannatie Ataie-2']. *Deutsche Welle Farsi* (5 December), https://p.dw.com/p/QKUt (last accessed 12 August 2020).

Jannatie-Ataie, Iraj (2011) 'Mafahim-e Tazriqi dar She'r: Goftogu ba Iraj Jannatie Ataie-3' ['Notions Injected into Poetry: An Interview with Iraj Jannatie Ataie-2']. *Deutsche Welle Farsi* (9 January), https://p.dw.com/p/Qorq (last accessed 12 August 2020).

Jannatie-Ataie, Iraj (2013a) *Bipardeh, Bita'arof ba Iraj Jannatie Ataie, Qesmat-e Avval* ['Candid and Frank with Iraj Jannatie Ataie, Part 1']. YouTube video

(1 November), https://www.youtube.com/watch?v=GAyOrZhNoxs (last accessed 5 September 2020).

Jannatie-Ataie, Iraj (2013b) *Bipardeh, Bita'arof ba Iraj Jannatie Ataie, Qesmat-e Dovvom* ['Candid and Frank with Iraj Jannatie Ataie, Part 2']. YouTube video (3 November), https://www.youtube.com/watch?v=lDuwb6gqp0Q&t=148s&ab_channel=khosrow222222 (last accessed 6 September 2020).

Jazani, Bijan (1976a) *Cheguneh mobarezeh-ye mosallahaneh tudehi mishavad* [*How Armed Struggle Becomes a Mass Movement*] (Germany: OIPFG).

Jazani, Bijan (1976b) 'Vahdat va Naqsh-e Estratezhik-e Cherikha-ye Fadai-e Khalq' ['Unification and the Strategic Role of the People's Fadai Guerrillas']. *19 Bahman-e Te'orik* 1 (December): 1–9.

Jazani, Bijan (1976c) '"Mashy-e siyasi" va "kar-e tudehi"' ['"Political Approach" and "Popular Activities"'] (*19 Bahman-e Te'orik*, No. 1 (December): 10–29.

Jazani, Bijan (1976d) 'Hezb-e tabaqeh-ye kargar dar Iran' ['The Working-Class Party in Iran']. *19 Bahman-e Te'orik*, No. 1 (December): 30–56.

Jazani, Bijan (1976e) *Panj resaleh* [*Five Essays*]. *19 Bahman-e Te'orik*, No. 8 (December).

Jazani, Bijan (1976f) *Jam'bandi-ye mobarezat-e si saleh-ye akhir dar Iran* [*Summation of the Struggles of the Past Thirty Years in Iran*]. *19 Bahman Te'orik*, Nos 5–6.

Jazani, Bijan (1978) *Nabard ba diktatori-ye Shah* [*War against the Shah's Dictatorship*] (n.p.: OIPFG).

Jeyhun, Ali (2017) 'Ali Ashraf Darvishian: Chehreh-ye Ranjur-e Adabiyyat-e Iran' ['Ali Ashraf Darvishian: The Suffering Face of Iranian Literature']. *BBC Persian* (27 October), https://www.bbc.com/persian/arts-41776949 (last accessed 6 December 2020).

Kabiri, Ali [Amir Parviz Puyan] (1968) 'Konun Rah-e Ou "bar Kodamin Bineshan Qolleh Ast, dar Kodamin Su"?' ['Now His Path "Stretches Which Way, to Which Unmarked Summit"?']. *Arash* 18 (November): 63–4.

Kar (Organ of the Organization of the Iranian People's Fadai Guerrillas) (1979) No. 9 (3 May).

Kar (Organ of the Organization of the Iranian People's Fadai Guerrillas) (1980a) No. 49 (5 March).

Kar (Organ of the Organization of the Iranian People's Fadai Guerrillas) (1980b) No. 50 (12 March).

Kar (Organ of the Organization of the Iranian People's Fadai Guerrillas) (1980c) No. 51 (19 March).

Kar (Organ of the Organization of the Iranian People's Fadai Guerrillas) (1980d) No. 52 (2 April).

Kar (Organ of the Organization of the Iranian People's Fadai Guerrillas) (1980e) No. 53 (9 April).

Karami, Hoda (2019) 'Dar Bab-e Romantisism Tondarkia ba Negahi bar Jahanbini-e Wagneri' ['Tondarkia's Romanticism through a Wagnerian World-view']. *Problematica* (4 October), http://problematicaa.com/tondar-kia-romanticism/ (last accessed 15 November 2019).

Karimi-Hakkak, Ahmad (1977) 'A Well Amid the Waste: An Introduction to the Poetry of Ahmad Shamlu'. *World Literature Today* 51(2): 201–6.

Karimi-Hakkak, Ahmad (1995) *Recasting Persian Poetry: Scenarios of Poetic Modernity in Iran* (Salt Lake City: University of Utah Press).

Karimi-Hakkak, Ahmad (2018) 'Continuity and Creativity: Models of Change in Persian Poetry, Classical and Modern', in A. A. Seyed-Ghorab (ed.), *The Layered Heart: Essays on Persian Poetry, a Celebration in Honor of Dick Davis* (Odenton, MD: Mage), pp. 25–54.

Karo (Karapet Derderian) (1955) *Shekast-e Sokut* [*Breaking the Silence*] (Tehran: Marjan).

Karo (Karapet Derderian) (1966) *Namehha-ye Sargardan* [*Wandering Letters*] (Tehran: Farrokhi).

Karo (Karapet Derderian) (2015) 'Baz Baran' ['Rain Again'], https://www.youtube.com/watch?v=NFpfgmQ8RP0 (last accessed 9 May 2021).

Kasra'i, Siavash (n.d.) 'Vietnami Digar' ['Another Vietnam']. *Rah-e Tudeh*, https://www.rahetudeh.com/rahetude/Kasrayi/HTML/chegouara.html (last accessed 15 May 2021).

Kasra'i, Siavash (2001) *Arash Kamangir* [*Arash, the Bowman*] (Tehran: Nader).

Katsiaficas, George (1987) *The Ideology of the New Left: A Global Analysis of 1968* (Boston: South End Press).

Kavusi, Houshang (1989) 'Sinema, Sinema; Bakhsh-e Nokhost – Aghaz-e Kar' ['Cinema, Cinema; Part One – the Beginnings']. *Ketab-e Sobh* 4 (Summer–Autumn): 161–6.

Kazemiyyeh, Eslam (1968) 'Chera Samad Mord?' ['Why Did Samad Die?']. *Arash* 18 (November): 3–4.

Khaksar, Nassim (2017) 'Baztab-e Mobarezeh-ye Cheriki dar Adabiyyat-e Dastani' ['Reflection of Guerrilla Struggle in Fiction Literature'], in T. Atabaki and N. Mohajer (eds) *Rahi Digar, 2* [*The Road Not Taken, Vol. 2*] (Berkeley, CA: Noghteh), pp. 619–39.

Kharrazy, Mohammad (2020) Interview by Peyman Vahabzadeh (Vancouver, Canada, 19 October).

Kho'i, Esma'il (trans. Ahmad Karimi-Hakkak and Michael Beard) (1995) *Edges of Poetry* (Santa Monica, CA: Blue Logos).

Khoshnam, Mahmoud (2017) 'Rastakhiz-e Taraneh' ['The Resurgence of Song'], in T. Atabaki and N. Mohajer (eds) *Rahi Digar, 2* [*The Road Not Taken, Vol 2*] (Berkeley, CA: Noghteh), pp. 641–53.

Kimiai, Massoud (2020) 'Bara-ye Taghir Payan-e 'Gavaznha' SAVAL Kardan Ferestad' ['To Change the Ending of *The Deers* SAVAK Sent a Director'. *TV Zone Plus Interview*, https://www.youtube.com/watch?v=_Qm1X3tndio (last accessed 23 January 2021).

Kushabadi, Ja'far (1979) *Khuchek Khan* (Tehran: Nil).

Laclau, Ernesto (2005) *On Populist Reason* (London: Verso).

Madani, Mostafa (2011) 'Siahkal: Ragbari Seylasa bara-ye Zamini Teshneh' ['Siahkal: A Deluge of Thundershowers for a Thirsty Earth']. *BBC Persian* (9 February), http://www.bbc.com/persian/iran/2011/02/110205_l13_siahkal_mostafa_madani.shtml (last accessed 10 June 2019).

Malek, Mehdi (2014) *In Taraneh Buy-e Nan Nemidahad: Sargozasht-e Taraneh-ye Mo'tarez-e Iran* [*This Song Smells Not of Bread: The Story of Iran's Protest Song*] (n.p.: Andishesara).

Mahmoud, Ahmad (1974a) *Gharibehha va Pesarak-e Bumi* [*Strangers and the Native Boy*] (Tehran: Amir Kabir).

Mahmoud, Ahmad (1974b) *Hamsayehha* [*The Neighbours*] (Tehran: Amir Kabir).

Mannheim, Karl (1969) *Ideology and Utopia* (London: Routledge & Kegan Paul).

Marcuse, Herbert (1969) *An Essay on Liberation* (Boston: Beacon Press).

Marighella, Carlos (1969) 'Mini-Manual of the Urban Guerrilla'. *Marxists Internet Archives*, http://www.marxists.org/archive/marighella-carlos/1969/06/minimanual-urban-guerrilla (last accessed 10 September 2013).

Matin-Asgari, Afshin (2002) *Iranian Student Opposition to the Shah* (Costa Mesa, CA: Mazda).

Mehrabi, Massoud (1992) *Tarikh-e Sinama-ye Iran az Aqaz ta Sal-e 1357* [*History of Iranian Cinema from the Beginning to 1979*] (Tehran: n.p.).

Mesghali, Farshid (2015) 'Roya Sad Qadam az Vaq'iyyat Jelotar Ast (Mosahebeh)' ['Dream Is a Hundred Steps Ahead of Reality (Interview)']. *Ketabak.org* (28 April), shorturl.at/rAH38 (last accessed 24 September 2020).

Mesghali, Farshid (2016) 'Mahi Siah-e Kuchulu, Mandegartarin Ketab-e Kudakan-e Tarikh-e Iran' ['*The Little Black Fish*, the Iran's Most Enduring Children's Book']. *Shahr-e Ketab* (3 March), http://www.bookcity.org/detail/7367/root/papers (last accessed 24 September 2020).

Milani, Abbas (2008) *Eminent Persians: The Men and Women Who Made Modern Iran, 1941–1979, Volume 1* (Syracuse, NY: Syracuse University Press and Persian World Press).

Mirzai, Shahab (2019) 'Firuz Shirvanlu: az Etteham-e Teror-e Mohammad Reza Shah ta Shenel Kanun-e Parvaresh-e Fekri-ye Kudakan va Nojavanan' ['Firuz Shrivanlu: From Being Charged with Mohammad Reza Shah's Assassination to the Mantle of the Centre for the Intellectual Cultivation of Children and Youth']. *BBC Persian* (20 February), https://www.bbc.com/persian/arts-47304965 (last accessed 8 December 2020).

Mohajer, Nasser, and Mehrdad Baba Ali [Vahabi] (2016) *Beh zaban-e qanun: Bijan Jazani va Hassan Zia-Zarifi dar dadgah-e nezami* [*In the Language of Law: Bijan Jazani and Hassan Zia-Zarifi in the Military Court*] (Berkeley, CA: Nashr-e Noghteh).

Mohammadi, Morteza (2016) *Taraneh-ye Mo'tarez-e Irani dar Gozar-e Tarikh, Pushineh Dovvom* [*Iranian Protest Songs in the Passage of History, Vol. 2*] (n.p., no pub.).

Mohammadian-Omriyan, Fereshteh, and Mohammad Reza Torki (2015) 'Barresi-ye Vizhegiha-ye Kalam-e Taraneh-ye Sonnatgara va Taraneh-ye Novin Farsi az Ta'sis-e Radio (1319) ta 1357' ['Investigating the Characteristics of Lyrics of Traditional and New Persian Songs from the Establishment of Radio (1940) until 1979']. *Adabiyyat-e Parsi-ye Mo'aser* 5(4) (Winter): 101–28.

Mohammadpour, Mohammad Amin (2014) 'Jonpesh-e Fadai dar She'r-e Mo'aser-e Iran' ['The Fadai Movement in Iran's Contemporary Poetry'. *Zamaneh Tribune* (20 May), https://www.tribunezamaneh.com/archives/49622 (last accessed 4 April 2020).

Mokhtari, Mohammad (1995) *Barg-e Goft-o-Shenid* [*Pages of Conversation*] (Toronto: Afra).

Monfaredzadeh, Esfandiar (2008) 'Kimiai bud, Man va Eshq-e Sinema' ['There Was Kimiai, I, and the Love of Cinema']. *Deutsche Welle Farsi* (4 November), https://p.dw.com/p/DgEP (last accessed 21 July 2020).

Monfaredzadeh, Esfandiar (2014) *Sirus Malakuti Interviews Esfandiar Monfaredzadeh, Chehreha 28*. YouTube video (9 September), https://www.youtube.com/watch?v=34pjkHjaez4 (last accessed 1 September 2020).

Monfaredzadeh, Esfandiar (2015a) *Az Hozur-e Netanyahu ta Majera-ye Film-s Safar-e Sang dar Goftogu ba Esfandiar Monfaredzadeh* [*From Netanyahu's Presentation to the Story of* Journey of the Stone *in Conversation with Esfandiar Monfaredza-deh*]. YouTube video (5 March), https://www.youtube.com/watch?v=70P6_NSOSF8&ab_channel=SaeedBehbahani (last accessed 4 March 2021).

Monfaredzadeh, Esfandiar (2015b) *Darbareh-ye Marasem-e Musiqi-ye Filmha-ye Kimiai dar Tehran va E'teraz-e Esfandiar Monfaredzadeh-Bakhsh-e Avval* [*On the Music Festival of Kimiai's Films and Esfandiyar Monfaredzadeh's Objection – Part One*]. YouTube video (31 July), https://www.youtube.com/watch?v=-boSoOBUex4 (last accessed 4 March 2021).

Monfaredzadeh, Esfandiar (2017) 'Negahi beh Posht-e Sar' ['A Glance at What Is Behind'], in T. Atabaki and N. Mohajer (eds) *Rahi Digar, 2* [*The Road Not Taken, Vol. 2*] (Berkeley: Noghteh), pp. 655–74.

Morris, Nancy (1986) '*Canto Porque es Necesario Cantar*: The New Song Movement in Chile, 1973–1983'. *Latin American Research Review* 21(2): 117–36.

Mosaddeq, Hamid (2010) *Abi, Khakestari, Siah* [*Blue, Grey, Black*]. *She'r-e Pars*, http://sherepars.blogfa.com/post/12 (last accessed 7 March 2020).

Nabard (Information Bulletin of the National Liberation Movement of Iran) (1971) No. 1 (April–May).

e Khalq (1975) Organ of OIPFG (January).

Nabdel, Ali Reza (1977) *Azerbaijan va Mas'aleh-ye Melli* [*Azerbaijan and the National Question*] (n.p., no pub.).

Naderi, Mahmoud (2008) *Cherikha-ye Fadai-ye Khalq: az nokhostin konesh ta Bahman-e 1357, jeld-e avval* [*People's Fadai Guerrillas: From Their First Acts until February 1979, Vol. 1*] (Tehran: Political Studies and Research Institutes).

Naficy, Hamid (2011a) *A Social History of Iranian Cinema: Volume 1, The Artisanal Era, 1897–1941* (Durham, NC and London: Duke University Press).

Naficy, Hamid (2011b) *A Social History of Iranian Cinema: Volume 2, The Industrializing Years, 1941–1978* (Durham, NC and London: Duke University Press).

Naficy, Majid (1997) *Modernism and Ideology in Persian Literature: A Return to Nature in the Poetry of Nima Yushij* (Lanham, MD: University Press of America).

Negahdar, Farrokh (2008) Interview by Peyman Vahabzadeh, 7–8 December.

Nobari, Ali Reza (1978) *Iran Erupts* (Stanford, CA: Iran–American Documentation Group).

Nooriala, Esma'il (1969) *Sovar va Asbab dar She'r-e Emrooz Iran* [*Imagination and Instruments in Iranian Poetry Today*] (Tehran: Bamdad).

Nooriala, Esma'il (1994) *Te'ori-ye She'r: az 'Moj-e No' ta 'She'r-e Eshq'* [*Theory of Poetry: On Iranian Contemporary Poetics*] (London: Ghazal).

OIPFG and OIPM (2014) *Ketab-e Goftogu-ye Sazman-e Cherikha-ye Fadai-ye Khalq Iran va Sazman-e Mojahedin-e Khalq Iran, Sal 1354* [*The Book of Exchanges between the Organisation of Iranian People's Fadai Guerrillas and the Organisation of Iranian People's Mojahdin, 1975*] (Paris: Andisheh va Peykar).

OIPF-M [Organization of Iranian People's Fadaiyan-Majority] (2010) 'The Organization of Iranian People's Fadaian (Majority): 1971–2001'. *Academic*, https://enacademic.com/dic.nsf/enwiki/2859167 (last accessed 5 June 2019).

OMCP (Office of Management and Communication of the President) (2000a) *Asnadi az Musiqi, Teatre, va Sinema dar Iran, 1300–1357, Jeld Dovvom [Documents on Music, Theatre and Cinema in Iran (1921–1979), Vol. 2]* (Tehran: Ministry of Culture and Islamic Guidance).

OMCP (Office of Management and Communication of the President) (2000b) *Asnadi az Musiqi, Teatre, va Sinema dar Iran, 1300–1357, Jeld Sevvom [Documents on Music, Theatre and Cinema in Iran (1921–1979), Vol. 3]* (Tehran: Ministry of Culture and Islamic Guidance).

Ostad Mohammad, Mahmoud (2014) 'Majera-ye Chaqukeshi-ye Nosrat Rahmani baraye Barahani' ['The Story of Nosrat Rahmani's Knifing Barahani']. *ISNA* (1 March), https://www.isna.ir/news/92121005979/ (last accessed 19 May 2020).

Parand (2011a) 'Yadman-e Esfandiyar Monfaredzadeh, Bakhsh-e Dovvom' ['About Esfandiyar Monfaredzadeh, Part Two']. *Ravi-ye Hekayat-e Baqi* (15 March), http://parand.se/?p=5345 (last accessed 21 May 2019).

Parand (2011b) 'Yadman-e Esfandiyar Monfaredzadeh, Bakhsh-e Sevvom' ['About Esfandiyar Monfaredzadeh, Part Three']. *Ravi-ye Hekayat-e Baqi* (15 March), http://parand.se/?p=8588 (last accessed 21 May 2019).

Parand (2012a) 'Mard-e Tanha (Seda-ye Biseda)' ['The Lonesome Man (Voiceless Voice)']. *Ravi-ye Hekayat-e Baqi* (10 September), https://web.archive.org/web/20120910153957/http://www.parand.se/tr-marde-tanha.htm (last accessed 21 July 2020).

Parand (2012b) 'Aftabkaran' ('Sun-Planters'). *Ravi-ye Hekayat-e Baqi* (19 September), https://web.archive.org/web/20120919192645/http://www.parand.se/tr-aftabkaran.htm (last accessed 13 September 2020).

Parsinejad, Iraj (2003) *A History of Literary Criticism in Iran (1866–1951)* (Bethesda, MD: IBEX).

Parvin, Naser al-Din (2007) 'She'r-e Morgh-e Sahar' ['Lyrics of Morning Bird']. *Bokhara Magazine* 55: 171–6.

Poudeh, Reza J., and M. Reza Shirvani (2008) 'Issues and Paradoxes in the Development of Iranian National Cinema: An Overview'. *Iranian Studies* 41(3): 323–41.

Pourshabanan, Ali Reza, and Amir Hossein Pourshabanan (2018) 'Barresi-e Tatbiqi-e Tahavvol-e Roman-e Tangsir Sadeq Chubak be Film Eqtebasi-ey Tangsir Amir Naderi' ['Comparative Study of the Transformation of the Novel *Tangsir* by Sadeq Chubak into the Film *Tangsir* by Amir Naderi']. *Pazhuheshha-ye Adabiyyat-e Tatbiqi* 6(1) (Spring): 132–57.

Puyan, Amir Parviz (1979) *Zarurat-e Mobarezeh-ye Mosallahaneh va Radd-e Teori-ye Baqa* [*The Necessity of Armed Struggle and the Refutation of the Theory of Survival*] (Tehran: Gam).

Puyan, Amir Parviz (2012) *Khandan ba Galu-ye Khunin* [*Singing with a Bloody Throat*] (n.p.: Nashr-e Alternative), https://altmag2011.files.wordpress.com/2012/07/pooyan2.pdf (last accessed 11 August 2021).

Rahmani, Nosrat (2000) *Dar Jang-e Bad: Bargozideh-ye Asar* [*Fighting the Wind: An Anthology*] (Tehran: Bozorgmehr).

Rohani, Seyed Hamid (1993) *Nehzat-e Emam Khomeini Jeld 3* [*Imam Khomeini's Movement, Vol. 3*] (Tehran: Centre of the Islamic Revolution Documents).

Sadr, Hamid Reza (2006) *Iranian Cinema: A Political History*. London: I. B. Tauris.

Sa'edi, Gholam Hossein (1968) 'Gejehdur! Bakh Gejedur!' ['It's Night! Look, It's Night!']. *Arash* 18 (November): 15–16, 106–7.

Sa'edi, Gholam Hossein (1991) *Azadaran-e Bayal* [*The Mourners of Bayal*] (Tehran: Qatreh).

Sa'edi, Gholam Hossein (1998) *Tars-o-Larz* [*Fear and Trembling*] (Tehran: Qatreh).

Salehi, Anush (2003) *Ravi-ye Baharan: Mobarezat va Zendegi-ye Karamatollah Daneshian* [*The Spring's Narrator: The Life and Struggles of Karamatollah Daneshian*] (Tehran: Nashr-e Qatreh).

Samakar, Abbas (2001) *Man yek shureshi hastam* [*I Am a Rebel*] (Los Angeles: Ketab).

Sarfaraz, Ardalan (2006) 'Man She'ram ra Zendegi Kardeham, Zendegiam ra She'r' ['I've Lived My Poems, Poetised My Life']. *Deutsche Welle Farsi* (27 November), https://p.dw.com/p/A6Br (last accessed 26 July 2020).

Sarkuhi, Faraj (2002) *Yas va Das: Bist Sal Rowshanfekri va Amniyyatiha* [*Jasmine and Sickle: Twenty Years of Intellectualism and the Security Forces*] (Spånga, Sweden: Baran).

Saussure, Ferdinand de (trans. P. Meisel and H. Saussy) (1959) *Course in General Linguistics* (New York: Columbia University Press).

Schürmann, Reiner (trans. Charles T. Wolfe) (1997a) 'Symbolic Difference', *Graduate Faculty Philosophy Journal* 19(2)–20(1): 9–38.

Schürmann, Reiner (trans. Charles T. Wolfe) (1997b) 'Symbolic Praxis', *Graduate Faculty Philosophy Journal* 19(2)–20(1): 39–65.

Setwat, Mariyam (2019) *Madi-ye Nomre Bist* [Canal Number Twenty] (Cologne: Forough).

Skocpol, Theda (1994) *Social Revolutions in the Modern World* (Cambridge: Cambridge University Press).

Seyed-Gohrab. A. A. and K. Talattof (eds) (2013) *Conflict and Development in Iranian Film* (Leiden: Leiden University Press).

Shabani, Mehdi (2019) 'Forough, Hedayat, va Behrangi: Chehrehha-ye Adabi Mo'aser-e Iran, Namadha-ye Roshanfekri-ye Torkiyyeh' ['Forough, Hedayat and Behrangi: Iran's Contemporary Literary Figures as Symbols of Intellectualism in Turkey']. *BBC Persian* (19 June), https://www.bbc.com/persian/blog-viewpoints-48690503 (last accessed 11 December 2020).

Shafi'i-Kadkani, Mohammad Reza (1971) *Dar Kucheh Baghha-ye Neshabur* [*In the Garden Alleys of Neishapur*] (Tehran: Tus).

Shafi'i-Kadkani, Mohammad Reza (2001) *Advar-e She'r-e Farsi az Mashrutiyyat ta Soqut-e Saltanat* [*Periods of Persian Poetry from Constitutionalism to the Fall of Monarchy*] (Tehran: Sokhan).

Shamlu, Ahmad, ed (1968a) *Khusheh: avvalin hafteh-ey she'r va honar* [*Cluster: The First Week of Poetry and Art*] (Tehran: Kavosh).

Shamlu, Ahmad (1968b) 'Preface', in A. Shamlu (ed.), *Khusheh: avvalin hafteh-ey she'r va honar* [*Cluster: The First Week of Poetry and Art*] (Tehran: Entesharat-e Kavosh), pp. i–iii.

Shamlu, Ahmad (1985) *Qat'nameh* [*Resolution*] (Tehran: Morvarid).

Shamlu, Ahmad (1993a) *Ebrahim dar atash* [*Ebrahim on Fire*] (Tehran: Zamaneh).

Shamlu, Ahmad (1993b) *Deshneh dar Dis* [*Dagger on a Tray*] (Tehran: Zamaneh).

Shamlu, Ahmad (1993c) *Hava-ye tazeh* [*Fresh Air*] (Tehran: Negah).

Shamlu, Ahmad (2010) *Majmu'eh Asar, Daftar-e Yekom: She'r-ha, 1323–1378* [*Collected Works, Vol. 1: Poems, 1944–1999*] (Tehran: Negah).

Shamlu, Ahmad (1978) 'Eykash in Hayula Hezar Sar Midasht' ['I Wish This Monster Had a Thousand Heads'], in *Samad Behrangi: ba Mojha-ye Aras beh Darya Peyvast* [*Samad Behrangi: He Reached the Sea by the Waves of Aras*] (Tehran: Aban), pp. 25–9.

Shams, Fatemeh (2015) 'The Dialectic of Poetry and Power in Iran'. *Dirasat 3* (February): 1–36.

Shams-Langarudi (Mohammad Taqi Javaheri Gilani) (1991a) *Tarikh-e tahlili-ye she'r-e no: jeld avval, 1284–1332* [*The Analytical History of New Poetry: Vol. 1, 1905–1953*] (Tehran: Nashr-e Markaz).

Shams-Langarudi (Mohammad Taqi Javaheri Gilani) (1991b) *Tarikh-e tahlili-ye she'r-e no: jeld dovvom, 1332–1341* [*The Analytical History of New Poetry: Vol. 2, 1953–1962*] (Tehran: Nashr-e Markaz).

Shams-Langarudi (Mohammad Taqi Javaheri Gilani) (1991c) *Tarikh-e tahlili-ye she'r-e no: jeld sevvom, 1341–1349* [*The Analytical History of New Poetry: Vol. 3, 1962–1970*] (Tehran: Nashr-e Markaz).

Shams-Langarudi (Mohammad Taqi Javaheri Gilani) (1991d) *Tarikh-e tahlili-ye she'r-e no: jeld chaharom, 1349–1357* [*The Analytical History of New Poetry: Vol. 4, 1970–1979*] (Tehran: Nashr-e Markaz).

Shannon, Matthew (2011) '"Contacts with the Opposition": American Foreign Relations, the Iranian Student Movement, and the Global Sixties'. *The Sixties* 4(1): 1–29.

Shahidani, Shahab, and Parvin Rostami (2019) 'Baztab-e E'terazha-ye Ejtema'i dar Filmha-ye Daheh-ye 1350' ['Reflections of Social Protests in the 1970s Films']. *Jame'ehshenasi-ye Tarikhi* 11(2) (Fall–Winter): 175–202.

Siahpoush, Hamid (ed.) (1994) *Bagh-e tanha'i: yadnameh Sohrab Sepehri* [*Garden of Solitude: Commemorating Sohrab Sepehri*] (Tehran: Nashr-e Soheil).

Siamdoust, Nahid (2017) *Soundtrack of the Revolution: The Politics of Music in Iran* (Stanford, CA: Stanford University Press).

Sho'aiyan, Mostafa (1969) '*Bazjui*' ['Interrogation']. *Jahan-e Naw* 24(1) (April): 160.

Sohrabi, Naghmeh (2019) 'Remembering the Palestine Group: Global Activism, Friendship, and the Iranian Revolution'. *International Journal of Middle East Studies* 51: 281–300. doi:10.1017/S0020743819000059.

Soleimani, Faramarz (1981) *She'r Shahadat Ast* [Poetry Is to Stand Witness] (Tehran: Moj).

Soltanpour, Said (n.d. 1) *Seda-ye Mira* [*Mortal Voice*] (n.p.: Arashkania).

Soltanpour, Said (n.d. 2) *Az Koshtargah* [*From the Abattoir*] (n.p.: Supporters of Fadaiyan Organization (Minority)).

Soltanpour, Said (2016) *Avazha-ye Band* [*Prison Songs*] (n.p.: Small Socialist Library).

Sorel, George (2004) *Reflections on Violence* (Nineola, NY: Dover).

Tabatabai, Ahmad (2014) 'Darbareh-ye Taraneh-ye "Bu-ye Khub-e Gandom"' ['On the Song "The Fine Scent of Wheat"']. *Navaye Fars* (18 July), http://www.navayefars.com/content/16 (last accessed 25 August 2020).

Tahbaz, Sirus (ed.) (2001) *Khorus Jangi-e bimanand: zendegi va honar-e Housang Irani* [*The Unique Fighting Cock: On the Life and Art of Houshang Irani*] (Tehran: Farzan).

Takhti, Babak (2019) 'Pedaram koshteh nashod, khodkoshi kard' ['My Father Was Not Killed; He Committed Suicide']. *Eghtesaad 24* (15 March), https://bit.ly/2JOi7Yk (last accessed 19 May 2019).

Talattof, Kamran (2000) *The Politics of Writing in Iran: A History of Modern Persian Literature* (Syracuse, NY: Syracuse University Press).

Tohidast Shafi', Marzieh (2017) 'Chapkhaneh-ye Makhfi' ['Secret Printshop'], in T. Atabaki and N. Mohajer (eds) *Rahi Digar, 1* [*The Road Not Taken, Vol. 1*] (Berkeley: Noghteh), pp. 257–77.

Tolstoy, Leo (trans. Ann Dunnigan) (1962) *Fables and Fairy Tales* (New York: New American Library).

Vahabzadeh, Peyman (2003) *Articulated Experiences: Toward a Radical Phenomenology of Contemporary Social Movements* (Albany, NY: State University of New York Press).

Vahabzadeh, Peyman (2007a) 'The Conditions of Subalternity: Reflections on Subjectivity, Experience and Hegemony'. *Socialist Studies/Études socialistes* 3(2) (Fall): 93–113.

Vahabzadeh, Peyman (2007b) *She'r, Rokhdad, Tajrobeh: beh suy-e padidarshenasi-ye she'r* [*Poetry, Event, Experience: Toward A Phenomenology of Poetry*] [five essays] (Vancouver: Subvision).

Vahabzadeh, Peyman (2010) *A Guerrilla Odyssey: Modernization, Secularism, Democracy, and the Fadai Period of National Liberation in Iran, 1971–1979* (Syracuse, NY: Syracuse University Press).

Vahabzadeh, Peyman (2015a) *Parviz Sadri: Namai az yek zendegi-ye siyasi* [*Parviz Sadri: A Political Biography*] (Vancouver: Shahrgon).

Vahabzadeh, Peyman (2015b) 'Rebellious Action and the "Guerrilla Poetry": Dialectics of Art and Life in the 1970s Iran', in Kamran Talattof (ed.), *Persian Language, Literature and Culture: New Leaves, Fresh Looks*; In Honor of Ahmad Karimi-Hakkak (London/New York: Routledge), pp. 103–22.

Vahabzadeh, Peyman (2015c) 'A Generation's Myth: Armed Struggle and the Creation of Social Epic in the 1970s Iran'. in Houchang Chehabi, Peyman Jafari and Maral Jefroudi (eds), *Iran in the Middle East: Transnational Encounters and Social History* (London: I. B. Tauris), pp. 183–98.

Vahabzadeh, Peyman (2015d) 'Phenomenology and Literature'. *Inquire: Journal of Comparative Literature* 4(2) (November), http://inquire.streetmag.org/articles/162 (last accessed 16 November 2019).

Vahabzadeh, Peyman (2019a) *Violence and Nonviolence: Conceptual Excursions into Phantom Opposites* (Toronto: University of Toronto Press).

Vahabzadeh, Peyman (2019b) *A Rebel's Journey: Mostafa Sho'aiyan and Revolutionary Theory in Iran* (London: OneWorld).

Vahabzadeh, Peyman (2021) 'Buseh bar Kakol-e Khorshid; Rokhdad va Jonbesh: Baztabha-ye Falsafi bar Siahkal' ['A Kiss on the Locks of the Sun; Event and Movement: Philosophical Reflections on Siahkal']. *Naqd-e Eqtesad-e Siyasi* (31 January), https://wp.me/p2GDHh-4IO (last accessed 31 January 2021).

Varon, Jeremy (2004) *Bringing the War Home: The Weather Underground, the Red Army Faction, and Revolutionary Violence in the Sixties and Seventies* (Berkeley/Los Angeles: University of California Press).

Vossoughi, Nasser (1963) 'Tangsir'. *Andisheh va Honar* 8: 662–6.

Wagner-Pacifici, Robin (2017) *What Is an Event?* (Chicago: University of Chicago Press).

Yaquti, Mansour (1972) *Kudaki-ye Man* [*My Childhood*]. (n.p., no pub.).

Yaquti, Mansour (1974) *Ba Bachehha-ye Deh-e Khodeman* [*With the Children of Our Village*] (Tehran: Ava).

Yaquti, Mansour (1977) *Pajush* (Tehran: Ayandeh).

Yaquti, Mansour (1978) *Yaddashtha-ye yek Mo'alem* [*Notes of a Teacher*] (n.p., no pub.).

Yousef, Saeed (1987) *No'i az Naqd bar No'i az She'r* [*A Particular Criticism of a Particular Poetry*] (Saarbrücken: Navid).

Yousef, Saeed (2017a) '*Goftogui ba Said Yusof*' ['An Interview with Said Yusof']. Interview by Vahid Davar. *Iranian Writers Association (in Exile)* (16 September), shorturl.at/gmHX3 (last accessed 31 March 2020).

Yousef, Saeed (2017b) 'She'ri Setayeshgar-e Shur' ['A Poetry Admiring Passion'], in T. Atabaki and N. Mohajer (eds) *Rahi Digar* [*The Road Not Taken*] (Berkeley: Noghteh), pp. 585–618.

Yunansian, Isaak (2013) 'Yadi az Soltan-e Jaz-e Iran, Vigen' ['Remembering Vigen, Sultan of Iranian Jazz']. *Peyman* 64, https://bit.ly/3fG1RoE (last accessed 9 August 2020).

Yushij, Nima (1962) 'From Diaries'. *Arash* 2 (January): 38–61.

Yushij, Nima (1989) *Arzesh-e ehsasat va panj maqaleh dar she'r va namayesh* [*The Value of Feelings and Five Essays on Poetry and Play*] (Saarbrücken: Nawid).

Yushij, Nima (ed. Sirus Tahbaz) (1991) *Majmu'eh-ye kamel-e ash'ar-e Nima Yushij* [*The Collected Poems of Nima Yushij*] (Tehran: Negah).

Yushij, Nima (2004) 'Nameh-i az Sha'r-e Yush be Mirzadeh Eshqi' ['A Letter from the Poet from Yush to Mirzadeh Eshqi'], *Iran Emrooz* (4 November), http://farhang.iran-emrooz.de/more.php?id=9202_0_13_0_M (last accessed 14 November 2019).

Yushij, Nima (2012) *Seh Nameh beh Sadeq Hedayat, Ehsan Tabari, Shin Partow* [*Three Letters to Sadeq Hedayat, Ehsan Tabari, Shin Partow*] (n.p.: Do-Library), http://do-lb.blogspot.com (last accessed 15 March 2021).

Zahedi, Parviz (1967) 'Chel Pellekan' ['Forty Stairs'], *Jahan-e Naw* 6–10 (November 1966–February 1967): 15–20.

INDEX OF NAMES AND SUBJECTS

MEDIA INDEX

Books

Cassette Tapes

Movies and TV Series

Periodicals

Plays and Radio Dramas

Poems

Radio Programmes

Short Fiction

Songs and Soundtracks

EU Authorised Representative:

Easy Access System Europe Mustamäe tee 50, 10621 Tallinn, Estonia

gpsr.requests@easproject.com

Printed and bound by CPI Group (UK) Ltd, Croydon, CR0 4YY

01/06/2026

02125115-0001